The Gospel Through the Ages

THE GOSPEL
Through the Ages

By

MILTON R. HUNTER
of the
First Council of the Seventy

Written and published under the direction of the General Priesthood Committee of the Council of the Twelve of the Church of Jesus Christ of Latter-day Saints.

STEVENS AND WALLIS, Inc.
SALT LAKE CITY, UTAH
1945

PRINTED IN U.S.A.

STEVENS & WALLIS, INC.

SALT LAKE CITY, UTAH

TO THE QUORUMS OF
THE MELCHIZEDEK PRIESTHOOD

The gospel of Jesus Christ was taught to Adam. This is a unique doctrine among the world's followers of Christ. Yet it is one of the basic truths revealed to the Prophet Joseph Smith by the Eternal Father.

This knowledge explains the course of human history. Man, from the beginning, was taught the gospel. The Lord did not initiate his work on earth by leaving man in darkness. But men, yielding to the temptations of the evil one, departed from the truth. Thus came a succession of apostasies and restorations.

Thus also it happens that the simple doctrines of the gospel of Jesus Christ appear, and have appeared, more or less perverted, in the religious beliefs of mankind. Fragments of the truth have been handed down through the ages.

This doctrine, amply substantiated in this book, becomes a powerful evidence for a common source of religious truths, and for the existence of gospel knowledge from the beginning of earth history.

Around the doctrine that Adam was taught the gospel, Dr. Hunter, who was assigned the task by the general authorities, has written a series of illuminating, interesting, and faith-building chapters. As the argument proceeds, almost every gospel truth is there touched upon in a somewhat new but sound manner.

The priesthood of the Church will find much satisfaction in studying this informative and enlivening priesthood course of study. It is hoped that all Melchizedek Priesthood quorums will avail themselves promptly of this new approach to gospel knowledge, and carry on the study throughout the year with intelligent discussions of the thoughts presented.

Sincerely your brother,

GEORGE F. RICHARDS
President of the Council of the Twelve

Explanation Regarding Footnotes
and Abbreviations

ibid.   From the Latin *ibidem,* meaning "the same reference as last cited."

op. cit.   From the Latin *opere citato,* meaning "the work cited more than one note previously."

e. g.   From the Latin *exempli gratia,* meaning "for example."

ff.   From the German *folgende,* meaning "and the pages following."

f.   Meaning "and the page following."

pp.   Meaning "pages."

p.   Meaning "page."

2:16; 3:10-12. Meaning "chapter two, verse sixteen; chapter three, verses ten to twelve."

PREFACE

This book is designed primarily for a course of study in the Melchizedek Priesthood quorums of the Church. It is to be used by all high priests', seventies', and elders' classes in their weekly meetings, beginning January 1, 1946. A second possible use of the book is for missionaries. The volume has been written and published under the direction of the General Authorities.

The Gospel Through the Ages presents the story of the plan of life and salvation which was instituted by our Heavenly Father and His Only Begotten Son in the spirit world before man was placed upon the earth; and it discusses the revelations of eternal truths from Adam's day forward. The relationship of paganism and world religions to the Gospel of Jesus Christ is shown. Also the story is told of how the human family has sought after salvation; and how all religious truths, regardless of where they were found, came originally from the same source—Jesus Christ and His Eternal Father.

The principal thesis which runs throughout the entire volume is that the Lord revealed the Gospel of Jesus Christ to Father Adam, and has continued to reveal His will to holy prophets from that day forward. Worldly doctrines, however, have from age to age adulterated divinely revealed truths; thus a succession of apostasies and restorations has occurred.

The most recent restoration took place a hundred years ago. At that time the Lord established the last and greatest of all the dispensations by revealing the Gospel of Jesus Christ to the Prophet Joseph Smith. Thus the true Church is now upon the earth with the promise that it shall never again be taken away.

The writer expresses sincere gratitude to Elder John A. Widtsoe, Elder Joseph Fielding Smith, Elder Ezra Taft Benson, and Elder Charles A. Callis for their careful perusal of the manuscript and for their kind and helpful

vii

suggestions throughout the entire time that this volume was being written and published.

Appreciation is also expressed to Elder George F. Richards, President of the Council of Twelve Apostles, for his message to the quorums of the Melchizedek Priesthood which serves as a foreword to this volume. Also, to all the General Authorities, including the First Presidency and the First Council of the Seventy, who have generously made it possible for the writer to have sufficient time to complete the assignment, sincere thanks is given.

The writer also expresses deep appreciation to Ferne G. Hunter who gave valuable assistance toward the preparation of this book for publication.

The writer wishes to dedicate this volume to all searchers after eternal truth and to all faithful Latter-day Saints who are desirous of helping to teach the Gospel of Jesus Christ at home and abroad. It is prayerfully and humbly hoped that through the study of this book the work of the Lord will be advanced.

MILTON R. HUNTER

Salt Lake City, Utah
October 25, 1945

CONTENTS

Chapter 1.

THE GOSPEL OF JESUS CHRIST

GOSPEL DEFINED

The Gospel of Jesus Christ is the "glad tidings" or "good news" concerning the Savior, the Kingdom of God, and the salvation of man.[1] It consists primarily of the teachings of Christ and of the apostles as recorded in the *New Testament* and *Book of Mormon,* and in revelations given through the holy prophets of God from the time the world began down to our day. These revelations and teachings are recorded in the holy scriptures.

Christians frequently use the word Gospel to designate their religion. Thought of in this light, the Gospel includes their theology. Fundamental in Christian theology are the doctrines of the eternal nature of man, the fall, and the atonement of Jesus the Christ; therefore, these are basic in the Gospel.[2] In fact, the Gospel gives answers to the questions of where we came from, why we are here, and where we are going.

Again, we may define the Gospel of Jesus Christ as the plan of salvation. It is built upon the principles of eternal truth; in fact, it is the foundation of all truth.[3] These truths are the standard by which God judges the actions of men.[4] The Gospel is the power of redemption of all human beings.[5] Paul, the famous Christian missionary, aptly stated his definition as follows:

> For I am not ashamed of the Gospel of Christ: for it is the power of God unto salvation to every one that believeth; to the Jew first, and also to the Greek. For therein is the righteousness of God revealed from faith to faith.[6]

[1] *Webster's New International Dictionary.*
[2] John A. Widtsoe, *Rational Theology,* p. 3.
[3] G. Homer Durham, *The Gospel Kingdom,* p. 92; John A. Widtsoe, *Discourses of Brigham Young,* p. 14.
[4] Romans 2:16; Galatians 6:7-8; *Doctrine and Covenants* 45:9; 130:20-21; 132:5.
[5] Joseph Fielding Smith, *Teachings of the Prophet Joseph Smith,* p. 59.
[6] Romans 1:16-17.

1

The Gospel also contains all of the covenants that God has made with His children from the time they were first placed on the earth to our day. Most of these covenants have been recorded in the holy scriptures. The Jews in Jesus' day referred to their sacred writings as "the Covenant." Later, after the Christians had produced a religious literature, they termed it the "New Covenant," and spoke of the Hebrew writings as the "Old Covenant." In the process of translating these sacred works into Latin, the names were changed by mistake to New and Old Testaments.

In a revelation to Joseph Smith, the Savior made definite mention of the ancient nature of the covenant and informed the Prophet that He had revealed to him the same covenant (Gospel). To quote the words of the Son of Man: "Wherefore, I say unto you that I have sent unto you mine everlasting covenant, even that which was from the beginning."[7] Today we speak of the covenant as the "new and everlasting covenant." Since the revelation on celestial marriage speaks of the "new and everlasting covenant of marriage," some Mormons are of the opinion that "the new and everlasting covenant" means merely temple marriage. But it embraces much more than that. In fact, it includes all of the principles and ordinances of the Gospel of Jesus Christ—all of the covenants that God has revealed to mortals or that He will ever reveal to them relative to their salvation. Thus the "new and everlasting covenant" and the Gospel of Jesus Christ are the same thing.

SCOPE OF THE GOSPEL

The Gospel of Jesus Christ is perhaps the most comprehensive subject that we can study. It embraces all truth.[8] Through it, we learn not only of conditions associated with the human family as they now exist, but also of the pre-existence—of the organization of this world and of other worlds. Through the eternal principle of revelation, the great purposes of God have been revealed from age to age and shall continue to be revealed. Furthermore, it teaches us regarding glorious rewards that our

---

[7] *Doctrine and Covenants* 49:9.
[8] Moroni 7:12, 16-17; Ether 4:12.

Father in Heaven has in store in the world to come for those who obey the Gospel while in mortality.

The Gospel is not only founded on unvarying certainties, but since it embraces all truth it must of necessity include the knowledge of all sciences. It possesses the key to the true philosophy of life. Although we do not understand the entire plan of life and purposes of God in our universe, yet the Gospel of Jesus Christ lays the foundation for men to learn little by little the great universal plan of human life.

Joseph Smith, Brigham Young, John Taylor, and all the other presidents and leaders of the Church have maintained that there are no limits nor bounds to the truths embraced within the Gospel of Jesus Christ. For the purpose of showing the viewpoint of latter-day prophets, we present two quotations from their teachings which are typical of many others. President Brigham Young emphatically declared:

Our religion is simply the truth. It is all said in this one expression—it embraces all truth, wherever found, in all the works of God and man that are visible or invisible to mortal eyes. . . . Mormonism embraces all truth that is revealed and that is unrevealed, whether religious, political, scientific, or philosophical. . . .

[It] embraces every principle pertaining to life and salvation, for time and eternity, no matter who has it. If the infidel has got truth, it belongs to Mormonism. The truth and sound doctrine possessed by the sectarian world, and they have a great deal, all belongs to this Church. As for their morality, many of them are morally just as good as we are. All that is good, lovely, and praiseworthy belongs to this Church and Kingdom. Mormonism includes all truth. There is no truth but what belongs to the Gospel. It is life, eternal life; it is bliss; it is the fullness of all things in the Gods and in the eternities of the Gods.[9]

President John Taylor expressed the same basic doctrine in the following words:

In regard to our religion, I will say that it embraces every principle of truth and intelligence pertaining to us as moral, intellectual, mortal and immortal beings, pertaining to this world and the world that is to come. We are open to truth of every kind, no matter whence it comes, where it originates, or who believes in it. Truth, when preceded by the little word "all," comprises everything that has ever existed or that ever will exist and be known by and among men in time and through the endless ages of eternity.[10]

---

[9] Widtsoe, *Discourses of Brigham Young*, pp. 2-4.
[10] Durham, *op. cit.*, p. 91.

Eternal Nature of the Gospel

"Truth abideth and hath no end."[11] This was the pronouncement of Jesus Christ to the Prophet Joseph Smith. Anything which has an end must of necessity have a beginning; therefore, truth had no beginning. It has always existed and it shall continue to exist eternally. Wherever there have been intelligences (i.e., the ego or life of men) in any world and at any stage of progression, such fundamental principles as good, evil, love, hate, choice (agency), will, faith, repentance, progression, and hundreds of similar verities have existed. They constitute the laws of God—the laws of eternal truth. Our Heavenly Parents have through aeons of time and a multitude of experiences gradually become acquainted with and applied in Their lives an untold number of these everlasting laws. As They learned these verities and how to operate them, these laws thereby became subject unto Elohim and henceforth were His laws—or, in other words, the Gospel of Jesus Christ. President John Taylor sustains and amplifies the foregoing doctrine in the following words:

The Gospel is a living, abiding, eternal and unchangeable principle that has existed co-equal with God, and always will exist, while time and eternity endure, wherever it is developed and made manifest. . . .

There is not a principle associated with the Gospel of the Son of God but what is eternal in its nature and consequences. . . . The principles of the Gospel being eternal, they were framed and originated with the Almighty in eternity before the world was, according to certain eternal laws, and hence the Gospel is called the Everlasting Gospel. . . . It reaches back into the eternities that are past; it exists in time and it stretches forward into the eternities to come, and everything connected with it is eternal.[12]

Light and Truth

All the knowledge of truths that exist comes from the same source—God the Eternal Father and His Only Begotten Son—the Divine Fountain of Truth. The ancient Nephite prophets positively maintained that all that is good, all that is true, comes from this one source.[13]

In revelations to the Prophet Joseph Smith, the Lord sustained the teachings of the Nephite prophets relative

---

[11] *Doctrine and Covenants* 88:66.
[12] Durham, *op. cit.*, pp. 88-90.
[13] Moroni 7:12, 16-17; Ether 4:12.

to their claim that all truths come from this one eternal source—the Godhead. The revelations declared that the power of God is "light and truth"; and it "proceedeth forth from the presence of God to fill the immensity of space." It is "the light which is in all things: which giveth life to all things: which is the law by which all things are governed."[14] This divine immanence of light and truth operates through the holy Priesthood and through the Holy Ghost. Thus through Jesus Christ and these eternal principles our eyes and our understandings are quickened and enlightened. In other words, we receive knowledge of truth; i.e., knowledge of "things as they are, as they were, and as they shall be."

Throughout this course of study, it is our purpose to present sufficient evidence to prove definitely that all truths come from the one divine source—the Godhead. Wherein religious teachings and practices in pagan and world religions resemble the true Gospel of Jesus Christ —although they may be perpetuated in adulterated and polluted forms—these teachings and practices came originally from the Divine Fountain of Truth.

SUPPLEMENTARY READINGS—CHAPTER 1

1. *Bible:* Isaiah 52:7; Romans 2:16; 1:16-17; Galatians 1:6-8; Hebrews 5:8-9; Ephesians 1:13; 6:14; Mark 16:15-18; Luke 9:6.
2. *Book of Mormon:* Alma 13:1-9; 22:13; Helaman 5:47; 3 Nephi 1:14; 26:5; 27:5-25; Ether 3:14; 4:12; Moroni, 7-12, 16-17.
3. *Doctrine and Covenants* 1; 18:23; 39:1-6; 45:1-10; 49:9; 68:1; 133:36-39; 128:19; 88:66.
4. G. Homer Durham (Compiler), *The Gospel Kingdom,* pp. 83-94.
5. Joseph F. Smith, *Gospel Doctrine,* pp. 11, 14, 90, 104, 114, 116, 121, 146, 150, 392.
6. Joseph Fielding Smith (Compiler), *Teachings of the Prophet Joseph Smith,* pp. 16, 59, 91, 138, 158, 166-168, 181, 264, 276, 308-310, 324, 328, 348.
7. Joseph Fielding Smith, *The Way to Perfection,* pp. 29-41.
8. John A. Widtsoe (compiler), *Discourses of Brigham Young,* pp. 1-17.
9. John A. Widtsoe, *Rational Theology,* pp. 1-11.

---

[14] *Doctrine and Covenants* 88:4-13.

Chapter 2.

THE WORK AND GLORY OF GOD

God's Work and Glory

Over 3,000 years ago God showed Moses in a vision the worlds which He had created (organized). The ancient Prophet beheld the earth and its inhabitants in their entirety. Then he asked the Lord to tell him why He had made all of these things. In reply, God explained by what power He did His creative work; and He also made it clear to Moses that there was a divine purpose back of all that He did. To quote the words of the Lord to the ancient Israelite prophet:

By the word of my power have I created them, which is mine Only Begotten Son, who is full of grace and truth. Worlds without number have I created; and I also created them for mine own purpose; and by the Son I have created them, which is mine Only Begotten.[1]

Then God concluded His explanation to Moses with the most significant and most marvelous statement regarding the work and glory of God to be found in religious literature. He declared:

For behold, this is my work and my glory—to bring to pass the immortality and eternal life of man.

Another declaration which is almost equally as important as the one just cited was given to the Prophet Joseph Smith by revelation. It is:

"The glory of God is intelligence, or, in other words, light and truth."[2]

These two revelations throw a flood of light on the activities of the Godhead—the Father, the Son, and the Holy Ghost—and all other intelligent beings, whether they be men or angels, that cooperate with the Gods.

One of the major functions of supreme beings is to prepare worlds for mortals to dwell on. If we meditate

[1] Moses 1:4, 8, 80-33, 89.
[2] *Doctrine and Covenants* 93:86.

6

on the history of mankind in this world, we readily see that there were natural resources carefully prepared beforehand which have fitted in well with the needs of every type of civilization which has existed here. Our age is a mechanical age. We have coal, iron, electricity, and every other resource which we need, and they are supplied in abundance. Even the precious metals appear in what seem to be their proper proportions. The same facts hold true for agricultural societies, nomadic groups, and even savage tribes. They also had natural resources, generously supplied, to fit their needs. This evidence bears testimony to the fact that a divine intelligence carefully planned and organized the world for His children, where they might work toward immortality and eternal life. The word of God confirms this evidence, and the holy prophets have proclaimed it to be true. To quote Nephi: "Behold, the Lord hath created the earth that it should be inhabited: and he hath created his children that they should possess it."[3]

We are informed in the two scriptures quoted that God's glory lies to a large degree in His ability to work, to create, to organize worlds. He has learned the eternal laws of truth (natural laws), and through controlling, regulating, and applying them as He sees fit, He has organized worlds as homes for His children. Through the power of the Priesthood—which was named after the Son of God—the Eternal Father creates worlds and accomplishes His divine designs.

God's glory is enhanced through His children's gaining eternal life. It is true that the larger the number of men who conform their lives to Gospel truths and thereby become glorified, the greater is the glory of their Heavenly Father. Naturally, a king who rules over a large kingdom of faithful subjects can accomplish more and has more power than one whose dominion is small. But we should not think for a moment that God has a selfish motive in glorifying mankind.

The life of the Eternal Father is the greatest in the universe, and that of the Only Begotten is comparable to the Father's. These two beings have experienced the deep-

---

[3] 1 Nephi 17:36; Alma 30:44; Deuteronomy 82:7-10.

est meaning of life and have attained the greatest intellectual and spiritual growth. God, being infinite in His
knowledge and power, is also infinite in His love. Therefore, He is inviting us to join Him in the development of
all human personalities. By cooperating with the Gods
and the holy angels, all men may move in the direction
of that Godlike life.

Since God is the all-wise One and the all-powerful
One, the commandments and instructions that He
gives to other intelligences are the wisest and the best
that can be given. These commandments, when followed,
bring about the greatest blessings, developing within man
a more joyful, kindly, sinless and Godlike behavior. The
things God tells His children to do we term the Gospel
of Jesus Christ. It is a plan, a philosophy, which when
applied will make mankind more like their Heavenly Father.

It is also true that God is the completely unselfish
One. His love is without bounds. Therefore He desires
that which is highest and best, not for Himself alone, but
for all of his children. What would be best for them, however, would also be best for Him. His glory, His power,
and His joy will be enhanced by bringing mortal beings
back into His presence and increasing their joy, power and
glory. In other words, God will increase His glory by
assisting His children to become as He is; thus His greatest work "is to bring to pass the immortality and eternal
life of man."

IMMORTALITY AND ETERNAL LIFE

There is a definite difference between "immortality"
and "eternal life." We are called mortal beings because
we are subject to death. But dwelling in each of us is a
spirit which is not subject to death, and therefore is immortal. In the plan of salvation, which was instituted before man was placed upon the earth, provisions were made
to bring about the resurrection of the physical body and
reunite it with the spirit, never again to be divided nor to
see corruption.[4]

---

[4] 2 Nephi 9:4-9; Alma 40:22-25.

The Lord was referring to the resurrection of the physical body when He told Moses that His work was to bring to pass the "immortality of man." In this sense, resurrection and immortality are synonymous. The holy prophets of God understood this doctrine thoroughly and taught it to the people. For example, Amulek instructed the Nephites as follows:

> I say unto you that this mortal body is raised to an immortal body, that is from death; even from the first death unto life, that they can die no more; their spirits uniting with their bodies, never to be divided; thus the whole becoming spiritual and immortal, that they can no more see corruption.[5]

The resurrection—or the bringing about of the immortality of man—was accomplished through the atonement of Jesus Christ. All men who have ever lived, regardless of how wicked or how righteous their lives have been, or who ever will live in this mortal world, will be made recipients of this great gift of the Savior's; that is, they will be resurrected and blessed with immortal existence.[6] Death was overcome or destroyed by the Savior of mankind, and the law of resurrection put into operation. Following the resurrection, men and women shall never again die a physical death. In the words of Elder Joseph Fielding Smith:

> Immortality is the gift of God, through Jesus Christ, to all men; by which they come forth in the resurrection to die no more, whether they have obeyed Him or rebelled against Him. This great gift is theirs; even the wicked receive it through the grace of Jesus Christ, and shall have the privilege of living forever, but they will have to pay the price of their sins in torment with the devil before they are redeemed.[7]

Eternal life, however, is a special blessing granted to a relatively few people because of their obedience to the Gospel of Jesus Christ.[8] The word of the Lord to His children is as follows: "If you keep my commandments and endure to the end you shall have eternal life, which is the greatest of all the gifts of God."[9] "He that hath eternal life is rich."[10] On another occasion the Lord explained both immortality and eternal life to the Prophet Joseph and definitely made it clear that they were entirely different things. He declared:

---

[5] Alma 11:45, 41; 12:13-16, 18; 40:26; 13:30; 1 Nephi 15:33-36; Jacob 3:11.
[6] Alma 11:44; 40:22-25; 2 Nephi 9:4-9; Helaman 14:16-19; Mormon 9:13-14.
[7] Joseph Fielding Smith, The Way to Perfection, p. 329.
[8] Alma 11:40-45; Doctrine and Covenants 132:21-25.
[9] Doctrine and Covenants 14:7.
[10] Ibid., 11:7.

And thus did I, the Lord God, appoint unto man the days of his probation—that by his natural death he might be raised in immortality unto eternal life, even as many as would believe; and they that believe not unto eternal damnation; for they cannot be redeemed from their spiritual fall, because they repent not.[11]

Just what is meant by eternal life? We read in the Gospel of John that *"this is life eternal to know Thee, the only true God, and Jesus Christ whom Thou hast sent."*[12] To know God is to have experienced His creative life to a large degree. Men must also know the full meaning of love, mercy, forgiveness, justice, intelligence, chastity and goodness in every respect by making those attributes part of their lives. In other words, they must through obedience to every word which comes from the mouth of their Heavenly Father learn to become like God. Regarding this subject, one of the eternal decrees of our Savior is as follows:

Strait is the gate and narrow is the way that leadeth unto the exaltation and continuation of the lives. . . . If ye receive me in the world, then shall ye know me, and shall receive your exaltation; that where I am ye shall be also. This is eternal lives—to know the only wise and true God, and Jesus Christ, whom he hath sent. I am he. Receive ye, therefore, my law.[13]

Eternal life is the kind of life possessed by the Heavenly Father and His Only Begotten Son; therefore, those mortals who attain it shall dwell in the presence of the divine beings. In a revelation to the Church members, the Savior declared, "If thou wilt do good, yea, and hold out faithful to the end, thou shalt be saved in the kingdom of God, which is the greatest of all the gifts of God; for there is no gift greater than the gift of salvation [eternal life]."[14]

In fact, the whole purpose of the Gospel of Jesus Christ and our existence is that we might aspire toward the more abundant and eternal life which is pointed out to us through the Gospel. Jesus declared, "I came that they might have life and that they might have it more abundantly. . . . I am the resurrection and the life: And whosoever believeth in me, though he were dead, yet shall he live; and whosoever liveth and believeth in me shall never die."[15]

The purpose and meaning of life are to be found in life itself. Lehi, the great ancient American prophet, de-

[11] *Ibid.*, 29:43-44.
[12] John 17:3.
[13] *Doctrine and Covenants* 132:22-24; 2 Nephi 9:15; 18; Mosiah 2:41.
[14] *Ibid.*, 6:13.
[15] John 11:25-26.

clared the purpose of life to be as follows: "Adam fell that men might be, and men are that they might have joy."[16] The deepest expression of joy and the most abundant life can be found in the Celestial Kingdom, where God dwells. Thus the Lord declared to Enoch that He had given mankind the Gospel in order that he might "enjoy the words of eternal life in this world and eternal life in the world to come, even immortal glory."[17]

To summarize, immortality means to live forever and the immortality given to every man and woman by the Savior is resurrection. Each of us will resurrect our body which will be united with the spirit, never to be separated again nor to disintegrate. Eternal life, on the other hand, is the condition of life that those who live righteous lives will enjoy throughout the ages in the Kingdom of God. In fact, it means exaltation. He who receives the greatest portion of eternal life becomes a God.

SUPPLEMENTARY READINGS—CHAPTER 2

1. *Bible*: John 10:10; 11:25-26; Romans 6:23; Genesis 1:2.
2. *Book of Mormon*: Alma 11; 12; 40; 41; 42; 1 Nephi 15:27-36; 2 Nephi 2:25; 9:4-9, 15, 18; Jacob 3:11; Mosiah 2:41; 16:7; Mormon 9:13-14.
3. *Doctrine and Covenants* 6:13; 11:7; 14:7; 29:43-44; 93:36; 132:21-25.
4. *Pearl of Great Price*: Moses 1:1-11, 24-42; 6:58; 2; 3:1-9; Abraham 4:5.
5. Joseph Fielding Smith, *The Way to Perfection*, pp. 328-333.
6. Joseph Fielding Smith (Compiler), *Teachings of the Prophet Joseph Smith*, pp. 166-167.
7. John A. Widtsoe (Compiler), *Discourses of Brigham Young*, pp. 147-152.

---

[16] 2 Nephi 2:25.
[17] Moses 6:58.

Chapter 3.

THE PLAN OF SALVATION

Eternal Progression of Man

The holy scriptures give an account of a great council which was held in the spirit world before man was placed on the earth. This meeting, known as the Council in Heaven, was presided over by God our Eternal Father; and those in attendance were His sons and daughters. It was one, perhaps, of many similar meetings held in the heavenly realm; but on this occasion the problems discussed and the decisions made were of such magnitude that God has seen fit to reveal to His prophets the main events that occurred there.

The principal purposes of the great gathering were to consider carefully the problem of the eternal progression of man and to present to the assembled throng the "Great Plan of Salvation."[1]

The law of growth or progression is one of the eternal laws of life. All other laws contribute to it. Our Eternal Father has attained His position of exaltation and Godhood by obedience to the great law of progression. We have risen to our present intelligent state by adherence to this law and by further compliance we will advance to a state of perfection.

The Great Plan

God the Eternal Father, who was the supreme intelligence at the great council, being more intelligent and more powerful than all the rest of the group combined, desired that His spirit-children should attain the same degree of glory that was then His. Since they had filled the measure of their spirit-existence, He knew that His purposes could be accomplished only by placing them on

[1] Joseph Fielding Smith, *Teachings of the Prophet Joseph Smith*, pp. 188, 354; Abraham 4:1-30.

12

a mortal world. After placing them there, God planned
to reveal to them the Gospel and give to them agency in
order that they might accept or reject its eternal truths.
Each mortal being would receive rewards based entirely
on valiancy, or obedience to the Gospel principles and ordinances. Thus the benevolent and Eternal Father explained to the assembled throng these and other conditions
of mortality and of the great "Gospel plan of salvation."

MEANS OF OBTAINING DIVINE VERITIES

The plan proposed by God for the government of
men and women in their earthly career was "based upon
eternal laws that always have been and always will be op-
erative." Since all forms of matter and energy are con-
trolled by laws, logic tells us that a plan formulated by
an eternal and intelligent being must be composed of laws.[2]
Many of these laws were the same as those obeyed in the
spirit world, and they are basically the same as the ones
we shall have opportunity to obey throughout eternity.
Thus the Gospel plan was laid upon a foundation of eternal
truth.

Among the laws to which all who come to earth were
to be subject are faith, repentance, baptism, confirmation,
love, charity, purity, industry, honesty, and many other
Gospel principles, ordinances and eternal realities.

BASED ON ETERNAL LAWS

God provided the gift of the Holy Ghost as a means
by which "a man may place himself in touch with the whole
universe and draw knowledge from it, including the beings
of superior intelligence that it contains."[3] The Spirit of
God was also provided to serve with the Holy Ghost as
another guide for man in helping him to establish communication with the Eternal Father.

According to the Prophet Joseph Smith, all truth was
to operate through the power of the Holy Priesthood. Man
was to be given that Priesthood, and through it God was
to reveal His will to mortals. To quote:

[2] *Doctrine and Covenants* 88:34-47; 130:20-21; 132:5; Abraham 3:1-15.
[3] John A. Widtsoe, *Rational Theology*, pp. 38-42.

[The Melchizedek Priesthood holds] the keys of the Kingdom of God in all ages of the world to the latest posterity on the earth; and is the channel through which all knowledge, doctrine, the plan of salvation and every important matter is revealed from heaven. Its institution was prior to the "foundation of the earth." . . . [It] is the highest and holiest Priesthood, and is after the order of the Son of God.[4]

THE FIRST SPIRITUAL DEATH

One important condition of mortal life provided in the great plan was that all spirits who come here must come in complete forgetfulness of their pre-mortal existence. The purpose of a veil being drawn over their past experiences was to start all of God's children out in mortality on as equal a basis as possible and let them live here by the principle of faith. Under these conditions each individual could face the world in faith and courage, and in vigor exercise his will in becoming acquainted with the realities that are here and in overcoming all obstacles.

Thus God's children, being placed upon a strange world and becoming mortal beings in almost complete forgetfulness of their Divine Parents, of the Gospel truths, and of all realities, would be spiritually dead. They would also be subject to physical death. In this condition God's sons and daughters would not have power to bring themselves back into His presence and thereby become glorified.

THE NEED FOR A SAVIOR

Knowing these facts, our Heavenly Father proposed as the center of the plan of salvation that one of His sons be appointed to be the Savior of the world. His work was to be the official revealer of Gospel truths to mortals. The Eternal Father decreed that angels should serve under the direction of this Savior as messengers to bring God's will to men. Thus His children would not be left in helpless ignorance, but they would be recipients of the Gospel. The Savior was to be endowed with power to break the bonds of death and thereby reunite the physical and spiritual bodies of men into a glorious resurrection. He was to be the light, the truth, and the life of the world. Only in and through His name could men be brought back into the pres-

---

[4] Joseph Fielding Smith, *Teachings of the Prophet Joseph Smith*, pp. 166-167.

ence of their Heavenly Parents. Thus He was to be a Divine Savior-God.

LEADERS CHOSEN

At the great council in heaven, God stood in the midst of His spirit-children and appointed "the noble and great ones" to future positions of leadership after they should become mortals.[5] In that assembled throng there was "one like unto God." This glorious personage volunteered to be the Savior of the world, humbly declaring, "Father, Thy will be done, and the glory be thine forever."[6] Thereupon the Father accepted His offer and foreordained Him to this great mission. This individual, while acting as the mediator, was none other than Jehovah of the Old Testament, and when He lived in mortality He was Jesus Christ of the New Testament. Michael the archangel, commonly known to us as Adam, was appointed to be the first mortal man; and Eve, a spirit of comparable brilliance and faithfulness, was assigned to be his helpmate—the "mother of all mortals." Abraham, Isaiah, Jeremiah, Joseph Smith, and others of the holy prophets were foreordained to positions of leadership in their respective dispensations, and Mary was chosen to be the mother of the Son of God.[7] These brilliant children of divine parents were chosen at the council in heaven for important work in the plan of salvation because of their intellectual superiority and their righteousness. They were foreordained but not predestined to their respective positions of leadership in mortality.

LUCIFER'S PLAN

The appointment of Jesus to be the Savior of the world was contested by one of the other sons of God. He was called Lucifer, son of the morning. Haughty, ambitious, and covetous of power and glory, this spirit-brother of Jesus desperately tried to become the Savior of mankind. At the great council he proposed a new plan of salvation, one which was not based on eternal truth. Regarding this event, the Lord revealed the following to Moses:

[5] Abraham 3:22-24.
[6] Ibid., 3:24.
[7] Ibid., Jeremiah 1:4-5; 2 Nephi 3:6, 15; 1 Nephi 11:13-21; Mosiah 3:8.

[Lucifer] came before me, saying, "Behold—here am I, send me, I will be thy son, and I will redeem all mankind, that one soul shall not be lost, and surely I will do it; wherefore give me thine honor."

But, behold, my Beloved Son, which was my Beloved and Chosen from the beginning, said unto me: "Father, thy will be done, and the glory by thine forever."

Wherefore, because that Satan rebelled against me, and sought to destroy the agency of man, which I, the Lord God, had given him, and also, that I should give unto him mine own power, by the power of mine Only Begotten, I caused that he should be cast down. And he became Satan, yea, even the devil, the father of all lies, to deceive and to blind men.[8]

FREE AGENCY

In contrast to Lucifer's plan of placing mortal beings on earth and bringing them back to God through no efforts of their own, Jesus sustained God's plan—the same one which had previously been followed in other worlds—of not interfering with the rights of intelligent beings to act for themselves. To Him free agency was basic in furthering the growth of human personality. Beginning with Adam, men were to be allowed to choose for themselves whether they learned much or little and whether they obeyed the laws of God or rejected them. In this way, and in no other, Jesus maintained, could men grow and eventually become Godlike.

INDIVIDUAL DIFFERENCES

Among the spirits assembled at that great council there were no two exactly alike. Some were more intelligent, more daring, more obedient than others. In fact, the law of individual differences operated there just as it does here in mortality. Since the Father respected man's free agency in the spirit world and since the group ranged in intelligence from God down to the least intelligent ones, it was but natural for a difference of opinion to develop over the two proposed plans of salvation. Lucifer vigorously campaigned for his plan, which was in opposition to the original Gospel pattern. His proposition, however, appealed to many of God's children, especially to the unadventurous ones. For them victory and salvation seemed to be assured if they followed Lucifer.

---

[8] Moses 4:1-6.

But not so with the great majority of the progressive spirits. They welcomed a world that offered real adventure and constant danger, where they could be agents unto themselves to cooperate with God in a great social scheme of learning and living truth—the laws of this new world. They were willing to accept God's law, as championed by Jesus Christ.

War in Heaven

The scriptures tell us the story as follows:

And there was war in heaven: Michael and his angels going forth to war with the dragon; and the dragon warred and his angels; and they prevailed not, neither was their place found any more in heaven. And the great dragon was cast down, the old serpent, he that is called the Devil and Satan.[9]

[Again we read] The devil . . . rebelled against me, saying, "Give me thine honor, which is my power; and also a third part of the host of heaven turned he away from me because of their agency; and they were thrust down, and thus came the devil and his angels.[10]

The Prophet Isaiah, lamenting this tragic event, exclaimed:

How art thou fallen from heaven, O Lucifer, son of the morning! How art thou cut down to the ground! . . . For thou hast said in thine heart, I will ascend into heaven, I will exalt my throne above the stars of God.[11]

Thus the plan of salvation as proposed by God and championed by Jehovah, Michael and other valiant men, was accepted by all the spirits who have been and who shall be permitted to come to this earth and take mortal bodies. Naturally some were not as valiant in the spirit world as were others; yet they all had their agency to choose for themselves. It is of importance to note that the free agency of man, as expressed in individual will, has continued in mortality as a basic principle in the eternal law of progression. That agency must be submissive, however, to the eternal laws of truth if we retain happiness and gain eternal life.

World War II, which recently came to a close, has proved once more that greater strength, power, leadership, and personal development are guaranteed to man by governments in which democracy and individual free-

---

[9] Revelation 12:7-9.
[10] *Doctrine and Covenants* 29:36-37.
[11] Isaiah 14:12-13.

dom are dominant principles than in governments wherein man does not have his free agency. Although all countries are more or less responsible for this terrible war, yet the fundamental principle we fought for was that the sons and daughters of God may retain their freedom of choice, just as the war in heaven was fought to preserve the same basic principle.

THE GOSPEL ORDINANCES

Operating in addition to and as part of natural laws are the Gospel ordinances. They were instituted by God the Eternal Father and His Son Jesus Christ before man was placed on this earth, for the purpose of assisting in bringing the sons and daughters of God back into Their presence. Such ordinances as baptism, confirmation, temple ordinances, priesthood ordinations, marriage, and others, are all part of the Gospel plan of salvation. All of these principles and ordinances of the Gospel are eternal. They were instituted before man was placed on the earth and are applicable to all human beings that live here. If any change or variation takes place in the Gospel plan of salvation, that change can be made only by the Father and His Only Begotten Son—the eternal Authors of that plan. Through the course of this study, these Gospel principles and ordinances will be discussed somewhat in detail.

As evidence of the truth of the facts just presented, the Prophet Joseph Smith declared:

If men would acquire salvation, they have got to be subject, before they leave this world, to certain rules and principles, which were fixed by an unalterable decree before the world was. . . .

The Gospel has always been the same; the ordinances to fulfill its requirements, the same, and the officers to officiate, the same; and the signs and fruits resulting from the promises, the same. . . .

He [God] set the ordinances to be the same forever and ever, and set Adam to watch over them, to reveal them from heaven to man, or to send angels to reveal them. . . . These angels are under the direction of Michael or Adam, who acts under the direction of the Lord. . . .

The ordinances, instituted in the heavens before the foundation of the world, in the priesthood, for the salvation of men, are not to be altered or changed. All must be saved on the same principles.[12]

Regarding the Gospel and its holy ordinances, the Lord has declared:

Verily, verily, I say unto you, he that receiveth my Gospel, receiveth me; and he that receiveth not my Gospel receiveth not me. And this

---

[12] Smith, *op. cit.*, pp. 324, 264, 168, 308.

is my Gospel: repentance and baptism by water, and then cometh the baptism of fire and the Holy Ghost, even the Comforter, which showeth all things, and teacheth the peaceable things of the kingdom.[13]

OBEDIENCE NECESSARY

From the beginning of history down to our day, God —even Jesus Christ—has been declaring through the mouths of His prophets that obedience to the Gospel plan is necessary for all who would attain eternal life. When the Man of Galilee was living among mortals, He definitely declared: "Not every one that saith unto me, Lord, Lord shall enter into the kingdom of heaven; but he that doeth the will of my Father who is in heaven."[14] Following are excerpts from the teachings of the Prophet Joseph Smith on this subject:

The question is frequently asked, "Can we not be saved without going through with all those ordinances?" I would answer, "No, not the fullness of salvation. . . . Any person who is exalted to the highest mansion has to abide a celestial law, and the whole law, too. . . ."

To get salvation we must not only do some things, but everything which God has commanded.[15]

Jesus Christ, the only perfect man who has lived on this earth, was perfect because He obeyed all the principles and ordinances of the Gospel in order that He "might fulfill all righteousness." He thereby set a pattern of life for mortals to follow. If they obey all the principles and ordinances of the Gospel, as did the Master, their growth will continue until they attain eternal life in the Kingdom of God.

SUPPLEMENTARY READINGS—CHAPTER 3

1. *Bible:* Isaiah 14:12-19; Revelation 12:7-12; Matthew 7:13-29.
2. *Book of Mormon:* 2 Nephi 2:17-18; 9:8-10; 24:12-19; Mosiah 3:17; 4:6-8; 18:13; Alma 12:25, 30, 32; 18:39; 40; 41; 42; 3 Nephi 27:5-25, 33.
3. *Doctrine and Covenants* 76:25-38; 29:36-41; 39:1-6; 63:5; 82:10; 89:18; 101:43; 130:19, 21; 132:37.
4. *Pearl of Great Price:* Abraham 3:22-28; Moses 4:1-4; 6:26-29, 50-67; 7:11-12; 8:19-30.
5. Lowell L. Bennion, *The Religion of the Latter-day Saints,* pp. 53-57, 82-86.
6. B. H. Roberts, *The Seventy's Course in Theology,* Second Year, pp. 13-27.
7. Joseph Fielding Smith, *The Way to Perfection,* pp. 28-38, 49-54, 178-186.
8. Joseph Fielding Smith (Compiler), *The Teachings of the Prophet Joseph Smith,* pp. 348-350, 308, 324, 168, 264, 138, 331-332, 199, 16.
9. John A. Widtsoe, *Rational Theology,* pp. 19-42.

---

[13] *Doctrine and Covenants* 1:5-6.
[14] Matthew 7:21.
[15] Smith, *op. cit.,* pp. 331-332, 199, 16.

Chapter 4.

JESUS AND THE GOSPEL

NAMING OF THE GOSPEL

As has been pointed out, at the great council in heaven, "when the morning stars sang together and all the sons of God shouted for joy,"[1] Jesus Christ was foreordained to be the Savior of the world.[2] Thereupon the Eternal Father bestowed upon His Beloved Son His divine power (Priesthood), in order that Jesus might in a valid way perform the works of the Redeemer and Mediator of the everlasting covenant and in the fullest degree be the Christ, the Savior of humanity. God honored the Only Begotten Son by naming this power *"the Holy Priesthood after the order of the Son of God."*[3] It was designated thus through the early Gospel dispensations down to the days of Abraham. But out of reverence to the name of the Supreme Being and to avoid its too frequent use, at this time the Church members changed the name to the Melchizedek Priesthood, calling it after the great high priest and king of Salem (Jerusalem).

Since Jesus was foreordained to be the Savior of mankind, God the Father also honored Him by naming the plan of salvation the *Gospel of Jesus Christ*. It makes no particular difference by what title this system of truth had been called on other worlds, it contains the same eternal verities which, through obedience to its principles, exalt human beings in any world, giving to them eternal life.

As a reward for the valiant work of the Son of Man, He shall eventually—when this earth is celestialized—become its God, King, and Ruler. The laws and the Priesthood which govern mankind shall be the laws and the Priesthood of the Gospel of Jesus Christ, and the God who will

---
[1] Job 38:7.
[2] Abraham 3:24; Moses 4:2.
[3] *Doctrine and Covenants* 107:1-4; Alma 13:1-31.

be directly responsible for the administration of those laws will be none other than the holy Man of Galilee.[4]

From the days of Adam to the present time, the Eternal Father has been declaring through His prophets that *"Jesus Christ is the only name which shall be given under heaven whereby salvation shall come unto the children of men."*[5] Paul, the Christian apostle, was so thoroughly convinced of that truth that he wrote these forceful words to the saints at Galatia:

I marvel that ye are so soon removed from him that called you into the grace of Christ unto another Gospel: Which is not another; but there be some that trouble you, and would pervert the Gospel of Christ. But though we, or an angel from heaven, preach any other Gospel unto you than that which we have preached unto you, let him be accursed.[6]

Who Jesus Was

Jesus is man's spiritual brother. We dwelt with Him in the spirit world as members of that large society of eternal intelligences, which included our Heavenly Parents and all the personages who have become mortal beings upon this earth or who ever shall come here to dwell. In that spirit-creation, when we became children of God, Jesus was the "first-born," and so He is our eldest brother.[7]

He was the most intelligent, the most faithful, and the most Godlike of all the sons and daughters of our Heavenly Father in the spirit world. He was so wise, so powerful, so good, that the scriptures speak of Him as "the author of eternal salvation."[8] He played such a dominant role in the pre-mortal world that He is referred to many times as "the creator of heaven and earth."[9] In fact, He worked as co-creator with the Eternal Father in preparing the world for man. Thus it is evident that in the pre-earth life, Jesus Christ shared richly in the life of His Eternal Father, and this prepared Him for the leading role in the work of God in bringing salvation to the human family. For these reasons He is the very center of the plan of salvation. In introducing Himself to the prophets, He says:

---

[4] Joseph Fielding Smith, *Teachings of the Prophet Joseph Smith*, p. 91.
[5] Moses 6:51; Mosiah 3:17; *Doctrine and Covenants* 18:23.
[6] Galatians 1:6-8.
[7] *Doctrine and Covenants* 93:23.
[8] Hebrews 5:9.
[9] *Doctrine and Covenants* 14:9; 29:1, 31; 76:24; Moses 1:32-33; 2:1, 5.

Hearken and listen to the voice of him who is from all eternity to all eternity, the Great I AM, even Jesus Christ, the light and the life of the world[10] . . . the same which looked upon the wide expanse of eternity, and all the seraphic hosts of heaven, before the world was made: the same which knoweth all things, for all things are present before mine eyes: I am the same which spake, and the world was made, and all things came by me. I am the same which have taken the Zion of Enoch into mine own bosom.[11]

The Jehovah of the Old Testament, the God who appeared to Abraham, Isaac and Jacob, the God who revealed the Gospel to the holy prophets from Adam's day down to the present time is Jesus Christ.[12] Among the numerous names by which He is known in the scriptures are the following: "the Lamb of God," "the Only Begotten Son of God," "Son of Man," "the Lord," "Immanuel," "Wonderful, Counselor, Mighty God, Everlasting Father, Prince of Peace."[13]

Sons and Daughters of Jesus Christ

The people of this earth are not only children of God the Eternal Father (being literally His offspring), but certain ones of them have also become in a particular sense the sons and daughters of Jesus Christ. In what respect, one may ask, are human beings Jesus' children, and why have the prophets sometimes referred to Him as "God the Father and the Son"? Many young Mormon elders have experienced difficulty in attempting to solve this problem.

We read in the Bible that during the early period of the earth's history "the sons of God saw the daughters of men that they were fair; and they took them wives of all which they chose."[14] According to the scriptures, the Lord was displeased with them for doing so. What is meant by this quotation? There are Christian writers who erroneously maintain that the antediluvian peoples recorded in the Bible false and childlike ideas regarding Gods and mortal beings; that they, like the ancient Greeks, believed that "gods" and the offspring of those "gods" married mortal beings. And this is the explanation of the foregoing scripture given by many writers.

---

[10] *Doctrine and Covenants* 39:1-2.
[11] *Ibid.*, 38:1-4.
[12] James E. Talmage, *Jesus the Christ*, pp. 1-2, 32.
[13] 1 Nephi 11:34-36; 13:26; Alma 13:11; 34:36; Helaman 6:5; Ether 13:10-11; Jacob 4:5, 11; Alma 12:33-34; 1 Nephi 11:7, 21; Moses 6:56; John 3:13-14; 6:27, 62; Luke 6:5; *Doctrine and Covenants* 20:21; 49:5; 76:13, 23.
[14] Genesis 6:2.

But the *Pearl of Great Price,* the *Book of Mormon,* and the *Doctrine and Covenants* throw brilliant light upon the foregoing text, as they do on many other ancient Gospel doctrines, explaining in what sense Jesus is the Father. These scriptures make it clear that in Adam's day part of his posterity accepted the Gospel of Jesus Christ, while others rejected it. Those who accepted it were called "the sons of God,"[15] while those who rejected it were termed "the sons of men."[16] For example, the Lord revealed to Adam that all people should have faith in Jesus Christ, repent and be baptized, and they would receive the Holy Ghost. This was the method definitely outlined by which all people could become the sons or daughters of Jesus Christ.[17] Further evidence is found in the same scripture wherein Enoch was teaching the people, saying: "Behold, our father Adam taught these things, and many have believed and become the sons of God."[18] Generations later we read that "Noah and his sons hearkened unto the Lord, and gave heed, and they were called the sons of God."[19] After the flood, the Savior appeared to the brother of Jared and declared:

Behold, I am he who was prepared from the foundation of the world to redeem my people. Behold, I am Jesus Christ. I am the Father and the Son. In me shall all mankind have light, and that eternally, even they who shall believe on my name; and they shall become my sons and daughters.[20]

This statement makes it very clear that mortals become the children of Jesus Christ (God) through affiliation with His Church. It also answers the difficult problem of how Jesus is both "the Father and the Son." Thus all mortals who accept the Gospel become the sons of Jesus Christ, and in this respect He is Father; but He is not the father of our spirits. God the Eternal Father is Jesus' Father and the Father of all the spirits of all men that come into mortality. The relationship of Father and children shall continue forever in that respect. But modern revelations confirm the declaration that Church members are also the sons and daughters of Jesus Christ;[21] and

---

[15] Moses 6:7, 67; 7:1; 8:13, 21.
[16] *Ibid.,* 5:52-53; 6:14.
[17] *Ibid.,* 6:7, 63-67.
[18] *Ibid.,* 7:1.
[19] *Ibid.,* 8:13.
[20] Ether 3:14.
[21] *Doctrine and Covenants* 39:1-6; 11:30; 34:3; 42:52; 45:8; 76:58; 128:23.

if they live the Gospel sufficiently well to gain celestial glory, they shall continue to be His children.

In the *Doctrine and Covenants* and the *Book of Mormon* we receive some additional ideas regarding the fatherhood of Jesus. Modern revelation tells us that Jesus became the Father by receiving a fullness of the glory of God the Eternal Father.[22] Abinadi, the ancient Nephite prophet, concluded that Jesus became the Father "because He was conceived by the power of God" and the Savior's will was swallowed up by the will of the Father.[23] Yet we must not get confused and think that the unity of the Father and the Son means that some mystical union of substance takes place. They are two separate and distinct persons, just as two mortal beings are separate and distinct persons.

SUPPLEMENTARY READINGS—CHAPTER 4

1. *Bible*: Job 38:7; Galatians 1:6-8; Hebrews 5:9; Isaiah 9:6; John 1; 8:13-14; 6:27, 62; 12:23, 31; Luke 6:5-9, 44; Genesis 6:2.

2. *Book of Mormon*: Mosiah 6:51; 3:17; 1 Nephi 11:7, 21, 34-36; 12:8-9; 13:26, 40; Alma 13:11; 12:33-34; 13:5, 11; 34:36; Helaman 3:28; 6:5; Jacob 4:5, 11; Ether 13:10-11; 3:14.

3. *Doctrine and Covenants* 107:3-4; 18:23; 93:23; 49:5, 9; 29:1, 31; 39:1-6; 38:1-4; 20:21; 11:30; 34:3; 42:52; 45:8; 128:23; 76:13, 23-24, 58.

4. *Pearl of Great Price*: Abraham 3:24, 27; Moses 4:2; 1:32-33; 2:1-5; 6:56, 67; 7:1; 8:13, 21; 5:52-53; 6:7, 14.

5. Joseph Fielding Smith (Compiler), *Teachings of the Prophet Joseph Smith*, pp. 91-92, 12.

6. Joseph Fielding Smith, *The Way to Perfection*, pp. 33, 24, 26, 231.

7. James E. Talmage, *Jesus the Christ*, pp. 1-41.

---

[22] *Ibid.*, 93:1-5, 15-17.
[23] Mosiah 15:1-9.

Chapter 5.

RELIGION IN HUMAN HISTORY

MAN'S SEARCH FOR TRUTH

Mormon theology maintains that the true religion, that is, the Gospel of Jesus Christ, is as old in this world as is human life. God revealed the Gospel to Father Adam— the first man—and since his day the dominant motive of human existence has been man's continuous search for truth —his quest for salvation. In fact, it has already been pointed out that the Gospel is eternal, and its truths were pursued by the sons and daughters of God in the spirit world before they were placed in mortality; and they have continued that search for truth after being placed on this earth.

Mormon theology maintains that the search for God, for the good life, and for salvation, is not only as old as human history, but is also world-wide. In all the records of human achievements there has not been found a more powerful, fundamental force than the Gospel in determining the actions of men and molding the events of history. It was the impelling power which caused a persecuted, exiled people to travel with ox teams and handcarts westward for hundreds of miles and to establish a commonwealth in the heart of a desert country. These people, under the driving urge of religion, engraved their names in history as the greatest colonizers the world has known. Other chapters of human history tell similar stories.

It is of value early in the course of study to define religion and theology and give evidence of their universality.

WHAT RELIGION IS

There is no one definition of religion which can be accepted as complete and authoritative. We all have our ideas of what is meant when religion is referred to; but we experience difficulty when we endeavor to define it satisfactorily. Religion, like love, testimony of the Gospel, appreciation of music, of art, of a beautiful sunset and many other finer things of life, is difficult of definition. Nevertheless, it is beneficial to offer explanation, discussion and definitions regarding it.

Religion has been defined as "the outreaching of the human heart for contact with the Deity"; also "as the expression of one's better self." William James stated: "In the broadest and most general terms possible one might say that religious life consists of the belief that there is an unseen order and that our supreme good lies in harmoniously adjusting ourselves thereto. This belief and this adjustment are the religious attitude in the soul."[1] Allen Menzies believes that "religion is the worship of higher powers from a sense of need."[2] And E. W. Hopkins concluded that "religion is squaring human life with superhuman life. . . . What is common to all religions is belief in a superhuman power and an adjustment of human activities to the requirements of that power, such adjustment as may enable the individual believer to exist more happily."[3]

It is the opinion of many people that religion is the highest expression of man's will to live and to have that life more abundantly. Religion is the outreaching of the human heart for the most worthwhile things that life offers. In fact, it is the highest aspect of our struggle for life, beauty and happiness. Religion is a drive in each of us to adjust our thoughts, feelings, and actions to God, to nature, and to all that is good and beautiful. Therefore, it is the impelling force which causes us to assume an attitude of profound seriousness towards life, towards God, and towards our eternal destiny.

An analysis of the definitions of religion that have been given shows that practically always three general factors appear in religion: first, the belief in a superhuman power is common to all religions; second, the worshipers have a desire for certain values, either material or spiritual;

---

[1] William James, *Varieties of Religious Experiences*, p. 53.
[2] Allen Menzies, *History of Religion*, p. 11.
[3] E. W. Hopkins, *History of Religion*, cited in Horace T. Houf, *What Religion Is and Does*, p. 2.

and third, they make certain adjustments in order to secure these values.

Let us conclude, then, that the true religion includes a knowledge of God, of the plan of salvation, and of all truths, as well as man's efforts to live in harmony with the eternal verities. In fact, religion interpreted in its broadest sense embraces all the attributes of godliness; or, in other words, it is the same thing as the Gospel of Jesus Christ applied in the lives of men. To the extent that mortals live in harmony with eternal truths and obey every commandment that has come from the mouth of God, they are truly religious.

THEOLOGY AND RELIGION

Theology and religion are closely related, but they are not identical. "The word 'theology' is of Greek origigin; it comes to us from *Theos*, meaning God, and *logos*— a treatise, or discourse."[4] Therefore, the word signifies a study or organized knowledge of divinity. It is the science that teaches us of God.

A person may be well-versed in theology and yet lack the principal traits which constitute a religious life. A religious man puts into practice his theological concepts. It is true that a thorough understanding of the plan of salvation—which could be accounted as theological knowledge — should strengthen and complement a man's religious living. For the purpose of illustrating the difference between religion and theology, let us

think of a triangle. Theology represents only one side of that triangle, which we shall designate as "Knowing." Religion, on the other hand, is much more inclusive. It embraces "Feeling," "Knowing," and "Doing," which would constitute the entire triangle.

---

[4] James E. Talmage, *The Articles of Faith*, p. 2.

Prophets Define Religion

In their definitions, the prophets of God have always stressed those three phases of religion—especially *Doing*. To quote James: "Pure religion and undefiled before God and Father is this, To visit the fatherless and widows in their affliction, and to keep oneself unspotted from the world."[5] Amos boldly declared: "Hate the evil, and love the good, and establish justice in the gate. . . . Let justice roll down as waters, and righteousness as a mighty stream."[6] Samuel's famous declaration to King Saul is as follows: "Hath the Lord as great delight in burnt offerings and sacrifices, as in obeying the voice of the Lord? Behold, to obey is better than sacrifice, and to hearken than the fat of rams."[7] The "Golden Text" of the Old Testament declares: "He [God] hath shewed thee, O man, what is good; and what doth the Lord require of thee, but to do justly, and to love mercy, and to walk humbly with thy God."[8] And Jesus, the author of the plan of salvation—quoting the Hebrew law[9]—summarized all of the Gospel teachings found in the holy scriptures in the following statement:

Thou shalt love the Lord thy God with all thy heart, and with all thy soul, and with all thy mind. This is the first and great commandment. And the second is like unto it, Thou shalt love thy neighbour as thyself. On these two commandments hang all the law and the prophets.[10]

Thus Latter-day Saints accept the foregoing teachings of the prophets and their definitions of religion as being true. They believe that the underlying force in religion is a deep, practical relationship with a superhuman being whom they call God. Their definition of religion will include, therefore, "a mode of behavior, a system of intellectual beliefs, and a system of feelings."

Universality of Religion

Historians agree with the Mormon concept that human beings have always been in constant search of God and salvation. Man's quest for salvation constitutes one

---

[5] James 1:27.
[6] Amos 5:15, 24.
[7] 1 Samuel 15:22.
[8] Micah 6:8.
[9] Deuteronomy 6:5; Leviticus 19:18.
[10] Matthew 22:37-40; Mark 12:30-33; Luke 10:27; Psalms 31:23.

of the major chapters in human history, as well as one of
the most powerful factors of social development. It has
frequently been stated regarding religion "that it is as
old as man in the universe and that it is universal."[11] An-
thropologists and historians claim that back in the period
of what they call unrecorded history, human beings distinguished themselves from other forms of earth-life by
their constant efforts to adjust their lives to the laws of
the unseen world and to find salvation. Dr. Robert Ernest
Hume states that "in the history of mankind there never
has been a tribe of men without some form of religion."[12]
Horace T. Houf and many other writers sustain Hume's
statement. To quote Houf:

> Religion is also very widespread. Not that religion in its fullest
> forms has always been. . . . But some features of religion have been
> found among all peoples, even the most backward. In the remotest,
> most isolated corners of the earth the tribes have practices or beliefs,
> or both, which would be so classified. To say that all known peoples,
> tribes, and groups have had religion in some form is not to assert that
> every individual person has had or does have. Investigators claim
> to have studied individuals who were non-religious. But the claim
> of universality seems to hold regarding all groups thus far found and
> studied. This means that religion would seem to be one of the most
> basal of human interests and a lasting part of man's life and culture.[13]

The statements of the foregoing authorities sustain
the revelations given to the Prophet Joseph Smith that
claim that religion is as old in this world as human life.
Although the non-Mormon scholars do not deal with religion as it operated in the pre-mortal world, they do maintain that men have had religious responses from the very
beginning of mortal history. In fact, reputable scholars
agree on the world-wide and world-old existence of religion.

SUPPLEMENTARY READINGS—CHAPTERS 5 AND 6

1. *Bible*: James 1:27; 1 Corinthians 13; Amos 5:15, 21-25; Isaiah 1:10-17; 58:5-7;
   Micah 6:1-8; 1 Samuel 15:22; Deuteronomy 6:5; Leviticus 19:18; Matthew
   22:37-41; Mark 12:30-33.
2. *Book of Mormon*: Alma 34:17-41; Mosiah 2:9-28; 4:10-30.
3. Horace T. Houf, *What Religion Is and Does*, pp. 3-31.
4. Robert Ernest Hume, *The World's Living Religions*, pp. 1-278.
5. William Warren Sweet, *The Story of Religion in America*, pp. 1-521.
6. James E. Talmage, *Articles of Faith*, pp. 1-4.
7. Harold Willoughby, *Pagan Regeneration*, pp. 1-307.

---

[11] Houf, *op. cit.*, p. 8.
[12] Robert Ernest Hume, *The World's Living Religions*, p. 1.
[13] Houf, *op. cit.*, p. 4.

Chapter 6.

MAN'S QUEST FOR SALVATION

PURPOSE

It is our purpose in this chapter to mention briefly the principal world religions, because later on throughout this course of study we shall have many occasions to compare some of the doctrines of these religions, especially those which have been believed in universally, with the true Gospel teachings. We shall also devote even more detailed attention to the pagan religions of the Mediterranean world which were rivals of Christianity—the Mystery Religions. Our purpose is to get acquainted with these cults, because in many of the chapters that follow, the relationship of these religions to Christianity and the effect that their rituals had upon the true Gospel established by Jesus Christ shall receive our careful consideration. It was the blending and mixing of the beliefs and practices of these pagan rivals of Christianity which resulted in the great apostasy. As the course proceeds, we shall become better acquainted with this religious syncretism, or blending together of religious beliefs and practices during the early Christian centuries, the net result of which was Catholicism.

RELIGIONS AND DENOMINATIONS

Human beings, in their quest for salvation, have established and fostered numerous religious systems. Some of them were very crude, while others contained many true principles. Several of the major world religions throughout history have multiplied and divided themselves into a number of different sects or churches. For example, in the United States in 1936 there were 256 Christian denominations.[1]

---

[1] *Religious Bodies, Denominations, A to J Statistics, History, Doctrine, Organization, and Work*, p. iii; William Warren Sweet, *The Story of Religion in America*, p. 1.

From the earliest times on, an untold number of pagan religions have flourished, some of which we have record of, while others have passed out of existence unrecorded. Dr. Frazer's voluminous work, *The Golden Bough*, gives many details of the story of paganism. Modern research and present-day writers have brought to light numerous facts regarding ancient religions.

The more thoroughly the extensive field of religious history is explored, the more evident it becomes that God is the center of human history and that one of the greatest endeavors of man has been his quest for salvation. A deity of some kind is an indispensable feature of religion and the very heart of each denomination. A pertinent fact in the history of religion is that what differentiates one particular religion from another is the interpretation the worshipers have had of God. Around their concept of the Deity they have in each religious denomination molded their human experiences, rituals, and creeds which appropriately fit their concept of the Supreme Being. Many of these beliefs and practices have been erroneous, however, while others have contained much truth. Thus human beings, in their quest for salvation, have practiced almost every conceivable type of ritual and have participated in a multitude of religious experiences.

WORLD'S MAJOR RELIGIONS

Robert Ernest Hume classifies the world's major religions into two groups—the dead and the living religions.' He lists twelve historical religions that have gone out of existence and eleven others that are prominent in the world today. The names of what Dr. Hume terms "the world's living religions" and their approximate church membership today are as follows: Christianity, 557 millions; Confucianism, 250 millions; Mohammedanism, 230 millions; Hinduism, 217 millions; Buddhism, 137 millions; Taoism, 43 millions; Shintoism, 16 millions; Judaism, 11 millions; Sikhism, 3 millions; Jainism, 1 million, and Zoroastrianism, 0.1 million.

The birthplace of every one of the eleven living religions was Asia. The following list of these religions

---

 Robert Ernest Hume, *The World's Living Religions*, pp. 12-17.

and their dates, arranged chronologically according to the
date of their founders, are quoted from Dr. Hume's book.
He points out that "for the two religions which had no
personal founder, the date assigned is the approximate or
traditional date of origin."[3]

Hinduism ....2000-1500 B.C. (Invasion of India)
Judaism ....1500-1200 B.C. (Approximate date of Moses)
Shintoism ....660 B.C. (First Japanese emperor)
Zoroastrianism ....660 B.C. (Latest possible date for Zoroaster)
Taoism ....604 B.C. (Nominal founder, Lao-Tze)
Jainism ....599 B.C. (Nominal founder, Mahavira)
Buddhism ....560 B.C. (Buddha's approximate birth date)
Confucianism ....551 B.C. (Confucius' approximate birth date)
Christianity ....4 B.C. (Jesus Christ's approximate birth date)
Mohammedanism ......570 A.D. (Mohammed's exact birth date)
Sikhism ....1469 A.D. (Guru Nank's exact birth date)

Hume makes the remark that "it is interesting to note
that about the sixth century before Christ there was a period
of unusual religious creativeness, when six of the world's
living religions originated. That same century was a period
of great importance to Judaism."[4]

It is equally as interesting to Latter-day Saints to
recall that in 600 B.C. God led a group of people from
Jerusalem to America under the direction of two great
prophets, Lehi and his son Nephi. Here for 1,000 years
flourished a great nation of people who understood the Gospel of Jesus Christ probably as well as any group of God's
children have done. Their history and their account of the
Gospel are recorded in the *Book of Mormon*.

RELIGIOUS CONDITIONS DURING THE EARLY CHRISTIAN CENTURIES

Probably at no time in history have all classes of people been more interested in religion than were the people of
the Mediterranean world during the early Christian centuries. The fact that people were conscious of the prevalence of evil and sin resulted in a hungering and yearning
for religious satisfaction. The aim of the good man was
"by means of a burning faith, by contempt for the world
and its standards, by ecstasy, suffering and martyrdom, to

---
[3] *Ibid.*, p. 13.
[4] *Ibid.*

be granted pardon for his unspeakable unworthiness, his immeasurable sins."[5]

During the early centuries A.D., people were demanding redemption, forgiveness of sins, freedom from existing or imaginary evils, and assurance of immortality. Thus any religion which professed to be able to procure forgiveness of sins for its members, to ward off many earthly evils, to assure the initiated of a life after death, to bring them back into the presence of Deity, and, most desirable of all, to deify them, such a religion became popular with the vast majority of the populace. The prevalence of the belief in fate, demons, sorcery, magic and superstition made any religion which offered salvation from these evils very popular.

Yet in the face of the deep religious attitude which prevailed throughout the entire Mediterranean world, Rome had nothing to offer the people that could satisfy them. Her old state religion was sterile; in fact, it had decayed. The old Greek Homeric religion, which had for hundreds of years furnished certain spiritual satisfactions to thousands of people, was now dead. Most of the citizens now looked upon that religion as being composed of idle myths. Even Greek philosophy had disintegrated to the point that the majority of the populace no longer sought shelter under its withering wings.

But a new day had dawned. The great Roman empire, established by Augustus Caesar in 27 B.C., extended its strong arms over a vast area, and gave tolerance of thought and freedom of action to its subject peoples on a larger scale than humanity had heretofore enjoyed. Having no religion of her own that could be made vital in the lives of her subjects, Rome was forced to throw the entire empire open to any religion or group of religions which could offer satisfaction to the people. In the words of Samuel Dill, "the world was in the throes of a religious revolution and eagerly in quest of some fresh vision of the Divine, from whatever quarter it might dawn."[6]

The Mystery Religions

In which direction were the people to look for a religion that would fill their needs and give to them complete

---

[5] Gilbert Murray, *Five Stages of Greek Religion*, p. 155.
[6] Samuel Dill, *Roman Society from Nero to Marcus Aurelius*, p. 82.

satisfaction? As Rome had nothing vital to offer, the populace turned to Christianity and the pagan cults of the Orient. Christ had just lived in the hilly country of Palestine and established the ancient Gospel on earth again. The Gospel was waiting for such men as Paul the apostle to take its glorious message to the inhabitants of Egypt, Syria, Asia Minor, Greece, and even Rome—the famous capital city.

But in addition to this virile religion, there were a number of vigorous cults in Asia Minor, Greece, Egypt, and even one which had migrated from far-off Persia, which offered salvation from the above-mentioned evils. They were known as the *Mystery Religions*. We shall also refer to them as the *pagan rivals of Christianity*. During the early centuries A.D. the mysteries spread throughout Italy and the Roman empire as the oncoming of a great wave, winning converts by the thousands.

Many factors, among which was emperor worship, contributed to the popularity of paganism during those early centuries. The fact that Christians refused to worship the Roman emperor as a god and also refused to worship any other individual except God the Eternal Father, while the Mystery Religions readily accepted the practice of worshiping the emperor and many other gods, gave paganism a distinct advantage over Christianity at first. Another important factor which served to make the Mystery Religions popular was the fact that these cults promised their devotees many of the things Christianity promised, such as the assurance of resurrection and a happy future life beyond the grave. They even promised that cult members could be exalted to godhood. They also had such doctrines as baptism, sacrament, atonement, sacrifices, and a belief in savior-gods. In fact, these pagan religions taught and practiced, in a distorted way, many doctrines which were directly related to the true Gospel of Jesus Christ. Even a casual glance at the doctrines of the Mystery Religions convinces one that they had come from the one common source of religious truths—the Gospel revelations given to Father Adam and the other holy prophets of God. Since many people failed to distinguish between the original and counterfeit brands of religion, the Mystery Religions became Christianity's strongest pagan rivals. The following quotation shows clearly this rivalry:

From Paul to Augustine . . . the fathers of the early church knew these cults as the strongest rivals that Christianity had, and with sour eloquence they testified to the popularity of the Mysteries among Gentile religionists.[7]

The Mystery Religions are of special interest to us in this course of study, since they affected the teachings of the Christian Church more than any other groups, resulting in drastically altering the teachings which Jesus had given and thereby bringing about the great apostasy. We shall give a brief statement of several of the most important cults which played such a dominant role in the religious history of the early Christian period. According to Dr. Willoughby, "it is a curious circumstance that the very cults which were most widely and genuinely popular in the Graeco-Roman world are the least known in detail to religio-historical students today";[8] therefore, we should become better acquainted with them.

The Mysteries of Mithra originated in Persia about 1500 B.C. and migrated westward, arriving in Rome 66 B.C. For more than a hundred years prior to Paul's birth, the worship of Mithra was the most popular religion at Tarsus, the apostle's home town, and it remained so for centuries thereafter. During the early Christian period, Mithraism became the most popular religion in the entire Roman empire; in fact, it became the state religion. It retained that position of importance until 312 A.D., when Constantine legalized Christianity; and then, in 392 A.D., it received its death blow when Theodosius outlawed all pagan religions. If it had not been for these important events, and especially for the sheer superiority of Christianity, much of the world might be worshiping Mithra today instead of Jesus, so powerful did this pagan cult become.

Egypt supplied the Mediterranean world with two important cults, the Mysteries of Isis and Hermeticism. The former religion had its inception early in Egyptian history. It went through various periods of transition, and finally, in its Hellenized form, it got a foothold in Rome

---
[7] Harold Willoughby, *Pagan Regeneration*, p. 26.
[8] *Ibid.*, pp. 23-24.

about 150 B.C. When Paul began his missionary work in Asia Minor, "he everywhere met with Isiac establishments that were already centuries old." This religion remained a power in the eastern Mediterranean world even to the last days of paganism, and it also won a place of importance in Italy. Hermeticism came into existence at least a century before Christ and reached its greatest popularity during the early Christian centuries. It also contributed its share to the religious complexity of the early Christian period.

Asia Minor's greatest contribution to paganism of the early Christian period was the Cybele-Attis (Great Mother) Mystery Religion. As early as the sixth century B.C. worshipers of this religion were practicing their orgies with a frenzy surpassing that of most other pagan devotees. During the Second Punic Wars (204 B.C.), the worship of the Great Mother was brought from Asia Minor to Rome by order of the Senate, with the hope that this goddess could help defeat Hannibal. Three years later the Carthaginian army was defeated and their city destroyed. The Great Mother had now won her place of prominence among the pagan cults. She retained that position until paganism came to an end.

Greece also supplied its Mystery cults to the Roman empire. The Eleusinian Mysteries were highly regarded at Athens long before the days of Socrates, and their influence was widespread throughout the Graeco-Roman world during the days of Jesus and thereafter. Cicero was of the opinion that "Athens had given nothing to the world more excellent or divine than the Eleusinian Mysteries."[9]

Greece also had its Dionysian or Bacchus Mysteries, whose members worshiped their god through excessive drunkenness and wild orgies. A reformed type of Dionysian worship was Orphism, a cult well known to Plato. Both of these religions remained prominent during the early Christian period until 392 A.D.

There were several other Mystery Religions of lesser importance which flourished in the Mediterranean world as rivals of Christianity, but space will not permit a discussion of them.

---

[9] *Ibid.*, 41.

Brief Description of Mystery Religions

By way of describing the Mystery Religions, one thing that was common to all of them was that they were secret organizations. That is their meaning of the word "mystery." Instead of being a religion of a state, a tribe, or a city into which people were born, these religions, like Christianity, were personal institutions into which individuals from any race could become initiated on condition of fulfillment of cult requirements. Membership was attained through initiation—a religious rebirth; thus the devotees felt a guarantee of personal salvation. These factors contributed to the popularity of the Mysteries during the early Christian age.

One of the most prominent features of a Mystery Religion was the great use it made of symbolism. Through the exhibition of statues of the cult deities, through public prayers, sacramental acts, myths and allegories, mystical experiences provoked the initiate to regeneration. He actually felt that he had been born anew. Some of the members brought about their religious experiences through drinking wine, dancing and violent whirling, bright lights, and other physically suggestive means. In the symbolism of the Mysteries, sometimes offensive to the early Christians and to people of our generation, these ancients were blindly grasping for the truths and realities of life.

There was a great variety of types of worship in the Mysteries, ranging from the most dissolute revelry to highly refined theology and rituals. Some rites were wild and barbaric, while others were meditative and refined. Thus, during the early Christian centuries, almost any type of individual could find things that appealed to him in one or another of these pagan cults. In fact, the worshipers, in their search for God and in their desire to gain salvation, participated in many weird religious practices. The main aim of the Mysteries was to appeal to the emotions. Through this appeal a psychic and mystic effect was produced which caused the participant to feel that he had experienced a new life.

Christianity vs. Paganism

Christianity moved westward from the Orient and spread throughout the Roman empire as a strong competitor of the Mystery Religions. It offered mankind all of the good things that the Mysteries promised, and in addition it also possessed the advantage of a superior code of ethics, a more definite and elaborate philosophy, and more refined ordinances and symbolism. Jesus of Nazareth had revealed to His followers the divine truths—the words and will of His Eternal Father—while the Mystery Religions were blindly seeking for those truths.

The world was in search of a Savior-God. Christianity supplied this in the divine historic person of Jesus Christ, while the Mystery Religions' savior-gods were but crude myths. The principles of Christian love and faith became a new force in religious life. Christianity during the early centuries possessed the ability to incorporate the social, ethical, and political aspects of life into religion, and to adjust to the needs of a changing world. Mystery cults lacked authoritative scriptures which Christianity possessed through its inheritance of the Old Testament and also its own writings, the New Testament. The latter gained the divine stamp equal in authenticity to the Hebrew scripture. No religion equaled the Church of the Master in offering moral content to humanity in time of the crises of life. Therefore, Christianity overcame all pagan rivals because of its superiority. The climax came when it received the support of the Roman government during the fourth century, and finally became the state religion in 392 A.D. But its ultimate triumph over paganism was not made without greatly altering the pure stream of Christian thought by the adoption of numerous heathenistic beliefs and practices.

Chapter 7.

COMMON SOURCE OF RELIGIOUS TRUTHS

SIMILARITIES IN RELIGIOUS BELIEFS AND PRACTICES

The study of comparative religions during the past one hundred years has brought to light a surprising and significant succession of similarities in the beliefs and practices of the major world religions as well as the Mystery Religions which were briefly presented in the last chapter. Men, in their worship of God and in their quest for salvation, have maintained certain beliefs and have performed numerous ceremonials that are seen in many religions regardless of the country or the century to which the worshipers belong. The people of Greece, Italy, Egypt, Palestine, Mesopotamia, and India, as well as the aborigines of America and the inhabitants of far-off China, had similar rituals and creeds. Scholars have marveled over this "golden thread," this trace of similarity, which can be followed throughout the religious history of man.

Among the world-wide concepts are: a belief in a golden age in the past and a Utopia in the future; a belief in a Messiah and the virgin birth of "savior-gods"; a belief in the overruling power of Deity; a belief in demons, sin, rewards, punishments, and in the efficacy of baptism and of the eucharist or sacrament.

All religions believe in some sort of immortality. The claim to priesthood is universal. The concept of the existence of a divine plan for the guidance of men to happiness is world-old and world-wide. Most of the religious groups have taught the brotherhood of man, cooperation, and the golden rule. The belief that growth comes as a result of self-control and self-effort has been commonly held throughout the ages.

The cardinal qualities of moral life, such as justice, temperance, patience, purity, truthfulness and love, played a dominant role in all religions. Spiritual sentiments, such as reverence, awe, worship and faith, are common to all; and in the varieties of religions there exists a passionate yearning to become perfect. Even the substance of the Ten Commandments has been fundamental in the beliefs of many peoples.

THEORIES ACCOUNTING FOR RELIGIOUS SIMILARITIES

There is ample proof that such religious similarities as have been mentioned exist, and many more examples might be cited; but why do they exist? What are the theories which explain their presence?

DEVIL THEORY

So similar were many of the pagan practices to those of early Christianity that Justin Martyr, about 150 A.D., after describing the Lord's Supper as given in the Gospels, remarked: "The wicked devils have imitated [it] in the mysteries of Mithra, commanding the same thing to be done."[1] Tertullian, another Christian teacher (160-220 A.D.), stated that "the devil, by the mysteries of his idols, imitates even the main part of the divine Mysteries. . . . He baptizes his worshipers in water and makes them believe that this purifies them from their crimes."[2]

Thirteen hundred years later, Las Casas (1474-1566 A. D.), a Spanish Catholic missionary, observing that the ceremonies of the Indians closely resembled those of the Christians, concluded that the devil had arrived in America ahead of the Christians and implanted in the minds of the natives many teachings closely akin to Christianity. It has been a Gospel teaching proclaimed by Jesus and the holy prophets that the devil has exerted a powerful influence upon mortal beings in bringing about sin and apostasy and in counterfeiting the true principles and ordinances of the Gospel. But it is also true that the complete responsibility for apostasies and also for the worldwide religious similarities cannot be placed upon the devil. Lucifer and his followers have merely contributed their share—in conjunction with other fundamental causes—in bringing about those conditions.[3]

[1] Justin Martyr, *Apologia* i, 66, cited in Harold Willoughby, *Pagan Regeneration*, p. 162.
[2] Tertullian, *De Praescriptione Haereticorum*, 40, cited in Willoughby, *Ibid.*, p. 160;
[3] *Doctrine and Covenants* 93:39.

Independent Development Theory

Another theory which is very popular among writers today in explaining such religious similarities in different lands and among different peoples has been termed the "independent development theory." Those who advocate it maintain that religious beliefs and practices have arisen spontaneously and independently in various countries. They hold that religious rituals and beliefs developed gradually as men evolved from savagery to civilization. Certain scholars point out that similar myths, legends, and folklore exist among all primitive peoples; and that these and primitive magic arose as a result of "fear," presence of death, reproduction, and other experiences that deeply stir the feelings of man.[4]

The theory of independent development also maintains that the founders of the various great world religions developed their creeds, beliefs and practices on their own foundation, independently of other religions. To quote:

The striking similarities that exist, despite independent origin, are explained by a "psychic unity that leads men independently . . . to arrive at the same destination." Some supporters of this theory speak of a "convergence" of human ideas towards the same conclusions. In short, the blind or chance operation of some mystic force explains the similarities appearing in the religious systems of the world.[5]

This explanation is also used to account for the world-wide similarities in art, mechanics, crafts and literature. Those who advocate this theory claim that all similarities in the general culture of mankind had an independent origin in different parts of the world.

Diffusion Theory

In contrast with the "independent development theory," a number of writers have maintained that the similarities in the religions and cultures of different peoples can be explained on the basis of having come from a common source or center and having been diffused throughout the world. Sir Edward Burnett Tylor and his followers are strong advocates of the "diffusion theory," having produced a large and convincing literature in its support. From the earliest times human beings have traveled by land and by

[4] Lewis Browne, *This Believing World;* James G. Frazer, *The Golden Bough.*
[5] John A. Widtsoe, *Evidences and Reconciliations,* p. 79.

sea very extensively, and through this intercourse their skills and learnings have passed from man to man and from land to land. There is an abundance of historical evidence to sustain the belief that ideas, handicrafts, arts, religious customs, and culture in general have been handed down from one generation to another and that races of people have borrowed all of these from each other.

In fact, one of the most important causes of the similarities of beliefs and rituals is this very fact, that people do hand down their customs to their children, and they in turn to their children. In such an important matter as religion, the fundamentals carry on from generation to generation. Also peoples of different countries in their social contacts borrow rituals from each other. During certain periods of history, conditions have been more favorable to the dispersal of human customs, beliefs and culture than during other periods. For example, the conquests of Alexander the Great and the spreading of Greek culture to foreign countries resulted in a mixture of Greek beliefs with those of the conquered nations. Historians speak of this activity as Hellenizing the world. Again the subsequent rise of the Roman empire was very conducive to the spread of ideas and the blending together of religious beliefs. This fusing and blending of theologies is termed "religious syncretism."

Mormons know that the Jaredites and the Nephites migrated to America, bringing with them from their former homes many social and religious customs and beliefs. Mohammedanism furnishes a good example of a religion spreading from Arabia throughout Asia and into parts of Europe and Africa. Christianity has been carried from one end of the world to the other. The diffusion of these latter two religions has taken place within historical times since the birth of Jesus of Nazareth; also the story of the former two peoples is clearly recorded in the *Book of Mormon.*

INDEPENDENT DEVELOPMENT AND DIFFUSION THEORIES EXPLAINED

All men and women born into the world are sons and daughters of God; therefore, they may all receive knowledge and guidance through His omnipresent Holy Spirit. One of the basic principles of the Gospel of Jesus Christ is revelation—God's will being communicated to man. Through various methods He gives mortals knowledge of light and truth. If the Lord should so desire, He could reveal the same truths to two men who lived in different parts of the world and who were completely inaccessible to each other. In fact, they could be separated also by hundreds of years of time. Mormons agree, therefore, that to a certain extent the theory of "independent development" can be accepted as partially accounting for the similarities in various religions.

This doctrine suggests that God has given to all peoples, regardless of their race, color or creed, the amount of religious truth that they were able to receive and willing to obey. The Nephite prophets maintained that the Lord has made known Gospel truths to every race of people according to their needs and ability to harmonize their lives with the divine will. In the words of King Benjamin: "And *the Lord God hath sent his holy prophets among all the children of men, to declare these things to every kindred, nation, and tongue.*"[6]

Alma stated that God is mindful of every people. He said: "*For behold, the Lord does grant unto all nations, of their own nation and tongue, to teach his word, yea, in wisdom, all that He seeth fit that they should have.*"[7]

Therefore, a certain amount of God's word was given in divers ways to the people of India, of Persia, of Babylon, of Arabia, of China, Greece, and Rome; and a great amount of it was given to the people of Palestine, to the inhabitants of ancient America, and to the Church of Jesus Christ of Latter-day Saints.

No prophet of God has ever presented these facts in a more beautiful and convincing way than did Nephi, the mighty preacher of old. To quote from his teachings and God's revelation to him:

Thus saith the Lord God: "I will give unto the children of men line upon line, precept upon precept, here a little and there a little; ... Unto him that receiveth, I will give more; and from them that shall

[6] Mosiah 3:12-13.
[7] Alma 29:8.

say, 'We have enough,' from them shall be taken away even that which they have.[8] . . .

"Know ye not that there are more nations than one? Know ye not that I, the Lord your God, have created all men, and that I remember those who are upon the isles of the sea; and that I rule in the heavens above, and in the earth beneath; and *I bring forth my word unto the children of men, yea, even upon all the nations of the earth?*

"Wherefore murmur ye because that ye shall receive more of my word? Know ye not that the testimony of two nations is a witness unto you that I am God, that I remember one nation like unto another? Wherefore, I speak the same words unto one nation like unto another. And when the two nations shall run together, the testimony of the two nations shall run together also.

"Wherefore, because that ye have a Bible, ye need not suppose that it contains all my words; neither need ye suppose that I have not caused more to be written: *For I commanded all men, both in the west, and in the north, and in the south, and in the islands of the sea, that they shall write the words which I speak unto them;* for out of the books which shall be written, I will judge the world, every man according to their works, according to that which is written.

"For behold, I shall speak unto the Jews, and they shall write; and I shall also speak unto the Nephites, and they shall write; and I shall also speak unto the other tribes of the house of Israel, which I have led away and they shall write it; and *I shall also speak unto all nations of the earth, and they shall write it.*"[9]

It seems, however, that historically the major portion of evidence favors the doctrine of diffusion from some central place of culture, beliefs, and customs as the principal explanation of the religious similarities among the various races of men. This belief is sustained by modern revelations given through Joseph Smith. The Prophet was informed that God revealed the plan of salvation to Father Adam, the first man. Gradually, as men drew further from their Heavenly Parents through sin and ignorance, the interpretation of Gospel truths was corrupted and changed; yet a resemblance to the original revelation persisted. At various times God renewed men's knowledge of truth by revelations to His prophets. Only those individuals or races who continued in harmony with Deity were able to draw divine verities from above. Thus the diffusion theory maintains that all religions had a common origin, that apostasies have diverted the truths, yet leaving enough verity in any religion to give it a resemblance to the teachings of the Master. This helps to account for the American

[8] I Nephi 17:35-40; 2 Nephi 28:29-30.
[9] *Ibid.*, 29:7-12.

Indians in 1492 having similar rituals and beliefs to the Christians, and in general, for the similarities in all religions.

In conclusion, therefore, the foregoing revelations quoted from the Nephite prophets definitely show that God has revealed His will to religious leaders all over the world. This gives us the key as to where the knowledge of truths came from in the support of the independent development theory. On the other hand, there has been one principal line of chosen people—beginning with Father Adam and running from him through Noah, Abraham, Isaac and Jacob, and then on through the Israelite prophets—through which God has revealed His will most generously. From the teachings of this central line of righteous prophets truths have filtered outward throughout the world. This, therefore, sustains the diffusion theory.

Thus both the independent development and diffusion theories can be accepted as answers to the problem of why there are resemblances in world religions. Doubtless there has been an interplay of these two forces operating throughout history. According to Dr. John A. Widtsoe, Mormons accept each of these theories as partial answers to this problem. To quote Dr. Widtsoe's words: "These two contending and opposite theories—the independent development and the diffusion theories—have followers of equal scholastic standing. . . . Latter-day Saints agree with both of these theories, in part, and differ with them in part."[10]

SUPPLEMENTARY READINGS—CHAPTERS 7 AND 8

1. *Bible:* John 1:1-16; Acts 17:26-32; Romans 10:11-15; Galatians 3:23-29; James 1:13-15; Matthew 24:14; Mark 16:15-18.
2. *Book of Mormon:* 1 Nephi 17:35-40; 2 Nephi 28:29-30; 29:7-12; Mosiah 3:12-13; 16:6-11; Alma 29:8; 5:40-42; 38:9; 3 Nephi 9:15-18; 15:9; Ether 4:12; Moroni 7:12-14.
3. *Doctrine and Covenants* 76:1-10; 29:34-35; 131:20-21.
4. Alfred W. Martin, *Seven Great Bibles,* pp. xviii, 1-277.
5. Joseph Fielding Smith (Compiler), *Teachings of the Prophet Joseph Smith,* pp. 218, 250-252.
6. Joseph F. Smith, *Gospel Doctrine,* pp. 36-40.
7. John A. Widtsoe, *Evidences and Reconciliations,* pp. 78-84.
8. John A. Widtsoe (Compiler), *Discourses of Brigham Young,* pp. 2-6.
9. Hugh McCurdy Woodward, *Humanity's Greatest Need,* pp. 1-321.

---

[10] Widtsoe, *op. cit.,* pp. 80-81; Sir G. Elliott Smith, *The Diffusion of Culture,* also *In the Beginning;* Ira. M. Price, *The Monuments and the Old Testament,* pp. 129-130.

Chapter 8.

DIVINE FOUNTAIN OF ETERNAL TRUTH

ALL TRUTH COMES FROM GOD

All that is good in the entire world, or that has been or that will be, comes from one divine source—the Godhead. These heavenly·beings constitute the Eternal Fountain of Law and Truth. The great scientists, the renowned philosophers, the famous poets and musicians, the teachers and prophets who have discovered truth and given it to humanity during any age of the world's history have received their inspiration from God. Thus Socrates, Plato, Aristotle, Kant, Shakespeare, Galileo, Copernicus, Edison, Burbank, Tennyson, Emerson, Beethoven and others received their revelations of new truths from the same source. Even the leaders of the great movements, such as Christopher Columbus, Abraham Lincoln, Susan B. Anthony, and Dorothea Dix, were divinely inspired. Also the forefathers in writing the Constitution were guided by the hand of God. All the great religious teachers of the world, such as Buddha, Confucius, Mohammed, Zoroaster and Lao-Tze wherein they taught virtue and truth, received the same from the divine fountain of truth. The Protestant reformers also received inspiration from God in carrying forward their work preparatory for the restoration of the Gospel of Jesus Christ. And it has been universally recognized in Christendom that the great prophets of the Old and New Testament periods were in close communion with the Supreme Being. The Latter-day Saints are of the opinion that no men who have lived in this world, with the exception of Jesus Christ, have drunk more deeply of the Fountain of Truth than did such individuals as Nephi, Alma the younger, and the Prophet Joseph Smith, especially the latter.

To go one step further, it is true that every man and woman receives a certain amount of guidance along the path of truth from the same source that the renowned leaders have received their inspiration. We all draw upon the Divine Fountain of Truth; however, some draw more heavily than others. Thus all truth comes from God.

THIS BELIEF CONFIRMED BY PRESIDENT SMITH

President Joseph F. Smith maintained that all truths come to men through the mediation of Jesus Christ; therefore, he confirmed the foregoing doctrine. To quote his words:

Christ, therefore, being the foundation of truth, is no imitator. He taught the truth first; it was his before it was given to man. When he came to the earth he not only proclaimed new thought, but repeated some of the everlasting principles which had been heretofore only partly understood and enunciated by the wisest of men. And in so doing he enlarged in every instance upon the wisdom which they had originally received from him, because of his superior abilities and wisdom and his association with the Father and the Holy Ghost. He did not imitate men. They made known in their imperfect way what the inspiration of Jesus Christ had taught them, for they obtained their enlightenment first from him.

Christ taught the Gospel to Adam, and made known his truths to Abraham and the prophets. He was the inspirer of the ancient philosophers, Pagan and Israelite, as well as of the great characters of modern times. Columbus, in discovery; Washington, in the struggle for freedom; Lincoln, in emancipation and union; Bacon, in philosophy; Franklin, in statesmanship and diplomacy; Stephenson, in steam; Watts, in song; Edison, in electricity; and Joseph Smith, in theology and religion, found in Christ the source of their wisdom and the marvelous truths which they advocated.

Calvin, Luther, Melanchthon, and all the reformers, were inspired in thoughts, words, and actions, to accomplish what they did for the amelioration, liberty and advancement of the human race. Their inspiration, as with that of the ancients, came from the Father, his Son Jesus Christ, and the Holy Ghost, the one true and living God. This may also truthfully be said concerning the Revolutionary fathers of this nation, and all who have in the ages past contributed to the progress of civil and religious freedom. There is no light nor truth which did not come to them first from him. Men are mere repeaters of what he has taught them. He has voiced no thoughts originating with man.

The teachings of Jesus did not begin with his incarnation; for, like truth, he is eternal. He not only inspired the ancients from the beginning, but when he came to earth he reiterated eternal, original truth, and added gloriously to the revelations men had uttered. When he returned to the Father he still took, and does take, an interest in his children and people, by revealing to them new truths, and by inspiring their actions; and, as men grow in the knowledge of God, they shall become more and more like him unto the perfect day, when his knowledge shall cover the earth as the waters cover the deep.[1]

---

[1] Joseph F. Smith, *Gospel Doctrine*, pp. 38-40.

This Doctrine Also Sustained by the Prophets

The Prophet Joseph Smith declared that "if there was anything great or good in the world, it comes from God."[2] This is also the doctrine of the holy scriptures. The Nephite prophets were especially emphatic in their pronouncements that all good comes from the Deity, while its opposite comes from the devil.[3] The Gospel of Christ, they taught, is the plan of salvation, Jesus being "the light and the life, and the truth of the world."[4] Many similar statements appear in the *Doctrine and Covenants*. It is reasonable to conclude, therefore, that religions resemble each other in those particular points which are true because all truth emanates from the same source—the great Fountain of Law and Truth, of which God is the head, because He has throughout the ages lived righteously and always worked in harmony with law and truth.

Religious Truths Revealed to the Righteous

In modern revelations, Jesus definitely promised to reveal His will and numerous truths to the people who serve Him diligently by keeping His commandments. For example, such revelations as the following appear in the *Doctrine and Covenants:*

I, the Lord, am merciful and gracious unto those who fear me, and delight to honor those who serve me in righteousness and in truth unto the end. Great shall be their reward and eternal shall be their glory. And to them will I reveal all mysteries, yea, all the hidden mysteries of my kingdom from days of old, and for ages to come will I make known unto them the good pleasure of my will concerning all things pertaining to my kingdom.

Yea, even the wonders of eternity shall they know, and things to come will I show them, even the things of many generations; and their wisdom shall be great, and their understanding reach to heaven: and before them the wisdom of the wise shall perish, and the understanding of the prudent shall come to naught; for by my spirit will I enlighten them, and by my power will I make known unto them the secrets of my will; yea, even those things which eye has not seen, nor ear heard, nor yet entered into the heart of man.[5]

Thus it is definite that in order to draw upon the fountain of truth one must live a righteous life. The more complete his obedience is to the principles of the Gos-

---

[2] Joseph Fielding Smith, *Teachings of the Prophet Joseph Smith*, p. 251.
[3] Alma 5:40-42; Omni 1:25; Moroni 7:12-14.
[4] Ether 4:12; Mosiah 16:6-11; Alma 38:9; 3 Nephi 9:15-18; 15:9.
[5] *Doctrine and Covenants* 76:1-10.

pel, the thinner the veil between him and the unseen world becomes. In other words, man must be in tune in order to receive revelation. For example, one morning in 1829, before Joseph Smith went upstairs to continue his work of translating the Nephite records, he had a disagreement with his wife. Then he and Oliver Cowdery went to their work. The Prophet's scribe sat, with pen in hand, for the seer to repeat the words from the ancient record. Finally, after many long minutes had passed, Joseph said, "Oliver, something is wrong. All is dark. I can't see a thing."[6]

Thereupon Joseph went out into the garden and remained about an hour praying. Then he returned to the house, where he and Emma made things right with each other. He was now spiritually in harmony with God and his mortal associates, and so he was able to resume his work as usual. This experience illustrates the absolute necessity of living righteously if we are to receive revelations from the Most High.

The fact that the Prophet Joseph Smith was in almost continuous communion with God, the veil always being very thin between himself and the unseen world, is positive proof of the perpetual righteousness of this great man. Therefore, those interpretations to the contrary of the Prophet's personality and character given by some anti-Mormon writers are grossly erroneous—in fact, wickedly false. Joseph Smith could not have continued to receive revelations from God and see and commune with heavenly beings up to the time of his death unless he was continuously living a pure life, both in thoughts and actions. And Latter-day Saints know that the American Prophet continued to commune with heavenly beings and that he received during his lifetime probably as many divine truths through revelation as any other mortal being ever received.

METHODS OF REVELATION

The members of the Godhead are forever reaching downward toward mortals and anxiously waiting for them to get in harmony so that they can receive knowledge of eternal truths. God has utilized divers channels through which to reveal His will to men. On certain occasions

---

[6] John Henry Evans, *The Heart of Mormonism*, pp. 58-59.

He has sent His Only Begotten Son to earth with messages to mortals and at other times angels have come. Through dreams and visions men have received light, and at times God has spoken directly from heaven to them. God has made available His Spirit and also that of the Holy Ghost to serve as guides toward all truths.

"The Holy Spirit is the power of intelligence, of wise direction, of development, of life. . . . Some measure of this power is given to all mankind."

The "force" of God's intelligence is permeating the universe, contacting and enlightening the intelligence of mortals. The foregoing doctrine is confirmed in modern revelation as follows:

For the word of the Lord is truth, and whatsoever is truth is light, and whatsoever is light is Spirit, even the Spirit of Jesus Christ; and the Spirit giveth light to every man that cometh into the world; and the Spirit enlighteneth every man through the world, that hearkeneth to the voice of the Spirit. And every one that hearkeneth to the voice of the Spirit, cometh unto God, even the Father.[7]

The Holy Ghost, on the other hand, functions almost exclusively with those individuals who have been baptized and confirmed members of the Church of Jesus Christ of Latter-day Saints.[8] Before His death, the Savior told His apostles: "I will pray to the Father and he shall give you another Comforter, that he may abide with you forever; even the Spirit of truth; whom the world cannot receive, because it seeth him not, neither knoweth him."[9] But even after members of the true Church receive the Holy Ghost, their righteousness determines the effectiveness with which this gift from God can operate through them.

It is encouraging to know that the Eternal Father and His Only Begotten not only see fit, but are very anxious for every nation to have all the truth that its development and nature will assimilate in harmonizing itself with law. The Eternal Beings have always revealed to men generously all the truth that they could live up to, and even more than most mortals have been able to obey.

---

[7] *Doctrine and Covenants* 84:45-47; 88:6-13.
[8] James E. Talmage, *The Articles of Faith*, pp. 168-179, 162-174.
[9] John 14:16-17.

LEARNING TRUTH THROUGH OBEDIENCE TO LAW

Mortals, aided by the Spirit of God and the Holy Ghost, have through obedience to law been able to discover many eternal truths. Thus great advancements have come all over the world in sciences, and through the prophets in religious concepts. In fact, since the Gospel of Jesus Christ was restored to earth, approximately one hundred years ago, light and truth have been shed forth upon mankind more generously than during the entire span of thousands of years of previous history. Even the terrific force contained in the atom has now been released by man and used for destructive purposes in bombing Japan. So tremendous is this power that man could easily destroy the world with it. Let us hope that this power may never be turned to evil, but Satan has taken over many of the discoveries and applied them in his service. On the other hand, man could harness this power for the purpose of doing the world's work. The amount of power in an atomic bomb staggers the limits of one's imagination. Some day, when all the laws of handling such an overwhelming force have been learned, this new agency of power can be used to replace or supplement all previously discovered sources of power, including electricity. Surely this atomic power will usher in a new age in science, industry, and social living. Once again the whole structure of human life will be revolutionized. God has once more placed in the hands of His children the knowledge of another of the great laws of His power.

Everything is governed eternally by law. *"There is a law irrevocably decreed in heaven before the foundation of this world, upon which all blessings are predicated; and when we obtain any blessing from God, it is by obedience to the law upon which it is predicated."*[10] This revelation refers to the laws of heaven, of earth, of nature, of science, of health and of brotherhood. They are God's spiritual laws.[11] Jesus became a God and reached His great state of understanding through consistent effort and continuous obedience to all the Gospel truths and universal laws. Whenever men put themselves in proper condition and obey, they also obtain the knowledge of truth. The whole

[10] *Doctrine and Covenants* 131:20-21.
[11] *Ibid.*, 29:34-35.

world is filled with the *Spirit of truth,* just as it is filled with
sunshine, electricity and other universal substances and
forces, waiting to touch the harmonizing chords of men's
understanding so they will obey the law and thereby gain the
knowledge and the blessing.

Throughout the entire course of human history, men
have as a rule been trying to get in harmony with law.
When mortals have strayed from the primeval Gospel
truths known by Father Adam and thereby, through apostasy, dropped into a condition of barbarism, they greatly
altered their modes of behavior and religious ceremonials
for their salvation, both temporal and spiritual. They
saved themselves to the extent that they placed themselves
beyond the power of their enemies. Their chief enemy was
ignorance—i. e., their inability to get in harmony with truth.
There are laws governing various levels of actions. If
barbarians could not harmonize their lives with the higher
order—which would give them greater freedom, knowledge,
and power—they adjusted themselves to many of the lower
laws and received salvation on that level. If their rituals
gave to their lives the deepest expression and greatest religious growth of which their natures were capable, then
they were in harmony with the laws that fit their immediate
salvation, but not in harmony with the higher laws of truth
that bring the greatest development and make men Gods.
The principal phase of this higher system of law is the
Gospel plan of salvation.

As these groups of people who had lost many Gospel
truths as a result of apostasies repented of many of their
sins and thereby progressed, members of their groups were
able to harmonize themselves with a greater number of
laws. Their intelligent natures were touched more easily
and more deeply by that eternal, universal truth which
naturally increased their knowledge. Then their rituals
took on a form more in consistency with that higher order
revealed by Jesus Christ.

God's Relationship to Man's Progression

We should keep in mind that throughout this whole
process of human history and men's quest for salvation,
God the Eternal Father and His Only Begotten Son have

been forever reaching downward to mortals to assist them in their eternal struggle for progression toward Godhood. These Eternal Beings have been the center, the principal motivating force of human history. The Godhead is the Divine Fountain of Eternal Truth from which all enlightenment throughout history has come to all peoples. The Lord has used numerous avenues through which to reveal truth for the purpose of enlightening His children and making possible their progression. The channels most universally used are the Spirit of God and the Holy Ghost.

God has always been an impartial ruler; therefore, all of His blessings are based upon the worthiness of the recipients. Thus the law of compensation operates throughout the entire universe. The responsibility is upon mortals, aided by God, to work out their own salvation through obedience to the principles and ordinances of the Gospel of Jesus Christ. The righteous men are the ones who shall receive rewards.

Chapter 9

APOSTASIES AND HOW THEY OCCUR

APOSTASIES

An apostasy is a falling away, altering, or rejecting the divinely revealed will of God. It is the substitution of man-made creeds and practices for the truths of the plan of salvation. It is the loss of light and truth by any person or group of people. All nations, tribes or clans in the world today as well as throughout the entire course of human history, have had many truths in their culture by which they lived. Every individual, also, is guided by a certain amount of truth. But when a nation, a race of people, or an individual loses the divine verities which have formerly been guides to their lives, and especially when they lose the power of the Priesthood of the Most High God, apostasy prevails.

There have been numerous apostasies throughout the course of history. Sometimes they have occurred with whole groups of people and at other times only individuals have been affected. When the holy Priesthood and the Holy Ghost are withdrawn from man, he is left in darkness; and in many instances races of people have dropped into savagery as a result. The pages of human history describe long periods of deplorable conditions of savagery and barbarism where the sons and daughters of God were groping in darkness. How have human beings and races reached that state? What are the underlying causes of apostasies?

THROUGH SIN AND IGNORANCE

Sin (i. e., human beings' refusing to live the laws of truth) has always been one of the most prevalent causes of apostasy. The first falling away from the revealed Gospel plan recorded in the holy scriptures took place in the first human family. Many of Adam and Eve's children loved sin and the things of the world more than they loved God and the way of eternal life; therefore, they refused to accept the Gospel teachings given to them by the Lord through their parents.[1]

When individuals or groups of people wilfully choose evil in preference to good, the Spirit of God is grieved and departs from them. They are then left to grope in darkness. Things which they have heretofore believed to be true they now doubt. The desire to study, learn truth, and progress becomes petrified within them. Degeneracy sets in, and soon they become a fallen people.

A good illustration in which this occurred to an extreme degree is found in the history of the Lamanites as presented in the *Book of Mormon*. Laman and Lemuel, with their families and friends, rebelled against God, against Lehi, against their brother Nephi, and against the eternal principles of truth. Within the short space of thirty years after the small colony left Jerusalem, complete degeneracy had set in. Nephi's description of the Lamanites at that time shows that they had degenerated almost to the level on which the more savage of the Indians were living when Columbus discovered America.[2] Sin was the cause which brought this people into apostasy and darkness. Then their children from generation to generation were kept in that condition through a combination of ignorance and sin.

THROUGH RELIGIOUS SYNCRETISM

Apostasies have also been brought about in various ages of the world as a result of a people who had the true religion intermarrying and mixing their culture and religious concepts with those of other peoples. At certain times a small group of people, possessing the true Gospel, would partially convert a much larger group to their church, but the converts would tenaciously cling to many of their former pagan beliefs and practices. After they had affiliated with the true religion, their false concepts became mixed with the true Gospel doctrine, so that the next generation inherited a fusion of the two. Therefore, these gradual

---

[1] Moses 5:12-13; Alma 29:4-5.
[2] 2 Nephi 5:20-23; Enos 1:20. Note the contrast of the condition of the Nephites with that of the Lamanites, 2 Nephi 5:8-18.

apostasies are brought about as a natural result of the social mixing of different races of people, or through a process of religious syncretism.

An excellent historical example of apostasy's being
brought about primarily through religious syncretism is
the merging together of Christian and pagan beliefs during the early Catholic period. The net result was neither
paganism nor Christianity as Christ had originally established it. Both systems of religious thought, with the accompanying rituals and doctrines, were altered so extensively that historians refer to the social process that occurred during the early portion of the Middle Ages, and
the net result of the process, as the Great Apostasy.

WORLD'S STREAM OF RELIGIOUS THOUGHT

To further explain how apostasies from the divine plan
of salvation have come about from Adam's day down to
our time, and also to show why pagans have had so many
beliefs resembling the true Gospel of Jesus Christ, we
present the following explanation:

In the beginning the Lord revealed the plan of salvation to Father Adam. Later a renewal of that revelation was given to the holy prophets at various times during the different Gospel dispensations, according to the
needs of the age and the ability of the prophets to harmonize their lives with the Divine Will.

This succession of Gospel dispensations can be lik-
ened to a great river of water flowing continuously from
generation to generation from the time of the first revelation of God's will to man. As pointed out in the last
chapter, the central Fountain of all Truth from which
these waters flow is Jesus Christ and His divine Father.

Meandering outward from the main river, there have
always been numerous streams and streamlets, disseminat-
ing truths among all peoples. But these streams also have
continued to pick up a variety of materials as they ran
along. The farther they traveled the more they became
contaminated or polluted through the sins and ignorance
of mortals and through man-made religious concepts. Thus
partial apostasies from the eternal verities were brought

about. In spite of these alterations in religious beliefs and practices, the streams of thought have always retained a semblance to the original revelation given to Adam.

Occasionally some of these small streams flowed back into the main river channel, thereby helping to pollute the original stream, bringing about a partial falling away from revealed truths. This necessitated a renewal of divine revelation.

At various times in history a great number of these polluted streams flowed back into the main river channel, adulterating almost completely the central supply of truth— or, in other words, instigating a rather pronounced apostasy from the Gospel of Jesus Christ. That is exactly what happened during the first four centuries of the Christian era. During the early centuries A.D., the Church established by Jesus rapidly became a depository of all the streams of thought—Hebrew and pagan—of the Graeco-Roman world which were flowing into the great river of truth, that is, into the teachings of the Man of Galilee. The alterations and modifications imposed on Christendom were numerous, especially as time moved forward from the days of Jesus and His apostles. Many of those changes will be discussed in this course of study.

SUPPLEMENTARY READINGS—CHAPTER 9

1. *Book of Mormon:* 2 Nephi 5:8-23; Enos 1:29; Alma 29:45; Ether 8:1-26; 9:1-13.
2. *Pearl of Great Price:* Moses 5:12-40, 47-55.

Chapter 10.

THE GOSPEL GIVEN TO FATHER ADAM

The Fall—A Spiritual Death

When Adam and Eve were first placed in the Garden of Eden they had intimate association with heavenly beings, because they were not yet mortals. They also understood the Gospel plan of salvation just as they had before being placed on the earth. When they partook of the forbidden fruit, however, a change came over them and they became mortal beings. Thereupon a veil was drawn over their minds, so they no longer remembered their pre-mortal experiences, nor could they recollect the Gospel principles and ordinances. Then God cast them out of Eden so they could go through the school of mortality. Therefore, after the fall our first parents were living in a temporal world and were cut off from the presence of God, who lives in a spiritual, celestial world.

The Nephite prophets spoke of this coming into mortality—or the banishment from the presence of God—as the first death, a spiritual death. Alma explained to the people that our first parents were cut off both temporally and spiritually from God's presence and were free to follow their own inclinations. Since men's spirits could never cease existing "and the fall had brought upon mankind a spiritual death as well as a temporal; that is, they were cast off from the presence of the Lord; it was expedient that mankind should be reclaimed from this spiritual death."[1] In other words, it was imperative that Adam and Eve receive the Gospel again.

Necessity of Divine Revelation

Under the conditions of mortality, unaided by a divine power or being, men did not have sufficient knowledge nor

---

[1] Alma 42:6-14; 12:22-24; Helaman 14:16; *Doctrine and Covenants* 29:41.

power to bring themselves back into the presence of God. The prophets also taught that as a result of Adam's fall "all mankind became a lost and fallen people," being "carnal, sensual, and devilish by nature."[2]   In fact, if men were never to receive revelations or aid from God, they would wander, as Lehi saw in a vision, "in a dark and dreary waste," without the possibility of escape from that depraved condition.   But the Eternal Father and His Son Jesus, in their love and mercy, provided an escape from this condition of spiritual and temporal death.   As has been pointed out, a plan of salvation was provided in heaven for mankind even before mortals were placed upon the earth.   Alma explained the interest that God had in Adam and Eve after they had been driven from the Garden of Eden as follows:

[God] saw that it was expedient that men should know concerning the things whereof he had appointed unto them; therefore, he sent angels to converse with them, who caused men to behold of his glory. And they began from that time forth to call on his name; therefore, God conversed with men, and made known unto them the plan of redemption, which had been prepared from the foundation of the world; and this he made known unto them according to their faith and repentance and their holy works.[3]

ADAM RECEIVED THE GOSPEL

Father Adam, called by Daniel the Ancient of Days, and by the Lord, Michael, the Prince, the Archangel, received through divine revelations the Gospel of Jesus Christ—the same Gospel with the same principles and ordinances that we have today.[4]   The Prophet Joseph Smith declared that God "set the ordinances to be the same forever and ever, and set Adam to watch over them."[5]   The *Pearl of Great Price, Book of Mormon, Doctrine and Covenants,* teachings of the Prophet Joseph Smith, with a lesser amount of evidence in the Bible, attest the foregoing statement to be positively true.

We shall now enumerate the various principles and ordinances that were revealed to Father Adam and discuss them briefly for the purpose of giving evidence that the first mortals received the same Gospel as was revealed

---

[2] Alma 12:22; 42:11; Moses 5:13.
[3] Alma 12:28-34; *Doctrine and Covenants* 29:42-45.
[4] Daniel 7:13-14; 12:1-3; *Doctrine and Covenants* 107:54; 27:11; 78:16; 116:1.
[5] Joseph Fielding Smith, *Teachings of the Prophet Joseph Smith,* pp. 166-170.

to the Prophet Joseph Smith and the same as has been
in the world during any dispensation. However, as we
proceed throughout this course of study, it will become
necessary to discuss the various Gospel principles and ordinances in separate chapters as they fit into the story of
the history of the Gospel through the ages. Therefore,
a certain amount of repetition will be unavoidable. On
each new topic, it will be necessary to begin with Adam's
reception of that Gospel doctrine.

Among the first Gospel principles that God revealed
to Adam and Eve was that of eternal marriage. When
they were first placed on earth, "God blessed them and
said unto them: 'Be fruitful, and multiply, and replen-
ish the earth, and subdue it'."[6] These instructions included
the Gospel principles of rearing families, and—through the
application of intelligence and industry—learning the laws
of the universe and controlling them for the good of men.
Men were to be the bread-winners, supporting their families "by the sweat of their faces," and women were to bear
children in sorrow and suffering.

Among the other Gospel verities which the scriptures
definitely point out as having been revealed to our first
parents are faith, repentance, baptism, and receiving the
Holy Ghost. The ancient records testify that our first
parents obeyed these principles and ordinances of the Gospel. Father Adam thoroughly understood the doctrines
of the fall, the atonement, free agency, and immortality.
He even knew that the Savior's name would be Jesus Christ.

God used diverse methods to reveal divine verities to
our first parents. At times "they heard the voice of the
Lord from the way toward the Garden of Eden, speaking
to them"; and on other occasions angels appeared unto them
to give them heavenly instructions. Little by little they
learned the Gospel truths, receiving and understanding this information gradually in the same manner as we
learn.

THE ADAMIC LANGUAGE

The ancient records also inform us that Adam and
his posterity were taught through the spirit of inspiration

---

[6] Moses 2:27-28; Genesis 1:28.

to read and write. They, in turn, taught their children. The language that they used is known as the Adamic language. The ancient records speak of it as being "a language which was pure and undefiled."[7] The record of Gospel teachings, revelations from God, and the genealogy of the people was kept in a book which they called the "Book of Remembrance."[8] Copies of this holy record were handed down from generation to generation. Abraham, the father of the faithful, claimed to possess "the records of the fathers" running back from his day to the beginning of the creation.

PRIESTHOOD GIVEN TO ADAM

Adam also received the keys of the holy Priesthood after the Order of the Son of God directly from Jesus Christ, and he in turn bestowed it upon his posterity.[9] Priesthood is probably the most important single item in the Gospel. Without it the ordinances could not be performed; neither could the true Church be established. Therefore, in the very beginning all the principles and ordinances of the Gospel were administered through the power of the Priesthood. Regarding this important subject, Joseph the Prophet proclaimed:

The Priesthood was first given to Adam; he obtained the First Presidency, and held the keys of it from generation to generation. He obtained it in the Creation, before the world was formed. . . . He had dominion given him over every living creature. He is Michael the Archangel, spoken of in the scriptures. Then to Noah, who is Gabriel; he stands next in authority to Adam in the Priesthood; he was called of God to this office, and was the father of all living in this day, and to him was given the dominion. These men held keys first on earth and then in heaven.[10]

The promise was made to Father Adam that "this same Priesthood, which was in the beginning, shall be in the end of the world also."[11] That promise was fulfilled when the Gospel of Jesus Christ was restored to the Prophet Joseph Smith.

[7] Moses 6:5-7.
[8] Abraham 1:28, 31; Moses 6:5-7, 45; 3 Nephi 24:16; Ether 8:9; *Doctrine and Covenants* 85:9.
[9] Moses 6:7; 8:19; Abraham 1:2, 4, 18, 26-27, 31; 2:9, 11; Alma 13:1-9; *Doctrine and Covenants* 84:6-17; 86:8; 76:57.
[10] Smith, *op. cit.*, p. 157.
[11] Moses 6:7; *Doctrine and Covenants* 2:1; 86:8-10; 84:107.

PEARL OF GREAT PRICE ACCOUNT

The most complete account that we have in any of the scriptures of Adam's receiving the Gospel of Jesus Christ is found in the *Pearl of Great Price*. If that record contained nothing but that important information, it would still be of untold worth to us. For the purpose of becoming personally acquainted with this excellent account as recorded by the ancients, let us quote the story directly from that sacred scripture:

And after many days an angel of the Lord appeared unto Adam, saying: "Why dost thou offer sacrifices unto the Lord?" And Adam said unto him, "I know not, save the Lord commanded me."

And then the angel spake, saying: "This thing is a similitude of the sacrifice of the Only Begotten of the Father, which is full of grace and truth. Wherefore, thou shalt do all that thou doest in the name of the Son, and thou shalt repent and call upon God in the name of the Son for evermore."

And in that day the Holy Ghost fell upon Adam, which beareth record of the Father and the Son, saying: "I am the Only Begotten of the Father from the beginning, henceforth and forever, that as thou hast fallen thou mayest be redeemed, and all mankind, even as many as will." . . .

And he called upon our father Adam by his own voice, saying: "I am God; I made the world, and men before they were in the flesh." And he also said unto him: "If thou wilt turn unto me, and hearken unto my voice, and believe, and repent of all thy transgressions, and be baptized, even in water, in the name of mine Only Begotten Son, who is full of grace and truth, which is Jesus Christ, the only name which shall be given under heaven, whereby salvation shall come unto the children of men, ye shall receive the gift of the Holy Ghost, asking all things in his name, and whatsoever ye shall ask, it shall be given you." . . .

And it is given unto them to know good from evil; wherefore they are agents unto themselves, and I have given unto you another law and commandment. Wherefore, teach it unto your children, that all men, everywhere, must repent, or they can in no wise inherit the kingdom of God, for no unclean thing can dwell there, or dwell in his presence; for, in the language of Adam, Man of Holiness is his name, and the name of his Only Begotten is the Son of Man, even Jesus Christ, a righteous judge, who shall come in the meridian of time.

Therefore, I give unto you a commandment, to teach these things freely unto your children, saying: "That by reason of transgression cometh the fall, which fall bringeth death, and inasmuch as ye were born into the world by water, and blood, and the spirit, which I have made, and so became of dust a living soul, even so ye must be born again into the kingdom of heaven, of water, and of the Spirit, and be cleansed by blood, even the blood of mine Only Begotten; that ye might be sanctified from all sin, and enjoy the words of eternal life in this world, and eternal life in the world to come, even immortal glory; for by the water ye keep the commandment; by the Spirit ye are justified, and by the blood ye are sanctified." . . .

And now, behold, I say unto you: "This is the plan of salvation unto all men, through the blood of mine Only Begotten, who shall come in the meridian of time." . . .

And it came to pass, when the Lord had spoken with Adam, our father, that Adam cried unto the Lord, and he was caught away by the Spirit of the Lord, and was carried down into the water, and was laid under the water, and was brought forth out of the water. And thus he was baptized, and the Spirit of God descended upon him, and thus he was born of the Spirit, and became quickened in the inner man.

And he heard a voice out of heaven, saying: "Thou art baptized with fire, and with the Holy Ghost. This is the record of the Father, and the Son, from henceforth and forever; and thou art after the order of him who was without beginning of days or end of years, from all eternity to all eternity. Behold, thou art one in me, a son of God; and thus may all become my sons." . . .

And in that day Adam blessed God and was filled, and began to prophesy concerning all the families of the earth, saying: "Blessed be the name of God, for because of my transgression my eyes are opened, and in this life I shall have joy, and again in the flesh I shall see God."

And Eve, his wife, heard all these things and was glad, saying: "Were it not for our transgression we never should have had seed, and never should have known good and evil, and the joy of our redemption, and the eternal life which God giveth unto all the obedient."

And Adam and Eve blessed the name of God, and they made all things known unto their sons and their daughters. . . .

And thus the Gospel began to be preached, from the beginning, declared by holy angels sent forth from the presence of God, and by his own voice, and by the gift of the Holy Ghost. And thus all things were confirmed unto Adam, by an holy ordinance, and the Gospel preached, and a decree sent forth, that it should be in the world, until the end thereof; and thus it was. Amen.[12]

JOSEPH SMITH'S VIEWPOINT

There are approximately a dozen revelations in the *Doctrine and Covenants* in which the Lord revealed to the Prophet of the last dispensation information about Father Adam. Through these declarations and other revelations which Joseph received from the Lord, the Prophet developed a strong and convincing doctrine on the Gospel of

---

[12] Moses 5:6-12; 6:50-51, 56-59, 61, 63-67; 5:58-59.

Jesus Christ being given to Adam, and from that point coming down through the various dispensations.

By direct revelation the Prophet learned that the Lord had sent forth angels to declare unto Adam and his posterity that they must repent, and through faith in the Only Begotten Son be redeemed and raised "in immortality unto eternal life."[13]   Following is an example of Joseph Smith's teachings on this subject:

Perhaps our friends will say that the Gospel and its ordinances were not known till the days of John, the son of Zacharias, in the days of Herod, the king of Judea.   But we will here look at this point: For our own part we cannot believe that the ancients in all ages were so ignorant of the system of heaven as many suppose, since all that were ever saved were saved through the power of this great plan of redemption, as much before the coming of Christ as since; if not, God has had different plans in operation (if we may so express it), to bring men back to dwell with Himself; and this we cannot believe, since there has been no change in the constitution of man since he fell. . . .

It will be noticed that, according to Paul,[14] the Gospel was preached to Abraham. . . . So, then, because the ancients offered sacrifice it did not hinder their hearing the Gospel; but served . . . to open their eyes, and enable them to look forward to the time of the coming of the Savior, and rejoice in His redemption. . . .

We may conclude that though there were different dispensations, yet all things which God communicated to His people were calculated to draw their minds to the great object, and to teach them to rely upon God alone as the author of their salvation, as contained in His law.

From what we can draw from the scriptures relative to the teaching of heaven, we are induced to think that much instruction has been given to man since the beginning which we do not possess now.[15]

BRIGHAM YOUNG'S STATEMENT

In his terse way of speaking, Brigham Young declared:

God was once known on the earth among His children of mankind, as we know one another.   Adam was as conversant with his Father, who placed him upon the earth, as we are conversant with our earthly parents. The Father frequently came to visit his son Adam, and talked and walked with him; and the children of Adam were more or less acquainted with Him, and the things that pertain to God and to heaven were as familiar among mankind in the first ages of their existence as our gardens are to our wives and children, or as the road to the western ocean is to the experienced traveler. *From this source mankind have received their religious traditions.*[16]

---

[13] *Doctrine and Covenants* 29:42-44.
[14] Galatians 3:8.
[15] Joseph Fielding Smith, *Teachings of the Prophet Joseph Smith*, pp. 59-62, 168-169.
[16] John A. Widtsoe, *Discourses of Brigham Young*, p. 159.

Conclusions

Thus we see that the holy scriptures declare that God the Father and His Son Jesus Christ revealed the Gospel to Father Adam. The Lord confirmed this truth in revelations to the Prophet Joseph Smith; and Latter-day Saints —from the Prophet's time to our day—have sustained that concept in their writings and teachings.

SUPPLEMENTARY READINGS—CHAPTER 10

1. *Bible*: Genesis 2:24; Daniel 7:13-14; 12:1-3; Matthew 19:5; Mark 10:7-8; Galatians 3:8.
2. *Book of Mormon*: Alma 42:6-14; 12:22-34; 13:1-19; Helaman 14:16; 2 Nephi 2:21.
3. *Doctrine and Covenants* 27:11; 29:42-45; 78:16; 84:6-17; 88:112-115; 107:53-57; 116:1; 121:36ff.
4. *Pearl of Great Price*: Moses 2:27-28; 3:24; 5:6-13, 58-59; 6:5-7, 45, 50-67; Abraham 1:2-4, 18, 26-31; 2:9-11.
5. G. Homer Durham (Compiler), *The Gospel Kingdom*, p. 91.
6. Joseph Fielding Smith (Compiler), *Teachings of the Prophet Joseph Smith*, pp. 59-62, 65-66, 157-160, 271.
7. Joseph Fielding Smith, *The Way to Perfection*, pp. 55-59, 67-69, 77-83.
8. John A. Widtsoe, *Evidences and Reconciliations*, pp. 82-84.
9. John A. Witdsoe (Compiler), *Discourses of Brigham Young*, pp. 156-161.

Chapter 11.

THE GOSPEL DISPENSATIONS

USE OF THE PHRASE

"Gospel dispensation" is a phrase which has been in common use in Mormon literature from the time of Joseph Smith to the present day. At least six revelations in the *Doctrine and Covenants* speak of them.[1] On numerous occasions in his sermons, the Prophet described the various dispensations, especially the "Dispensation of the Fullness of Times." Mormon writers, following the pattern set by Joseph, have discussed rather fully the various Gospel dispensations. The various leaders of the Church of Jesus Christ of Latter-day Saints have contributed their share toward amplifying this subject. Elder B. H. Roberts presented it so thoroughly that some people are of the opinion that he originated the theory of dispensations. Such an idea is erroneous. The phrase was in common use among the Protestant groups before the Gospel was restored to the Prophet Joseph Smith. The concept came into use at least as early as the days of Paul, the Christian apostle. In three of his letters he speaks of Gospel dispensations.[2] Mormons believe that one of his principal statements refers definitely to our day. It is as follows:

[God] having made known unto us the mystery of his will, according to his good pleasure which he hath purposed in himself: that in the dispensation of the fullness of times he might gather together in one all things in Christ, both which are in heaven, and which are on earth; even in him.[3]

MEANING OF DISPENSATIONS

Various definitions of dispensations have been given by Christian writers. For example, we read in *Webster's*

---

[1] *Doctrine and Covenants* 27:5, 13; 64:30, 37; 112:28ff.; 121:31; 128:18-21; 36:37.
[2] I Corinthians 9:16-17; Ephesians 1:10; 3:1-5; Colossians 1:25-26.
[3] Ephesians 1:10.

New International Dictionary that a theological definition is as follows:

a. The distribution of good or evil by God to man, or, more generally, the acts and modes of His administration; the divine ordering of the affairs of creation. b. A system of principles, promises, and rules ordained and administered; scheme; economy; as, the Patriarchal, Mosaic, and Christian dispensations.[4]

The following definition is given in a Bible encyclopaedia:

Dispensations are called "the ways of God," and denote those schemes or methods which are devised and pursued by the wisdom and goodness of God, in order to manifest his perfections and will to mankind, for the purpose of their instruction, discipline, reformation and advancement in rectitude of temper and conduct, in order to promote their happiness. . . .

The sacred scriptures reveal and record several dispensations of Divine Providence, which have been directed to the promotion of the religious principles, moral conduct and true happiness of mankind. These have varied in several ages of the world, and have been adapted by the wisdom and goodness of God to the circumstances of his intelligent and accountable creatures. In this sense the various revelations which God has communicated to mankind at different periods, and the means he has used, as occasion has required, for their discipline and improvement, have been justly denominated divine dispensations.[5]

ADAM'S PLACE IN THE GOSPEL PLAN

Following the great council in heaven at which Lucifer and his hosts revolted against the Gospel plan of salvation as laid down by God the Father and advocated by His Only Begotten Son, Adam—who was known as Michael the Archangel—led the righteous ones in heaven in sustaining the eternal Gospel plan and Jesus as the Christ. In Revelation we read: "And there was war in heaven: Michael and his angels fought against the dragon; and the dragon fought and his angels, and prevailed not; neither was their place found any more in heaven."[6]

Without doubt, Adam was one of the most intelligent, one of the most obedient and valiant of all the sons and daughters of God in the spirit world. For this reason he stood in a position of leadership at and following the Great Council, being perhaps the strongest personality—except the Father and the Son—in advocating the

---

[4] *Webster's New International Dictionary*, Second Edition, Unabridged.
[5] *The Popular and Critical Bible Encyclopaedia*, vol. 1, p. 532.
[6] Revelation 12:7-8.

Messiahship of Jesus. Thus the Father appointed Adam to a position of power and leadership, that of being the father of the human family in this world.[7] Since he was chosen to be the "first man" in mortality, he stood among the council of the Gods and helped plan this world for humanity. In other words, he was one of the creators of this earth, working in conjunction with the Father and the Son.[8]

Since he was foreordained to be the father of the human family, Adam was appointed by the Savior to hold the keys of the Priesthood [9] throughout all Gospel dispensations until the Son of Man should come to reign.[10] Therefore, whenever the Priesthood has been withdrawn from the earth through apostasy, the keys have been brought back from heaven by Adam's authority.[11] When angels are sent as messengers to restore the ordinances of the Gospel and the Priesthood, "these angels also are under the direction of Michael or Adam, who acts under the direction of the Lord."[12]

Just prior to the second coming of the Savior, an important council meeting will be held at Adam-Ondi-Ahman, Missouri.[13] Jesus, Michael, Gabriel, and all the great high priests who have held the keys of the Priesthood from Adam's day down to this dispensation will be in attendance. At this meeting, Adam will surrender his authority—or the keys of the Priesthood — to Christ, but will retain his standing as head of the human family.[14] He will be crowned as the prince over his posterity to reign eternally in that position. Jesus Christ will be officially received as King of kings, and Lord of lords. Throughout the Millennium the Savior will reign. "Christ is the Great High Priest; Adam next," and, according to the Prophet Joseph Smith, Noah or Gabriel "stands next to Adam in the Priesthood."[15] In fact, each great prophet who held keys of the Priesthood over a dispensation will continue to hold that same authority and blessing. Thus Joseph

[7] *Doctrine and Covenants* 27:11; 29:34-35.
[8] John A. Widtsoe, *Evidences and Reconciliations*, pp. 287-290.
[9] *Ibid.*, 84:16; 78:16.
[10] *Ibid.*, 88:112-115; 128:21; Smith, *Teachings of the Prophet Joseph Smith*, pp. 167-168.
[11] Smith, *Ibid.*, p. 157.
[12] *Ibid.*, p. 168.
[13] Joseph Fielding Smith, *The Way to Perfection*, pp. 289-290.
[14] Joseph Fielding Smith, *The Progress of Man*, pp. 479-482.
[15] Smith, *Teachings of the Prophet Joseph Smith*, pp. 157, 158, 168-169.

Smith will retain his position as the head of the Dispensation of the Fullness of Times.

ADAMIC DISPENSATION

The last chapter told the story of the Gospel's being revealed to Adam and Eve. These first mortals begat sons and daughters, who paired off two by two and began to inhabit various parts of the earth. Adam and Eve rejoiced in the knowledge of the Gospel truths which they had received through divine revelations, and made definite efforts to teach those principles to their children and grandchildren. According to the record, however, they succeeded very poorly at first. Their older children and grandchildren rejected the Gospel.

Adam and Eve, however, continued to hearken unto the voice of God and to call upon their children to repent. Eventually two more children, named Cain and Abel, were born into the family. Unfortunately, when they grew to manhood, Cain also rejected the counsel of God and that of his parents and slew his brother Abel. Finally, Adam's and Eve's hearts were made to rejoice in the birth of a child, whom they named Seth, because he grew up to be a "perfect man like unto his father, Adam, in all things." It was through Seth's posterity that the Gospel was handed down from generation to generation.[16] This is a brief statement of the first or Adamic dispensation.

DISPENSATION OF ENOCH

The story of the dispensation of Enoch is told in chapters six and seven of the Book of Moses. The record states that as early as the days of Seth "the children of men were numerous upon all the face of the land. And in those days Satan had great dominion among men, and raged in their hearts; and from thenceforth came wars and bloodshed; and a man's hand was against his own brother, in administering death, because of secret works, seeking for power."[17]

Enoch, however, came through a righteous line of patriarchs, of which he was seventh in number, counting Father Adam. Each of his ancestors held the Priesthood. Since they were affiliated with the true Gospel of Jesus Christ,

---

[16] Moses 5:1-59; 6:1-20; *Doctrine and Covenants* 107:53-56.
[17] Moses 6:14.

they were known as the "sons of God." But a special dispensation of the Gospel seems to have been given to Enoch. He was called of God to preach the plan of redemption to the "sons of men" (non-Church members). The scripture presents Enoch's call as follows:

> It came to pass that Enoch journeyed in the land, among the people; and as he journeyed, the Spirit of God descended out of heaven, and abode upon him. And he heard a voice from heaven, saying: "Enoch, my son, prophesy unto this people, and say unto them—Repent, for thus saith the Lord: I am angry with this people, and my fierce anger is kindled against them; for their hearts have waxed hard, and their ears are dull of hearing, and their eyes cannot see afar off; and for these many generations, ever since the day that I created them, have they gone astray, and have denied me, and have sought their own counsels in the dark; and in their own abominations have they devised murder, and have not kept the commandments, which I gave unto their father Adam.[18]

Enoch accepted the call and became a powerful preacher of righteousness. An examination of the scriptures shows plainly the fact that the Gospel doctrines as taught by Enoch are exactly the same as we teach today.[19] It reveals how complete was the dispensation of the Gospel committed to Enoch. He understood thoroughly the doctrine of the fall, the atonement, and the accompanying principles and ordinances of the Gospel. So righteous was Enoch that God on numerous occasions came to earth and visited him. In the words of that great prophet: "I saw the Lord; and He stood before my face, and He talked with me, even as a man talketh one with another, face to face."[20]

In vision, Enoch beheld the inhabitants of the earth and their history down to the second coming of the Son of Man, when He should dwell on earth in righteousness for the space of a thousand years. At that day a holy city would be built which, Enoch learned, would be called "Zion, a New Jerusalem."

Enoch was so successful in proclaiming the Gospel that he converted a multitude of people and gathered them together in a city known as the "City of Holiness, even Zion," "because the people were of one heart and one mind." A successful economic order was established in that city,

[18] *Ibid.*, 6:25-27.
[19] *Ibid.*, 6:20-67; 7:1-69.
[20] *Ibid.*, 7:4.

known as the Order of Enoch, or consecration, which resulted in doing away with all poverty. Peace and righteousness prevailed. In the words of B. H. Roberts: "Doubtless among all the dispensations of the Gospel committed to man the dispensation given to Enoch was one of the most glorious."[21] It ended in triumph, as follows:

And all the days of Zion, in the days of Enoch, were three hundred and sixty-five years. And Enoch and all his people walked with God, and he dwelt in the midst of Zion; . . . and lo, Zion, in process of time, was taken up into heaven. And the Lord said unto Enoch: "Behold mine abode forever." . . . And it came to pass that Zion was not, for God received it up into his own bosom; and from thence went forth the saying, "ZION IS FLED."[22]

Thus the righteous people were taken from the earth, except Methusaleh, the son of Enoch, and he was left "that the covenant of the Lord might be fulfilled which he made to Enoch; for he truly covenanted with Enoch that Noah should be of the fruit of his loins."[23] In this spectacular way the dispensation of Enoch came to a close.

SUPPLEMENTARY READINGS—CHAPTER 11

1. *Bible*: Genesis 4; 5; 6:1-7; 1 Corinthians 9:16-17; Ephesians 1:10; 3:1-5; Colossians 1:25-26; Revelation 12:7-8.
2. *Doctrine and Covenants* 27:11-13; 78:16; 84:16; 88:112-115; 107:1-3; 128:20-21.
3. *Pearl of Great Price*: Moses 4; 5; 6; 7; 8:1-7.
4. G. Homer Durham (Compiler), *The Gospel Kingdom*, pp. 95-103.
5. B. H. Roberts, *The Seventy's Course of Theology*, Second Year, "The Adamic Dispensation," pp. 37-72; "Dispensation of the Gospel Committed to Enoch," pp. 73-85.
6. Joseph Fielding Smith (Compiler), *Teachings of the Prophet Joseph Smith*, pp. 157-159, 167-168, 170-171.
7. Joseph Fielding Smith, *The Way to Perfection*, pp. 60-72, 78-83.
8. Joseph Fielding Smith, *The Progress of Man*, pp. 67-72, 93, 178-182, 479-482.
9. John A. Widtsoe, *Evidences and Reconciliations*, pp. 287-290.
10. John A. Widtsoe (Compiler), *Discourses of Brigham Young*, pp. 153-169.

---

[21] B. H. Roberts, *The Seventy's Course of Theology*, Second Year, p. 74.
[22] Moses 7:21, 68-69; Genesis 5:22-24.
[23] Moses 8:2.

Chapter 12.

GOSPEL DISPENSATIONS FROM NOAH TO JESUS

Noah, the Second Father of Humanity

Noah, the great-grandson of Enoch, was born during a period in the world's history when practically all the inhabitants of the earth were corrupt except his particular family. But Noah and his three sons, Ham, Shem and Japheth, "hearkened unto the Lord, and gave heed, and they were called the sons of God."[1] It is evident from the following excellent quotation that Noah taught the same Gospel principles and practiced the same ordinances as did Father Adam and the other men of God who preceded him; and he carried on his Gospel dispensation under the same divine power and guidance as did the other holy prophets. Noah also taught the same Gospel as we have today, namely, the Gospel of Jesus Christ. The following quotation from the ancient records gives definite proof that the foregoing statements are true:

And it came to pass that Noah prophesied, and taught the things of God, even as it was in the beginning. . . . And the Lord ordained Noah after his own order, and commanded him that he should go forth and declare his Gospel unto the children of men, even as it was given unto Enoch. And it came to pass that Noah called upon the children of men that they should repent; but they hearkened not unto his voice. . . .

God saw that the wickedness of men had become great in the earth; and every man was lifted up in the imagination of the thoughts of his heart, being only evil continually.

And it came to pass that Noah continued his preaching unto the people, saying: "Hearken, and give heed unto my words; believe and repent of your sins and be baptized in the name of Jesus Christ, the Son of God, even as our fathers, and ye shall receive the Holy Ghost, that ye may have all things made manifest; and if ye do not this, the floods will come in upon you." Nevertheless they hearkened not.[2]

---

[1] Moses 8:13.
[2] *Ibid.*, 8:16, 19-20, 22-24.

According to the accounts given in the scriptures, the people continued to live wicked lives in spite of Noah's persistent preaching and teaching of the word of God. It became necessary, therefore, for the Lord to cleanse the earth with a flood. Since all the people were destroyed except Noah's family, the great patriarch now became the second father of humanity; and he, like Father Adam, was given the keys of the holy Priesthood.[3]

THE PATRIARCHAL DISPENSATION[4]

The scriptures do not contain much information regarding the religious history of the human family from Noah's day to Father Abraham's; but they do give enough of the story in the account of the tower of Babel to let us know that at that time an apostasy had occurred which necessitated divine revelations from God to restore the Gospel to earth again. These revelations came to Abraham.

The story of this ancient patriarch opens with an account of his experiences in the city of Ur, located in the land of the Chaldees among a group of pagans; but fortunately he came into possession of "the records of the fathers, even the patriarchs, concerning the right of the Priesthood," and also "a knowledge of the beginning of the creation, and also of the planets, and of the stars, as they were made known unto the fathers."[5]

Abraham—by nature being a follower of righteousness—desired to become a high priest, which was his right by birth under the patriarchal order.[6] He also diligently sought after knowledge; and among his greatest desires was to learn the will of God and keep His commandments.

The Lord accepted of Abraham's righteous desires and gave unto him a dispensation of the Gospel of Jesus Christ. He appeared unto the ancient patriarch and said:

Abraham, my son . . . behold, I will lead thee by my hand, and I will take thee, to put upon thee my name, even the Priesthood of thy father, and my power shall be over thee. As it was with Noah so shall it be with thee; but through thy ministry my name shall be known in the earth forever, for I am thy God.[7]

[3] Joseph Fielding Smith, *Teachings of the Prophet Joseph Smith*, p. 157.
[4] B. H. Roberts, *The Seventy's Course in Theology*, Second year, p. 86, refers to this Gospel dispensation as "the Abrahamic Dispensation."
[5] Abraham 1:31.
[6] *Ibid.*, 1:2.
[7] *Ibid.*, 1:17-19.

Later, after Abraham had migrated westward to the land of Canaan to establish a new home, God's promises were all fulfilled. The "father of the faithful" received the Priesthood from Melchizedek, the king of Salem.[8] Abraham reported the event as follows:

It was conferred upon me from the fathers; it came down from the fathers, from the beginning of time, yea, even from the beginning, or before the foundation of the earth to the present time, even the right of the first-born, on the first man, who is Adam, our first father, through the fathers unto me. I sought for mine appointment unto the Priesthood according to the appointment of God unto the fathers concerning the seed.[9]

The fact that Abraham, Isaac, Jacob, Joseph, Melchizedek, and other ancient patriarchs held the High Priesthood bears witness to the fact that they had the Gospel, since that Priesthood exists (according to the word of the Lord) for the purpose of "administering the Gospel and [it] holdeth the keys of the mysteries of the kingdom, even the key of the knowledge of God. Therefore, in the ordinances thereof, the power of godliness is manifest. And without the ordinances thereof, and the authority of the Priesthood, the power of godliness is not manifest unto men in the flesh; for without this no man can see the face of God, even the Father, and live."[10] In the words of B. H. Roberts:

Therefore, wherever this Priesthood is found there also will a knowledge of the Gospel be had. If, then, the patriarchs after Abraham had the Priesthood they undoubtedly had also the Gospel.[11]

Among the numerous things that God revealed to Abraham was an extensive knowledge of the Universe, its planets and movements. In fact, He informed the Patriarch regarding the preparation of the earth for man's abode, and told him of the advent of Adam upon it. To quote:

Thus I, Abraham, talked with the Lord face to face, as one man talketh with another; and he told me of the works which his hands had made; and he said unto me: "My son, my son" (and his hand was stretched out), "behold I will show you all these." And he put his hand upon mine eyes and I saw those things which his hands had made, which were many; and they multiplied before mine eyes, and I could not see the end thereof.[12]

---

[8] *Doctrine and Covenants*, 84:6-18; Alma 13.
[9] Abraham 1:3-4.
[10] *Doctrine and Covenants* 84:19-22.
[11] Roberts, *op. cit.*, p. 91.
[12] Abraham 3:11-12.

God also revealed to Abraham the great doctrine of the eternal nature of time, of space, and of matter, and of the eternal existence of intelligences. He was shown a vision of the great council in heaven, where the plan of salvation was presented and the Son of Man was selected to become the Savior of the world. At that council the Heavenly Father made a covenant with his children to give them eternal life on condition of their obedience to the Gospel.[13]

From what has been presented, it seems evident that the whole Gospel plan of salvation was thoroughly understood by Abraham. The *Pearl of Great Price* clearly gives us that picture and it is confirmed by the *Doctrine and Covenants* and the *New Testament*.[14] ·

Probably the most far reaching event in the Abrahamic Dispensation was the covenant entered into between God and the ancient Patriarch, a covenant which God reconfirmed with Isaac, Jacob, and Joseph. Following are the main points of the covenant: (1) Abraham was to be the father of a great nation;[15] (2) his descendants were to be as numerous as the stars of the heavens or the dust of the earth;[16] (3) they were to inhabit Palestine as an everlasting possession;[17] (4) kings and nations were to come from his descendants;[18] (5) many of his descendants should bear the name of God, even the holy Priesthood;[19] (6) in him and that Priesthood all families of the earth were to be blessed;[20] (7) circumcision was to be the sign of the covenant;[21] (8) the covenant was to be an everlasting one, or a Gospel covenant;[22] (9) in return for all of the foregoing blessings, Abraham and his posterity were to serve the Lord and keep all of His commandments.

In addition to his lineal descendants, the righteous of the earth should be accounted among Abraham's posterity through adoption. God declared to Abraham, "For as many as receive this Gospel shall be called after thy name, and

---

[13] *Ibid.*, 3:24-26.
[14] *Doctrine and Covenants* 132:29, 37; Galatians 3:8.
[15] Genesis 12:3.
[16] *Ibid.*, 13:15; 15:5.
[17] *Ibid.*, 13:14, 15.
[18] *Ibid.*, 17:6.
[19] Abraham 2:9.
[20] Genesis 12:3.
[21] *Ibid.*, 17:10-14.
[22] *Ibid.*, 17:7.

shall be accounted thy seed, and shall rise up and bless thee, as their father."[23]

THE "CHOSEN PEOPLE" CONCEPT

Probably the most powerful force which came out of the covenant concept and which exerted its influence in every generation of Jewish history is the belief that the descendants of Abraham are the "chosen people"—a "peculiar people." From the day that God changed Jacob's name to Israel and made a covenant with him similar to that which He had formerly made with Abraham, Jacob's descendants have been known as Israelites and have regarded themselves as the chosen people. The Old Testament teachers and the Nephite prophets have used this concept as their central theme in their endeavors to get the people to live righteous lives. In fact, the sacred scriptures of these two races are impregnated with the chosen people concept.

The belief has been held from age to age that Abraham and his descendants through his son Jacob were to be the witnesses for God and the Gospel truths unto all nations. The Priesthood and the doctrine of the plan of salvation would be carried forward through these people. Even the Son of God, the ancients were told through revelation, would come through Abraham's seed. Therefore, in addition to being a motivating force throughout Jewish history, the chosen people concept played a dominant role in early Christendom, and has also been one of the most powerful factors in Mormon history.[24] In fact, no greater dynamics have been engendered in religious history than the covenant concept. Thus this belief is another of those age-old concepts which has persisted for thousands of years.

THE NEW LEADER OF ISRAEL

It was Moses, the dominant and famous ancient lawgiver, through whom the Lord remembered His people and the covenants He had made with Abraham as well as the

---

[23] On April 3, 1836, a heavenly messenger bestowed upon modern Israel through Joseph Smith and Oliver Cowdery the same blessings, covenants, and promises which had been made approximately 4,000 years ago to Father Abraham. The revelation (*Doctrine and Covenants* 110:12), states that "Elias appeared, and committed the dispensation of the Gospel of Abraham, saying, that in us, and our seed, all generations after us should be blessed."

[24] *Doctrine and Covenants* 133:1-74; 1:1-39; 61:24-29; 38:33; 39:11; 84:98-102; 103:13-20.

promise He had made to Jacob that He would surely bring the "chosen people" back from Egypt to the promised land.[25]

Moses' career may be divided into three periods of forty years each. The first period was spent as an adopted son of Pharaoh's daughter. During this period he became well acquainted with the best in Egyptian education and culture.[26] During the second forty years he worked as a sheep herder in the Sinai Peninsula for Jethro, the High Priest (President) of the Midianite worshipers of Jehovah. It was during these years that Moses received the High Priesthood from his father-in-law, Jethro, and became thoroughly acquainted with the Gospel plan of salvation.[27] The period was climaxed by the Lord's calling to Moses from the burning bush and commissioning him to deliver the covenanted people from bondage. The story of Moses' successful accomplishment of this assignment constitutes the third period.

MOSES AND THE GOSPEL

Moses' receiving the Gospel begins another dispensation, known as the Mosaic Dispensation. The first five chapters of the Book of Moses give a clear account of his knowledge of the Gospel of Jesus Christ. Exodus, Leviticus, Numbers and Deuteronomy also graphically tell the story of Moses' great accomplishments and his numerous intimate contacts with God. For example, the following quotation bears testimony to the fact that Moses was taught the Gospel, and he held the Melchizedek Priesthood, which is necessary for administering the Gospel principles; otherwise he could not have withstood the presence of God, the Father, and live:

Moses was caught up into an exceeding high mountain, and he saw God face to face, and he talked with him, and the glory of God was upon Moses; therefore Moses could endure his presence. And God spake unto Moses, saying: "Behold, I am the Lord God Almighty, and Endless is my name. . . . Behold, thou art my son. . . . I have a work for thee, Moses, my son; and thou art in the similitude of mine Only Begotten; and mine Only Begotten is and shall be the Savior, for he is full of grace and truth.[28]

Moses reported the foregoing experience in the following words:

---

[25] Genesis 46:1-4.
[26] Acts 7:22; Josephus, *Works of Josephus*, Book I, pp. 62-68.
[27] *Doctrine and Covenants* 84:6-16, 25.
[28] Moses 1:1-6.

But now mine own eyes have beheld God; but not my natural, but my spiritual eyes, for my natural eyes could not have beheld; for I should have withered and died in his presence; but his glory was upon me; and I beheld his face, for I was transfigured before him.[29]

Thus the Lord conversed with Moses and taught him regarding the fall, the atonement, faith, repentance, baptism, confirmation, and the other Gospel truths.

MOSES AND THE LAW

When Moses brought the Israelites out of Egypt, they made their headquarters near Mt. Sinai during the first year. It was here that the Israelites received the Ten Commandments; and the Lord made a covenant with them to make of them "a kingdom of priests and a holy nation" if they would hearken unto His voice and keep His covenant.[30] The story of God's making this covenant with the Israelites at Sinai is vividly told in Exodus. The prophet-leader is pictured as being always in close communication with the Lord.

Moses put forth every effort within human possibility to teach the Gospel of Jesus Christ to the children of Israel and thereby make of them "a kingdom of priests and a holy nation"; but he—even with the Lord's help—failed to accomplish that goal. As a result of their many years of bondage, the Israelites had adopted numerous pagan practices and beliefs from the Egyptians, thereby contaminating the truths of the Gospel that their forefathers had known and observed. Finally, it became necessary for the Lord, through His servant Moses, to substitute for some of the higher Gospel truths a code of living of lesser value, known as the law of Moses. It is often referred to as "the law of carnal commandments."

The Apostle Paul declared that "God . . . preached before the Gospel to Abraham, saying, 'In thee shall all nations be blessed'." The Christian preacher then asked the question, "Wherefore then serveth the law?" That is, if the Gospel was given to Abraham, and later to Moses, how came the Law of Moses into existence? Why did it become binding on ancient Israel? Then Paul answered this important question as follows:

[29] *Ibid.*, 1:11.
[30] Exodus 19:3-9.

It was added because of transgression, till the seed should come to whom the promise was made. . . . Wherefore the law was our schoolmaster to bring us unto Christ, that we might be justified by faith. . . . For as many of you as have been baptized into Christ have put on Christ. . . . And if ye be Christ's, then are ye Abraham's seed, and heirs according to the promise.[31]

The author of Hebrews speaks of Moses' attempt to give the Israelites the Gospel as follows:

For unto us was the Gospel preached as well as unto them: but the word preached did not profit them, not being mixed with faith in them that heard it.[32]

The whole matter of Moses and the law is plainly set forth in a revelation to the Prophet Joseph Smith.[33] Also the Nephite prophets boldly taught that salvation could not come to mankind through the "Law of Moses" alone, but it must come through living the Gospel of Jesus Christ.[34]

After forty years of leadership of the children of Israel in the wilderness, during which time he functioned effectively as one of the greatest prophets and lawgivers known to history, Moses passed on into the other world. So outstanding were his accomplishments that a Bible writer later remarked: "There arose not a prophet since in Israel like unto Moses, whom the Lord knew face to face."[35] Today the membership of three great religions—Christian, Jewish and Mohammedan—regard Moses as an outstanding prophet of God. One writer concluded that "it is quite probable that in almost any list of the ten greatest men in the world, Moses' name would be included."

FROM MOSES TO JESUS

Many of the Gospel truths were taught and practiced by the Hebrews after the death of Moses and before the coming of the Son of Man. At times, however, their religion was on a high plane and at other times many false doctrines were believed in and practiced.

The Bible gives an account of a dark period of Israel's history during the days of the Judges when the Israelites were fusing their culture with the people of the land of Canaan. For a number of years many of the Gospel truths

---

[31] Galatians 3:8, 19, 27-29.
[32] Hebrews 4:2.
[33] *Doctrine and Covenants* 84:18-28.
[34] Mosiah 13:27-28, 33.
[35] Deuteronomy 34:10.

were adulterated by pagan beliefs and practices. Human sacrifice, sex immorality, worshiping of idols, and other heathenistic practices were frequently followed by many of the Israelites.[36] The complete moral tone of the nation was lowered.

But finally a prophet-judge named Samuel rose up, who talked with the Lord frequently and gave His divine will to the people.[37] Great prophets of God were again in Israel, instructing the populace in the same Gospel truths which had been taught by Moses, Abraham, Enoch and Adam. Although the Jewish church in general was operating under the Law of Moses, yet such prophets as Elijah, Amos, Hosea, Micah, Isaiah, Jeremiah and others were attempting to instruct the people in many of the Gospel truths. According to the Prophet Joseph Smith, this great line of prophets held the Melchizedek Priesthood, which Priesthood holds the keys to administer the spiritual ordinances of the Gospel of Jesus Christ.[38]

It is true that following the days of these great Old Testament prophets, the Jews did make their religion more static, adulterating the Gospel truths with many man-made concepts. Yet when Jesus came into the world, the religious philosophy of this people was probably nearest to the truth of any race of people then existing, with the possible exception of the Nephites.

OTHER EARLY PEOPLES WHO HAD THE GOSPEL

If we had their records we would probably find that there have been many groups of people upon the earth, about whom we know little or nothing, who have had the Gospel. One of the early Roman popes, Leo the Great (440-461 A.D.), maintained that the Gospel had been preached among men from the beginning. To quote:

Let those who with impious murmurings find fault with the divine dispensations, and who complain about the lateness of our Lord's nativity, cease from their grievances, as if what was carried out in this last age of the world had not been impending in time past. . . . What the apostles preached, the prophets had announced before, and what has always been believed cannot be said to have been fulfilled too late.

---

[36] Judges chapters 1 to 21; 2 Kings 16:3; 21:6; Judges 11:39; 2 Chronicles 28:1-3; Micah 6:7; Jeremiah 7:21; Ezekiel 16:20; 20:26; 2 Kings 21:1-18.
[37] 1 Samuel chapters 1 to 16.
[38] Smith, op. cit., p. 181.

. . . God has not provided for the interests of men by a new counsel or by a late compassion; but He had instituted from the beginning for all men one and the same path of salvation.[39]

There is sufficient information in the scriptures to show definitely that Melchizedek, to whom Abraham paid tithes, had the Gospel of our Master. The scriptures declare:

[He was a High Priest] according to the holy order of God. He preached repentance unto the people. And, behold, they did repent; and Melchizedek did establish peace in the land in his days; therefore he was called the Prince of Peace, for he was the king of Salem; and he did reign under his father. Now, there were many before him, and also there were many afterwards, but none were greater; therefore, of him they have more particularly made mention.[40]

Jethro, who was the High Priest of the Midianites, a branch of Abraham's family, instructed Moses in the principles of the Gospel and ordained him to the Priesthood. Thus we see that there have been other dispensations which our records tell us little about, and there may be many others of which we do not have record.

SUPPLEMENTARY READINGS—CHAPTER 12

1. *Bible*: Genesis chapters 5:29-32 to 50; Exodus, entire book; scan Leviticus, Numbers, Deuteronomy, Judges; 1 Samuel Chapters 1 to 16; Galatians 3:1-29; Hebrews 3:5-19; 4:1-4; 1 Corinthians 10:1-6; 2 Kings 16:3; 21:6, 18; 2 Chronicles 28:1-3; Micah 6:7; Jeremiah 7:21; Ezekiel 16:20; 20:26.

2. *Doctrine and Covenants* 84:6-27, 98-102; 132:29, 37; 110:12; 133:1-74; 1:1-39; 61:24-29; 38:33; 39:11; 103:13-20.

3. *Pearl of Great Price*: Moses chapter 8; Abraham chapters 1 to 15.

4. B. H. Roberts *The Seventy's Course in Theology*, Second year, "The Dispensation of the Gospel Given to Noah," pp. 77-85; "The Abrahamic Dispensation," pp. 86-90; "The Mosaic Dispensation," pp. 91-106.

5. Joseph Fielding Smith (Compiler), *Teachings of the Prophet Joseph Smith*, pp. 157, 181.

6. Joseph Fielding Smith, *The Way to Perfection*, pp. 84-96.

7. Sidney B. Sperry, *The Spirit of the Old Testament*, pp. 84-96.

8. John A. Widtsoe, *Rational Theology*, pp. 50-60.

---

[39] Cited in Roberts, *op. cit.*, p. 94.
[40] Alma 13:1-31; Genesis 14:18-24.

Chapter 13.

GOSPEL DISPENSATIONS IN ANCIENT AMERICA

JAREDITE GOSPEL DISPENSATION

The Book of Ether gives a brief account of what we could term the Jaredite Gospel Dispensation. It began at the time the Lord confounded the language of the people when they were building the tower of Babel. The great prophet, who received many revelations from the Lord and who inaugurated this dispensation, was called in the ancient record the brother of Jared; but Joseph Smith tells us that his name was Mahonri Moriancumer.[1]

So great was the faith of this ancient prophet that, when the Savior of the world stretched forth His hand to touch some stones in order that they might radiate light in response to a prayer uttered by Moriancumer, he saw the finger of the Lord. Jesus declared:

"Never has man come before me with such exceeding faith as thou hast; for were it not so, ye could not have seen my finger. Sawest thou more than this?"

The prophet answered, "Nay, Lord, shew thyself unto me." . . .

And when he had said these words, behold, the Lord shewed himself unto him, and said, "Because thou knowest these things, ye are redeemed from the fall; therefore ye are brought back into my presence; therefore I shew myself unto you. Behold I am he who was prepared from the foundation of the world to redeem my people. Behold, I am Jesus Christ. . . . In me shall all mankind have light, and that eternally, even they who shall believe on my name; and they shall become my sons and my daughters."[2]

Then the Lord gave unto the brother of Jared a vision of the history of the world from its beginning to its end; "and there never were greater things made manifest, than that which was made manifest unto the brother of Jared."[3]

---

[1] *Improvement Era*, vol. 8, p. 705; *Juvenile Instructor*, vol. 27, p. 282.
[2] Ether 3:4-20.
[3] *Ibid.*, 4:4.

God taught him many Gospel truths, and commanded him to write all that he had seen and heard and seal them up to be brought forth in our dispensation of the Gospel. The Lord declared that the writings which were sealed should come forth when the people had learned, accepted, and were living the teachings given in the *Book of Mormon*. Two-thirds of the record given to the Prophet Joseph Smith was sealed. The Prophet translated and published the other third. The Lord is trying us out on it to prepare us for the greater teachings contained in the sealed record. Some day the writings of the brother of Jared will go forth among the Gentiles and be read through the power of Christ from the housetops. This shall take place in that day when the people shall have faith in God, "even as the brother of Jared did, that they may become sanctified in Me, then will I manifest unto them the things which the brother of Jared saw, even to the unfolding unto them all my revelations, saith Jesus Christ, the Son of God."[4]

Moroni read what the brother of Jared wrote, and made the following comment: "Behold thou [O Lord] hath not made us mighty in writing like unto the brother of Jared, for thou madest him that the things he wrote, were mighty even as thou art, unto the overpowering of man to read them."[5]

In this marvelous way God inaugurated the Jaredite Gospel Dispensation. He commanded Moriancumer to take his brother, their families and friends, and go under His direction to a promised land (America). There He would make of them a great nation. Following is the promise made by the Lord to the Jaredites and the everlasting decree which he placed upon this country:

I will go before thee into a land which is choice above all the land of the earth. And there will I bless thee and thy seed, and raise up unto me of thy seed, and of the seed of thy brother, and they who shall go with thee, a great nation. And there shall be none greater than the nation which I will raise up unto me of thy seed, upon all the face of the earth. . . .

Behold, this is a choice land, and whatsoever nation shall possess it, shall be free from bondage, and from captivity, and from all other nations under heaven, if they will but serve the God of the land,

---

[4] *Ibid.*, 4:6-7.
[5] *Ibid.*, 12:24.

who is Jesus Christ. . . . Whatsoever nation shall possess it shall serve God, or they shall be swept off when the fullness of his wrath shall come upon them. And the fullness of his wrath cometh upon them when they are ripened in iniquity.

For behold, this is a land which is choice above all other lands; wherefore, he that doth possess it shall serve God, or shall be swept off; for it is the everlasting decree of God.[6]

In accordance with the covenant that Jesus made with Mahonri Moriancumer and the eternal decree that He placed on America, the Jaredites migrated to America and built up a great nation which lasted approximately 2,000 years.

Throughout all of the Jaredite history, the Gospel of Jesus Christ was a standard by which the prophets of God endeavored to get the people to live. At times a marked degree of success was attained, and during other periods of their history wickedness prevailed.

During the 2,000 years, the Jaredite history went in cycles. When the people were in poverty they were industrious and righteous. The natural result of this type of life, however, was gradually to make them wealthy. Then, with an excessive amount of leisure time and worldly goods on their hands, they became very wicked, which resulted in war, famine, disease, and almost complete destruction of the people. Finally, when reduced to poverty, they began the cycle over again. One of these cycles resulted in such extreme wickedness that the whole race of people was destroyed in a war, leaving only two men—Coriantumr, the king, and Ether, a great prophet. The king wandered southward and discovered another race of people, the Mulekites, whom God had brought to this land. Ether recorded the history of his people and left the record, written on "twenty-four gold plates," on the battlefield. Later it was discovered by the Nephites, and they abridged it and incorporated it into the *Book of Mormon*.[7]

NEPHITE GOSPEL DISPENSATION

The Lord instructed a prophet named Lehi, who lived in Jerusalem in 600 B.C., to take his family and migrate to America to replace the Jaredites, who had become ripe

---

[6] *Ibid.*, 1:42-43; 2:12, 9-10.
[7] Mosiah 8:15-21; 21:25-28; 28:11-20.

in iniquity and were shortly to destroy themselves by their
last great war.   God made the same promises and covenants with Lehi and Nephi regarding this land that He
had made with the brother of Jared.[8]   Appropriate to the
call to found a new Gospel dispensation, the Lord appeared
to Lehi and to his son Nephi and revealed to them the plan
of salvation.   Time and time again these two prophets,
especially Nephi, were visited by heavenly beings and taught
the Gospel truths.   Nephi saw a vision of the history of
the world, comparable perhaps in many respects to the one
witnessed by the brother of Jared.   We have the record
of Nephi's wonderful experience.[9]   In this way the Lord
commenced the Nephite Gospel Dispensation.

This people, known as Nephites, descendants of these
two prophets, inhabited America for a thousand years.
Throughout the course of their history, the center of their
civilization was religion.   The people were ruled by their
great prophets and teachers.   Following Nephi, such men
as Jacob, King Benjamin, King Mosiah II, the two Almas,
Abinadi, Amulek, Ammon, Helaman, Nephi the Second,
Samuel the Lamanite, Nephi the Third, Mormon and Moroni loom up in history as outstanding prophets of the true
and living God.

If ever men were God-centered and had the religious
motive as the one dominating and controlling purpose of
existence, the Nephites were those men.   To begin with,
direct revelations from heaven, which intensified the religious drive, caused Lehi and his family and friends to leave
Jerusalem and immigrate to the other side of the world.
The Lord was the strength and support of these holy men
in all that they did.   The prophets and the word of the Lord
were the guiding factors in the lives of the people.   Through
the course of their history they were fortunate in having
in their midst a prophet or prophets.

Their story is recorded in the *Book of Mormon,* which
record shows a very high interpretation of religious concepts running throughout the entire course of the 1,000
years from Lehi to Moroni.   Each of the great leaders
taught the Gospel with a depth of understanding.   Their
religious thinking did not go up and down in moral inter-

[8] 1 Nephi 2:19-22; 18:22-23; 2 Nephi 1:4-12; 10:10-14, 19.
[9] 1 Nephi 11; 12; 13; 14.

pretations, as did the religious thought recorded in the Old
Testament.

God declared on several occasions, and His statements
are recorded in the *Doctrine and Covenants,* that the *Book
of Mormon* contains the true plan of salvation. Such statements as the following are found in modern revelation:
"The *Book of Mormon* . . . contains the truth and the word
of God."[10] "[It] contains a record of a fallen people, and
the fullness of the Gospel of Jesus Christ to the Gentiles
and to the Jews also."[11]

Practically all of the religious truths taught and practiced in any Gospel dispensation are given in a clear and
forceful way in the *Book of Mormon.* In fact, many of the
principles are presented more clearly in that record than
in any of the other ancient scriptures. For example, the
concept of the mission of the Messiah, the belief in immortality, an understanding of the Godhead, the true order of
baptism, sacrament, and Mormon's famous discourse rejecting infant baptism are presented more vividly and forcefully than in the other ancient scriptures.[12]

LAW OF MOSES AND THE GOSPEL

The Nephites came from Jerusalem and brought with
them the practices of the Law of Moses; yet it seems that
their religious life was governed during the first 600 years
by a combination of the Law of Moses and the Gospel of
Jesus Christ. Beginning with Nephi, the actual founder
of the institutions and leader of the people, the prophets
boldly taught the first principles and ordinances of the
Gospel—faith, repentance, baptism and receiving the Holy
Ghost. Christ, Nephi claimed, had "commanded all men
that they must repent and be baptized in His name, having perfect faith in the Holy One of Israel, or they cannot be saved in the Kingdom of God."[13] The Prophet
Abinadi boldly declared to wicked King Noah and his
priests that the Law of Moses was not sufficient to save the
people.[14]

---

[10] *Doctrine and Covenants* 19:26-27.
[11] *Ibid.,* 20:8-9; 27:5; 42:12; 135:3; 17:1, 5-6, 9.
[12] Berrett, Hunter, Welker, Fitzgerald, *A Guide to the Study of the Book of Mormon,*
    pp. 55-116.
[13] 2 Nephi 9:23.
[14] Mosiah 13:27-28, 33.

The fact that the Nephites offered sacrifices and observed other religious rituals under the direction of the Aaronic Priesthood, as did their progenitors the Jews, and that they performed the spiritual ordinances through the Melchizedek Priesthood, is another evidence that they lived under a combination of the Law of Moses and the Gospel before the coming of Christ. However, after the Son of Man was resurrected, He appeared unto the inhabitants of ancient America and taught them the same Gospel truths that He had given to the Jews while living in mortality, declaring: "Ye shall offer unto me no more the shedding of blood; yea, your sacrifices and your burnt offerings shall be done away. . . . And ye shall offer as a sacrifice unto me a broken heart and a contrite spirit."[15]

CHURCH AND THE NEPHITES

It is important to know that the *Book of Mormon* gives evidence of the Nephites having had a well-established Church throughout most of their history, which functioned under the direction of the Melchizedek Priesthood.[16] Nephi held that Priesthood and was a prophet, seer and revelator. He consecrated his brothers, Jacob and Joseph, to be priests and teachers. Jacob acted with much efficiency in this capacity. He taught the people the plan of salvation in almost as comprehensive a manner as did his brother Nephi.

The Nephites had built a temple in less than thirty years after leaving Jerusalem, and later they built many other temples. In this first structure, Nephi and Jacob taught the people the Gospel of Jesus Christ. It was also used as a place in which sacrifices were offered in compliance with their custom of observing the Law of Moses preparatory for the coming of the Savior.

Even in the days of Nephi his people took upon themselves the name of Christ when they were baptized. An especially significant statement regarding it appears in one of that prophet's discourses: "Wherefore, my beloved brethren, I know that if you shall follow the Son, repenting of your sins, witnessing unto the Father that ye are willing to take upon you the name of Christ by bap-

---

15 3 Nephi chapters 9 to 30.
16 Alma 13:1-31.

tism . . . behold, then shall ye receive the Holy Ghost."[17]
Since the observance of the ordinance of baptism is requisite for entrance into the Church of Jesus Christ, it is quite probable that even at that early date the name of the Nephite Church was the Church of Christ.

Over 400 years later (147 B.C.), Alma established at the waters of Mormon in the land of Nephi a church named "the Church of Christ."[18] Twenty-three years thereafter, King Benjamin held a great religious revival in front of the temple at Zarahemla. At this revival, the people experienced an unusual spiritual awakening. They entered into a covenant to serve God henceforth and took upon themselves the name of Christ.[19] Each of these peoples acted independently of the other. Both groups had the Priesthood. Alma definitely named the Church he founded the "Church of Christ," while Benjamin gave his people the "name of Christ." The Church members were called Christians, which is a very significant fact, since it seems that the followers of Jesus on the eastern hemisphere were not called Christians until 46 A.D., at Antioch.[20]

After the Savior's resurrection and appearance to the Nephites, the people were concerned as to what the official name of the Church should be. The Master appeared to the twelve disciples (apostles) and said: "Have they not read the scriptures, which say ye must take upon you the name of Christ, which is my name? for by this name shall ye be called at the last days."[21] Then He instructed them to take the name of the "Church of Christ."

JESUS' TEACHINGS IN THE BOOK OF MORMON

The period following the personal appearances of Jesus to the Nephites as recorded in Third Nephi is one of the highlights in the religious history of man. This scripture contains the best account available of many of Jesus' teachings. Only a portion of the Master's instruc-

---

[17] 2 Nephi 31:13.
[18] Mosiah 5:7-15.
[19] *Ibid.*, 18:1-29; 26:15-39; 27:1-37.
[20] Alma 46:13-16; 48:10; Acts 11:26; Benjamin Willard Robinson, *The Life of Paul*, pp. 68-70, 221.
[21] 3 Nephi 26:17-21; 27:1-33. Jesus' prediction was fulfilled on April 6, 1830, when the "Restored Church" was placed upon the earth through the Prophet Joseph Smith and named the "Church of Christ," the official name coming by revelation (*Doctrine and Covenants* 21:1). Later, however, in order to distinguish the church in this Gospel dispensation from other dispensations, the Lord revealed to the Prophet that its name should be the "Church of Jesus Christ of Latter-day Saints." (*Doctrine and Covenants* 115:3).

tions as found in the New Testament appear in the *Book of Mormon,* yet that which is given is more complete than similar material contained in the Hebrew scripture. It clarifies the New Testament teachings by giving additional information or by giving more accurately the exact words of the Master.[22]

And what is even more unusual than the excellent way in which Jesus' teachings are recorded is the astounding effect that the Gospel had upon the lives of the people. A beautiful account is given of how the Nephites lived in perfect harmony and righteousness for 165 years after the resurrection of the Savior of the world.[23]

CONCLUDING EVENTS

But there came a day when the people rejected the Savior, who is the God of this land, and indulged in all manner of sins. About 400 A.D. this chapter of human history closed when the Nephite race was destroyed by the Lamanites in a great war. Of this great people, only Moroni was left, and it became his task to complete the religious record and, 1,400 years later, restore it to the Prophet Joseph Smith as part of our dispensation.

SUPPLEMENTARY READINGS—CHAPTER 13

1. *Book of Mormon:* Ether chapters 1 to 15; 1 Nephi 1; 2; 11; 12; 13; 14; 18:22-23; 2 Nephi 1:4-12; 10:10-14, 19; 9:23; 31:13; 27:10-11; Mosiah 8:5-21; 21:25-28; 28:11-20; 13:27-33; 5:7-15; 18:1-29; 26:15-39; 27:1-37; Alma 13:1-31; 46:13-16; 48:10; 3 Nephi 9:15-20; 13:24-34; 23:6-14; 26:17-21; 27:1-33; 4 Nephi 1:1-24.

2. *Doctrine and Covenants* 19:26-27; 20:8-9; 27:5; 42:12; 135:3; 17:1-9; 20:1; 115:3.

3. Berrett, Hunter, Welker, Fitzgerald, *A Guide to the Study of the Book of Mormon,* pp. 55-116.

4. James E. Talmage, *The Articles of Faith,* pp. 261-307.

---

[22] 3 Nephi 13:23-24; 23:6-14.
[23] 4 Nephi 1:1-24.

Chapter 14.

THE MERIDIAN AND FULLNESS OF TIMES

CHRISTIAN DISPENSATION

All of the holy prophets from Adam's time forward rejoiced in the knowledge that the Son of Man was eventually coming to earth to establish a Gospel dispensation in which He Himself was to set the pattern of life and point out the road to salvation. All truth and righteousness were to center in the life and the teachings of this one divine man—even Jesus Christ.

Nearly 2,000 years ago the Savior of mankind was announced into mortality by angels from heaven, accompanied by radiant light appropriate to His great mission. God the Father declared Him to be "my beloved Son, in whom I am well pleased." Even the skeptical Jews were caused to marvel and to remark, "Never man spake like this man."[1] "The people were astonished at his doctrine: For he taught them as one having authority, and not as the scribes."[2] He communed with God daily and declared that He did nothing and said nothing except that which He had been commanded of the Father. Finally He sealed His teachings with His blood; after which He triumphed over death to a glorious resurrected immortality. Thereafter He appeared unto His apostles and others and assured man of a blessed life eternal on condition of obedience to the Gospel plan of salvation.

EXPLANATORY NOTE

The writer has purposely given only a brief statement regarding the Christian dispensation, which is one of the greatest in history since it was inaugurated by the Son of God. The reason for not giving a more complete presenta-

[1] John 7:46.
[2] Matthew 7:28-29.

tion at this point is that throughout the entire book we shall refer to the conditions, teachings and practices of Christ, the apostles, and the other early Christians.

In fact, the New Testament contains the glorious teachings and a brief account of the life of the Man of Galilee. This book, therefore, will be our standard of judgment or the norm by which we measure the Gospel truths of all the dispensations.

THE GREAT APOSTASY AND THE REFORMATION

As has been previously mentioned, the glorious Gospel truths proclaimed by the Savior were corrupted by pagan teachings and practices to such an extent that Isaiah's prophesy was completely fulfilled wherein he declared: *"The earth is defiled under the inhabitants thereof; because they have transgressed the laws, changed the ordinance, broken the everlasting covenant."*[3]

These facts became apparent to a number of good men, such as Martin Luther, John Calvin, William Tyndale, the Wesley brothers, and others, who inaugurated what is known as the Reformation. Through sincere and diligent efforts they attempted to restore the Gospel teachings and practices to what the Master had given. But none of them held the holy Priesthood of God, which was absolutely essential if they were officially to establish the true Church of Jesus Christ. Until a divine restoration of the Priesthood and many of the Gospel ordinances came from heaven, therefore, the best that any of the reformers could hope to do was to rectify the more obviously adulterated Christian practices. In their efforts to do this, they did not receive divine revelations from God on vital points of doctrine, nor did they receive a restoration of the Priesthood. As time passed the Christian teachers violently disagreed with each other on many points of doctrine, with the result that numerous Christian denominations came into existence. What was badly needed—in fact, positively essential—was the restoration of the Priesthood from heaven and a new revelation of God's will.

---

[3] Isaiah 24:5.

RALPH WALDO EMERSON'S OBSERVATIONS

During the early part of the nineteenth century and after the Protestant Reformation had run its course, the religious condition of Christendom was so deplorable that Ralph Waldo Emerson—one of America's most brilliant men—became displeased and resigned his position as a minister of the Unitarian Church. He became a teacher of philosophy. On July 15, 1838, he described to the senior class of the Divinity School at Harvard University the religious condition of Christendom:

It is my duty to say to you that the need was never greater for new revelation than now. From the views I have already expressed, you will infer the sad conviction, which I share, I believe, with numbers, of the universal decay and now almost death of faith in society. The soul is not preached. The Church seems to totter to its fall, almost all life extinct. On this occasion, any complaisance would be criminal which told you, whose faith and commission it is to preach faith in Christ, that the faith of Christ is preached. . . .

In how many churches, by how many prophets, tell me, is man made sensible that he is an infinite soul? . . . Where shall I hear words such as in older ages drew men to leave all and follow—father and mother, house and land, wife and child? . . .

Men have come to speak of revelation as somewhat long age given and done, as if God were dead. The injury to faith throttles the preacher; and the godliest of institutions becomes an uncertain and inarticulate voice.[4]

On another occasion Emerson declared:

We are now so far from the road of truth, that religious teachers dispute and hate each other, and speculative men are esteemed unsound and frivolous. . . .

Our age is retrospective. It builds the sepulchres of the fathers. . . . The foregoing generations beheld God and nature face to face; we, through their eyes. Why should not we also enjoy an original relation to the universe? Why should not we have a poetry and philosophy of insight and not of tradition, and a religion by revelation to us, and invite us by the powers they supply, to action proportioned to nature, why should we grope among the dry bones of the past, or put the living generation into masquerade out of its faded wardrobe?[5]

I look for the hour when the supreme Beauty which ravished the souls of those Eastern men, and chiefly of those Hebrews, and through their lips spoke oracles to all times, shall speak in the West also. . . . I look for the new Teacher that shall follow so far those shining laws that he shall see them come full circle; shall see the world to be the mirror of the soul; shall see the identity of the law of gravitation with

[4] Frederic I. Carpenter, *Ralph Waldo Emerson*, pp. 79-80.
[5] *Ibid.*, pp. 10-11.

purity of heart; and shall show that the Right, the Duty, is one thing with Science, with Beauty, and with Joy.[6]

DISPENSATION OF THE FULLNESS OF TIMES

The gleams of prophetic light which flashed across Emerson's mind were shining forth with full radiance right at that time in another section of America. God the Eternal Father and His Son, Jesus Christ, had already spoken to that "new teacher"—the Prophet Joseph Smith—and had, through him, inaugurated another Gospel dispensation. The decree had gone forth from the heavens that the Gospel of Jesus Christ was given to this Prophet "never to be taken from earth again nor given to another people." The God of heaven and earth had proclaimed that:

Unto him [Joseph] I have committed the Keys of my Kingdom, and a dispensation of the Gospel for the last time; and for the fullness of times, in the which I will gather together in one all things, both which are in heaven and which are in earth.[7]

To Joseph Smith and the other general authorities of the Church the Lord declared:

For unto you, the Twelve, and those, the First Presidency, who are appointed with you to be your counselors and your leaders, is the power of this Priesthood given, for the last days and for the last time, in the which is the dispensation of the fullness of times. Which power you hold, in connection with all those who have received a dispensation at any time from the beginning of the creation; for verily I say unto you, the keys of the dispensation, which ye have received, have come down from the fathers, and last of all, being sent down from heaven unto you.[8]

It is evident from the scriptures that the dispensation of the Gospel in the latter days is to be one of restoration and restitution. Nephi predicted that "all things which have been revealed unto the children of men shall at that day be revealed."[9] Peter declared that the Lord "shall send Jesus Christ, which before was preached unto you: whom the heavens must receive until the times of restitution of all things, which God hath spoken by the mouth of all the holy prophets since the world began."[10] And Paul predicted "that in the dispensation of the fullness of times he [God] might gather together in one all things in Christ,

[6] Ibid., p. 88.
[7] Doctrine and Covenants 27:13.
[8] Ibid., 112:30-32.
[9] 2 Nephi 30:18.
[10] Acts 3:20-21.

both which are in heaven, and which are on earth; even in him."[11]

So important is this dispensation in the grand scheme devised by the Father and the Son that these two heavenly beings appeared to the Prophet Joseph Smith in the spring of 1820 and gloriously opened the Dispensation of the Fullness of Times. Following this visitation, such heavenly beings as the angel Moroni, John the Baptist, Peter, James and John, Elijah, Moses, Elias, and others appeared unto the American Prophet and gave him the keys of their dispensations. In the words of Joseph:

Now, what do we hear in the Gospel which we have received? A voice of gladness! A voice of mercy from heaven; and a voice of truth out of the earth; a voice of gladness for the living and the dead; glad tidings of great joy. . . . And the voice of Michael, the Archangel; the voice of Gabriel, and of Raphael, and of divers angels, from Michael or Adam down to the present time, all declaring their dispensation, their rights, their keys, their honors, their majesty and glory, and the power of their Priesthood; giving line upon line, precept upon precept; here a little and there a little; giving us consolation by holding forth that which is to come, confirming our hope! . . .

For it is necessary in the ushering in of the dispensation of the fullness of times, which dispensation is now beginning to usher in, that a whole and complete and perfect union, and welding together of dispensations, and keys, and powers, and glories should take place, and be revealed from the days of Adam even to the present time. And not only this, but those things which never have been revealed from the foundation of the world, but have been kept hid from the wise and prudent, shall be revealed unto babes and sucklings in this, the dispensation of the fullness of times.[12]

The Prophet Joseph Smith not only received the keys of the Priesthood from those in authority who held them last in each of the Gospel dispensations, but he also was given revelation upon revelation explaining the various principles and ordinances of the Gospel. Through this American Prophet, Jesus Christ again established His Church upon the earth and endowed it with all the power requisite for the salvation of the human family. He made it the depository of all true doctrines, principles and practices that have been revealed to men or that shall be revealed. Therefore, the Church of Jesus Christ of Latter-day Saints is the only organization in the world which is

---

[11] Ephesians 1:10.
[12] *Doctrine and Covenants* 128:18-21; 121:31; 136:37; Smith, *Teachings of the Prophet Joseph Smith*, pp. 231-232, 193, 61, 264, 159, 171-178, 228; 2 Nephi 22:7-16.

officially recognized by God as having the power, authority, ordinances and doctrines requisite to bring men back into the presence of the Eternal Father and the Only Begotten Son and to exalt them with a glorious eternal life.

Therefore, the Dispensation of the Fullness of Times is the greatest of all, because into it will flow all other dispensations. It will be in this dispensation that Christ will come to reign for one thousand years.

As we move forward through the course of study we shall have occasion in a number of the chapters to discuss the various principles and ordinances of the Gospel and plan of salvation as practiced in former dispensations and as revealed to the Prophet Joseph Smith in what God has termed the Dispensation of the Fullness of Times.

SUPPLEMENTARY READINGS—CHAPTER 14

1. *Bible*: Genesis 14:18-24; John 7:46; Matthew 7:28-29; Isaiah 24:5; Acts 3:20-21; Ephesians 1:10.
2. *Book of Mormon*: Alma 13:1-31; 1 Nephi 22:7-15; 2 Nephi 30:18.
3. *Doctrine and Covenants* 27:13; 112:30-32; 128:18-21; 121:31; 136:37; 110.
4. G. Homer Durham (Compiler), *The Gospel Kingdom*, pp. 106-107, 121-125.
5. B. H. Roberts, *The Seventy's Course in Theology*, Second Year, pp. 107-232.
6. Joseph Fielding Smith (Compiler), *Teachings of the Prophet Joseph Smith*, pp. 231-232, 193, 61, 264, 159, 171, 173, 228.
7. Joseph Fielding Smith, *The Restoration of All Things*, pp. 11-46.
8. Joseph Fielding Smith, *The Way to Perfection*, pp. 142-148.

Chapter 15.

CHILDREN OF GOD

MEN THE OFFSPRING OF DEITY

A Gospel truth which is as old as the human race and which appears in the theologies of numerous religions throughout history is that all mortals are literally sons and daughters of God. They were His offspring in the spirit world. Although expressed in a variety of ways by the various religious teachers, there is an almost universal agreement that man has within himself a divine spark. A portion of man is spirit, which is eternal and closely related to Deity.

In addition to the concept that mortal beings are the spirit children of God there has been running through history as a golden thread the eternal verity that human beings were created and placed here upon this earth by a divine power or being, known to us as God the Eternal Father. Practically every religion throughout history has had its own version of the origin of man, and basically they have agreed on the two foregoing points, namely, that mortals are not only the spirit-children of God, but that He also placed them upon this earth.

ORIGIN OF CHILDREN OF GOD BELIEF

This golden thread of religious truth is accounted for on the ground that the Lord revealed to Father Adam, the first man, that Adam was a son of God, and thereby divine and eternal. He also informed our first parents that they were placed upon this earth by heavenly beings— God the Father and His Only Begotten Son.[1]

According to a revelation given to Moses and re-revealed to the Prophet Joseph Smith, the first creation of man was a "spiritual creation." The Lord declared: "And

---

[1] Moses 2:26-27; Genesis 1:27; Abraham 4:26-31.

96

I, the Lord God, had created all the children of men; and
not yet a man to till the ground; for in heaven created I
them; and there was not yet flesh upon the earth, neither
in the water, neither in the air."[2]   This eternal truth was
confirmed by revelations to several of the ancient prophets.
For example, more than 2,000 years before the Savior was
born into mortality, He appeared to the brother of Jared
and said: "Behold, I am Jesus Christ. . . . This body, which
ye now behold, is the body of my spirit; and man have I
created after the body of my spirit; and even as I appear
unto thee to be in the spirit, will I appear unto my people
in the flesh."[3]   This statement and a revelation given to
the Prophet Joseph definitely tell us that spirit beings in
appearance are like the Gods and also like earthly bodies.[4]

Following the spiritual creation of God's children came
the mortal organizing of their physical bodies. The story
of the organizing of the first man is told in the scriptures
as follows: "And I, the Lord God, formed man from the
dust of the ground, and breathed into his nostrils the breath
of life [i. e., put into his physical body his spirit], and man
became a living soul; . . . nevertheless, all things were before created; but spiritually were they created and made
according to my word."[5]   These divine revelations definitely
proclaim that mortal man is composed of a spirit body, made
of eternal spiritual matter, and a mortal body, made of the
elements of the earth. Thus from this original revelation
kindred ideas have spread throughout many religions, as
we shall point out later.

BELIEF SUSTAINED BY OLD TESTAMENT PROPHETS

The Old Testament prophets thoroughly understood
that all people of the earth are literally the sons and daughters of God the Eternal Father, since He begat their spirit
bodies. The following statements confirming this viewpoint appear in the ancient Hebrew records: "Let the
Lord, the God of the spirits of all flesh, set a man over the
congregation."[6] "And they fell upon their faces, and said,
'O God, the God of the spirits of all flesh, shall one man

---

[2] Moses 3:4-5; Abraham 3:27; 4:5; Genesis 1:27; 2:5-9.
[3] Ether 3:14-16.
[4] *Doctrine and Covenants* 129:1-9.
[5] Moses 3:7-9; Abraham 5:7-8; Genesis 2:7.
[6] Numbers 27:16.

sin, and wilt thou be wroth with all the congregation'."[7]
Again we read, "I said, Ye are gods, and all of you sons
of the Most High."[8] And the author of Ecclesiastes points
out this constant truth: "Then shall the dust return to the
earth as it was, and the spirit shall return unto God who gave
it."[9]

TEACHINGS OF JESUS AND HIS APOSTLES

The Man of Galilee throughout His entire ministry
proclaimed that mortals are the children of God. He taught
His apostles to pray as follows: "Our Father which art in
heaven"; and this was the pattern for all of us to follow.
Shortly after the Master's resurrection, He said unto Mary
Magdalene: "Touch me not, for I am not yet ascended
to my father: but go to my brethren, and say unto them,
*I ascend unto my Father, and your Father; and to my God,
and your God.*"[10]

The Savior taught this doctrine of the Fatherhood of
God so thoroughly to His apostles that in their writings
are found some of the most pertinent statements of this concept. Such declarations as the following are indicative of
the belief and teachings of the early Christians:

Furthermore we have had fathers of our flesh which corrected
us, and we gave them reverence: shall we not much rather be in subjection
unto the Father of spirits, and live.[11]

The Spirit itself beareth witness with our spirit, that we are the
children of God: and if children, then heirs; heirs of God, and joint-heirs
with Christ; if so be that we suffer with him, that we may be also glorified together.[12]

MORMONS' CONCEPT OF HEAVENLY PARENTS

When light burst forth from heaven in revelations to
the Prophet Joseph Smith, a more complete understanding
of man—especially regarding his personal relationship to
Deity—was received than could be found in all of the holy
scriptures combined. The stupendous truth of the existence of a Heavenly Mother, as well as a Heavenly Father,
became established facts in Mormon theology. A complete
realization that we are the offspring of Heavenly Parents—
that we were begotten and born into the spirit world and
grew to maturity in that realm—became an integral part

---

7 *Ibid.*, 16:22.
8 Psalm 82:6.
9 Ecclesiastes 12:7.
10 John 20:17.
11 Hebrews 12:9.
12 Romans 8:16-17.

of Mormon philosophy. Those verities are basic in the Gospel plan of eternal progression.

The prophets of our dispensation have clearly explained the doctrine of heavenly parenthood. In the words of President Joseph F. Smith, and his counselors, John R. Winder and Anthon H. Lund: "Man, as a spirit, was begotten and born of Heavenly Parents, and reared to maturity in the eternal mansions of the Father prior to coming upon the earth in a temporal body to undergo an experience in mortality."[13] President Brigham Young read the two verses in Genesis 1:26-27, which declared that God created man, and then he told the congregation:

I believe that the declaration made in these scriptures is literally true. God has made His children like Himself to stand erect, and has endowed them with intelligence and power and dominion over all His works, and given them the same attributes which He Himself possesses. He created men, as we create our children; for there is no other process of creation in heaven or on the earth, in the earth, or under the earth, or in all the eternities, that is, that were, or that ever will be.[14]

The crowning glory of exaltation received by every man and woman who obeys all of the Gospel principles and ordinances is centered directly in the doctrine of parenthood in the celestial degree of glory. This sublime doctrine will be discussed in the following chapter.

Eliza R. Snow Smith, in her famous poem, "O My Father," expressed beautifully the doctrine of a Father and Mother in heaven. In fact, she gives several pertinent truths regarding pre-mortal life, and a convincing hope of immortality and the future union with our Heavenly Parents in such a classical way that we shall quote her entire poem for the student's careful consideration:

O MY FATHER
Eliza R. Snow Smith

O my Father, Thou that dwellest
  In the high and glorious place!
When shall I regain Thy presence,
  And again behold Thy face?
In Thy holy habitation,
  Did my spirit once reside;
In my first primeval childhood,
  Was I nurtured near Thy side.

---

[13] Joseph F. Smith, *Improvement Era*, vol. 13, p. 80.
[14] Brigham Young, *Journal of Discourses*, vol. 11, p. 122.

For a wise and glorious purpose
   Thou hast placed me here on earth,
And withheld the recollection
   Of my former friends and birth,
Yet ofttimes a secret something
   Whispered, "You're a stranger here";
And I felt that I had wandered
   From a more exalted sphere.

I had learned to call Thee Father,
   Thru Thy Spirit from on high;
But until the Key of Knowledge
   Was restored, I knew not why.
In the heav'ns are parents single?
   No; the tho't makes reason stare!
Truth is reason, truth eternal,
   Tells me I've a Mother there

When I leave this frail existence,
   When I lay this mortal by,
Father, Mother, may I meet you
   In your royal courts on high?
Then at length, when I've completed
   All you sent me forth to do,
With your mutual approbation
   Let me come and dwell with you.

COMPARATIVE RELIGIONS' CONCEPT OF MAN

Not only have the prophets of God throughout the various dispensations declared that mortals are the children of Heavenly Parents and that God placed mankind into mortality; but the pagan religions preserved in their theologies kindred doctrine. The ancient Greek poets and philosophers, the Mystery Religions, and even the first settlers of the Mesopotamian Valley proclaimed these divine truths.

In Paul's famous speech at Athens, which was inspired by the inscription "To the Unknown God," the apostle to the Gentiles quoted the Greek poet Aratus—who had lived near Tarsus, Paul's birthplace—as having written: "For we are also his [God's] offspring."[15]

In the Cybele-Attis cult, which originated in central Asia Minor, the supreme deity was known as the "Great Mother." She was believed to be the mother not only "of all the gods," but *of all men* as well. Several other cults

---

[15] Acts 17:26-28; Benjamin William Robinson, *The Life of Paul*, p. 132.

which were pagan rivals of Christianity had beliefs similar to those of the Cybele-Attis cult, each of which maintained that men were the offspring of heavenly beings.

For example, the Mithraic religion, which had its rise in Persia as early as 1,500 B.C. and which eventually became the strongest pagan rival of Christianity, proclaimed the doctrine that man had a spirit which was composed of immortal substance and his physical body was of earthly materials. Cult members believed, as did Father Abraham, that the Gods placed human beings upon the earth and were their protectors.

The belief that each human being is composed of a physical body and a spirit—the latter composed of divine, eternal substance—is a concept that was held by practically all ancient peoples. This belief of the dualism of man was as universally held by Greeks as it was by the prophets and teachers of the Gospel during the various dispensations. It is nothing more than the pagan version of the spirit of man being a child of God and his body being made of earthly substance.

Pindar, the Greek poet, stressed the divine origin and nature of the human spirit in contradistinction to the mortality of the human body. He wrote: "While the body of all men is subject to over-mastering death, an image of life remains alive, for it alone comes from the gods."[16] The Stoic philosophers, some of whom Paul encountered at Athens, "believed that every man possessed within him a spark of the divine reason and so is in a sense akin to God."[17] Plato, the famous Greek philosopher, represented Socrates, his master teacher, as saying shortly before his death: "There is a doctrine whispered in secret that a man [i.e., the spirit of man] is a prisoner who has no right to open the door and run away; that is a great mystery which I do not quite understand. Yet I, too, believe that the gods are our guardians and that we are a possession of theirs."[18]

The Orphic mystery worshipers, pagan rivals of Christianity, believed that men were created originally from the ashes of the Titans who had been blasted to pieces by Zeus. The Titans were of the earth and were beings similar in

[16] Pindar, *Threnodies*, p. 131.
[17] Robinson, *op. cit.*, p. 130; Acts 17:18.
[18] Plato, *Phaedo*, p. 62.

their evil nature to devils. The Orphic myth claimed that just prior to their destruction, the Titans had eaten the god Dionysus. Since man was believed to have been created from the ashes of the Titans, he was a compound of two natures, one Dionysian and immortal, the other Titanic and mortal. This sharp contrast of dualism of spirit and body appears in many of the Orphic writings. Recorded on the Petelian tablets in southern Italy during the third century B.C., the spirit asserts its divine nature as follows: "I am a child of Earth and Starry Heaven; but my race is of Heaven." The following inscription appeared on another Orphic tablet: "Pure Queen of Them Below . . . I avow me that I am of your blessed race."[19]

The foregoing Orphic doctrine was widespread throughout the Mediterranean world during the period of the rise of Christianity. The following inscription was found in a Sabine village, dating in the second century A. D.: "The soul is immortal, for it came from God. The body is the garment of the soul. Honor the God in me"[20] This Orphic inscription, which confirms the belief of the divine nature of man, was taken from the grave of an ancient Greek: "Hermes gathers me with the sons of the gods, and I have not drunk the water of Forgetfulness."[21]

As previously mentioned, the belief that God created man is also universal. A good example of an ancient people having this concept is found on the Babylonian tablets. Marduk, the god of this people, is purported to have declared: "Blood will I create, and bone will I cause to be. I will set up man, indeed, man shall be his name. I will create man, even man. They (men) shall worship the gods; they (the gods) shall be appeased."[22] The Sumerian-Babylonian tablets (the Sumerians being the oldest race of Mesopotamia) proclaimed that Marduk "formed mankind. The goddess Aruru, with him, made the seed of mankind."[23] Doubtless these stories are corruptions of the Bible creation story.

[19] Harold Willoughby, *Pagan Regeneration*, pp. 96-97.
[20] Cited in *Ibid.*, p. 111.
[21] Cited in *Ibid.*, p. 112.
[22] Cited in Ira M. Price, *The Monuments and the Old Testament*, p. 103.
[23] Cited in *Ibid.*, p. 106.

Conclusions

Ample evidence has been given to demonstrate thoroughly that human beings throughout the entire history of the world have maintained not only that they were created by God, but that they were the spiritual children of Heavenly Parents. This blessed Gospel truth, which has been revealed to the holy prophets throughout the various dispensations, was disseminated among pagan peoples. Although it appears in their theologies in a degenerated form, yet they maintained enough of the original revelation to know that they were of divine origin, and hence by very nature eternal. This concept has been one of the most dynamic motivating forces in religious history.

SUPPLEMENTARY READINGS—CHAPTERS 15 AND 16

1. *Book of Mormon:* 2 Nephi 9:4-10, 22; Alma 11:41-45; 18:34; 22; 3 Nephi 26:4-5; 1 Nephi 2:12; 17:36; Mosiah 2:20-23; 7:27.
2. *Doctrine and Covenants* 76:58; 131:2; 132:17-20, 37.
3. Joseph Fielding Smith, *The Restoration of All Things*, pp. 56-64.
4. Joseph F. Smith, "The Origin of Man," *Improvement Era*, vol. 13, pp. 75-81.
5. John A. Widtsoe, *Rational Theology*, pp. 23-38, 61-65.
6. John A. Widtsoe, *An Understandable Religion*, pp. 10-28.
7. Harold Willoughby, *Pagan Regeneration*, pp. 84-85, 106-112, 126, 191-194.

Chapter 16.

MEN MAY BECOME GODS

INTRODUCTORY STATEMENT

It is our purpose in this chapter to show that since mortal beings are the spirit children of Heavenly Parents, as pointed out in the last chapter, the ultimate possibility is for some of them to become exalted to Godhood. After presenting the doctrine as revealed by God to the holy prophets and proclaimed by the scriptures, we shall follow it as it appears somewhat universally in the pagan religions.

GOD AN EXALTED BEING

The Gospel of Jesus Christ teaches that God the Eternal Father is an exalted being. "In the language of Adam, Man of Holiness is his name, and the name of his Only Begotten is the Son of Man, even Jesus Christ, a righteous Judge."[1] Mormon prophets have continuously taught the sublime truth that God the Eternal Father was once a mortal man who passed through a school of earth life similar to that through which we are now passing. He became God—an exalted being—through obedience to the same eternal Gospel truths that we are given opportunity today to obey.

For the purpose of giving a clear understanding of the teachings of the latter-day prophets, we shall quote some of their statements. President Joseph F. Smith declared that "God himself is an exalted man, perfected, enthroned and supreme."[2] Elder Orson Hyde, a member of the Quorum of the Twelve, said: "Remember that God our Heavenly Father was perhaps once a child, and mortal like we are, and rose step by step in the scale of progress, in the school of advancement; has moved forward and over-

[1] Moses 6:56.
[2] Joseph F. Smith, John R. Winder, Anthon H. Lund, *Improvement Era*, vol. 13, p. 81.

come until He has arrived at the point where He now is."[3]
And Daniel H. Wells concluded: "God is a being of agency
and He has passed along the path He wishes us to tread,
and has attained to His exaltation just as He wishes us
to attain to ours."[4] But probably the most forceful and
explicit statement declaring God to be an exalted man was
made by the Prophet Joseph Smith. To quote:

> God Himself was once as we are now, and is an exalted man, and
> sits enthroned in yonder heavens! That is the great secret. If the
> veil were rent today, and the great God who holds this world in its
> orbit, and who upholds all worlds and all things by His power, was
> to make Himself visible—I say, if you were to see Him today, you
> would see Him like a man in form—like yourselves—in all the person,
> image, and very form as a man; for Adam was created in the very
> fashion, image, and likeness of God, and received instruction from and
> walked, talked and conversed with Him, as one man talks and com-
> munes with another. . . .
>
> It is the first principle of the Gospel to know for a certainty the
> character of God, and to know that we may converse with Him as
> one man converses with another, and that He was once a man like us,
> yea, that God Himself, the Father of us all, dwelt on an earth, the
> same as Jesus Christ Himself did.[5]

Men May Become Gods

As early as February 16, 1832, the Lord revealed to
the Prophet Joseph Smith the sublime truth that *"men may
become gods."* Among many other important truths revealed to Joseph and Sidney Rigdon that day, God showed
them a vision of the three degrees of glory and explained
to them who should be assigned to each degree. In speaking of those who should inhabit the celestial world, the Lord
said:

> They are they who are the church of the first-born. They are
> they into whose hands the Father has given all things—they are they
> who are Priests and Kings who have received of his fullness, and of
> his glory; And are Priests of the Most High, after the order of
> Melchizedek, which was after the order of Enoch, which was after the
> order of the Only Begotten Son; Wherefore, as it is written *they are
> Gods,* even the sons of God. . . . These shall dwell in the presence of
> God and his Christ for ever and ever.[6]

In June, 1840, Lorenzo Snow formulated the following famous couplet: *"As man is, God once was; as God is,*

[3] Orson Hyde, *Journal of Discourses*, vol. 1, p. 123.
[4] Daniel H. Wells, *Millennial Star*, vol. 26, p. 786.
[5] Joseph Fielding Smith, *Teachings of the Prophet Joseph Smith*, pp. 345-346.
[6] *Doctrine and Covenants* 76:54-59; *Moses* 6:66-67.

man may become."[7]   This doctrine, when first announced
by the Prophet and later restated by Elder Snow, was astounding to Christendom, since the teachers as well as the
laity had long ago ceased to regard man as a being of such
magnitude.   Even today it is still a doctrine understood
primarily by members of the Church of Jesus Christ of
Latter-day Saints.

Following the earlier pronouncements of this doctrine, much more light came to earth through the prophets
of the last dispensation.   For example, in a revelation given
to Joseph Smith on May 6, 1833, he learned of Jesus' development in the spirit world and of the unfoldment of His
personality in mortality and glorification in post-mortal
life wherein "He received a fullness of the glory of the
Father."[8]   Then the following promise was made to mortals:

For if you keep my commandments you shall receive of his [God's]
fullness, and be glorified in me as I am in the Father; therefore, I
say unto you, you shall receive grace for grace.[9]

The glory that Christ received was that of Godhood;
therefore, for men to receive the same glory they also shall
become Gods.   In fact, when the Church leaders during
the early period of Mormondom searched the scriptures more
carefully, it became very clear to them that the ultimate
goal of eternal progression is to receive eternal life, i. e.,
to become as God is.   For this cause the Gospel of Jesus
Christ was instituted before the foundation of the world
and revealed to mankind from age to age by a gracious
Heavenly Father.   Of course, it is generally understood
that a vast majority of the children of our Heavenly Parents will not obey the Gospel principles and ordinances to
the degree requisite to finally exalt themselves unto Godhood, but the possibility is that there are many individuals
who will attain that desired goal.   For example, Abraham,
Isaac and Jacob "have entered into their exaltation according to the promises, and sit upon thrones, and are not
angels but are Gods."[10]

President Joseph F. Smith beautifully expressed the
foregoing doctrine, as follows:

[7] Lorenzo Snow, *Millennial Star*, vol. 54, p. 404; LeRoi C. Snow, "Devotion to a Divine
   Inspiration," *Improvement Era*, vol. 22, (June, 1919), pp. 653-662.
[8] *Doctrine and Covenants* 93:1-17.
[9] *Ibid.*, 93:20.
[10] *Ibid.*, 132:37.

Man is the child of God, formed in the divine image and endowed with divine attributes; and even as the infant son of our earthly father and mother is capable in due time of becoming a man, so the undeveloped offspring of celestial parentage is capable by experience through ages of aeons of evolving into a God.[11]

In the words of Dr. John A. Widtsoe, "God and man are of the same race, differing only in their degrees of advancement."[12] Additional light is thrown on the subject by Charles W. Penrose:

To know God we must know ourselves. All the personal attributes which are ascribed to God by inspired men, we find in ourselves. . . . Mormonism does not tend to debase God to the level of man, but to exalt man to the perfection of God.[13]

DOCTRINE OF THE PLURALITY OF GODS

The first question that may arise in one's mind is, "How can mortals ever become Gods when there is already a supreme being?" As it is possible for several sons here in mortality to eventually become fathers, so is it just as possible for the sons of God to reach the station of perfection that He has attained. Of course, at that time He will still be God, and even a greater Deity than He is today. This is the doctrine of the plurality of Gods.

Here and there in the holy scriptures the prophets confirmed the doctrine that there is a plurality of Gods and that men may become Gods. The creation story as recorded in the Book of Abraham uses the term "Gods" throughout the entire text.[14] St. John begins his Gospel by saying: "In the beginning was the Word, and the Word was with God, and the Word was God. The same was in the beginning with God."[15] This sentence proves that there were at least two Gods who created this world, and is that not a plurality of divine beings? The authors of Psalms declared: "I will praise thee with my whole heart: before the gods will I sing praises unto thee."[16] "For the Lord is a great God, and a great King above all gods."[17] Again we read: "God standeth in the congregation of the mighty; he judgeth among the gods. . . . I have said,

---

[11] Joseph F. Smith, *Improvement Era*, vol. 12, p. 81.
[12] John A. Widtsoe, *Rational Theology*, p. 61.
[13] Charles W. Penrose, *Millennial Star*, vol. 23, pp. 180-181.
[14] Abraham 4:5.
[15] John 1:1-3.
[16] Psalm 138:1.
[17] *Ibid.*, 95:3.

'Ye are gods; and all of you are children of the Most High.' "[18] Thus all of these scriptures proclaim a plurality of the Gods.

When the Man of Galilee was speaking to the Jews, He claimed to be the Son of God, and He accepted the doctrine that those who obeyed the Gospel could some day become Gods. Thereupon the Jews became exceedingly angry and threatened to stone the Master. In defense of this doctrine, He explained unto them:

Is it not written in your law, "I said, ye are gods"? If he called them gods, unto whom the word of God came, and the scriptures cannot be broken; Say of him, whom the Father hath sanctified and sent into the world, "Thou blasphemist"; because I said, "I am the Son of God."[19]

Paul in his letter to the Corinthians recognized the plurality of the Gods. He wrote: "For though there be that are called gods, whether in heaven or in earth (as there be gods many, and lords many), but to us there is but one God, the Father, of whom are all things, and we in him."[20]

In reference to the last quoted scripture, the Prophet Joseph Smith declared: "Paul says there are Gods many and Lords many; and that makes a plurality of Gods. . . . You know and I testify that Paul had no allusion to the heathen gods. I have it from God, and get over it if you can. I have a witness of the Holy Ghost, and a testimony that Paul had no allusion to the heathen gods in the text."[21] As was pointed out in the last chapter, Paul also taught that all the members of the true Church who lived righteous lives were "heirs, heirs of God, and joint-heirs with Christ." Since Jesus has attained Godhood, to be a joint-heir with Him would be to attain a similar glory. Thus there are a plurality of Gods, and it is possible for men to become like the Supreme Being.

DOCTRINE TAUGHT BY THE CHRISTIAN FATHERS

During the early Christian centuries, the Church retained as part of its doctrine the divine verity previously proclaimed by Jesus and His apostles, that "men may become Gods." The teachings on this doctrine as given by the

---

[18] *Ibid.*, 82:1, 6.
[19] John 10:34-36.
[20] 1 Corinthians 8:5-6.
[21] Joseph Fielding Smith, *op. cit.*, 371.

early Christian fathers are so nearly identical with those of the Latter-day Saint prophets that one would find difficulty in trying to tell which came from which age. It is logical that these teachings should be identical, since the early Christians still retained many Gospel truths and the same verities were revealed to the Prophet Joseph Smith. For example, Methodius, the Greek father, emphatically declared that "every believer must, through participation in Christ, be born a Christ," and he also taught dogmatically that "He was made man that we might be made Gods."[22] Lactantius (about 325 A.D.) affirms that the chaste man will become "identical in all respects with God."[23] Clement of Alexandria employed a language that is well understood by John the Beloved and the Mormons alike.[24] The following statement, taken from Clement's teachings, shows that he had a comprehensive understanding of the doctrine of men's becoming Gods:

"If anyone knows himself he shall know God, and by knowing God he shall be made like unto him"; and again, "that man with whom the Logos dwells . . . is made like God and is beautiful. . . . That man becomes God, for God so wills it"; and "the Logos of God became man that from man you might learn how man may become God." Further, that the true Christian Gnostic "has already become God."[25]

PAGANS' BELIEFS OF DEIFICATION

The teachings of these early Christian fathers were compatible with the doctrines taught by the contemporary pagan philosophies and religions. Eternal truths had come down through the stream of time and had spread outward throughout the pagan cults of the Mediterranean world. It has been claimed that "through the course of Greek religious thought a single thread may be traced, in the essential unity of man and God."[26] During the early period in Greece and Italy "there were legends of men who, by conspicuous deserts, had been promoted to gods, as there were also legends of gods who had descended to earth. The Roman dead became *Manes,* and so divine. Greek heroes had, after death, been accorded divine honours."[27] Leo, an Egyptian priest, informed Alexander the Great "that

[22] S. Angus, *The Mystery Religions and Christianity*, pp. 106-107.
[23] Cited in *ibid.*, p. 106.
[24] John 17:3; *Doctrine and Covenants* 132:24.
[25] Angus, *op. cit.*, p. 106.
[26] Mrs. Adam, *Greek Ideals of Righteousness*, p. 67.
[27] Angus, *op. cit.*, p. 107.

heroes and gods alike had been elevated from the ranks of humanity." Later Hecataeus, under Ptolemy I, asserted that such gods as "Zeus and Isis had been mortals divinized because of their beneficent deeds to mankind." Euhemerus, in his epochal *Sacred History,* denied the existence of Gods "as a species, so to speak, distinct from man."[28]

The close kinship of Deity and man was a pertinent concept proclaimed by the Greek and Latin philosophers. Such prominent Latin writers as Seneca, Epictetus, and Cicero, who lived near the time of Jesus, were pronounced in their viewpoints on the divine nature of man. Dr. S. Angus quotes from these ancient philosophers as follows:

> Seneca says that "a good man differs only in point of time from God, whose disciple and imitator he is." Epictetus speaks eloquently of the security accruing to man from the fact that God is his Father: "Do you suppose that God would suffer His own son to be enslaved?" "Know, then, that thou art a god," says Cicero, "and inferior in no whit to the celestials save in immortality."[29]

DEIFICATION DOCTRINE TAUGHT BY MYSTERY RELIGIONS

The Mystery Religions, pagan rivals of Christianity, taught emphatically the doctrine that "men may become Gods." Hermeticism, which had its rise in Egypt in the second or third centuries B.C., was a prominent religion in the Mediterranean world during the period of the rise of Christianity. Its literature, the *Corpus Hermeticum,* professes to be revelations to Hermes from his divine father and teacher. Hermes declared: "We must not shrink from saying that a man on earth is a mortal god, and that God in heaven is an immortal man."[30] This thought very closely resembles the teachings of the Prophet Joseph Smith and of President Lorenzo Snow.

This religion taught that it was perfectly possible for man, even while living in mortality, to become a god. It also maintained, as does the true Gospel doctrine, that the spirit of the man who had become deified was immortal. To quote from Hermetic literature: "The natural body can be dissolved, the spiritual body cannot be."[31] The worshiper was taught that after he left this

[28] *Ibid.,* pp. 107-108.
[29] *Ibid.*
[30] Cited in Harold Willoughby, *Pagan Regeneration,* p. 220.
[31] *Ibid.,* pp. 219-220.

mortal life he would "be brought into the troops of the gods and the souls that have attained bliss."[32]

Such teachings as the following appear in the theology of Orphism—another prominent pagan rival of Christianity: " 'Happy and Blessed One, you shall be God instead of mortal.' . . . Thus the initiated, having lived a life of Orphic purity, finally became 'God from man'."[33]

Archaeological evidence furnished by sepulchral art and grave inscriptions illustrates that the members of this cult believed that the status of divinity was attained after death. For example, at Guthaeum a first-century (A.D.) statue, obviously a portrait-statue of a youth, represented him as being a god—a Dionysus. "A priest of Thasos dedicated an inscription to his dead wife as 'an incarnate goddess', and a man by the name of Lucius consecrated a monument to his child of four years with these words: 'To my sweetest child and personal God who hearkens to my prayers'."[34]

The Isiac Mystery Religion's initiation ceremony was for the purpose of deifying the initiate. The ancient records tell of the initiation of a man named Lucius. "At midnight he saw the sun brightly shine and saw likewise the gods celestial and the gods infernal." At sunrise the following morning he was dramatically dressed in sacred clothing, covered with symbolical figures, and seated on a pedestal in the middle of the temple before the statue of the goddess herself. In his hand was a lighted torch and on his head a rayed crown. The curtains were drawn aside and he was exposed to public view. "The faithful contemplated him with the admiration and devotion due a god." In fact, he was hailed as Osiris-Ra. "Reborn through the rite of initiation, the mystic believed himself born again to a superhuman life, the immortal life of the gods."[35]

The Great Mother Mystery Religion furnishes another example which deified its cult members. All holders of the priesthood, the *Galli,* were eunuch-priests and were regarded as gods. Each one was also called Attis, the name of the male god in this religion. "Just as Attis was be-

---

[32] *Ibid.*
[33] *Ibid.*, pp. 107-108.
[34] *Ibid.*, pp. 110-111.
[35] *Ibid.*, pp. 186-195.

lieved to have attained the state of deity by the passion of
emasculation, so by the way of self-mutilation, the *Gallus*
became a god instead of mortal."[36]

In the same religion, as well as in the Mithraic Mysteries, a baptism in blood, known as *taurobolium,* was practiced. As the neophyte emerged from the trench, drenched
and dripping with blood, he presented himself to the expectant throng of worshipers. "They did obeisance to
him as to a god, as to one who had been born again to a
divine life."

CONCLUSIONS

Much evidence has been presented which shows that
throughout history human beings had the belief that "men
may become Gods." During certain periods the prophets
have thoroughly understood this sublime truth; and at other
times the doctrine has practically vanished from the earth.
For example, during the early centuries A.D., both Christians and pagans accepted this doctrine wholeheartedly.
Then there came a period, which lasted for hundreds of
years, in which the "divine-man doctrine" was lost, except
as it was applied to kings. During this period, often spoken
of as the "Dark Ages," a drastic phase of the Great Apostasy was the loss of the true interpretation of this Gospel
truth and its warped and adulterated application to the families of earthly royalty.

Therefore, during the early part of the nineteenth
century, it required divine revelations from God to the
Prophet Joseph Smith and other Mormon leaders to restore to mankind in all of its purity and majesty the eternal
truth that the goal of human life is that *"men may become
Gods."*

MAN'S DESTINY, *by Lorenzo Snow*

The following poem was composed by President Lorenzo Snow on January
11, 1892, and first published by his son, LeRoi C. Snow, in the *Improvement Era,*
June, 1919. The poem was addressed to Apostle Paul, and was written in reply
to the apostle's epistle to the Philippians:

"Let this mind be in you, which was also in Christ Jesus, who, being in the
form of God, thought it not robbery to be equal with God."[37]

[36] *Ibid.*, pp. 125-126.
[37] Philippians 2:5-6. The poem as originally composed by President Snow contains four
more verses.

MAN'S DESTINY

Dear Brother:

Hast thou not been unwisely bold,
Man's destiny to thus unfold?
To raise, promote such high desire,
Such vast ambition thus inspire?

Still, 'tis no phantom that we trace
Man's ultimatum in life's race;
This royal path has long been trod
By righteous men, each now a God:

As Abra'm, Isaac, Jacob, too,
First babes, then men—to gods they grew.
As man now is, our God once was;
As now God is, so man may be,—
Which doth unfold man's destiny. . . .

The boy, like to his father grown,
Has but attained unto his own;
To grow to sire from state of son,
Is not 'gainst Nature's course to run.

A son of God, like God to be,
Would not be robbing Deity;
And he who has this hope within,
Will purify himself from sin.

You're right, St. John, supremely right:
Whoe'er essays to climb this height,
Will cleanse himself of sin entire—
Or else 'twere needless to aspire.
                                    —Lorenzo Snow.

Chapter 17.

"THEN SHALL THEY BE GODS"

INTRODUCTORY STATEMENT

Since, as pointed out in the last chapter, "men may become Gods," what are the requirements to reach such an exalted station? In what respects do Gods differ from other intelligent beings? How did the Eternal Father become God? And, finally, what road must mortals follow in order for them to become as He is? These are among the pertinent questions which arise when we think on the doctrine of our exaltation.

THE PERSONALITY OF GOD

We accept the fact that God is the Supreme Intelligent Being in the universe. He has the greatest knowledge, the most perfect will, and the most infinite power of any person within the realm of our understanding. To us, His love, His justice, His mercy, and His control over the universe are all infinite. We know that God absolutely transcends the finite understanding of mortals. He possesses all the virtues that mankind possesses in such an enhanced degree that when we attempt to define Him we fail, because He is infinitely greater than the most complete picture that mortals can give of Him.

HOW HE BECAME GOD

Yet, if we accept the great law of eternal progression, we must accept the fact that there was a time when Deity was much less powerful than He is today. Then how did He become glorified and exalted and attain His present status of Godhood? In the first place, aeons ago God undoubtedly took advantage of every opportunity to learn the laws of truth and as He became acquainted with each new verity He righteously obeyed it. From day to day He

114

exerted His will vigorously, and as a result became thoroughly acquainted with the forces lying about Him. As he gained more knowledge through persistent effort and continuous industry, as well as through absolute obedience, His understanding of the universal laws continued to become more complete. Thus He grew in experience and continued to grow until He attained the status of Godhood. In other words, He became God by absolute obedience to all the eternal laws of the Gospel—by conforming His actions to all truth, and thereby became the author of eternal truth. Therefore, the road that the Eternal Father followed to Godhood was one of living at all times a dynamic, industrious, and completely righteous life. There is no other way to exaltation.

How Men May Become Gods

Thus all men who ascend to the glorious status of Godhood can do so only by one method—by obedience to all the principles and ordinances of the Gospel of Jesus Christ. Fundamental in the process of obedience to truth is knowledge. We must first learn true principles before we are capable of intelligent obedience. The word of the Lord came to the latter-day Prophet as follows: "Behold, ye are little children and ye cannot bear all things now; ye must grow in grace and in the knowledge of truth."[1] Also, "It is impossible for a man to be saved in ignorance."[2] And again the Lord declared, "Men are saved no faster than they gain knowledge." The Prophet Joseph described the process of going on toward Godhood as follows:

When you climb up a ladder, you must begin at the bottom, and ascend step by step, until you arrive at the top; and so it is with the principles of the Gospel—you must begin with the first, and go on until you learn all the principles of exaltation. But it will be a great while after you have passed through the veil before you will have learned them.[3]

No prophet of record gave more complete and forceful explanations of the doctrine that men may become Gods than did the American Prophet, and, furthermore, he definitely pointed the course which men must follow. A small portion of his teachings is as follows:

[1] *Doctrine and Covenants* 50:40.
[2] *Ibid.*, 131:6.
[3] Joseph Fielding Smith, *Teachings of the Prophet Joseph Smith*, p. 348.

Here, then, is eternal life—to know the only wise and true God; and you have got to learn how to be Gods yourselves, and to be kings and priests to God, the same as all Gods have done before you, namely, by going from one small degree to another, and from a small capacity to a great one; from grace to grace, from exaltation to exaltation, until you attain the resurrection of the dead, and are able to dwell in everlasting burnings, and to sit in glory as do those who sit enthroned in everlasting power. . . .

They shall be heirs of God and joint heirs with Jesus Christ. What is it? To inherit the same power, the same glory and the same exaltation, until you arrive at the station of a God, and ascend the throne of eternal power, the same as those who have gone before. What did Jesus do? "Why; I do the things I saw my Father do when worlds came rolling into existence. My Father worked out his kingdom with fear and trembling, and I must do the same; and when I get my kingdom, I shall present it to my Father, so that he may obtain kingdom upon kingdom, and it will exalt him in glory. He will then take a higher exaltation, and I will take his place, and thereby become exalted myself."

So that Jesus treads in the tracks of his Father, and inherits what God did before; and God is thus glorified and exalted in the salvation and exaltation of all of his children.[4]

Thus we do not become Godlike in this world, nor Gods in the world to come, through any miraculous or sudden gift, but only through the slow process of natural growth brought about as a result of righteous living. Some people may think that when they die they will instantaneously get rid of all their bad habits and become purified. Such is not the case. We can become purified in this world, and the same holds true in the next life, only through repentance; that is, overcoming our faults and sins and replacing them with virtues. Charles W. Penrose sustains these thoughts in the following words: "Men become like God not by some supernatural or sudden change, either in this world or another, but by the natural development of the divinity within. Time, circumstances, and the necessary intelligence are all that are required."[5]

Knowing Deity an Avenue to Godhood

In chapter two we pointed out that "this is life eternal to know Thee the only true God, and Jesus Christ whom Thou hast sent." If to obtain eternal life means to enjoy the same type of life that God lives and to experience sim-

---

[4] *Ibid.*, pp. 344-348.
[5] Charles W. Penrose, *Millennial Star*, vol. 23, p. 181.

ilar experiences, then those people who receive it to the fullest degree shall actually be Gods. To explain further, the principal avenue of learning is experience; therefore, we know best the things which we have had the most experience with. The person who drinks deeply of the fountain of such virtues as love, honesty, kindness, industry, chastity, cheerfulness, and all other things that are good, making those virtues part of his personality and eliminating all vice and sins from his thoughts and actions, is following the avenue to Godhood. Therefore, the most Godlike people know Deity best. Interpreted in this light, to know the Father and the Son is the avenue to Godhood.

PAGANS' CONCEPT OF KNOWING GOD

Even the doctrine of a knowledge of God as the avenue to Godhood made its way outward from the Divine Fountain of Truth into the heathenistic religions of the Mediterranean world. The teachings of the Hermetic pagan cult sound quite familiar to those who are acquainted with the doctrine taught by Jesus, by John the Beloved, by Paul, and by Joseph Smith the American Prophet. They have a close kinship to the true Gospel which came to earth through the holy prophets of God. For example, Hermes declared: "And this alone, even the knowledge (*gnosis*) of God, is man's salvation. This is the ascent to Olympus, and by this alone can a soul become good."[6] This religion taught, as did the Prophet Alma, that man must experience a rebirth. The Hermetic rebirth involved nothing less than deification. "This is the good; this is the consummation for those who have got *gnosis*—they enter into God"; so declared the Hermetic teacher.

Cult members believed that such knowledge came about as a special mental or spiritual enlightment which came to them as a gift of God. (Compare this thought with John 14:16-18, 26; 15:26; 16:13.) They also maintained that demons were forever present to lead the ungodly man into unrighteous desires and habits. "But to the holy and good, the pure and merciful who lived piously, the spirit was ever present to help them win the Father's love by their upright lives."[7]

---

[6] Cited in Harold Willoughby, *Pagan Regeneration*, pp. 218-221. Compare the Hermetic statement with John 17:3; *Doctrine and Covenants* 132:22-24.
[7] Willoughby, *ibid*. Compare with John 8:12, 31-32.

Note the close resemblances between the foregoing pagan teachings and those of the true Gospel. For example, the doctrine of the Holy Ghost and Spirit of God being forever present to guide the righteous man along the path of truth and light and to give him a testimony of the Gospel and divinity of Jesus the Christ is closely related to the Hermetic doctrine of spiritual enlightenment through the Spirit of God. Thus we see that the true doctrine of knowing the Lord as the pathway to Godhood was revealed to man as part of the knowledge of the divine plan of salvation; and, like many other Gospel truths, it was disseminated among pagan worshipers.

CELESTIAL MARRAIGE—THE CROWNING GOSPEL ORDINANCE

The crowning Gospel ordinance requisite for Godhood is celestial marriage. The doctrine of celestial marriage, as taught and practiced in the Church of Jesus Christ today, means temple marriage. It does not necessarily mean plural marriage, as some are prone to believe, although at times in Gospel history plural marriage has been included in the law of celestial marriage. The point of importance, however, is the fact that those who enter into this holy covenant of marriage do so in purity and continue to live worthily enough that they may be sealed by the "Holy Spirit of promise." Every Latter-day Saint should be so familiar with the doctrine of celestial marriage and value it so highly that there would be nothing in the world that could induce him to enter into the covenant of marriage on any other basis.

Abraham, Isaac, Jacob, David, Solomon, Moses, and—according to the Lord—"also many others of my servants from the beginning of creation until this time," have known and practiced the law of celestial marriage.[8] Paul the apostle taught that "neither is the man without the woman, neither the woman without the man, in the Lord."[9] Jesus, the Master of life and exaltation, declared:

He who made them at the beginning made them male and female, and said, "For this cause shall a man leave father and mother, and shall cleave to his wife: and they twain shall be one flesh." Where-

[8] *Doctrine and Covenants* 132:37-40.
[9] 1 Corinthians 11:11.

fore they are no more twain but one flesh. What therefore God hath joined together, let no man put asunder.[10]

Jesus' statement shows definitely that in the very beginning, when Adam and Eve were placed upon the earth, God gave unto them the law of celestial marriage. They were to love each other so devotedly and live in harmony with each other so perfectly—being true to each other in every respect through complete obedience to the principles of the Gospel—that they would become as one in thoughts, in purposes, and in all their activities. In this way man and woman would become one flesh. Divorce would be impossible if they lived completely the eternal plan of God.

This blessed Gospel doctrine was lost by mankind during the period of the apostasy following the Apostolic Age, and in its place a man-made system of marriage—"until death do ye part"—was established. In fact, a portion of the Christian world became so warped in their knowledge of truth that they accepted as church dogma the doctrine that marriage is evil or sinful. However, as part of the restoration of the Gospel to the Prophet Joseph Smith, God condemned that wicked and false dogma and re-revealed the true doctrine of the sacredness and eternal nature of the marriage covenant. This revelation is found in section 132 of the *Doctrine and Covenants*. Following are the words of the Lord regarding the sanctity of marriage:

Verily, I say unto you, that whoso forbiddeth to marry is not ordained of God, for marriage is ordained of God unto man. Wherefore, it is lawful that he should have one wife, and they twain shall be one flesh, and all this that the earth might answer the end of its creation; and that it might be filled with the measure of man, according to his creation before the world was made.[11]

Marriage is not only a righteous institution, but obedience to this law is absolutely necessary in order to obtain the highest exaltation in the Kingdom of God. The word of the Lord came to the Prophet Joseph Smith on this subject, as follows: "In the celestial glory there are three heavens or degrees: and in order to obtain the highest, a man must enter into this order of the Priesthood (meaning the new and everlasting covenant of marriage)."[12] If men

---

[10] Matthew 19:4-6; Genesis 2:24; Moses 2:27-28; 3:24.
[11] *Doctrine and Covenants* 49:15-17.
[2] *Ibid.*, 131:1-2.

and women obey all the other laws of the Gospel except
that of celestial marriage, they "are appointed angels in
heaven, which angels are ministering servants, to minister for those who are worthy of a far more, and an exceeding, and an eternal weight of glory." The revelation con-
tinues as follows:

For these angels did not abide my law; therefore, they cannot
be enlarged, but remain separately and singly, without exaltation, in
their saved condition, to all eternity; and from henceforth are not Gods,
but are angels of God forever and ever. . . .

And again, verily I say unto you, if a man marry a wife by my
word, which is my law, and by the new and everlasting covenant, and
it is sealed unto them by the Holy Spirit of promise, by him who is
anointed, unto whom I have appointed this power and the keys of this
Priesthood [and if they commit no sin to break that seal]; they shall
pass by the angels, and the Gods, which are set there, to their exaltation and glory in all things, as hath been sealed upon their heads, which
glory shall be a fullness and a continuation of the seeds forever and
ever: *then shall they be Gods.*[13]

Later Joseph explained what the revelation meant by
the statement, "Which glory shall be a fullness and a continuation of the seeds forever and ever." He explained
that the Gods were to be parents of spirit children just
as our Heavenly Father and Heavenly Mother were the
parents of the people of this earth. To quote his own words:

Except a man and his wife enter into an everlasting covenant and
be married for eternity, while in this probation, by the power and
authority of the Holy Priesthood, they will cease to increase when
they die; that is, they will not have any children after the resurrection.
But those who are married by the power and authority of the Priesthood in this life, and continue without committing the sin against the
Holy Ghost, will continue to increase and have children in the celestial
glory.[14]

Thus we see that celestial marriage is the crowning
Gospel ordinance. If men and women have obeyed this
holy ordinance and all the other principles of the Gospel,
following the resurrection and the great judgment day,
"then shall they be Gods."

PAGANS' CONCEPT OF CELESTIAL MARRIAGE

Since the Gospel ordinance of celestial marriage was
revealed to Father Adam and was practiced by him, and
by the other ancient prophets of God, we would naturally

[13] *Ibid.*, 132:16-19.
[14] Smith, *op. cit.*, pp. 300-301.

expect to find that doctrine in a modified form in some of the ancient pagan cults.[15] Such is the case.

The eunuch-priests of the Great Mother pagan religion believed themselves to be gods as a result of the initiation into the priesthood of their cult. Each priest became the husband of the cult goddess—the Great Mother. As part of the initiation into the priesthood, a ceremony was performed in the marriage chamber of the temple in which the new priest became the bridegroom of the goddess. Thereafter he was often called "bridegroom," and a common name for him was Attis, who was the immortal god-husband of the Great Mother.

According to Clement of Alexandria, a Christian father, the laity, as well as the priests in this pagan cult, were also united to the Great Mother by a marriage ceremony. But it is probable that their godhood was postponed until they reached the other world.[16]

CATHOLIC PRACTICE OF CELESTIAL MARRIAGE

During the early Christian period, the Catholic church, like its pagan rivals, also had a practice of marrying certain of its members to the Christian Savior-God. One of the orders of nuns had a ceremony performed which made the sisters in a mystical sense betrothed to Jesus. As a token of becoming the brides of the Son of God, the nuns who entered this order wore plain gold band rings. This custom dates to an early period in Christian history. For proof, the following is quoted from the *Catholic Encyclopedia:*

St. Ambrose (340-397) speaks as though it were a received custom for virgins consecrated to God to wear a ring in memory of their heavenly Spouse. . . . Wedding rings, or more strictly, rings given in the betrothal ceremony, seem to have been tolerated among Christians under the Roman Empire from quite an early period. The use of such rings was of course of older date than Christianity.[17]

It seems that the interpretation placed upon the nuns' becoming the brides of Jesus which was held during the early Christian centuries was almost identical with that of the *Galli* (priests) becoming bridegrooms of the Great Mother. According to St. Jerome, who was a contemporary

---

[15] *Doctrine and Covenants* 132:32-40.
[16] Willoughby, *op. cit.*, pp. 126-127, 134.
[17] Charles G. Herbermann, and others, editors, *The Catholic Encyclopedia*, vol. 13, p. 60.

of St. Ambrose and did his writing toward the close of the fourth century A.D., certain nuns were actually and literally regarded as brides of Jesus and their mothers were referred to as mothers-in-law to God. Salomon Reinach, in his book *Orpheus,* gives the following explanation regarding St. Jerome, and then quotes this pertinent statement taken from one of the letters of this early Christian father:

St. Jerome, who was born in Dalmatia, revised the Latin translations of the Scriptures by order of Pope Damasus, and made use of his personal influence, which was as considerable as his talent, to win over the ladies of the Roman aristocracy to a conventual life. *"Thou hast become the mother-in-law of God,"* he wrote to one of them, whose daughter had entered a nunnery, and was therefore the bride of God.[18]

Even down to the present time the custom has persisted in the Catholic church to betroth nuns who enter certain orders to their heavenly spouse—Jesus. The modern interpretation of the Catholics, however, maintains that the betrothal ceremony entered into by the nuns does not marry them to Jesus in the sense that we regard marriage, but in some sort of mystical sense they become His brides for the purpose of carrying forward His work. This concept is a distinctly modified form of the true celestial marriage doctrine as given by the Lord to the holy prophets, but it is almost identical with the pagan belief in the Great Mother cult. This close similarity to paganism can be seen in the following statement made by Dr. Willoughby:

[The experiences of the *Galli* (priests) in becoming the bridegrooms of the Great Mother] were interpreted as a process of mystical union with the Great Goddess herself, and by means of certain obscure ritual acts there was developed a sense of intimate divine communion on the part of the devotee. . . . It made him realistically and mystically one with the goddess.[19]

The evidence seems to indicate that the Catholic doctrine was borrowed directly from the pagan practice of marrying the priests to the Great Mother, and both the pagan and the Catholic practices are altered forms of the true doctrine of celestial marriage. The principal difference, however, is that the pagan deity was a woman, while the Christian God was a male. Therefore, in the Catholic practice, women became the brides of Jesus, while in

---

[18] Salomon Reinach, *Orpheus, a General History of Religions* (translated from French to English by Florence Simmonds), p. 263.
[19] Willoughby, *op. cit.*, pp. 126-127.

the Great Mother religion men became the bridegrooms of their goddess.

CONCLUSIONS

Other examples of pagan conceptions of celestial marriage could be given, all of which indicate that the true Gospel doctrine persisted in paganism in a degenerated form. Originally it came from the common source of truth through the holy prophets, but men through the ages adulterated those truths. However, a semblance to the divine revelation persisted even to the present day in the Catholic practice. But God in His mercy has revealed again to man through the Prophet Joseph Smith the true eternal marriage covenant with a clear explanation of the blessings attached thereto.

SUPPLEMENTARY READINGS—CHAPTER 17

1. *Bible*: Matthew 1:4-6; Genesis 2:24; 1 Corinthians 11:11.
2. *Doctrine and Covenants* 132:1-66.
3. *Pearl of Great Price*: Moses 2:27-28; 3:24.
4. Joseph Fielding Smith (Compiler), *Teachings of the Prophet Joseph Smith*, pp. 300-301, 344-348.
5. Harold Willoughby, *Pagan Regeneration*, pp. 126-127, 134, 218-219.

Chapter 18.

THE IMMORTALITY OF MAN

UNIVERSAL BELIEF IN IMMORTALITY

There is in the breast of each of us no human hope stronger than that of continuing to live. Man, being a rational creature, has faith that there is a continuation of life hereafter in a world even more beautiful and glorious than this earth. To exist eternally is his dream.

History affirms that a belief in the immortality of man has always been universally accepted. From the savages of the jungles to the most highly civilized nations, men have maintained that, although death overtake them, they shall live on eternally. This concept has been one of the most dynamic motivating forces in religious thought and action from the advent of man upon the earth until the present day. It has been the very center around which theological creeds have been constructed. The master teachers of all the great world religions have given humanity a definite assurance of a life beyond the grave. It is this star of hope that has inspired humanity to study their philosophies and to adopt their plans of life. Something deeply rooted in human nature causes mankind to feel that he is composed of eternal substance—that he will live forever. In the words of M. Lynn Bennion:

"When God wants to carry a point with His children," says one writer, "He plants His arguments in their instincts." This, it seems to me, is what Jesus recognized when He described the issue of immortality in that singularly simple but suggestive statement, "If it were not so, I would have told you." By these statements the Master sought to place our confidence in the persistence of personality, not upon some dogmatic utterance, but upon the deepest instinct of humanity, which instinct, in the last analysis, is far better than head knowledge.[1]

In his drama of ancient Rome, Joseph Addison (1672-1719 A.D.) had Cato—a devout student of Plato, the Greek

---

[1] M. Lynn Bennion, "The Challenge of Immortality," *Week Day Religious Education*, IV:6 (Salt Lake City, March, 1940).

philosopher, who fervently taught the doctrine of the immortality of man—say:

It must be so,—Plato, thou reasonest well! Else whence this pleasing hope, this fond desire, this longing after immortality? Or whence this secret dread, and inward horror of falling into naught? Why shrinks the soul back on herself, and startles at destruction? 'Tis the divinity that stirs within us; 'tis Heaven itself that points out an hereafter, and intimates eternity to man. Eternity! thou pleasing, dreadful thought!
. . .

The soul, secure in her existence, smiles. . . . The stars shall fade away, the sun himself grow dim with age, and Nature sink in years; but thou (the soul) shalt flourish in immortal youth unhurt amidst the war of elements, the wreck of matter, and the crush of worlds.[2]

THE PROPHETS' TEACHINGS OF IMMORTALITY

While the majority of God's children place their faith and hope of immortality upon feeling and reason, a few of His elect have had definite knowledge of the reality of a life after temporal death and of the ever-enduring qualities of human personality. Having received their information through divine revelation, those individuals can say with Jacob, or with Job, "Wherefore I know that ye know that our flesh must waste away and die; nevertheless, in our bodies we shall see God."[3]

The holy men of the Lord, such as the beloved Prophet Joseph Smith, who understood the unseen world beyond the veil of mortality, not only had a firm conviction that life is eternal, but had a comprehensive philosophy of the stages of progression that men pass through. Shortly before the Prophet's death he expounded in a masterful sermon the Mormon philosophy of progressive-eternalism. "As a teacher he reached the climax of his career in this discourse. After it there was but one thing more he could do—seal his testimony with his blood. This he did in less than three months."[4]

Quoting directly from the Prophet's discourse:

I have another subject to dwell upon, which is calculated to exalt man. . . . It is associated with the subject of the resurrection of the dead—namely, the soul—the mind of man—the immortal spirit. Where did it come from? All learned men and doctors of divinity say that God created it in the beginning; but it is not so; the very idea lessens

---

[2] Joseph Addison, cited in John Bartlett, editor, *Familiar Quotations*, p. 195.
[3] 2 Nephi 9:4; Job 19:25-26.
[4] Brigham H. Roberts, cited in Joseph Fielding Smith, *Teachings of the Prophet Joseph Smith*, p. 256.

man in my estimation. I do not believe the doctrine; I know better. Hear it, all ye ends of the world; for God has told me so. . . .

We say that God Himself is a self-existent being. Who told you so? Who told you that man did not exist in like manner upon the same principles? . . .

The mind or the intelligence which man possesses is co-equal (co-eternal) with God Himself. I know that my testimony is true; hence, when I talk to these mourners, what have they lost? Their relatives and friends are only separated from their bodies for a short season; their spirits which existed with God have left the tabernacle of clay only for a little moment, as it were, and they now exist in a place where they converse together the same as we do on the earth.

I am dwelling on the immortality of the spirit of man. Is it logical to say that the intelligence of spirits is immortal, and yet that it had a beginning? The intelligence of spirits had no beginning, neither will it have an end. . . .

Intelligence is eternal and exists upon a self-existent principle. It is a spirit from age to age, and there is no creation about it.[5]

ETERNAL NATURE OF MAN

Man "is a spirit from age to age," i.e., "an entity, a person, an individual."[6] "It is now inconceivable that a particle of matter should either come into existence or lapse into non-existence." What exists now has always existed in one form or another, and will continue to exist eternally. "All spirit is matter," and it is also self-enduring.[7]

Life, intelligence, mind, the "light of truth," or whatever name one gives to the center of the personality of man, is an uncreated, eternally existent, indestructible entity.[8] "He—for that entity is a person—. . . is eternal as God is; co-existent, in fact, with God; of the same kind of substance or essence with Deity, though confessedly inferior in degree of intelligence and power of God."[9] The Lord called this eternal entity an "intelligence," which quality is its chief characteristic. "Man was also in the beginning with God. Intelligence, or the light of truth, was not created or made, neither indeed can be."[10]

---

[5] Smith, *ibid.*, pp. 352-355.
[6] Roberts, *op. cit.*, p. 354.
[7] *Doctrine and Covenants* 93:33; 131:7; 29:31-34; Smith, *op. cit.*, pp. 350-356, contains in the footnote some excellent quotations from various authorities on matter's being indestructible.
[8] Smith, *ibid.*, pp. 342-360; *Doctrine and Covenants* 93:29-33, 36, 23-24; Roberts, *Seventy's Course in Theology*, (Second Year, 1908), pp. 7-32.
[9] Roberts, "Immortality of Man," *Improvement Era*, vol. 10, pp. 406, 401-423, (Salt Lake City, April, 1907).
[10] *Doctrine and Covenants* 93:29.

Eternally Existent Intelligences

Revelations were given by the Lord to the Prophet Joseph relative to several phases of the eternal progression of man. In the first stage, man was an eternally existent being termed an intelligence. In that sphere of existence each individual was naturally conscious. "He must have the power to distinguish himself from other things—the 'me' from the 'not me'. He must have power of deliberation, by which he sets over one thing against another; with power also to form a judgment that this or that is a better thing or state than this or that."[11] In short, he must have the power of choosing one thing instead of another and acting upon that choice. In that realm, as in all other states of immortal existence, natural law, good and evil, love and hate, truth and error, and free agency exist. They are all eternal and closely connected with immortal man as he ascends the ladder of progression.[12]

We do not know how long we lived in this first realm, but it must have been ages and ages. There came a time, however, when we completed our work in that realm and were permitted to go forward in the eternal process of progression.

The Spirit World

The next realm where man dwelt was the spirit world. According to Mormon concept eternally existing intelligences were clothed with spirit bodies in the mansion of their Eternal Father. As was definitely pointed out in an earlier chapter, numerous sons and daughters were begotten and born of heavenly parents into that eternal family in the spirit world. In the likeness of God Himself, these spirit children were organized, possessing divine, eternal, and godlike attributes, inherited from their Heavenly Father and Mother. There in the spirit world they were reared to maturity, becoming grown spirit men and women prior to coming upon this earth.[13]

Four thousand years ago, Father Abraham knew that God's children lived in the pre-mortal world and that they

---

[11] Roberts, *Era, op. cit.*, p. 107.
[12] 2 Nephi 2:1-30; *Doctrine and Covenants* 88:5-30; 29:34-35; 130:20-21; 132:5; John A. Widtsoe, *Rational Theology*, pp. 1-44.
[13] Joseph F. Smith, John R. Winder, Anthon H. Lund, "The Origin of Man," *Improvement Era*, vol. 13, p. 80; Widtsoe, *op. cit.*, pp. 27, 64-65.

were eternal. He was shown in vision the spirit world and the intelligences which had been organized into spirit beings before this world was created. The Lord told Abraham that He had selected the most progressive, righteous, and highly developed spirits to become the rulers in mortality. Then God told the ancient prophet, "Abraham, thou art one of them; thou was chosen before thou wast born."[14] The Lord also said unto Abraham:

If there be two spirits, and one shall be more intelligent than the other, yet these two spirits, notwithstanding one is more intelligent than the other, have no beginning, they exist before, they shall have no end, they shall exist after, for they are *gnolaum,* or eternal.[15]

The Mortal Probation

Following his stay in the spirit world, man comes on earth in a probationary state preparatory to the eternal existence beyond the mortal confines of this world. Here he receives a physical body and undergoes the experiences of mortality. It is true that when we are born into mortality a veil is drawn over our minds, so that we have forgotten our pre-mortal life; yet we come here with the amount of potential development that we had attained in the spirit world. Since mortality is a continuation of a previous existence, children learn very rapidly during the early years of their mortal lives. This is largely an unfoldment of their pre-mortal development. At times it seems to each of us that we have a dim recollection of some bygone age or world, some previous experiences which we may have had. The poet Wordsworth beautifully expressed the foregoing divine doctrine when he wrote the following:

> Our birth is but a sleep and a forgetting;
> The soul that rises with us, our life's star,
> Hath had elsewhere its setting,
> And cometh from afar;
> Not in entire forgetfulness,
> And not in utter nakedness,
> But trailing clouds of glory do we come
> From God who is our home.
> —*Ode on the Intimations of Immortality.*

Post-Mortal Life

Eventually, however, mortal death comes upon all. The eternal spirit goes to the spirit world to await

---

[14] Abraham 4:22-28.
[15] *Ibid.,* 8:18.

resurrection and judgment. In due time, all will rise from
the grave and stand before the judgment seat of Jesus
Christ. There they shall be assigned to the glory that they
have merited according to the lives that they have lived
while in mortality and the changes that they have wrought
upon their characters while in paradise. Some will receive
telestial glory; others, terrestrial, while those who are recorded in "the Lamb's book of life" will enter celestial glory.
There some of them will become angels and others priests
and kings, or, in other words, Gods.[16]

Regardless of the degree of glory to which one attains,
human personality will persist. In the words of Jacob,
the Nephite prophet, following resurrection "all men become incorruptible and immortal, and they are living souls."[17]
Abinadi added the following thought: "Even this mortal
shall put on immortality, and this corruption shall put on
incorruption. . . . If they [personal beings] be good, to the
resurrection of endless life and happiness; and if they be
evil, to the resurrection of endless death."[18]

SUPPLEMENTARY READINGS—CHAPTERS 18 AND 19

1. *Bible*: Daniel 12:2; Ecclesiastes 12:7; Job 19:25-26; 1 Corinthians 15:1-58;
   Matthew 27:52-53; 2 Timothy 1:9-10.
2. *Book of Mormon*: 2 Nephi 2:19-29; 9:1-44; Mosiah 16:1-12; Alma 11:34-46;
   18:26-35; 34:1-16, 31-38; 40; 41; 42; Helaman 5:18-52; 3 Nephi 9:1-22; 11:1ff.
3. *Doctrine and Covenants* 29:31-50; 76:16-119; 88:14-31; 93:29-33; 132:1-66.
4. Joseph Fielding Smith (Compiler), *Teachings of the Prophet Joseph Smith*,
   pp. 350-360, 256, 181.
5. John A. Widtsoe, *Rational Theology*, pp. 9-31.

---

[16] *Doctrine and Covenants* 76:54-59, 62.
[17] 2 Nephi 9:13.
[18] Mosiah 16:10-11.

Chapter 19.

UNIVERSALITY OF THE BELIEF IN IMMORTALITY

INTRODUCTORY STATEMENT

This chapter is a continuation of the subject presented in the last lesson. By way of introduction, we previously pointed out that the belief in immortality is universal (a theme which will be enlarged upon in this lesson); and then we devoted our attention to the doctrine of eternal progression, following the various stages or realms in which we have lived or shall live according to the revelations given to the Prophet Joseph Smith. The last lesson, then, was devoted primarily to the Latter-day Saints' concept of immortality.

The purpose of this chapter is to show that the belief of immortality is as old as man and as widespread as the human race. A belief in some kind of future life, it will be shown, is the central hope in practically every religion in history. This belief is another of those golden threads of religious truths which link all of mankind to that one divine source—Jesus Christ.

DOCTRINE OF IMMORTALITY REVEALED TO ADAM

Father Adam received through revelation a knowledge of the doctrine of the immortality of man, just as he did of the other Gospel principles. The Holy Ghost bore testimony to him that he and his posterity should be redeemed from their fallen condition if they would accept and live the Gospel of Jesus Christ. In regards to Adam's and Eve's definite knowledge of immortality, the ancient record states:

The Holy Ghost fell upon Adam . . . and Adam blessed God and was filled, and began to prophesy [saying] . . . "In this life I shall have joy, and again in the flesh I shall see God."

And Eve, his wife, heard all these things and was glad, saying: "Were it not for our transgression we never should . . . have known good and evil, and the joy of our redemption, and the eternal life which God giveth unto the obedient."[1]

BIBLE TEACHINGS OF IMMORTALITY

Of all the scriptures accepted by the Mormons, the Old Testament contains the least information on the doctrine of the immortality of man. Only glimpses of that eternal truth are found in the Hebrew scripture, one of the most clear-cut statements being recorded in Daniel: "And many of them that slept in the dust of the earth shall awake, some to everlasting life, and some to shame and everlasting contempt."[2] The words of Isaiah are equally as forceful as are Daniel's. To quote: "Thy dead men shall live, together with my dead body shall they arise. Awake and sing ye that dwell in dust: for thy dew is as the dew of herbs, and the earth shall cast out the dead."[3] But there are enough references to this doctrine given by the prophets and in Psalms to prove beyond doubt that the Jews did conceive of man as being eternal. For example, a great Hebrew poet, the divinely inspired prophet who recorded the experiences of Job, declared: "For I know that my Redeemer liveth, and that he shall stand at the latter days upon the earth: and though after my skin worms destroy this body, yet in my flesh I shall see God."[4] The ancient Jewish philosopher who wrote Ecclesiastes left us this consoling thought: "Then shall the dust return to the earth as it was: and the spirit shall return unto God who gave it."[5]

The New Testament, however, is literally filled with the doctrine of the immortality of man, containing evidence of the pre-existence as well as post-mortal life. One of Jesus' central themes was that of immortality. For example, He told His apostles, "In my Father's house are many mansions; if it were not so I would have told you. I go to prepare a place for you."[6] Shortly before His crucifixion He earnestly prayed, "O Father, glorify thou me with thine own self with the glory which I had with thee before the world was."[7]

[1] Moses 5:9-11.
[2] Daniel 12:2.
[3] Isaiah 26:19.
[4] Job 19:25-26; *Doctrine and Covenants* 121:10.
[5] Ecclesiastes 12:7.
[6] John 14:1-3.
[7] *Ibid.*, 17:5.

A splendid example of the early Christian concept of immortality is Paul's famous discourse written to the saints at Corinth. Among many other fine things, he said:

> For as in Adam all die, even so in Christ shall all be made alive.
> . . . The last enemy that shall be destroyed is death. . . . The dead shall be raised incorruptible, and we shall be changed. For this corruptible must put on incorruption, and this mortal must put on immortality.[8]

NEPHITES' KNOWLEDGE OF IMMORTALITY

Equally as clear, forceful, and detailed as the New Testament's teachings on the immortality of man is the philosophy of the Nephite prophets.[9] They had a positive belief in the eternal nature of personality; in fact, they considered temporal life as merely a probationary state in which to prepare for the greater existence beyond the grave.[10] If one studies the aggregate information on eternalism contained in the *Book of Mormon*, he may be surprised to find that the Nephite record contains a more comprehensive explanation of the Gospel teachings on immortality than does any other ancient record. A good example of its teachings follows:

> I say unto you that this mortal body is raised to an immortal body, that is from death, even from the first death unto life, that they can die no more; their spirits united with their bodies, never to be divided; thus the whole becoming spiritual and immortal, that they can no more see corruption.[11]

ANCIENT RELIGIONS' IMMORTALITY CONCEPTS

All the religions that became popular in the ancient world were the ones that assured their worshipers a happy, glorified life beyond the grave. Religions that have been vital forces in the lives of salvation seekers and have made positive contributions to human happiness are those that offer means of obtaining salvation and give an assurance of life eternal.

The ancient Chinese, Indian, Persian, Egyptian, Mesopotamian, Greek and Roman religions all taught the doctrine of the immortality of man; yet each had its own interpretation regarding the final condition of the eternal

[8] 1 Corinthians 15:1-58.
[9] Berrett, Hunter, Welker, Fitzgerald, "Book of Mormon Concept of Immortality," *A Guide to the Study of the Book of Mormon*, pp. 79-90.
[10] 2 Nephi 2:19-29.
[11] Alma 11:45.

essence of which he is composed. The Chinese philosopher, Lao-Tze (600 B.C.), taught: "Therefore, does the wise man provide for the soul and not for the senses. He ignores the one and takes the other with both hands. . . . Being of Tao he endures forever; for though the body perish, yet he suffers no hurt."[12] Confucius, a contemporary of Lao-Tze, is credited with having said: "Man never dies. It is because men see only their bodies that they hate death."[13] The Buddhist literature, as well as the Persian Zoroastrian Avesta, taught immortality—with an accompanying heaven and hell—just as specifically as does Christian theology. The following command is given in the Hindu bible: "Go give to the plants and to the waters the body which belongs to them; but there is an immortal portion of thee. Transport it to the world of the holy."[14] In India the ultimate end of one's living the good life was to lose his individual identity by becoming absorbed in the great "world-soul"; and in this way man attained his final immortality.

Conversely, as early as 3,000 years B.C., the Egyptians were embalming their deceased preparatory to a literal resurrection of the body. Their chief deity was Osiris. "From the earliest times he was regarded as the god-man who suffered, died, rose again, and reigned eternally in heaven. He was the king of eternity, lord of the everlastingness, . . . whose existence is everlasting."[15] He promised resurrection to his faithful followers and rewards for their righteousness. Even until after the advent of Jesus, initiation into the cult of Osiris "meant the certain hope of a happy immortality" to its thousands of devotees.[16] In fact, the most indubitable item of this faith was its assurance to the worshipers that they would live eternally. In the words of Aquelius, an ancient writer:

[Osiris is] the savior and leader of souls, leading them to the light and receiving them again. . . . We can never escape his sway, but he will save us, and even after death we shall be the objects of his providence.[17]

A Sumerian burial practice, in many respects resembling the ancient Egyptian custom, was to put gold, sil-

---

[12] Cited in Hugh M. Woodward, *Humanity's Greatest Need*, p. 293.
[13] *Ibid.*, p. 294.
[14] *Ibid.*, p. 292.
[15] *A Guide to the Egyptian Collection in the British Museum*, p. 139.
[16] Harold Willoughby, *Pagan Regeneration*, p. 139.
[17] Cited in *ibid.*, p. 194.

ver, food, and many other supposedly useful articles in the
tombs of the deceased. These "Royal Tombs" date back
over 5,000 years. Thus a cardinal precept in the oldest
known Mesopotamian civilization was that of immortality
of the soul.

Even the Greek philosophers taught the eternal nature
of life. Socrates is purported to have said, "When death
attacks a man, his immortal part retreats before death,
and goes away safe and indestructible."[18]

IMMORTALITY HOPE OF THE MYSTERY RELIGIONS

The Mystery Religions, pagan rivals of Christianity
during the first four centuries A.D., were constructed
around the concept of a glorified immortality of cult members with accompanying formulas of how worshipers could
achieve that glorification. Members of the Eleusinian Mysteries declared: "To us alone is there joyous light after
death, who have been initiated and who lived in pious fash-
ion as touching our duty to strangers and private people."[19]

Herodotus, the Greek historian, stated in regards to
the Thracians who instituted the worship of Dionysus:
"They believed themselves immortal; they think that they
do not die, but that the dead go to join their god Zalmoxis."[20]

It was commonly accepted Ophic doctrine that "the
soul is immortal, for it came from God. The body is the
garment of the soul."[21]

Dating from nearly 600 B.C. to 400 A.D., the worshipers of the Great Mother Mysteries held a passion drama
celebrating the resurrection of Attis, their savior-god. "The
resurrection of the god brought with it the assurance of
salvation for men, and this chiefly included the promise
of happy immortality."[22]

Mithraism, the strongest pagan rival of Christianity,
recorded in its literature, "Though I was born a mortal from
a mortal mother . . . having been sanctified by the sacred
ceremonies, I am about to gaze with immortal eyes on the
immortal aeon."[23]

---

[18] M. Lynn Bennion, "The Challenge of Immortality," *Week-Day Religious Education*
[19] Aristophanes, *Ranae*, p. 455ff, cited in Willoughby, *op. cit.*, pp. 64-65.
[20] Herodotus, vol. 4, p. 93ff.
[21] Kaibel, *Inscriptiones Graecae Sicilae et Italiae*, No. 651.
[22] Firmicus Maternus, *De Errore*, 22, cited in Willoughby, *op. cit.*, p. 123.
[23] *Bibliotheque National*, Suppl.; Gr. p. 574. See Dieterich, *Eine Mithasliturgie*, cited
in Willoughby, *op. cit.*, pp. 163-164.

Scientists' Testimonies of Immortality

Since the concept of immortality is so old and so universal, one may wonder what the effect of the rise of modern science has had on this belief. We shall let two of the most eminent scientists speak for themselves, and their conclusions are typical of the opinions of many outstanding men in their profession. The famous nineteenth century scientist, Charles R. Darwin (1809-1882), gave his belief in immortality as follows:

Believing as I do that man in the distant future will be a far more perfect creature than he now is, it is an intolerable thought that he and all other sentient beings are doomed to complete annihilation after such long-continued slow progress. To those who fully admit the immortality of the human soul, the destruction of our world will not appear so dreadful.[24]

Nearly one hundred years later, Dr. Arthur H. Compton, one of America's foremost scientists, said:

No cogent reason remains for supposing the soul dies with the body. . . . We (scientists) found strong reasons for believing that man is of extraordinary importance in the cosmic scheme. . . . What would we say is the most important thing about a noble man? Not the strength of his body, not the brilliance of his intellect, but the beauty of his character. It takes a lifetime to build the character of a noble man. The exercise and discipline of youth, the struggles and failures of maturity, the loneliness and tranquillity of age—these make the fire through which he must pass to bring out the pure gold of his soul. Having been thus perfected, what shall Nature do with him, annihilate him? What infinite waste! As long as there is in heaven a God of love there must be for God's children *everlasting life!*[25]

Common Source of the Immortality Doctrine

The fact should be clear to all of us that all religions that have taught the doctrine of the immortality of man have sipped of the Divine Fountain of Truth. Whether they be pagan or Christian, their beliefs have a kinship to those revealed to Father Adam. In the words of the scripture:

I, the Lord God, gave unto Adam and unto his seed, that they should not die as to the temporal death, until I, the Lord God, should send forth angels to declare unto them repentance and redemption, through faith on the name of mine Only Begotten Son,[26] . . . that

---

[24] Charles Darwin, cited in John Bartlett, editor, *Familiar Quotations*, p. 449.
[25] Dr. Arthur H. Compton, professor of Physics at the University of Chicago, in 1928 was the Nobel Prize winner in Physics.
[26] *Doctrine and Covenants* 29:42.

[they] might be sanctified from all sin, and enjoy the words of eternal life in this world, and eternal life in the world to come, even immortal glory.[27]

Like a perpetual stream of water, this divine assurance of immortality flowed downward through the ages. The testimony of this verity was strengthened from time to time by revelations from God to the holy prophets. Hundreds of their statements appear in the scriptures bearing witness to the validity of the doctrine of the persistence of personality. Also, ideas filtered outward from the main channel of truth, giving hope to many pagan souls.

Christians' Knowledge of Immortality Became Hazy

It is a well-known fact that the doctrine of immortality throughout the long period of Catholic dominance and on has been a paramount teaching of the religious leaders through Protestantism. It is also a fact that, although the belief of immortality persisted in Christendom, the people's understanding of the conditions of post-mortal life became warped, confused, and very hazy. This loss of knowledge made it necessary for God to speak from heaven again and re-reveal this ancient Gospel truth. Many revelations came to Joseph Smith on this important subject, but since we have already discussed the Prophet's knowledge of immortality in the last chapter, we need not do so here.

Evidences of Immortality

Before leaving our study of immortality of man, however, we should examine some of the direct evidence that life is eternal. The most convincing evidence given to man came when Jesus the Christ rose from the dead and appeared to many of the faithful among the Jews, to the multitude of the Nephite nation, and, later, to Joseph Smith, the American Prophet.

Definite evidence is given in the New Testament and confirmed by the *Doctrine and Covenants* to the effect that many of the saints of old who had passed beyond the veil arose from the grave at the time of Christ's resurrection.[28] The *Book of Mormon* record relates that a similar event

---

[27] Moses 6:28b.
[28] Matthew 27:52-53; *Doctrine and Covenants* 132:37.

occurred in distant America.[29] Modern revelation also testifies to the immortality of man by affirming that Moroni, John the Baptist, Moses, Elijah, Elias, and others who lived during the distant past appeared to the Mormon Prophet. President Wilford Woodruff testified as to the immortality of the latter-day prophets:

> After the death of Joseph Smith I saw and conversed with him many times in my dreams in the night season. One occasion he and his brother Hyrum met me when on the sea going on a mission to England. . . . The Prophet talked freely to me about the mission I was then going to perform, and he also talked to me with regard to the mission of the Twelve Apostles in the flesh, and he laid before me the work they had to perform; and he also spoke of the reward they would receive after death. . . . I have had many interviews with Brother Joseph until the last fifteen or twenty years of my life. I have not seen him for that length of time. . . . I had many interviews with President Young and with Heber C. Kimball, George A. Smith and Jedediah M. Grant, and many others who are dead. They attended our conferences. They attended our meetings . . . and I believe myself that these men . . . had this mission left with them, that is, to watch over the Latter-day Saints.[30]

CONCLUSIONS

The immortal beings who appeared to the Prophet Joseph Smith brought from the unseen world keys of the Priesthood and instructed the Prophet relative to salvation for the dead. Thus the blessed doctrine of the immortality of man reaches its culminating point in temple work—salvation for both the living and the dead. In the House of the Lord various sealings are effected by the "Holy Spirit of promise" to endure eternally. These sealings are the capstone of all Gospel principles.[31]

The knowledge that the Latter-day Saints have of the Gospel truth of immortality is probably the most dynamic, vital and comforting force in their lives. It is a beacon light guiding the faithful in the path of godliness. It gives comfort in time of grief, fortitude in time of temptation, and it offers a goal of incalculable value toward which to work—that of Godhood.

---

[29] 3 Nephi 23:9-10.
[30] *Journal of Discourses*, vol. 21, p. 317.
[31] *Doctrine and Covenants* 132:1-66; 124:25-41; 127:5-12; 128; Smith, *Teachings of the Prophet Joseph Smith*, pp. 356, 362-363.

Chapter 20.

WE SHALL BE JUDGED

OUR MORAL RESPONSIBILITY

Just as surely as we live, each of us at a future day shall stand in the presence of the Great Judge to give account of the life we have lived while in mortality. The prophets have declared that following resurrection we shall all be held accountable for our deeds in accordance with the opportunities we have had for righteousness.[1]

If our actions have been good, a compensation of happiness, advancement, and glory is the result; if they have been evil, misery, shame, and spiritual death close in upon the human soul. No better summary of this eternal truth has been given by mortal teachers than the following pertinent statement made by Apostle Paul:

Be not deceived; God is not mocked: for whatsoever a man soweth that shall he also reap. For he that soweth unto his flesh shall of the flesh reap corruption; but he that soweth unto the Spirit shall of the Spirit reap life everlasting.[2]

The same great religious leader warned the Christians in Rome of the destructive nature of sin in the following words:

For if ye live after the flesh, ye must die; but if by the spirit ye put to death the deeds of the body, ye shall live. . . . For the wages of sin is death; but the free gift of God is eternal life in Christ Jesus our Lord.[3]

REIGN OF LAW

It is true that character is built and that we receive rewards and punishments from day to day according to our diligence in obedience to eternal verities. The law of compensation operates universally. A moral order ex-

---

[1] *Doctrine and Covenants* 75:21-22; 2 Nephi 9:25-39; Alma 29:5; 32:18-20; 9:14-18, 23; 3 Nephi 27:23-27.
[2] Galatians 6:7-8.
[3] Romans 8:13; 6:23.

ists which is just as exacting as the physical order, and the blessings received in each realm come through obedience to the laws which control those orders. God revealed to the Prophet Joseph Smith that rewards and punishments invariably and automatically follow our obedience or disobedience to the eternal laws of truth. Quoting from the revelation:

There is a law, irrevocably decreed in heaven before the foundation of this world, upon which all blessings are predicated. And when we receive any blessing from God, it is by obedience to that law upon which it is predicated.[4]

THE JUDGMENT DAY

The decree—that there shall be a universal judgment—has gone forth from the mouth of the Father and His Only Begotten Son, and it "shall not return," but must be fulfilled.[5] In the words of Apostle Paul: "We shall all stand before the judgment seat of Christ. . . . 'As I live,' saith the Lord, 'to me every knee shall bow, and every tongue confess to God'."[6]

The word of the Lord came to the Prophet Joseph Smith as follows:

Every knee shall bow and every tongue shall confess . . . saying: "Fear God, and give glory to him who sitteth upon the throne, for ever and ever; for the hour of his judgment is come."[7]

On the American continent, the Prophet Amulek was very explicit and detailed in his teachings on the judgment. Some of his doctrine is as follows:

For behold, the day cometh that all shall rise from the dead and stand before God, and be judged according to their works. . . .

Now, this restoration shall come to all, both old and young, both bond and free, both male and female, both the wicked and the righteous; . . . and [they] shall be brought and be arraigned before the bar of Christ the Son, and God the Father, to be judged according to their works, whether they be good or whether they be evil.[8]

The adjudication will be perfectly just and fair, "so that men shall say, 'Verily there is a reward for the righteous: Verily there is a God that judgeth in the earth.' "[9] In the words of the Psalmist, "Jehovah sitteth as king forever:

[4] *Doctrine and Covenants* 130:20-21; 132:5; 88:34-47.
[5] Isaiah 45:23; Moses 5:59.
[6] Romans 14:10.
[7] *Doctrine and Covenants* 88:104.
[8] Alma 11:41-44; *Doctrine and Covenants* 29:30; 76:68, 73.
[9] Psalms 58:11.

He hath prepared his throne for judgment; and he will judge the world in righteousness."[10]   Again it is written, "And the heavens shall declare his righteousness; for God is judge Himself."[11]

The God who is the judge of mankind is none other than Jesus Christ. He works in harmony with the other members of the Trinity. Quoting Apostle Peter:

> God anointed Jesus of Nazareth with the Holy Ghost and with power. . . . He [Jesus] commanded us to preach unto the people, and to testify that it is he which was ordained of God to be the Judge of quick and dead.[12]

According to the evangelist John, Jesus taught the following doctrine:

> The Father judgeth no man, but hath committed all judgment unto the Son: That all men should honour the Son, even as they honour the Father. . . . For as the Father hath life in himself, so hath he given to the Son to have life in himself; and hath given him authority to execute judgment also, because he is the Son of God.[13]

ACCOUNTABLE FOR OUR THOUGHTS, WORDS, AND ACTIONS

People usually neglect to take into consideration the fact that we shall be held accountable for each word that we speak while in mortality. Furthermore, even the secret thoughts of our hearts will rise up at the judgment day to condemn or to honor us. Alma the younger, speaking to the wicked people of Ammonihah, stated that when we are "brought before the bar of God to be judged according to our works . . . our words will condemn us, yea, all our works will condemn us; we shall not be found spotless, and our thoughts will also condemn us."[14]

One needs only to turn to the New Testament to find verification of this in the teachings of the Man of Galilee and the apostle to the Gentiles. Jesus has left mankind with no excuse for not knowing the law of judgment. He declared:

> I say unto you that every idle word that men shall speak, they shall give account thereof in the day of judgment. For by thy words thou shalt be justified, and by thy words thou shalt be condemned.[15]

---

[10] *Ibid.*
[11] *Ibid.,* 50:6.
[12] Acts 10:38, 42.
[13] John 5:22-23, 26-27, 30; *op. cit.,* Moses 6:56.
[14] Alma 12:12-14.
[15] Matthew 12:36-37; Romans 2:16.

For there is nothing covered, that shall not be revealed; neither hid, that shall not be known. Therefore, whatsoever ye have spoken in darkness shall be heard in the light; and that which ye have spoken in the ear in closets shall be proclaimed from the house-tops.[16]

Terrifying as these statements may sound to the sinner, they are true, "for the Lord is our judge, the Lord is our lawgiver, the Lord is our King," and He has proclaimed these facts.

Here is John the Revelator's word-picture of the great judgment:

And I saw a great white throne, and him that sat on it, from whose face the earth and the heaven fled away; and there was found no place for them. And I saw the dead, small and great, stand before God; and the books were opened: and another book was opened, which is the book of life, and the dead were judged out of those things which were written in the books, according to their works. . . . And whosoever was not found written in the book of life was cast into the lake of fire.[17]

UNIVERSALITY OF FINAL JUDGMENT CONCEPT

Not only did the worshipers of Jehovah believe such a doctrine, but practically all the important religions of antiquity taught a similar concept, Confucianism being a possible exception. This doctrine was a vital part of ancient paganism. Like a golden thread of truth, the concept of a final judgment connected all important religious devotees with that divine revelation given by the Lord to His holy prophets.

As early as several hundred years B.C., in far-off India, the theory was taught that "a great and final day of judgment" was inevitable. Krishna, a crucified savior-god, was to be the "judge of the dead."[18] His followers believed that he would reward or punish them according to the lives they had lived while in mortality.

[Also] from the earlier times the Egyptians appear to have believed firmly that the righteous would be rewarded in the other world, and the wicked punished.[19]

[Osiris was] "Lord of the Underworld and Ruler of the Dead." Here he presided at the bar of judgment and assigned to the souls of the departed their proper reward for virtue or punishment for sin.[20]

[16] Luke 12:2-3.
[17] Revelation 20:11-15.
[18] Kersey Graves, The World's Sixteen Crucified Saviors, pp. 262-269; John P. Jones, India's Problem, Krishna or Christ, pp. 75-76.
[19] A Guide to the Egyptian Collection in the British Museum, p. 142.
[20] Plutarch, De Iside et Osiride, p. 79, cited in Harold Willoughby, Pagan Regeneration, p. 170.

In the Judgment Hall of Osiris sat the great judge of the dead. The soul of every man was brought there and weighed in the "Great Balance" in his presence, by Thoth, the scribe of the gods. The soul was represented by the heart, and was weighed against the feather, symbolic of righteousness. If the heart failed to counterbalance the feather it was cast to an animal monster Am-mit, i. e., "Eater of the Dead," which was part crocodile, part lion, and part hippopotamus. When the heart and the feather balanced exactly, Thoth announced the fact to the gods of his company, and then the soul of the deceased was taken by Horus into the presence of Osiris, who rewarded him according to his desserts.[21]

The Zoroastrian faith of ancient Persia maintained that after death the "Conscience Daena" accuses man of the wrong he has done while in mortality. In the words of E. Washburn Hopkins:

His conscience meets him on the third day after death, in the form of a fair maid or a foul hag, and as his conscience accuses or acquits him, so he fares forth into the world of spirits, accompanied by pleasant or unpleasant surroundings, till the soul's deeds are weighed in the balance and it is sent to heaven or hell or purgatory.[22]

At the judgment of each individual at death, "man's destiny was determined by his religion, and by his thoughts, words, and deeds in this life."[23]

The Old Testament contains very little relative to a final judgment, but the writer of Ecclesiastes closed his book with the following excellent statement: "Let us hear the conclusion of the whole matter: Fear God, and keep his commandments: for this is the whole duty of man. For God shall bring every work into judgment, with every secret thing, whether it be good, or whether it be evil."[24]

The later Jewish writings—dating near the advent of Jesus—picture a final judgment for each individual. A similar doctrine is taught in abundance in the New Testament, and it became one of the paramount teachings of Christianity. Six hundred years following the death of the Man of Galilee, Mohammed taught Islam the doctrine of "the weighing in the balance of each man's evil and good deeds." Dr. Moore thinks that Mohammed obtained that doctrine from Christianity.[25]

[21] A Guide, op. cit., pp. 140-141.
[22] E. Washburn Hopkins, The History of Religions, p. 393.
[23] George Foot Moore, History of Religions, vol. 2. p. 55; vol. 1, pp. 375, 398ff; George A. Barton, The Religions of the World, pp. 135-137.
[24] Ecclesiastes 12:13-14.
[25] Moore, op. cit., pp. 64, 387, 475.

CONCEPT HELD BY THE MYSTERY RELIGIONS

One of the cardinal concepts of the Mystery Religions was that following death came a judgment day, at which men were held responsible for their lives. Even before the Mysteries of Mithra had arrived in Rome, Mithra had been elevated to the position of the god who sat upon a throne and judged the souls of the deceased. If these souls were stained with impure lives, Ahriman (the devil) or his emissaries dragged them down to the infernal depths, but if they were found worthy they were borne aloft to the regions of the heavens.[26]

According to the teachings of the Eleusinian cult, the deceased descended into Hades, where Pluto sat upon his throne and directed activities. Persephone, the queen of the underworld, was the goddess of death. "Sitting beside Pluto, she directs the Furies, and, like her husband, is cruel, unyielding, inimical to youth and life and hope."[27] Speaking of Demeter, the goddess mother of the Eleusinian Mysteries, and of Persephone and Pluto, Lewis R. Farnell said:

These deities, the mother and the daughter and the dark god in the background, were the powers that governed the world beyond the grave; those who had won their friendship by initiation in this life would by the simple logic of faith regard themselves as certain to win blessings at their hands in the next. And this, as far as we can discern, was the ground on which flourished the Eleusinian hope.[28]

Assisting the major deities of the underworld were minor gods. According to Gayley:

Before the judges of the lower world—Minos, Aeacus and Rhedamanthus—the souls of the dead were brought to trial. The condemned were assigned to regions where all manner of torment awaited them at the hands of monsters dire—the fifty-headed Hydra and the avenging Furies.[29]

The main effort of the Orphic pagan worshiper was to free himself from the wheel of successive reincarnation, as the theory of transmigration of the soul was one of the principal beliefs of that religion. Following a life of rigid Orphic asceticism and discipline, the post-mortal cult member drank of the waters of the "Lake of Memory," situated at the left of the House of Hades. After drinking

[26] Franz Cumont, The Mysteries of Mithra; Cumont, Oriental Religions in Roman Paganism, pp. 135-161; Willoughby, op. cit., pp. 143-168; Hopkins, op. cit., p. 386.
[27] Charles M. Gayley, Classic Myths, pp. 46-54; Willoughby, op. cit., pp. 86-87.
[28] Louis R. Farnell, Cults of the Greek States, vol. 3, p. 197.
[29] Gayley, op. cit., p. 51.

he was able to remember the post-mortal ritual and rules of conduct when he appeared before Persephone to be judged. This resulted in a favorable judgment, which broke the cycle of reincarnations.[30]

TRUTH'S COMMON SOURCE

Examples could be multiplied almost indefinitely of various important religions from one end of the world to the other which taught the doctrine of a final judgment.[31] The universality of the concept bears witness to its truth. God revealed the doctrine to his holy prophets from the time of Adam to that of Joseph Smith. He gave to all peoples and nations the amount of religious truth that they were capable of receiving.[32] Thus mankind knows that he is to be held accountable at the great judgment day for the life he has lived and the thoughts that have been his. This knowledge came from the "common source of religious truth"—Jesus Christ, the Lord of heaven and earth and the author of the eternal plan of salvation.

SUPPLEMENTARY READINGS—CHAPTER 20

1. *Book of Mormon:* 1 Nephi 10:20; 12:9-10; Alma 5:15-44; 9:12-30; 11:43-45; 12:1, 8-19; 29:5; 32:18-20; 40:21-24; 41:1-15; 42; 2 Nephi 33:7; 9:18-54; Jacob 6:13; Mosiah 3:11, 24-25; 16:1-15; 3 Nephi 27:14-16; 15:9-10; 20:23-26; 26:4-5; Mormon 3:18-22; 8:1-30; 9:14.

2. *Doctrine and Covenants* 10:23; 19:3; 38:5; 64:11; 75:22; 76:68, 73; 82:4, 23; 84:87; 88:99, 104; 128:6ff.

3. Joseph Fielding Smith, *The Way to Perfection*, pp. 340-347.

4. Joseph Fielding Smith (Compiler), *Teachings of the Prophet Joseph Smith*, pp. 257, 69.

5. James E. Talmage, *The Articles of Faith*, pp. 54-66.

6. John A. Widtsoe, *An Understandable Religion*, pp. 80-89.

7. John A. Widtsoe (Compiler), *Discourses of Brigham Young*, pp. 584-592.

---

[30] Willoughby, *op. cit.*, pp. 90-107.
[31] Gaius G. Atkins, *Procession of the Gods*, pp. 1-575.
[32] 2 Nephi 28:26-30; 29:1-14.

Chapter 21.

THE MESSIANIC HOPE

INTRODUCTORY STATEMENT

The next four lessons are devoted to the world-old and world-wide belief in a Savior-God, each discussing a different phase of this subject. This chapter presents the teachings of the prophets regarding the coming of a Savior, summarizing the most outstanding points that were known during the early Gospel dispensations.

Messiah is a Hebrew word (Mahsiah), which means "the expected king and deliverer." He was to be "the Anointed One" or "the Christ, the divinely sent Savior of the world." Therefore, the chapter title, "The Messianic Hope," means the belief held by the prophets from age to age that the Messiah (Savior) would come to redeem mankind from his fallen condition by teaching him the Gospel and breaking the bonds of death, thereby opening a pathway for mortals to come back into the presence of God.

ORIGIN OF THE MESSIANIC HOPE

As has been pointed out earlier in this book, the Eternal Father ordained His Only Begotten Son to be the Savior, even before men were placed upon the earth; therefore, the Messianic concept was instituted at the great council in heaven.

Since the heart of the plan of salvation is this Savior-God and the great work and mission He performed in providing for the redemption of mankind, one of the first and paramount Gospel truths revealed to mortals was the mission of the Messiah. The story of this revelation coming to Father Adam is beautifully told in the *Pearl of Great Price*. An angel of the Lord appeared unto him and said: "Why dost thou offer sacrifice unto the Lord?"

Adam replied, "I know not, save the Lord commanded me."

Then the heavenly messenger explained unto him that "This thing is a similitude of the sacrifice of the Only Begotten of the Father, which is full of grace and truth," who would come into the world to redeem mankind from his fallen and mortal condition. Adam was also told that the name of God's Only Begotten Son was "the Son of Man, even Jesus Christ . . . the only name which shall be given under heaven whereby salvation shall come unto the children of men."[1] Christ was to come to earth in the meridian of times to be a righteous Judge and the Savior that (to quote) "as thou hast fallen thou mayest be redeemed, and all mankind, even as many as will" obey the Gospel truths. By way of summary and also prophesy, the ancient record declared:

And thus the Gospel began to be preached, from the beginning, being declared by holy angels sent forth from the presence of God, and by his own voice, and by the gift of the Holy Ghost . . . and a decree sent forth that it should be in the world until the end thereof.[2]

UNIVERSALITY OF THE MESSIANIC HOPE

Adam and Eve rejoiced in what they had learned concerning the Messiah and the great part He would play in the plan of salvation.

And they made all things known unto their sons and their daughters. And Satan came among them, saying: "I am also a son of God"; and he commanded them saying: "Believe it not"; and they believed it not, and they loved Satan more than God. And men began from that time forth to be carnal, sensual and devilish.[3]

Even though the children of men began at that early date to fall away from the revealed Gospel truths, yet a belief in a Savior has never been lost by mortals. This thread of persistence of Gospel truths—although stretched at times almost to an infinitesimal thinness through evil, ignorance, and sins of man—has such tensile strength that it has never been broken; hence one finds human beings, pagan and Christian, reaching up towards God and relying on a Savior for assistance.

---

[1] Moses 5:5-9; 6:56, 51.
[2] Ibid., 5:58-59; Alma 12:28-30.
[3] Ibid., 5:12-13.

In addition to this persistence of the Messianic concept which has filtered outward and downward through the ages, God has renewed men's knowlege of the Savior through revelations to His holy prophets. This became necessary because at certain times during history many of the truths regarding the Messiah were changed or lost through apostasies. The Eternal Father has always been so anxious to give His children immortality and eternal life that He has used many avenues through which to inform them that Jesus is the Christ and that salvation can come only in and through His name,[4] and these are basic facts in the Messianic hope.

Therefore, most of the races of the earth have had some sort of concept relative to a Redeemer who should save them from the evils of mortality. This information may have come to them as a social heritage from the days when Adam and his posterity understood the Gospel principles, or the ideas may have been borrowed from some other race of people who had received divine revelation, or it may have come directly to the prophets from the Lord.

The Messianic Hope of Enoch and the Jaredites

Throughout the entire history of the world the holy prophets of God have, one after another, received divine revelations regarding a Messiah—a Savior—who should come and redeem mankind from his fallen condition and make possible his entrance into the kingdom of God. Enoch saw in vision the principal events in the history of the world. For the purpose of showing the main points regarding Enoch's knowledge of the Messiah which he received directly from the Lord, we shall quote from this revelation, as follows:

Enoch saw the day of the coming of the Son of Man, even in the flesh; and his soul rejoiced, saying: "The Righteous is lifted up, and the Lamb is slain from the foundation of the world." . . .

And the Lord said: "Blessed is he through whose seed Messiah shall come"; for he saith—"I am Messiah, the King of Zion, the Rock of Heaven, which is broad as eternity; whoso cometh in at the gate and climbeth up by me shall never fall; wherefore, blessed are they of whom I have spoken, for they shall come forth with songs of everlasting joy."

---

[4] *Ibid.,* 1:39; *Doctrine and Covenants* 18:22-25; Mosiah 3:7; Acts 4:12.

And it came to pass that Enoch cried unto the Lord, saying: "When the Son of Man cometh in the flesh, shall the earth rest? I pray thee, show me these things."

And the Lord said unto Enoch: "Look"; and he looked and beheld the Son of Man lifted up on the cross, after the manner of men; And he heard a loud voice, and the heavens were veiled, and all the creations of God mourned, and the Saints arose, and were crowned at the right hand of the Son of Man, with crowns of glory; And as many of the spirits as were in prison came forth, and stood on the right hand of God; and the remainder were preserved in chains of darkness until the judgment of the great day. . . . And Enoch beheld the Son of Man ascend up unto the Father.[5]

Several hundred years after this event occurred, the brother of Jared was favored of the Lord with a vision similar to the one experienced by Enoch. In the course of the vision, the Savior appeared to him and said: "Behold, I am Jesus Christ. . . . In me shall all mankind have light, and that eternally, even they who shall believe on my name; and they shall become my sons and my daughters."[6] Then He told the brother of Jared of His future advent on earth and of His work for the salvation of man. Therefore, through this vision the Jaredites obtained a Messianic hope which remained a dominant doctrine in the religious history of this people for over 2,000 years.

Messianic Hope of the Hebrews

The belief that a Savior, even the Christ, the Anointed One, would come to earth among the Hebrew people, was one of the strongest forces in the history of that race. As early as the time of Moses, the ancient lawgiver, this belief was cherished. Doubtless it was a heritage from earlier Gospel ages. The Lord, however, through this great prophet, instituted the Feast of the Passover and enlarged the people's vision of the mission of the Messiah. It is a significant fact that one of the principal purposes of this ancient Jewish feast was to remind the people of the future advent of the Messiah. In fact, the paschal lambs of the Feast of the Passover were symbolical of the Lamb of God, whose blood should be shed for the sins of man. Through revelation the Hebrews had been informed that at the time of Christ's death no bones would be broken

[5] Moses 7:47, 53-59.
[6] Ether 3:14-16.

in His body. Since the paschal lambs, being without spot
or blemish, symbolized the purity and holiness of the Savior
in His life, so in their death no bones were broken in their
bodies.

Throughout the course of Old Testament history,
many prophecies were made regarding the coming of the
Savior. It was definitely understood that He would be a
Jew and a descendant of King David.[7] He would be born
of a virgin; and His birthplace would be Bethlehem.[8]
Isaiah told the people that this Savior would be despised
and rejected of men, afflicted and smitten.

> As a lamb that is led to the slaughter, and as a sheep that before
> its shearers is dumb, so he opened not his mouth. . . . He poured out
> his soul unto death, and was numbered with the transgressors: yet he
> bare the sin of many, and made intercession for the transgressors.[9]

The Old Testament prophet who left the most numerous statements regarding the Messiah was Isaiah. Many
of his predictions, however, referred to the second coming
of the Son of Man. As the Messianic hope of the Jews
developed, there was a complete fusing together of the
predictions relative to His first coming and those statements regarding the second coming and the millennial
reign. For this reason, when the Man of Galilee came
among the Jews, He failed to fulfill the prevalently accepted Jewish Messianic hope.[10] Therefore, they rejected
Him and crucified Him.

BIBLE AND BOOK OF MORMON MESSIANIC VIEWS COMPARED

The New Testament gives its readers a beautiful and
enlightening story of Jesus while in mortality and His
message of love and salvation; and the Nephite record gives
a similar account obtained from Jesus following His resurrection. The fact is definite, however, that the Bible as
a whole does not contain as comprehensive and detailed a
picture of Christ's work before His birth into mortality nor
as complete a picture of the plan of redemption as does
the *Book of Mormon.*

---

[7] Isaiah 9:6-7; 11:1-10; 16:5.
[8] Isaiah 7:14-15; Micah 5:2.
[9] Isaiah 53:1-12.
[10] William R. Van Burkirk, *The Saviors of Mankind,* pp. 342-349.

Nephites' Knowledge of the Messiah

The Nephites had a very comprehensive and thorough knowledge regarding the Messiah. In fact, no people have left us a more complete record of the birth, life, mission, death, resurrection, and glorification of the Son of God than did these people; and it is important to know that their knowledge was almost as complete before Jesus lived in mortality as it was after that event. God began the Nephite Messianic hope by revealing to Lehi and also to his son Nephi numerous facts regarding the coming of the Christ.[11] They learned that He was to be a universal Savior-God, and that He would redeem all mankind from their sins if they would obey His Gospel. Referring to his father's teachings, Nephi wrote:

Yea, even 600 years from the time that my father left Jerusalem, a prophet would the Lord God raise up among the Jews; even a Messiah; or in other words, a Savior of the world. And he also spake concerning the prophets, how great a number had testified of these things, concerning this Messiah, of whom he had spoken, or this Redeemer of the world. Wherefore all mankind were in a lost and in a fallen state, and ever would be, save they should rely on this Redeemer.[12]

God favored Nephi with one of the most marvelous visions that mortal man has experienced. In the course of that vision, Nephi saw a beautiful virgin and was informed that she would be the mortal mother of the Messiah. The virgin held a baby in her arms, and the angel said unto Nephi, "Behold the Lamb of God, yea, even the Son of the Eternal Father!" Then the prophet saw the Savior, the Redeemer of the world, go down to the river to be baptized of John. Following this, the entire ministry of the Master was shown to Nephi. He recorded his vision, and the main facts of Christ's life agree identically with the record made by the New Testament writers after Jesus had lived among the Jews. For the purpose of illustrating the definite knowledge that Nephi had regarding the mission of the Christ, the following is quoted:

And I beheld that he went forth ministering unto the people, in power and great glory; and the multitudes were gathered together to hear him; and I beheld that they cast him out from among them. . . . And I looked and beheld the Lamb of God that he was taken by the people; yea, the Son of the everlasting God was judged of the

---
11 1 Nephi 1:7-15.
12 *Ibid.*, 10:4-6.

world; and I saw and bear record that he was lifted up upon the cross, and slain for the sins of the world.[13]

Nearly 500 years after Nephi had experienced his vision the Lord enlarged the Messianic concept of those ancient Americans by sending an angel to King Benjamin. By quoting a portion of the message received by this prophet-king we can obtain a clearer understanding of the Nephites' knowledge of the Messiah. The angel said:

For behold, the time cometh, and is not far distant, that with power, the Lord Omnipotent who reigneth, who was, and is from all eternity to all eternity, shall come down from heaven, among the children of men, and shall dwell in a tabernacle of clay, and shall go forth amongst men, working mighty miracles, such as healing the sick, raising the dead, causing the lame to walk, the blind to receive their sight, and the deaf to hear, and curing all manner of disease. . . .

And he shall be called Jesus Christ, the Son of God, the Father of heaven and earth, the Creator of all things, from the beginning; and his mother shall be called Mary.

And lo, he cometh unto his own, that salvation might come unto the children of men, even through faith on his name; and even after all this, they shall consider him a man, and say that he hath a devil, and shall scourge him, and shall crucify him. And he shall rise the third day from the dead; and behold, he standeth to judge the world.[14]

These and many other glorious truths regarding the life, mission, death, and resurrection of Jesus Christ and the eternal plan of salvation were revealed to the Nephite prophets.[15] Their knowledge of the life and mission of the Savior is almost as complete as ours today, even after Christ has lived upon the earth. There is no indication in the *Book of Mormon* that the Nephites restricted their conception of the Christ to that of Savior of Jews and Nephites only. They at once and throughout their history acclaimed Him to be the universal Messiah of mankind—even Jesus Christ, the Savior of the world.

SUPPLEMENTARY READINGS—CHAPTER 21

1. *Bible*: Isaiah 7:14-15; 9:6-7; 11:1-10; 16:5; 25:6-9; 32:1-8; 53:1-12; Micah 5:2.
2. *Book of Mormon*: 1 Nephi 1:4-11; 10:17; 11:1-36; 12:1-8; 19:8-12; 22:20-28; 2 Nephi 2:1-30; 11:3-7; 6:9; 9:4-41; 10:3; 25:12-30; 26:1-9; Jacob 4:1-18; Mosiah 3:1-27; 14:15-16; Alma 5:48-51; 7:7-16; 9:26-29; 12:1-37; 39:15-19; 40; 41; 42; 11:21-46; 34:1-41; Helaman 14:1-31; 3 Nephi 1:1-25; 2:14-16; 9:12-22; 11:1ff.
3. *Pearl of Great Price*: Moses 1:6, 13, 17-19, 32-33; 2:1, 26-27; 4:1-4; 6:51-67; 7:45-69; Abraham 3:22-28.

[13] *Ibid.*, 11:11-36.
[14] Mosiah 3:1-12.
[15] 2 Nephi 9:4-41; Jacob 4:1-18; Mosiah 14:15, 16; Alma 5:48-51; 12:1-37.

Chapter 22.

THE BELIEF IN A SAVIOR-GOD [1]

INTRODUCTORY STATEMENT

The purpose of this lesson is to show that practically every ancient world religion and pagan cult of importance believed in a savior-god, and that all of these savior-god beliefs had a definite relationship to the divine revelations received by Father Adam and the other prophets of God regarding Jesus the true Redeemer of mankind. In fact, the purpose of the following two chapters will be to show definitely that Jesus of Nazareth is the Messiah and the only true Savior-God.

In order to be able to arrive at a correct interpretation, while studying this lesson it will be helpful to observe carefully the similarities of the pagan traditions of their savior-gods to the revelations of what transpired in connection with the life of the Only Begotten Son of God; because, as was pointed out in the last chapter, the prophets knew all of the principal details of Christ's life hundreds of years before He came to the earth.

UNIVERSALITY OF BELIEF IN A SAVIOR-GOD

The belief in a savior is another of those religious concepts that is world-old and world-wide. Human beings have always built their religious rituals around their concept of a redeemer—a humanized savior. Kersey Graves lists over thirty-five different individuals who were worshiped as savior-gods before the birth of Jesus of Nazareth.[2] On the other hand, people in several different countries were anxiously waiting for the earthly advent of a divine deliverer at the time the Son of God was born in Bethlehem.

---

[1] The term "Savior-God" denotes practically the same thing as that of a "Messiah," but we used the latter name in the last chapter because it was commonly known to the Hebrews.

[2] Kersey Graves, *The World's Sixteen Crucified Saviors*, pp. 31-32.

152

Seneca, Hesid, and other ancient writers left us accounts of the crucifixion of Prometheus—the Caucasus savior-god—and of his subsequent resurrection. The crucifixion is reported to have occurred on a cross near the Caspian Straits, about 547 B.C. "The cause for which he suffered was his love for the human race." The following claim is made:

[At the time of his crucifixion] the earth shook, the rocks were rent, the graves were opened, and in a storm, which seemed to threaten the dissolution of the universe, the solemn scene forever closed, and "Our Lord and Savior" Prometheus gave up the ghost.[3]

Buddha (about 600 B.C.), in far-off India, is purported to have said: "Let all the sins that are in the world fall on me, that the world may be delivered,"[4] a promise made from the very beginning by Jesus Christ to all people who would repent.

"His [Buddha's] followers always speak of him as one with God from all eternity." His most common title was "the Savior of the World." He was also called "the Benevolent One," "the Dispenser of Grace," "The Source of Life," "the Light of the World," and "the True Light."

[Tradition claims that] his mother was a very pure, refined, pious and devout woman; never indulged in any impure thoughts, words or actions. She was so much esteemed for her virtues and for being the mother of a God, that an escort of ladies attended her wherever she went. The trees bowed before her as she passed through the forest, and flowers sprang up wherever her foot pressed the ground. She was saluted as "the Holy Virgin, Queen of heaven."[5]

Regarding Buddha, Dr. Robert E. Hume concluded:

Not only has Buddha been deified, but he has been made a member of a Buddhist Trinity. It is one of the ironics of history that he whose main message and very last words before dying were a call to a self-reliant, ethical life, as over against dependence upon any kind of a Divine Being, should himself be subsequently worshiped with larger and more numerous images than exist of any other person in the history of the world.[6]

It is obvious that the traditions regarding Krishna, a Hindu deity, were altered forms of the true revelations regarding the Messiah as given to the holy prophets. In fact,

[3] *Ibid.*, pp. 124-125. Observe the many similarities between Enoch's vision as quoted in the last chapter and the traditions of Prometheus and also keep in mind that Enoch lived probably 3,000 years before the traditional date of Prometheus.
[4] Max Muller, *History of Sanskrit Literature*, p. 80.
[5] Graves, *op. cit.*, pp. 116-117; Isaiah 7:14-15; Micah 5:2; 1 Nephi 11:11-36; Mosiah 3:1-12. Recall the prophesies made by Nephi, King Benjamin, Isaiah and other prophets reported in the last chapter regarding the virgin birth of Jesus and the beauty and purity of Mary, the mother of the Son of God.
[6] Robert Ernest Hume, *The World's Living Religions*, p. 29.

the very name *Krishna* seems to be merely another form of *Christ*. This god, it is claimed, "became incarnate for the protection of good men, for the destruction of evildoers, for the re-establishment of piety."[7] Tradition has it that he came into the world as a result of "a divine immaculate conception," his mother being "overshadowed by the supreme god, Brahma." He met his death by crucifixion; and, furthermore, the Hindu tradition claims, that after having risen from the dead, he appeared to his disciples. To quote:

"He ascended to Voiacantha (heaven), to Brahma," the first person of the trinity (he himself being the second), and that as he ascended, "all men saw him, and exclaimed, 'Lo, Krishna's soul ascends to his native skies'."[8]

The holy scriptures claim that Enoch, thousands of years B.C., knew that Christ would be crucified, resurrected, and then ascend to heaven, as was pointed out in the last chapter. Thus we find the original source of the pagan traditions of the crucifixion, resurrection, and ascension of savior-gods.

The ancient Chinese religious records contain a Messianic prophecy. It is as follows: "The Holy One, when he comes, will unite in himself all the virtues of heaven and earth. By his justice the world will be established in righteousness. He will labor and suffer much . . . and will finally offer up a sacrifice worthy of himself."[9] The people of ancient China even had their savior-god. There came a time when they attached this prophecy to one of their holy men. "Tien, the Holy One—one with God and existing with Him from all eternity — died to save the world."[10]

On the other side of the world, in Mexico, "Quetzalcoatl, the savior, was born of a virgin, was tempted, and fasted forty days, was done to death, and his second coming looked for so eagerly that when Cortez appeared, the Mexicans, poor things, greeted him as the returning God! In Peru and among the American Indians, north and south of the equator, similar legends are, or were, to be found."[11] Members of the Church of Jesus Christ of Latter-day

---

[7] *Ibid.*, p. 29.
[8] Cited in Graves, *op. cit.*, pp. 145, 152-155, 103.
[9] Martinus, *History of China;* Halde, *History of China.*
[10] Edward Carpenter, *Pagan and Christian Creeds*, pp. 203-204.
[11] *Ibid.;* Josiah E. Hickman, *The Romance of the Book of Mormon*, pp. 185-197; Kingsborough, *Mexican Antiquities*, vol. 6.

Saints know from the *Book of Mormon* history, that the savior-god beliefs held by the American Indians are actually altered forms of the Savior's appearances to the Nephites following His resurrection.

SAVIOR-GODS OF THE PAGAN RIVALS OF CHRISTIANITY

All of the pagan religions which were vital rivals of early Christianity—especially the Mystery cults—had their savior-gods. The Egyptian "Osiris was claimed to be the savior of the world, both in his life and death."[12] His devotees believed that he had wrought many noble benefits for mankind while in life, and that through his death he had overcome the powers of darkness. Following his death he became the "Lord of the Underworld and Ruler of the Dead."[13] As a result of his resurrection and the observance of the cult rituals, the worshipers were promised a glorious resurrection and that, if they so chose, they could become gods. "Many a man so privileged was specifically called 'Osiris' after his death."[14] The following Egyptian text testifies to the future hope of the initiate: "As truly as Osiris lives, he also shall live; as truly as Osiris is not dead, shall he not die; as truly as Osiris is not annihilated, shall he not be annihilated."[15] These are all pertinent beliefs in the ancient prophets' knowledge of the life and mission of the Son of God and the rewards received by the faithful saints.

The Egyptian mother-goddess, Isis, the "eternal saviour of the race of men," promised her worshipers:

Thou shalt live in blessedness; thou shalt live glorious under my protection. And when thou hast finished thy life-course and goest down to the underworld, even there in that lower world thou shalt see me shedding light in the gloom of Acheron and reigning in the inmost regions of Styx: thou thyself shalt inhabit the Elysian fields and shalt continually offer worship to me, ever gracious.[16]

It so happened in this pagan cult that Isis acted in conjunction with Osiris as savior-gods, while in the true Gospel the Savior of the world and the Judge of the dead was a male God. This is further evidence of the alterations made in paganism.

---

[12] Carpenter, *op. cit.*, pp. 203-204.
[13] Cited in Harold Willoughby's *Pagan Regeneration*, p. 170.
[14] *Ibid.*, p. 175.
[15] Erman, *Die Aegyptische Religion*, pp. 96-97, cited in *ibid.*, p. 175.
[16] Samuel Angus, *The Mystery Religions and Christianity*, p. 139.

It was believed that the Greek "Bacchus or Dionysus, born of the virgin Semele to be the liberator of mankind, was torn to pieces," died, resurrected, immortalized, and deified.[17] After this "Dionysus functioned in Hellenistic cults as god of the underworld, and his devotees had the same expectation in relation to him that the ancient Getae had concerning Zalmoxis," i. e., "they believe themselves immortal; they think that they do not die, but that the dead go to join their god Zalmoxis."[18]

It was claimed that Bacchus, Dionysus-Zagreus and Persephone—three savior-deities—were begotten by Zeus, the chief of the Greek gods, and born to mortal virgins. Obviously this belief was an adulterated version of Jesus Christ being the Only Begotten Son of God, a fact known and proclaimed by all the holy prophets beginning with Adam. Dionysus-Zagreus was purported to have been the son of Persephone, while Persephone was the daughter of Demeter. Following death, each of these three individuals were deified and became rulers of the dead and gods of the underworld, just as Jesus became judge and ruler of the next world.[19]

According to the Cybele-Attis Myth, the Great Mother of the gods loved the youthful, virgin-born shepherd named Attis, who died a violent death. Thereupon the Great Mother buried him in a cave, mourned for her dead lover, and finally effected his resurrection.[20] Thus Attis became deified and immortal. Priests of Attis told the worshipers, "Be of good cheer, you of the Mystery; your god is saved; for us also shall be salvation from ills."[21]

Mithraism, the Mystery cult which promised during the early Christian centuries to make itself the universal religion, proclaimed Mithra to be a mediator between God and man and also a savior, just as Jesus of Nazareth was both Mediator and Savior. He was regarded by his devotees as a divine being, a humanized savior-god.[22] After performing a number of unusual feats, according to tradition he ascended to heaven and became "the god of light,

---

[17] Carpenter, op. cit., p. 130.
[18] Willoughby, op. cit., p. 84.
[19] Cited in ibid., p. 107.
[20] These pagan traditions closely resemble the facts that the prophets had long taught about the true Messiah.
[21] Angus, op. cit., p. 60; Willoughby, op. cit., pp. 127-128.
[22] Willoughby, ibid., pp. 143-168; Franz Cumont, The Mysteries of Mithra.

the upholder of truth and the enemy of error," and the judge of the dead. To quote:

As the beneficent god of light, Mithra was the dispenser of physical blessings. . . . He was the one who gave to man an abundance of material possessions, good health, and a numerous progeny. . . . Being the "ever-waking, ever-watchful" god, who, with his "hundred ears and hundred eyes," constantly watched the world, Mithra naturally became the guardian of truth and the preserver of good faith. . . .

The wrath of Mithra was as terrible as his blessings were rich and full; for he was the implacable foe of all evil who, "never sleeping, wakefully maintains the creation of Mazda." He was engaged in ceaseless combat with the spirits of evil, and to wicked men brought endless troubles.[23]

Nowhere in ancient paganism was there a god who in his functions resembed more closely the true Savior of mankind than did Mithra. In fact, the entire religion of this ancient mythical god had numerous beliefs and practices resembling the Gospel of Jesus Christ. By the time Mithraism reached the Mediterranean world, its beliefs and practices were greatly adulterated; yet the evidence is extensive enough to show beyond question that this ancient religion was a modified form of the true Gospel and that its roots extended back into the divine revelations from heaven.

There were a number of pagan religions which flourished in Syria and Asia Minor during the early Christian period and with which Paul, the Christian apostle, had early familiarity and contacts that were intimate. Each of them had its savior-god. Fundamentally they were closely related to the Great Mother cult, prominent primarily throughout Asia Minor and Italy. In each of these pagan cults, a mother goddess fell in love with a virgin-born youth who met a violent death and then was resurrected by the goddess. Each of these youths became savior to his respective cult members, breaking the bands of death and bringing about resurrection. The mother-goddesses are adulterated forms of God the Eternal Father, while the virgin-born youths are altered forms of Jesus Christ.

In Phoenicia the mother-goddess was named Ashtart and her consort was Eshmun. It was claimed that these two deities were simultaneously glorified and they had promised glorification to cult members.

---

[23] Willoughby, *op. cit.*, pp. 144-145.

Citizens of the Greek world were familiar with Aphrodite and Adonis, "the goddess of love and her impetuous young husband." Adonis, an ardent young hunter, was killed by a wild boar. The grief of his goddess lover brought about his resurrection; and thereafter cult members were promised that they also would rise from death. Obviously this was another drastically altered form of the true Savior doctrine.

The Syrian goddess Atargatis and her consort Hadad gained considerable prominence in the Roman world. Hadad, like many of the other pagan savior-gods, was said to have died a violent death to save mankind. An elaborate show of grief was a characteristic factor in the ritual of this cult. The prophet Zachariah was acquainted with the lamentations of Hadad.[24]

The Babylonian goddess Ishtar, the deified personification of motherhood, was known to Bible writers as Ashtoreth. With her was associated a young and active deity called Tammuz. He was crucified, it was claimed, and afterwards resurrected and deified; and thereupon, becoming a savior, he promised similar blessings to cult members.[25] As in the case of Attis, Adonis and Hadad, "lamentations formed an important part of his worship. In Ezekiel's day this practice was adopted by Jews even, and among the 'abominations' which the prophet saw perpetrated at the very gate of the Jerusalem temple was the weeping of women for Tammuz!"[26] A poet has perpetuated the memory of this savior-god as follows:

> Trust, ye saints, your Lord restored,
> Trust ye in your risen Lord;
> For the pains which Tammuz endured
> Our salvation have procured.[27]

The traditional date of Tammuz is approximately 1160 B.C. The following statement was translated from a Greek text by Mr. Godwin: "Trust ye in God, for out of his loins salvation has come unto us." Julius Firmicus speaks of Tammuz as "rising from the dead for the salvation of the world."[28]

---

[24] Zachariah 12:11.
[25] Graves, op. cit., p. 120.
[26] Ezekiel 8:14; Willoughby. op. cit., p. 137.
[27] Cited in ibid.
[28] Cited in ibid., p. 121.

SOURCE OF PAGANS' SAVIOR-GOD CONCEPTS

Members of the Church of Jesus Christ of Latter-day Saints know through revelations from God to the holy prophets—especially to Joseph Smith—that all of the savior-gods of paganism and world religions contributed nothing toward bringing about the resurrection and eternal life of man. Jesus Christ was declared even before the foundation of the world to be the only name which would ever be given whereby mankind could ever gain immortality and exaltation. All of these other saviors were counterfeits.

Mormons also know, as has been pointed out definitely in this course of study, that shortly after God placed Adam and Eve on earth, He revealed to them the Gospel. Gradually, as mortals, drew farther away from their Heavenly Parents and their Savior through sin and ignorance, the truths were corrupted and changed; yet a likeness to the original revelations persisted. At various times throughout history the Lord renewed men's knowledge of the Gospel truths through revelations to His prophets. Only those individuals or peoples who continued in harmony with the Godhead were able to draw verities from above. Thus all religions containing eternal truths came from the one true religion that God taught Father Adam.

From these purer sources of truth—the holy prophets—ideas disseminated outward in every direction among pagan nations. Through a process of religious syncretism, or blending together of religious beliefs, savior-god concepts became common property of all peoples. These groups who remained more directly in tune with God through a succession of prophets—as did the Nephites and Hebrews—retained a more pure and unadulterated Messianic hope; while, on the other hand, it was natural for the pagan groups who had obtained information relative to the mission of the Redeemer to project the idea of the Savior (yet unborn) into one of their mythological characters with the claim that the Messiah had lived, died, and had been resurrected and immortalized, thereby assuring the devotees of a blessed life eternal.

Therefore, through apostasies—which have been brought about through borrowing and lending of religious practices and beliefs and adopting from time to time man-made creeds—the Gospel truths have been diverted, leaving only enough truth in paganism to give it a resemblance to the teachings of the Master. This accounts for the numerous savior-gods in history, the universality of the concept, and the world-wide presence of certain other religious doctrines and practices.

But it should not be assumed for a moment that just because many principal beliefs and practices found in Christianity today were present in most of the great religions of the world as well as in the minor pagan cults of antiquity that all religions are of equal moral and spiritual worth. The waters of truth sparkle divinely in the Church of Jesus Christ as they gush forth from the great Fountain of Truth —even Jesus Christ, "the light and life of the world"; while, on the other hand, the sluggish streams of paganism—adulterated and teeming with error—contain only glimmers of the original Gospel.

SUPPLEMENTARY READINGS—CHAPTER 22

1. Josiah E. Hickman, *The Romance of the Book of Mormon*, pp. 185-197.
2. Harold Willoughby, *Pagan Regeneration*, pp. 41-49, 69-74, 90, 114-118, 136-146, 169-171, 176-179.

Chapter 23.

THE ONE DIVINE SAVIOR-GOD

ATTEMPTS TO DISCREDIT THE DIVINITY OF CHRIST

Ever since it has been recognized that human beings in their search for God and their quest for salvation have had certain concepts and practices in common, regardless of the country or the century to which the worshipers belong, many Christians have lost faith in their religion. In fact, there has been a growing tendency during the past century for many people to reject the most vital Christian doctrines, such as the validity of divine inspiration or revelation in religion and the belief of the efficacy of the atonement of Jesus Christ.

A number of books and articles have been written with the avowed purpose of proving that Christianity is pagan in its origin, that Jesus is not the only Begotten Son of God, and that the account of His miraculous and holy conception is merely a myth on a par with those found in paganism. Some writers have gone so far as to maintain that the universal reality of the savior-god concept disproves the divine nature of Jesus Christ, making of Him not the Only Begotten of the Father, but a mythological character around whom were collected pagan myths, refined and recorded by early Christian writers.[1]

DIVINITY OF JESUS CHRIST

The responsibility of the true Christian today is to weigh the evidences regarding the divinity and historicity of Jesus. The most reputable scholars of early Christian history maintain that the four gospels and the letters of Paul are reliable, trustworthy and relatively accurate his-

---

[1] Kersey Graves, *The World's Sixteen Crucified Saviours;* Edward Carpenter, *Pagan and Christian Creeds.*

tory.[2] They agree as to the historicity of Jesus. In fact, the evidence presented by Dr. Shirley J. Case, dean of the Divinity School of the University of Chicago, effectively counteracts any and all negative arguments presented by radical critics claiming Jesus to be a mythological Christ.[3] In the words of Henry M. Battenhouse, "There is one point on which Christian opinion is unanimous; it is that Jesus is indisputably the Christ."[4]

Dr. Sidney Angus emphatically states:

Christianity had an unique advantage over all of its competitors, including even Judaism, in having an historic Person as Founder, whose Person was greater than His teachings. . . . No other religion could "placard" a real Being in flesh and blood who had lived so near to God and brought men into such intimate soul-satisfying union with the Father. . . . The Mystery Religions could offer only myths.[5]

Mormons know beyond doubt through the evidence presented in their holy scriptures, especially the *Book of Mormon* and the *Doctrine and Covenants,* that Jesus is the Christ and the only name given whereby mankind can receive salvation.

Indeed, the revealed purpose of the Nephite record is to be another witness to the divinity and mission of Jesus. It sustains and amplifies the testimony of the Bible, and even confirms the hopes which arose in the breasts of the ancient pagans relative to the reality of God, the efficacy of the Savior, and an assurance of eternal life. . . . From Nephi to Moroni, the avowed purpose of each of the writers was to produce a work *"to the convincing of the Jew and the Gentile that Jesus is the Christ, the Eternal God, manifesting Himself unto all nations."*[6]

Not only did the prophets of old give testimony that Jesus is the only true Messiah, but new light came in modern times to the Prophet Joseph Smith. In his words:

We beheld the glory of the Son, on the right hand of the Father, and received of his fullness; and saw the holy angels, and them who are sanctified before his throne, worshiping God, and the Lamb, who worship him forever and ever.

And now, after the many testimonies which have been given of him, this is the testimony, last of all, which we give of him: *That he lives! For we saw him, even on the right hand of God; and we heard the voice bearing record that he is the Only Begotten of the Father—That by him,*

---

[2] Charles Gore, "Are the Gospels Trustworthy?" *Jesus of Nazareth,* pp. 175-211; Edgar J. Goodspeed, *The Story of the New Testament,* pp. 1-147; Ernest Findlay Scott, *The Literature of the New Testament,* pp. 1-300.
[3] Shirley Jackson Case, *The Historicity of Jesus,* pp. 1-300.
[4] Henry M. Battenhouse, *New Testament History and Literature,* pp. 176-177.
[5] Angus, *op. cit.,* pp. 309-311.
[6] Berrett, Hunter, Welker, Fitzgerald, "Book of Mormon Concept of the Mission of Christ," *A Guide to the Study of the Book of Mormon,* pp. 62-78.

and through him, and of him, the worlds are and were created, and the inhabitants are begotten sons and daughters unto God.[7]

Thus we see that there is only one divine Savior-God, even Jesus Christ.

Signs of the Birth and Death of the Savior

Christ's divinity was of such significance and His mission of such importance that His advent into mortality and His exodus from this life were heralded by unusual signs in nature. Five years before the birth of the Savior, Samuel, the Lamanite, stood on the wall of the city of Zarahemla and prophesied many things regarding the coming of the Messiah, among which were definite signs which should announce His birth and others which should indicate that He had died. In order that we might get the story first-hand we shall quote directly from the ancient Nephite record. The Prophet Samuel said:

I give unto you for a sign at the time of his coming; for behold, there shall be great lights in heaven, insomuch that in the night before he cometh there shall be no darkness, insomuch that it shall appear unto man as if it was day. Therefore there shall be one day and a night, and a day, as if it were one day, and there were no night. . . . And behold there shall a new star arise, such an one as ye never have beheld; and this shall be a sign unto you. . . .

But behold, as I said unto you concerning another sign, a sign of his death, behold, in that day that he shall suffer death, the sun shall be darkened and refuse to give his light unto you, and also the moon, and the stars; and there shall be no light upon the face of this land, even from the time that he shall suffer death, for the space of three days, to the time that he shall rise again from the dead.[8]

Then he proceeded to describe to them the terrible storm that should occur with great violence at the time of the crucifixion of the Son of Man. And he prophesied that "many graves shall be opened, and shall yield up many of their dead; and many saints shall appear unto many" at the time of the resurrection of the Savior of the world. Anyone who is familiar with the *Book of Mormon* story knows that these prophesies were all fulfilled exactly as they were spoken of by the mouth of God's prophet.[9] Matthew also testified of darkness and a storm occurring in Palestine at the death of Jesus and of the resurrection of many saints immediately following the resurrection of the Master.[10]

---

[7] *Doctrine and Covenants* 76:20-24.
[8] Helaman 14:1-8, 20-28.
[9] 3 Nephi 1:8-21; 8:3-25; 9:1-22; 23:6-13.
[10] Matthew 27:45-53.

The unusual phenomenon of light in nature symbolized Christ's coming into mortality, and very appropriately symbolized His teachings and example to mankind while here. In the words of Alma: "He [Christ] is the light and life of the world; yea, a light that is endless, that can never be darkened; yea, and also a life which is endless, that there can be no more death."[11]

The signs of the death of the Master, i.e., the engulfing of the world in darkness with the accompanying storm and earthquakes, symbolized very aptly the end of the life of Jesus and His immediate influence going out of the world, thereby leaving the world temporarily in darkness. This condition lasted in the Nephite country during the three days while the Lord's body was in the tomb, but when He was resurrected the darkness gave way to the light of another calm, beautiful day.

BELIEF IN THE STAR AS A SIGN

Pagans in various lands had as part of their traditions the belief that a new star appeared at the birth of several of their savior-gods. One writer stated: "Among the ancients there seems to have been a very general idea that the arrival of Gods and great personages who were expected to come, would be announced by a star. And the cases of Abraham, Cacsar, Pythagoras, Yu, Krishna and Christ may be cited in proof of this declaration."[12] Chalcidus, a second century A.D. writer, in his *Comments on the Times of Plato,* speaks of "a star which presaged neither disease nor death, but the descent of a God amongst men, and which is attested by Chaldean astronomers, who immediately hastened to adore the new-born Deity, and present him gifts."[13]

We know from Abraham's experiences, as recorded in the *Pearl of Great Price,* that the ancients had a very comprehensive understanding of the heavenly bodies; therefore, God was able to reveal many truths to them through the stars.[14] Doubtless the original source of the sign of a new star was the revelations of God to His holy prophets.

[11] Mosiah 16:9.
[12] Graves, *op. cit.,* p. 58.
[13] Chalcidus, *Comments on the Times of Plato,* cited in Graves, *op. cit.,* p. 37.
[14] Abraham 3:1-22.

As time passed, pagan traditions attached this sign to their heroes and savior-gods.

ZOROASTER'S PROPHESY AND THE WISE MEN

As early as Nephi's time, Zoroaster, the Persian prophet, is reputed to have predicted that a new star should appear in the heavens as a sign of the birth of the Savior of the world. In the words of this ancient religious teacher:

A virgin should conceive and bear a son, and a star would appear blazing at midday to signalize the occurrence. "When you behold the star," said he to his followers, "follow it whithersoever it leads you. Adore the mysterious child, offering him gifts with profound humility. He is indeed the Almighty Lord, which created the heavens. He is indeed your Lord and everlasting King."[15]

The story told in the gospel of Matthew of the wise men (Magi) from the east who visited Palestine at the time of the birth of Jesus is evidence that the sign of a new star had been given to those of a foreign land. These Magi were probably recipients of Zoroaster's prophecy or they had been informed through some other divine source of that particular sign's being given to announce the birth of the Christ-child. Upon their arrival in Jerusalem, they asked King Herod: "Where is he that is born King of the Jews? *for we have seen his star in the east and are come to worship him.*"[16] They were instructed to go to Bethlehem, for the prophets had predicted that there the Messiah, the Son of God, would be born.[17] When they arrived at Bethlehem "they saw the young child with Mary, his mother, and fell down, and worshiped him, and when they had opened their treasures, they presented unto him gifts; gold, frankincense and myrrh."[18] Thus the sign of a new star which had been revealed to the prophets guided the humble seekers to the home of the new-born King of kings; and, as Zoroaster had instructed, they did "adore the mysterious child, offering him gifts with profound humility." This baby was the one divine Savior-God.

CONCLUSIONS

The time will come when everyone who worshiped a savior-god other than Jesus the Christ will learn that the

---

[15] Faber, *History of Idolatry*, vol. 2, p. 92.
[16] Matthew 2:2, 11.
[17] Micah 5:2; Matthew 2:4-7.
[18] Matthew 2:2, 11.

creed he followed contained only a semblance of the divine truths revealed through the holy prophets of God. He will realize that his savior-god was but a counterfeit of the true Messiah. But a vestige of truth from a common source connects him and all other searchers for life eternal with that original Messianic revelation given to Adam, the first man, in accordance with the decree of God, that Gospel truths "should be in the world until the end thereof."[19] He will also learn that in order to gain eternal life in the celestial glory of God he must become a member and live the Gospel principles and ordinances of the true Church of the Master—which is the Church of Jesus Christ of Latter-day Saints, restored to earth through divine revelations to the Prophet Joseph Smith.

SUPPLEMENTARY READINGS—CHAPTER 23

1. *Bible*: Matthew 2:1-23; 27:33-66; 28:1-20; Acts 7:54-60; 9:1-20.
2. *Book of Mormon*: Helaman 14:1-8, 20-28; 3 Nephi 1:8-21; 8:3-25; 9:1-22; 11:1-17ff.
3. *Doctrine and Covenants* 76:20-24.
4. *Pearl of Great Price*: "The First Vision."
5. James E. Talmage, *Jesus the Christ*, pp. 1-800.

---

[19] Moses 5:59.

Chapter 24.

JESUS AND THE SORROWS OF HUMANITY

INTRODUCTORY STATEMENT

The work that Jesus performed as the Savior of the world involved a number of different phases, but space will permit the discussion of only a few of the major points, one being the problem of suffering. Human suffering is as old and universal as mankind, and practically every religion has attempted to answer some of the problems growing out of the sorrows of humanity. Common to all religions is the belief that their savior-gods were required to suffer intensely in order that through their sacrifice the sorrows and suffering of mankind might be alleviated. In chapter twenty-two it was shown that intense suffering, a violent death, and a triumphant resurrection were beliefs connected with most of the pagan savior-gods. The purpose of this lesson is to show that such concepts had their origin in the revelations to the prophets that Jesus Christ would suffer, die, and be resurrected. The problem will be discussed, however, primarily from the standpoint of what actually happened in Jesus' life. An effort will be made to show that Jesus Christ was the true Messiah and answered the needs of humanity for a savior-god, who suffered and who by so doing helped all human beings in times of sorrow.

PROBLEM OF HUMAN SUFFERING

Jesus Christ, through His suffering and His teachings, put meaning into the sorrow and distress of humanity and marked out the course whereby mankind may gain immortality and eternal life.

Before the birth of the Savior the world was full of superstition, doubt, disease, distress, fear, sorrow and suffering. Where was man to go to receive comfort? Almost

every avenue in human experience was searched in order
to find comfort for sorrowing humanity. Sages arose in various countries and tried to give hope to man by answering
the question: "Why do men suffer—the righteous as well
as the wicked?" Some masterful Hebrew prophet skill-
fully presented numerous truths relative to the universal
problem of human suffering when he told in a dramatic
poem the experiences of God's righteous servant Job.

MORTAL DEVELOPMENT OF JESUS

The problem remained unsolved. The world waited
to learn the purpose of suffering until there was born a
babe in a little town in Palestine, who was taught by good
Jewish parents to love his associates and to care for those in
distress. At His birth angels from heaven sang, "Glory
to God in the highest, and on earth peace, good will toward
men"; for this was the babe who had been selected before
man was placed on earth to be the Savior, the Christ, the
Redeemer of mankind. He was the one "like unto God
the Father" who stood in the council of the Gods and volunteered to be the Savior of the world and to do at all times
the will of the Father. He was the one to whose coming
all the holy prophets since Adam's time had looked forward, and many of them had predicted the signs of His
advent. No wonder heaven and earth joined in their ex-
pressions of joy and praise at His birth. Yet the great
Augustus Caesar in Rome, the famous world's capital, did
not realize that in the hilly country of Palestine was at
that time a lowly Nazarene who was destined to mark out
the course whereby millions would find comfort in their
suffering. Nor did he know that this Christ-child would,
through His life and teachings, point out to mankind the
course to follow in order to have joy in this life and exaltation in the Kingdom of God, even eternal life and a similar glory to that enjoyed by our Heavenly Parents.

Jesus had no easy road to follow. At a very early
age He was the main support of a widowed mother, four
brothers, and at least two sisters.[1] Day by day He worked
in His carpenter shop to eke out an existence for His de-
pendents. Thus as an artisan He belongs to the great army

---

[1] Mark 6:3.

of world workers, which links Him in sympathy with all working people.

This boy's mind was ever alert. While He swung the adz in His carpenter shop He saw and felt the griefs of His associates. He heard the cry of the suffering multitudes. The pains of humanity became His pains, its joys His joys. Into His life He wove the deepest feelings for mankind.

Just how widely the information of Jesus being the long-looked-for Messiah was scattered throughout Nazareth and other sections of Galilee during His childhood is not definitely known, but the evidence presented in the New Testament, although scanty, seems to indicate that Mary very wisely kept all such information within the limits of the family circle while she prudently taught the Christ-child those things that would prepare Him for His divine mission. In fact, the reports in the scriptures of the birth of Jesus, the visitation of the angels to the shepherds, followed by the shepherds' coming to the stable in Bethlehem to see the holy child, are summarized in this significant remark: "But Mary kept all of these things and pondered them in her heart."[2] Even the unusual events which occurred at the Jerusalem temple when the Savior was 12 years old are reported as follows: "But his mother kept all these sayings in her heart."[3] Thus unhampered by public prejudice and in a natural way Jesus was permitted to grow and develop just as any other boy develops—learning to do by doing. The same laws we must obey the Master Himself obeyed, since God has declared that obedience to all the laws is required of him who "fulfills all righteousness."[4]

The only statement that the holy scriptures make regarding Jesus' life from the time He was 12 until He became a man definitely proclaim that He grew not only physically, but also mentally and spiritually. Following are the exact words given in the scriptures: "Jesus increased in wisdom and stature, and in favour with God and man."[5] Gradual growth and development, then, mark

[2] Luke 2:19.
[3] Luke 2:51.
[4] Matthew 3:15.
[5] Luke 2:40.

the story of His life, as recorded in the New Testament, until He was 30 years old.

In Section 93 of the *Doctrine and Covenants* a description is given of Christ's pre-mortal, mortal and post-mortal life. The portion of that revelation which deals with His experiences in mortality seems to sustain the thesis of a gradual growth and unfolding of His personality. To quote:

He [Jesus] received not of the fullness at the first, but received grace for grace; and he received not of the fullness at the first, but continued from grace to grace, until he received a fullness.[6]

John continued the description of Jesus' natural development up to the occasion of His baptism and the announcement of His Messiahship by the Eternal Father. Then John said:

And I, John, bear record that he received a fullness of the glory of the Father; And he received all power, both in heaven and on earth, and the glory of the Father was with him, for he dwelt in him.[7]

Summary Statement

By way of summary, then, this Man of Galilee went through the school of life in a natural way, learning and developing by work and obedience and through spiritual contacts with heavenly forces. Finally such a complete unfolding of character and personality—and of His pre-mortal development and glory—took place that He became the most perfect type of manhood that has ever existed in this world. God was here on earth dwelling among mortals. In such perfect likeness was He to the Father that He was able to say, "Those who have seen me have seen my Father." Since Jesus was a humanized Savior-God as well as a divine being, He was in a position to establish a pattern of life which mortals could, through diligence, attain. If the Savior had been entirely immortal, then mortals would feel that there would be no need of trying to follow His pattern of life, since such perfection could not be attained by a mortal.

Jesus the True Messiah

One day Jesus went down to the Jordan River, where an unusual man was teaching the doctrine of repentance and baptism. When He made application for baptism with

---

[6] *Doctrine and Covenants* 93:12-13.
[7] *Ibid.*, 93:1-20.

this prophet and teacher, "John forbad him, saying, 'I have need to be baptized of thee and comest thou to me?' "[8] But Jesus understood that even He, the Savior, must obey all laws if He received all blessings;[9] and so He replied: "Suffer it to be so now: for thus it becometh us to fulfill all righteousness."[10]   Then John immersed the Master in the water.

And Jesus, when he was baptized, went up straightway out of the water: and, lo, the heavens were opened unto him, and he saw the Spirit of God descending like a dove, and lighting upon him: And lo, a voice from heaven, saying: "This is my beloved Son, in whom I am well pleased!"[11]

John the Baptist testified that the descending of the Spirit of God like a dove on Jesus was a special sign given to him to let him know the Messiah. To quote:

The next day John seeth Jesus coming unto him, and saith, "Behold the Lamb of God, which taketh away the sin of the world. This is he of whom I said, 'After me cometh a man which is preferred before me'; for he was before me. And I knew him not: but that he should be made manifest to Israel, therefore am I come baptizing with water."

And John bare record, saying, "I saw the Spirit descending from heaven like a dove, and it abode upon him. And I knew him not; but he that sent me to baptize with water, the same said unto me, 'Upon whom thou shalt see the Spirit descending, and remaining on him, the same is he which baptizeth with the Holy Ghost.' And I saw, and bare record that this is the Son of God."[12]

JESUS AND THE JEWISH MESSIANIC HOPE

In all history no other announcement had the significance of this one by the Father that He, Jesus of Nazareth, was His Only Begotten Son—the long-looked-for Messiah or Christ, the Savior of the World. What! He, Jesus, the Son, the Messiah? Imagine the problems that immediately presented themselves to Him. How was He to proceed in order to fulfill the Jewish Messianic hope? The Jews were looking for a temporal ruler who would sit upon a throne in power and glory and make all other nations subject to Him and the Jewish nation. Their Messianic hope at that time consisted of a mixture of the prophecies which related to Jesus' first coming and those of His second coming, plus some erroneous hopes. Such Hebrew

---

[8] Matthew 3:14.
[9] *Doctrine and Covenants* 130:20-22; 132:5.
[10] Matthew 3:15.
[11] *Ibid.*, 3:16-17; *Doctrine and Covenants* 93:15; Mark 1:10-11.
[12] John 1:29-34.

prophecies as the following played a major role in their Messianic hope:

> For unto us a child is born, unto us a son is given: and the government shall be upon his shoulder. . . . Of the increase of his government and peace there shall be no end, upon the throne of David, and upon his kingdom, to order it, and to establish it with judgment and with justice from henceforth and forever. The zeal of the Lord of hosts will perform this.[13]

> And there was given him dominion, and glory and a kingdom, that all people, nations, and languages should serve him; his dominion is an everlasting dominion, which shall not pass away, and his kingdom that which shall not be destroyed.

To sit upon a throne and rule the Jewish nation and subject peoples might have been at first thought a pleasing idea. Yet, Jesus immediately realized that His whole development and training were directly opposed to such a career. Never in His life had He dreamed of controlling armies and men. To be clad in fine linen, dyed with the purple of Syrian vats, shod with the gold of Ophir, were not in accord with His inherent tastes. How could He fulfill the Jewish Messianic hope? There must be some course of action that the Messiah could follow other than that prevailing among the Jews.

JESUS CHOOSES HIS COURSE

Jesus made his way to the wilderness. For forty days and forty nights He stayed there fasting, meditating, and praying. One course would bring Him honor, power, gold and silver, houses and lands, pomp and armies, worldly glory and praise of men. The other would lead Him to the homes of the poor, the needy and sick, the lowly and despised, and finally to persecution and to Calvary.

Having completely withstood the alluring temptations of the devil and having been ministered to by angels, Christ came forth from the wilderness victorious. He knew that His course lay not with armies, powers and kingdoms, but with the afflicted and despised. He was to taste of life's bitterness. He was to stoop below all in order that He might rise above all. In the synagogue at Nazareth, shortly after returning from the wilderness, He announced His course by reading the following quotations from Isaiah:

---

[13] Isaiah 9:6-7; 15:5.

The Spirit of the Lord is upon me, because he hath anointed me to preach the Gospel to the poor; he hath sent me to heal the broken-hearted, to preach deliverance to the captives, and recovering of sight to the blind, to set at liberty them that are bruised, to preach the acceptable year of the Lord.[14]

Was He prepared for this life of sorrow and to be a great teacher? No other man by consistent, natural development, by obedience to law, by suffering and walking the path of mortals, has so completely prepared himself for such a work as had this Nazarene, now proclaimed Jesus the Christ, the Son of the true and living God. So thoroughly and completely had been His training, so rationally had He followed the laws of the creation—the eternal plan of salvation—that He stood as a perfect prototype of God the Father. And coupled with all this was His glorious pre-mortal development and His earthly divinity by being the Only Begotten Son. Here was a man who could naturally fit Himself into the very hearts and lives of millions of people—yes, all humanity.

Hope Given to Suffering Humanity

This Man-God was now Master of the proper course to follow. He was able to give moral content to the sorrows and perplexities of humanity better than could any other teacher who had ever lived. He put into suffering a meaning, a purpose, through His promises of rewards for diligent efforts and a glorious exaltation in His Father's kingdom for those who obeyed the Gospel teachings. In fact, no other message ever given has contained the hope, the encouragement, and the light of true direction that are found in the Sermon on the Mount and in Jesus' other teachings. Christ gave to the world not only a satisfying message for its sorrows by His teachings; but both by example and precept He marked out a course of self-sacrifice and of detachment from the vanities of the world that was not rivaled by any of the contemporary religions. The Master declared:

If a man wishes to come after me, let him deny himself, and let him take up his cross and follow me. Whoever wishes to save his life shall destroy it, but whosoever shall lose his life for my sake and the Gospel's, shall save it. For what shall a man be profited if he shall gain

---
[14] Luke 4:18-19; Isaiah 61:1-3.

the whole world and loseth his soul?[15] Blessed are they that mourn: for they shall be comforted.[16]

He also said:

Come unto me, all ye that labor and are heavy laden, and I will give you rest. Take my yoke upon you and learn of me; for I am meek and lowly in heart; and ye shall find rest unto your soul. For my yoke is easy, and my burden is light.[17]

What a hopeless place the world was for millions before Christ attached such a meaning to sorrow! Almost any religious teacher can succeed in times of joy and happiness. But in times of sorrow, if he can offer no satisfying message, his teachings are doomed to decay. Humanity will seek consolation elsewhere. Christ, the Lord and Master of life eternal, touched the hearts of millions by His teachings, and by His actions established serenity in suffering that could not fail to make His plan of salvation universal. Here was a Savior that appealed to the masses —a really divine human, a suffering God. Many a Christian has taken hope when he was burdened with grief by merely thinking of the supreme example set by Jesus Christ.

JESUS A SUFFERING SAVIOR

Indeed, a distinctive phase of Christ's life is that of suffering and grief. The Prophet Isaiah described Him aptly:

He is despised, and rejected of men; a man of sorrows and acquainted with grief: and we hid as it were our faces from him; he was despised, and we esteemed him not. Surely he hath borne our griefs, and carried our sorrows: yet we did esteem him stricken, smitten of God, and afflicted. But he was wounded for our transgressions, he was bruised for our iniquities: the chastisement of our peace was upon him, and with his stripes we are healed. . . . He was oppressed, and he was afflicted, yet he opened not his mouth: he is brought as a lamb to the slaughter, and as a sheep before her shearers is dumb, so he openeth not his mouth. . . . He was cut off out of the land of the living: for the transgression of my people was he stricken. And he made his grave with the wicked, and with the rich in his death; because he had done no violence, neither was any deceit in his mouth.[18]

His bitter tears and agony in Gethsemane and His intense pain on Calvary were so severe that no other mortal could have borne them. His mental and spiritual suffering were so severe that while He was praying to the

---

[15] Matthew 16:24-26.
[16] Ibid., 5:4.
[17] Ibid., 11:28-30.
[18] Isaiah 53:1-12.

Father in the garden of Gethsemane "His sweat became as it were great drops of blood falling down upon the ground."[19]

This intense suffering in Gethsemane can be accounted for by the fact that Christ was going through His last great contest with Lucifer, the son of the morning.[20] In some mystical way He was taking upon Himself the sins of the world and preparing for victory over that last great enemy—death and the grave. The Son of Man revealed to the Prophet Joseph Smith the following facts:

For, behold, the Lord your Redeemer suffered death in the flesh; wherefore he suffered the pain of all men, that all men might repent and come unto him. And he hath risen again from the dead, that he might bring all men unto him, on conditions of repentance.[21]

THE DIVINE SAVIOR-GOD

At the time Christ died on Calvary the world was in search of a symbol and a savior-god who could feel its agony and know its distress. The pagan religions—especially the Mystery Religions—tried to picture their deities as humanized, sympathetic gods, but their teachings were doomed to failure, because their deities were merely myths. Jesus supplied the need for a suffering God by being crucified for the sins of the world.

In contrast to the pagan savior-gods, the Man of Galilee was a real historical character. He was a perfect man and was required to suffer greatly; therefore, those who are not perfect can take consolation when they are called upon to suffer even if they do not know all of the reasons why. But we do know that there was a purpose in Jesus' excessive suffering. He was to become the Judge, the Ruler, and Lord of this earth. By no method other than by passing through the experiences of life could He be trained so thoroughly for the work of a sympathetic, loving, impartial judge. Christ, in order to gain a fullness of joy and exaltation, must partake of the experiences of this life—both the bitter and the sweet. He was the Son of God, "yet he learned obedience by the things he suffered."[22]

---

[19] Luke 22:44; *Doctrine and Covenants* 19:16-18; Mosiah 3:7.
[20] Isaiah 14:12.
[21] *Doctrine and Covenants* 18:11-12.
[22] Hebrews 5:8-9.

In no other way could He have become the author of eternal salvation unto all who would obey His teachings.

CHRIST ASSURES MAN OF IMMORTALITY

The Savior not only taught a satisfying theology and suffered and died, but He rose from the grave and thereby became the "first fruits of the resurrection." He arose into a glorious immortality.[23] His was a victory over death and sin. Through this victory over the grave, He assured all men a similar triumph—a promise of immortality—and, upon condition of obedience to the Gospel, eternal life. Nothing within the range of human experience has had such a tremendous effect upon friends of the deceased as has the assurance of immortality.[24] Tears have been wiped away and aching hearts have been healed through the assurance the Master gave us that all shall live again and associate with friends and loved ones eternally. The assurance of immortality is the most potent force in religious history. A complete understanding of sorrow and healing of griefs of humanity could never have been realized just through the life and death of Jesus of Nazareth, but the final essential was resurrection. Herein lies the power and beauty of the Christian message. A God who had power over death—who assured men of immortality—was the only Savior-God who could give meaning to the sorrows of humanity. This was accomplished by Jesus Christ and it marks the climax of the atonement.

---

[23] 1 Corinthians 15:1-58; Matthew 28:1-20; Mark 16:1-20; Luke 24:1-53; John 20; 21; 3 Nephi Chapters 9-28; "The First Vision."
[24] Joseph Fielding Smith (Compiler), *"Teachings of the Prophet Joseph Smith,"* pp. 342-376.

Chapter 25.

ATONEMENT THROUGH SACRIFICE

INTRODUCTORY STATEMENT

The use of blood as a means to extricate one from sin and also the belief that blood is charged with life-giving qualities has played a dominant role in religious history, especially prior to the advent of Jesus Christ. In fact, in Adam's day men believed that the shedding of blood cleansed humanity from sin and was effective in bringing about the atonement. The origin of such beliefs is a revelation regarding the atonement given by the Lord to the first mortal being. God declared to all humanity through this holy prophet, Father Adam: "Ye must be born again into the kingdom of heaven, of water, and of spirit, and *be cleansed by the blood of mine Only Begotten,* that ye might be sanctified from all sin . . . [for] by the blood ye are sanctified."[1]

In Biblical days the doctrine was widely taught that the life of an individual or of an animal was in its blood. In the days of Noah, God gave the following commandment: "But flesh with the life thereof, which is the blood thereof, shall ye not eat."[2] This law was reiterated from generation to generation in ancient Israel.[3] The reason why it became necessary for the Lord to warn His people from age to age against the eating and drinking of blood was because this abomination was so prevalently practiced among the numerous pagan groups. They had adulterated the true doctrine of the atoning blood of Jesus Christ and had applied it in a number of forms of blood-sanctifying rites. The prophets of God worked hard to save the children of Israel from these pagan beliefs and practices, yet at times the people partook of them.

---

[1] Moses 6:58-59.
[2] Genesis 9:4.
[3] Leviticus 17:10-16; 19:26; Deuteronomy 12:16, 23; 1 Samuel 14:32-33; Acts 15:20, 29.

The purpose, therefore, of this and the following chapter will be to show that the numerous beliefs held throughout history relative to atonement, through the shedding of blood and the eating and drinking of blood have a definite relationship to the shedding of Jesus' blood for the sins of the world. They all root in that divine doctrine which was revealed to man from the beginning. Although there are a number of vital phases of the Gospel doctrine of atonement, we shall center our attention on the various concepts held relative to the efficacy and use of blood in atoning for the sins of mankind.

The Fall and the Atonement

The atoning blood of the Man of Galilee washes away the sins of all mortals who—through faith, repentance, and baptism, and through living every other Gospel principle to the best of their ability—have done everything within their power to bring about their own redemption. In the words of a Nephite prophet:

According to the great plan of the Eternal God, there must be an atonement made, or else all mankind must unavoidably perish. . . . For it is expedient that there should be a great and last sacrifice; yea, not a sacrifice of man, neither of beast, neither of any manner of fowl; for it shall not be a human sacrifice; but it must be an infinite and eternal sacrifice.

Now there is not any man that can sacrifice his own blood which will atone for the sins of another. . . . Therefore, there can be nothing which is short of an infinite atonement which will suffice for the sins of the world.[4]

The fact that man is mortal — spiritually dead and banished from the presence of his Heavenly Parents—necessitated the sacrifice of a Son who was completely pure and holy, one endowed with divine powers to the extent that He could break the bands of death and put into effect the law of universal resurrection.

The doctrine of atonement is based upon the concept known in the scriptures as the fall. When placed upon the earth, Adam and Eve died a spiritual death, or, in other words, a veil was drawn over their minds which prevented them from remembering their pre-existence and the Gospel of Jesus Christ.[5]

---

[4] Alma 34:9-12.
[5] Alma 12:20-37; 42:2-10; 2 Nephi 2:1-30; 9:1-10.

The very fact that Adam and Eve and all of their descendants were mortals living in a temporal world cut them off from the presence of God, who is living in a spiritual, celestial world. The fall interpreted in this sense includes people other than just Adam and Eve. Every child of God that leaves his heavenly abode through birth into mortality is cut off from the presence of the Lord; therefore, he becomes spiritually dead and also subject to a temporal death.

JESUS AND THE ATONEMENT

Under the conditions of mortality and unaided by divine power or the Divine Being, men did not have sufficient knowledge or power to bring themselves back into the presence of their Creator. As has been previously pointed out, the Heavenly Father, knowing fully the conditions of mortality, devised a plan for the redemption of His children even before He placed them upon the earth.[6] A Savior, a Redeemer, "One like unto God himself," was chosen from among the spirit children, and foreordained to come into mortality fully endowed with divine powers requisite for bringing about the atonement of mankind. The Master, the Lord of heaven and earth, was the one chosen.

He, Jesus Christ, being literally the Only Begotten Son of God, was endowed with a double portion of divine attributes. He received a comparable proportion of divinity in the spirit world that we received through being spirit children of God, and He was also the offspring of the Eternal Father in mortality—thus He possessed a double portion of God's power. Therefore, it was He who was chosen to die and shed His blood that we might live. To quote the *Doctrine and Covenants: "Jesus, the mediator of the new covenant . . . wrought out this perfect atonement through the shedding of his own blood."*[7]

No individual other than the Nazarene who has ever lived in this world possessed the innate power to perform such an "infinite and eternal sacrifice," since He was the only one among the earth's inhabitants who had an immortal Father. These glorious Gospel truths were understood throughout the various dispensations. The Nephites taught

[6] Alma 12:25, 29-30.
[7] *Doctrine and Covenants* 76:69.

this doctrine extensively. In the words of Amulek to the inhabitants of Ammonihah:

I do know that Christ shall come among the children of men, to take upon him the transgressions of his people, and that he shall atone for the sins of the world; for the Lord God hath spoken it. . . . The righteous shall sit down in the kingdom, to go no more out; *but their garments shall be made white through the blood of the Lamb.*[8]

ATONEMENT DOCTRINE REVEALED

Shortly after Adam and Eve were banished from the Garden of Eden the Lord "saw that it was expedient that men should know concerning the things whereof he had appointed unto them; therefore he sent angels to converse with them. . . . [Also] God conversed with men, and made known unto them the plan of redemption, which had been prepared from the foundation of the world."[9] Thus, through divers ways, the Eternal Father and His Only Begotten Son taught mortals the Gospel of Jesus Christ, instructing them to hearken unto the voice of the Son of God, who was to offer Himself freely as a sacrifice for mankind.

But men were informed that only they who repented, received baptism and confirmation, and faithfully obeyed the Gospel teachings, had a positive and full claim on the sanctifying and atoning blood of the Master. The Lord in definite terms told Father Adam, *"This is the plan of salvation unto all men, through the blood of mine Only Begotten, who shall come in the meridian of time."*[10]

Therefore, whenever the true Gospel plan has been understood by mortals, the belief has been held that the Savior —the Only Begotten Son of God—should willingly sacrifice His life and shed His blood to rescue man from sin and the grave. As a result of His suffering and death, and through His power of Godhood, which is life eternal, all mortals will eventually be resurrected—Jesus Himself being the "first fruits." While living in mortality, the Nazarene declared:

I am the resurrection and the life: he that believeth in me, though he were dead, yet shall he live: And whosoever liveth and believeth in me shall never die.[11]

---

[8] Alma 34:1-16, 36.
[9] *Ibid.*, 12:28-30.
[10] Moses 6:57-67; 5:57.
[11] John 11:25-26.

When you have lifted up the Son of Man, then shall ye know that I am he, and that I do nothing of myself; but as my Father hath taught me, I speak these things.[12]

THE LAW OF SACRIFICE

In order for mankind to remember constantly the great atoning sacrifice of the Master, God gave to Adam and his posterity the law of sacrifice, which law was observed until the coming of the Son of Man in the flesh.[13] At His advent, however, sacrifice was replaced by sacrament.

An explanation of the true meaning of sacrifice came to Adam one day when he was offering unto the Lord the firstlings of his flocks. He was informed by an angel:

This thing is a similitude of the sacrifice of the Only Begotten of the Father, which is full of grace and truth. Wherefore, thou shalt do all that thou doest in the name of the Son, and thou shalt repent and call upon God in the name of the Son for evermore.[14]

Thus in the very beginning the offering of the sacrificial animal was regarded by Adam and his successors as an act symbolical of the sacrifice of the Lamb of God. The blood of the animal had no efficacious powers.

THE HEBREWS' PRACTICE OF SACRIFICE

The Old Testament is rather replete with descriptions of sacrifices as carried on by Moses and his Israelite successors preceding the advent of Christ. Most of the time the blood of the animal-victim was sprinkled on the altar;[15] however, in connection with certain rites, it was sprinkled on the worshipers.[16]

To what extent the Hebrews believed that blood contained potent attributes for cleansing them from sin is not made exactly clear in much of the Old Testament. The evidence therein seems to indicate that at certain times in their history at least some of the people attributed a considerable amount of saving grace to blood.[17] That was especially true during the eighth and seventh centuries B.C., when, due to pagan influences, many of the priests and laity had a warped understanding of the Gospel. However,

---

[12] *Ibid.*, 8:28-29.
[13] Moses 5:5-9; 6:56; 8 Nephi 9:15-22.
[14] Moses, *op. cit.*
[15] Leviticus 3:8, 13; 4:17-18; 7:2; 8:15.
[16] *Ibid.*, 8:30; Exodus 24:5-8; Hebrews 9:18-21.
[17] Leviticus 16:14-15; Exodus 12:7-30.

182 THE GOSPEL THROUGH THE AGES

several of Israel's great prophets firmly maintained that the sacrifice of animals was merely symbolical of the atoning sacrifice of Jesus—the blood of the animal-victim being shed in similitude of the "blood of the Lamb of God slain from the foundation of the world." In violent protest to those Jewish priests who attached too much saving effect to the sacrifices and neglected the ethical aspects of true religion, Amos (speaking for the Lord) said:

I hate, I despise your feasts, and I will take no delight in your solemn assemblies. Yea, though ye offer me your burnt offerings and meal-offerings, I will not accept them; neither will I regard the peace-offerings of your fat beasts. Take thou away from me the noise of thy songs; for I will not hear the melody of thy viols.

But let justice roll down as waters, and righteousness as a mighty stream.[18]

In the "Golden Text" of the Old Testament, Micah made a similar protest.[19] Hosea, the prophet of love, acting as mouthpiece for God, also said: "For I desire goodness, and not sacrifice; and the knowledge of God more than burnt offerings."[20]

SHEDDING OF JESUS' BLOOD

The night preceding His crucifixion, Jesus Christ willingly suffered so intensely that "blood cometh from every pore, so great [was] . . . his anguish for the wickedness and the abominations of his people."[21] "In some manner, actual and terribly real, though to man incomprehensible, the Savior took upon Himself the burden of the sins of mankind from Adam to the end of the world."[22]

Why was it necessary for the Savior to shed His blood? His own answer to this interrogation is the best that could be given. Quoting His words to the Prophet Joseph Smith:

For behold, I, God, have suffered these things for all, that they might not suffer if they would repent. But if they would not repent, they must suffer even as I, which suffering caused myself, even God, the greatest of all, to tremble because of pain, and to bleed at every pore.[23]

Further light was thrown upon this subject in a pertinent statement made by the Lord to Brigham Young rel-

[18] Amos 5:21-24, 4:4f.
[19] Micah 6:1-8; Jeremiah 6:19-21; 7:21-24.
[20] Hosea 6:6; Isaiah 58:1-7.
[21] Mosiah 3:7.
[22] James E. Talmage, *Jesus the Christ*, p. 613.
[23] *Doctrine and Covenants* 19:16-18; Luke 22:39-44; Mosiah 3:7.

ative to the martyrdom of the Prophet Joseph Smith. "It was needful that he should seal his testimony with his blood, that he might be honored, and the wicked might be condemned."[24]

John the Revelator understood the doctrine of atonement through sacrifice in Jesus and rejoiced in its expiating grace. He wrote regarding the Man of Galilee:

And they sang a new song, saying, "Thou art worthy to take the book, and to open the seals thereof: for thou wast slain, and hast redeemed us to God by thy blood out of every kindred, and tongue, and people, and nation; and hast made us unto our God kings and priests: and we shall reign on the earth."[25]

Jesus, therefore, preceding crucifixion, had His last great struggle, while in mortality, with Satan and with death and came forth victorious. As the Father had life in Himself, so had the Son. Thus through the death of the Master an expiatory sacrifice was offered. Justice was satisfied, the will of God fulfilled, and the Son became the Master of life eternal. "For as in Adam all die, even so in Christ shall all be made alive."[26] Through the power of light and life which was in Him, all men shall be resurrected. Thus in Gethsemane and at Golgotha the blood of the Lamb of God was shed in order that we might live.[27]

EFFICACY OF JESUS' SACRIFICE

It may be true that some of the Hebrew worshipers over-estimated the efficacy of animal blood in atoning for sin, but when the Man of Galilee re-established the Gospel truths upon the earth in the meridian of time, His followers clearly understood that it was impossible for animal blood to free them from guilt. They believed (as Adam had earlier) that sacrifice was merely symbolical of the infinite and eternal sacrifice of the Master. The law of Moses was looked upon as being "a schoolmaster to bring them unto Christ." In the words of the writer of Hebrews:

It is impossible that the blood of bulls and goats should take away sin, . . . [yet] according to the law, I may almost say, all things are cleansed with blood, and apart from shedding of blood there is no redemption. . . .

[24] *Doctrine and Covenants* 136:39b.
[25] Revelation 5:9-10.
[26] 1 Corinthians 15:21-22.
[27] John Taylor, *Mediation and Atonement*, pp. 1-205; Talmage, *op. cit.*, pp. 17-31, 610-614; Talmage, *Articles of Faith*, pp. 76-97.

But Christ . . . through his own blood, entered in once for all into the holy place, having obtained eternal redemption. . . . We have been sanctified through the offering of the body of Jesus Christ, once for all . . . having therefore, brethren, boldness to enter into the holy place by the blood of Jesus.[28]

The same doctrine was taught by the writer of First Peter:

Ye know that ye were not redeemed with corruptible things . . . but with the precious blood of Christ, as of a lamb without blemish and without spot: who verily was foreordained before the foundation of the world.[29]

John the Revelator contributed the thought that Lucifer and his followers were overcome "by the blood of the Lamb . . . slain from the foundation of the world."[30]

---

[28] Hebrews 9:11-28; 10:1-31; Romans 3:21-27; Ephesians 1:7.
[29] 1 Peter 1:18-21.
[30] Revelation 12:11; 13:8.

Chapter 26.

PAGAN BELIEFS OF ATONEMENT THROUGH SACRIFICE

INTRODUCTORY STATEMENT

As was pointed out in the last lesson, the doctrine of atonement through sacrifice relative to the sacrifice of Jesus and the shedding of His blood is pertinent in the plan of salvation. This doctrine—first revealed to Father Adam and later to the holy prophets during the various Gospel dispensations—found its way outward throughout the world and downward through the ages as a golden thread of truth. As it was disseminated outward from the original source, alterations from the true concept occurred. Therefore, a great variety of beliefs—some true and others false—have been held relative to the efficacy of sacrifice and of blood in cleansing man from sin and in helping to assure him immortal and eternal life. However, these various concepts and practices are rooted in the Messianic revelations given to the first mortal and to the other holy prophets of the Lord. They come from the common source of truth, which is the Gospel of Jesus Christ.

In this chapter the beliefs and practices of paganism wherein the worshipers ate and drank blood and were baptized in it, and shed the blood of human beings as well as that of animals for the purpose of atonement and bringing about their salvation, will be presented. The purpose will be to show that those pagan rites are adulterated forms of the true Gospel doctrine of atonement and shedding of the blood of Jesus Christ. Valid historical evidence will be given.

PAGAN CONCEPTS OF ATONEMENT

At the time Christianity was spreading throughout the world—yes, and from the date of the first apostasy from the true Gospel in the days of Adam to the final triumph

of Christianity over paganism in 392 A.D.—the majority
of the heathenistic religions attributed a pronounced saving efficacy to blood. Some cults, in order to utilize its
potent, life-giving qualities, washed or sprinkled their devotees with it.[1] Each one of the candidates who was being
initiated in the Eleusinian mysteries purified himself and a
sucking pig by immersion in the waters of the sea. Then
the pig was sacrificed and the blood sprinkled on the initiate.[2]

Some pagans even drank blood for the purpose of ef-
fecting a rebirth or regeneration. A part of the initiation
ceremony in the ancient Orphic religion was for the initiates
to eat the raw flesh and drink the blood of the sacrificial bull
in which they believed their god Zagreus to be ritualistically
incarnate. After once partaking of this "red and bleeding
feast" they henceforth abstained from eating meat.[3]

The worshipers of Dionysus, a pagan cult of
Paul's day, believed that their god, during the period
of their festivals, was temporarily resident in animals. The kind of animal in which Dionysus dwelt varied
according to locality. The people of a goat-raising district looked upon Dionysus as a goat and those of a cattle district as a bull. He was also pictured as a kid, a fawn,
or a deer.

All of the initiates participated in the devouring of
these animals. Firmicus Maternus, a writer of the early
Christian period, stated that at his time, in Crete the populace would "rend a living bull with their teeth, and they sim-
ulate madness of soul as they shriek through the secret places
of the forests with discordant clamors."[4] Euripides (480-
406 B.C.), one of the greatest Greek dramatists, wrote a
play entitled "The Bacchae," in which he described the practices in the Dionysian Mysteries. Part of his description
reads as follows:

> The joy of the red quick fountain,
> The flood of the hill-goat torn.
> (They) quaff the goat's delicious blood,
> A strange, a rich, a savage food.[5]

---

[1] Exodus 24:5-8; Harold Willoughby, *Pagan Regeneration*, pp. 45, 129-132.
[2] *Ibid.*, 36-67.
[3] *Ibid.*, 90-113.
[4] Firmicus Maternus, *De Errore Profanarum Religionum*, vi. 5, cited in *ibid.*, p. 76.
[5] Euripides, *Bacchae*, p. 140.

Euripides gives a vivid account of an attack of the female worshipers upon a herd of cattle. To quote:

Down swooped they then
Upon our pasturing kine with swordless hand,
Then had you seen your mother with her hands
Rend a deep uddered heifer bellowing loud:
And others tore the calves in crimson shreds.
Ribs had you seen and cloven hoofs far hurled
This way and that, and flakes of flesh that hung
And dripped all blood bedabbled, 'neath the pines.
Bulls chafing, lowering fiercely along the horn
Erewhile, were tripped and hurled upon the earth
Dragged down by countless clutching maiden hands.
More swiftly was the flesh that lapped their bones
Stripped, than you could have closed your kingly eyes.[6]

The point of significance in this barbaric ceremonial was that the worshipers believed that their god was present temporarily in the animal victim. In order for them to enter into a direct and realistic communion with him, they must devour and assimilate the god before he escaped. Especially was the warm blood of the animal sacred blood because it contained the divine life of Dionysus. In fact, the worshipers believed that dripping, raw, quivering flesh was where the divine life was to be found. They made haste, therefore, in drinking the blood and eating the flesh before the divinity resident therein had time to escape.

Just as Jesus' blood was shed for the atonement of mankind these ancient pagans believed that by eating the blood of their god, Dionysus (the animal victim), they, too, would receive divine grace and forgiveness for their sins.

Another altered form of the sacrifice of the Son of God —especially as interpreted by the ancient pagans—was that of human and animal sacrifices. The majority of those heathenistic religions offered sacrifices of victims ranging from their most beautiful youths and most perfect babies to that of divers animals. The concept underlying the practice was that the Divine Ruler required the shedding of blood to extricate man from sin and win for him heavenly grace. Therefore, they believed that on certain important occasions God could be appeased only through the sacrificing of their most perfect child. Pagan influences at certain

---
[6] *Ibid.*, p. 736.

times caused even God's chosen people, Israel, to offer their little children as an oblation for sin. Naturally such an apostate practice was strenuously opposed by the holy prophets.[7]

What was the origin of such a ghastly rite? It is probable that the offering of youths and maidens is an adoption of the ideas underlying the atonement of Jesus Christ. Just as the Eternal Father willingly gave His Only Begotten Son to expiate penitent mortals, so were pagans convinced that they must sacrifice their children to atone for their transgressions. Hence the true and original concept dates back to the first Messianic revelation given to Father Adam.

TAUROBOLIUM AND CRIOBOLIUM

Another very pertinent religious practice which claimed saving grace for the devotees comparable to the atonement of the Man of Galilee was that of *taurobolium* (bath in bull's blood), and its variant, *criobolium* (bath in ram's blood). The Great Mother Mysteries and Mithraism promised salvation to proselytes who cleansed themselves in the sacred blood of the bull or ram.

Prudentius, a Christian poet who is purported to have been an eyewitness to the rite, recorded a description of it.[8] His description of *taurobolium* gives us an understanding of how the pagans performed this rite during the second, third and fourth centuries A.D. Wearing a golden crown and with his body wreathed with flowers, the one being initiated descended into a trench which was covered with a platform of perforated planks. A magnificent bull, decorated with gold and flowers, was led on the platform and there stabbed to death with the consecrated spear. "It's hot reeking blood poured in torrents through the apertures, and was received with devout eagerness by the expectant worshiper" below.[9] He "receives the falling drops on his head, clothes and body. He leans backward to have his cheeks, his ears, his lips, and his nostrils wetted. He pours the liquid over his eyes and does not even spare his palate, for he mois-

[7] Ezekiel 20:30-31; 26; Leviticus 18:21; 20:2-5; 19:4-5; 2 Kings 17:17; 16:3; 21:1-17.
[8] Prudentius, *Peristephanon*, vol. 10, p. 1011ff, cited in Willoughby, *op. cit.,* 131.
[9] Edward Carpenter, *Pagan and Christian Creeds*, p. 43; S. Angus, *Mystery Religions and Christianity*, pp. 94-95.

tens his tongue with blood and drinks it eagerly";[10] so runs
the description given by an eyewitness.

After this baptism, the neophyte emerged drenched,
dripping, and scarlet from head to foot. He was greeted
by the spectators as one who "had been born again to a divine life for eternity." The bath in blood was "believed
to purify him from the sins and evils of his old life and make
him a new man, or rather a divinized human."[11]

There were many similarities between this pagan practice and the Christian's concept of baptism and atonement of
Christ. For example, the initiate's going down into the
trench and coming forth again very aptly symbolized death
and rebirth, and the efficacy attached to the blood of the
holy bull or ram was believed to have as much saving effect
as Christian baptism and the atonement of Jesus. In the
words of Dr. Samuel Dill:

In *taurobolium* there was developed a ritual in which, coarse and
materialistic as it was, paganism made, in however imperfect a form, its
nearest approach to the religion of the Cross.[12]

The fundamental concept in *taurobolium* and *criobolium* had a kinship to the divine revelation on baptism and
atonement as given to Adam, wherein the Lord said:

Ye must . . . be cleansed by blood, even the blood of mine Only
Begotten; that ye might be sanctified from all sin, and enjoy the words
of eternal life in this world, and eternal life in the world to come, even
immortal glory; for . . . by the blood ye are sanctified.[13]

"WASHED IN THE BLOOD OF THE LAMB"

J. M. Robertson came to the following conclusion:

In the procedure of *taurobolia and criobolia,* which grew very popular in the Roman world, we have the literal and original meaning of
that phrase "washed in the blood of the lamb"; the doctrine being that
resurrection and eternal life were secured by drenching or sprinkling
with the actual blood of a sacrificial bull or ram.[14]

It is true that in washing with ram's blood the pagans did put a very literal and realistic interpretation on
the foregoing phrase, but the evidence contained in the
Book of Mormon is positive to the effect that in *taurobolium*
and *criobolium* we do not find the origin of the statement

[10] Prudentius, *op. cit.*
[11] Willoughby, *op. cit.*, p. 131.
[12] Samuel Dill, *Roman Society From Nero to Marcus Aurelius*, p. 155.
[13] Moses 6:57-60.
[14] J. M. Robertson, *Pagan Christs*, p. 315.

"washed in the blood of the lamb." That phrase did not originate with either the pagans nor the Nephites. Both groups inherited it from an earlier source—from the doctrine of atonement instituted before man was placed upon the earth. In fact:

> Enoch saw the day of the coming of the Son of Man, even in the flesh; and his soul rejoiced, saying, "The righteous is lifted up, and the Lamb is slain from the foundation of the world."[15]

The *Book of Mormon* makes clear two important points, i. e., that the phrase "washed in the blood of the Lamb" is extremely old, and that the prophets who lived in ancient America understood its true meaning. The Jaredites who came to America shortly following the flood were familiar with it. Ether, their last prophet, predicted that a "New Jerusalem" would be built upon this the American continent, and those who should inhabit the Utopian city are "they whose garments are white through the blood of the Lamb."[16] According to the prophets, the Old Jerusalem should eventually undergo a transformation and also become a holy city filled with righteousness. At that time those who reside in that city are "they [who] have been washed in the blood of the Lamb."[17]

Another race of people who inhabited ancient America taught the same doctrine. Nephi (600 B.C.), in speaking of the redeemed, said: "Their garments are made white in his blood";[18] while Alma (nearly 500 years later) proclaimed the same concept.[19]

The foregoing phraseology, therefore, was merely figurative language, as the Nephites did not believe or teach that there would be a literal washing of human beings in Christ's blood. The meaning behind that phrase was that the people who, through faith, repentance, baptism, confirmation, and righteous living, merited celestial glory were the ones who were "washed in the blood of the Lamb." They are the ones who shall be found numbered in the membership of the Church of the Firstborn, and they shall dwell in the Kingdom of God as priests, kings and holy angels. In reference to the wicked, Alma declared:

---

[15] Moses 7:47; Revelation 5:6; 13:8.
[16] Ether 13:10-11.
[17] *Ibid.*
[18] 1 Nephi 12:10.
[19] Alma 5:21; 13:11.

I say unto you, ye will know at that day [Judgment day] that ye cannot be saved; for there can no man be saved except his garments are washed white; yea, his garments must be purified until they are cleansed from all stain, through the blood of him of whom it has been spoken by our fathers who should come to redeem his people from their sins.[20]

When the Master visited the Nephites following His resurrection, He confirmed Alma's doctrine in the following important remark, making clear how one can be washed in the blood of Lamb: "No unclean thing can enter into his kingdom; therefore nothing entereth into his rest, save it be those who have washed their garments in my blood, because of their faith, and the repentance of all their sins, and their faithfulness unto the end."[21]

Therefore, in conclusion it is very evident that the basis of the ancient practice of offering sacrifices—both of animals and of human beings—and that of all types of blood atonement doctrines and practices was the infinite and eternal sacrifice and the shedding of the blood of the Only Begotten Son of God, who was indeed the Christ and the one true Savior of the world.

---

[20] Ibid.
[21] 3 Nephi 27:18-27; Doctrine and Covenants 76:69.

Chapter 27.

THE TRUE ORDINANCE OF BAPTISM

BAPTISM INSTITUTED

One must look heavenward to find the origin of baptism and also to ascertain the origin of the other principles and ordinances of the Gospel of Jesus Christ. For the earliest revelations of the plan of salvation to mortals one should look to Father Adam—the first man of our race.

Since the Gospel was instituted by God and not by man, its requirements are just as constant and exacting in their composition and operation as are the laws of health or other laws of nature. If any alteration takes place, it can be made only by the Almighty Author of the laws. The Lord has said:

All who will have a blessing at my hands shall abide the law which was appointed for that blessing, and the conditions thereof, as were instituted from before the foundation of the world.[1]

The ancient religious records possessed by our generation are so brief that it is impossible to reconstruct in detail the Gospel as lived in the Adamic and other early dispensations. There is, however, enough information preserved to give conclusive evidence that baptism is one of the most vital ordinances of the plan of salvation and that it is positively a requisite—fixed and unalterable—for those who enter into the kingdom of God.[2] "Strait is the gate, and narrow is the way, which leadeth unto life,"[3] and "the gate by which ye should enter is repentance, and baptism by water; and then cometh a remission of your sins by fire and by the Holy Ghost."[4]

---

[1] *Doctrine and Covenants* 132:5; 130:20-21.
[2] Moses 6:49-67; John 3:1-8.
[3] Matthew 7:14; 3 Nephi 14:13; 27:33.
[4] 2 Nephi 31:4-21.

By heavenly messengers, Adam was taught the doctrine concerning this ordinance. He heard the voice of God saying:

"If thou wilt turn unto me and hearken unto my voice, and believe, and repent of all thy transgressions, and be baptized, even in water, in the name of mine Only Begotten Son, who is full of grace and truth, which is Jesus Christ, the only name which shall be given under heaven whereby salvation shall come unto the children of men, ye shall receive the gift of the Holy Ghost." . . .

And it came to pass, when the Lord had spoken with Adam, our father, that Adam cried unto the Lord, and he was caught away by the spirit of the Lord, and was carried down into the water, and was laid under the water, and was brought forth out of the water.

And thus he was baptized, and the Spirit of God descended upon him, and thus he was born of the Spirit, and became quickened in the inner man. And he heard a voice out of heaven, saying: "Thou art baptized with fire, and with the Holy Ghost. This is the record of the Father, and the Son, from henceforth and for ever. . . . Behold, thou art one in me, a son of God; and thus may all become my sons."[5]

Thus through faith, repentance, baptism and confirmation, Adam received a spiritual rebirth and was initiated into the Kingdom of God.[6] He taught the principle of baptism to his children and they in turn to their children.[7] In this way the knowledge and the practice of this holy ordinance was carried on among the children of men from generation to generation as a golden thread to which they must cling in order to bring about their own redemption.

BAPTISM TAUGHT BY ENOCH AND NOAH

We learn from the *Pearl of Great Price* that Enoch, hundreds of years after Adam's day, administered the same order of baptism to his people that had been practiced by his ancestors. He is the prophet who gives us the account of Adam's receiving this holy ordinance. To quote a divine revelation to Enoch:

The Lord said unto me: "Go to this people, and say unto them—Repent, lest I come out and smite them with a curse, and they die." And He gave unto me a commandment that I should baptize in the name of the Father, and of the Son, which is full of grace and truth, and of the Holy Ghost, which beareth record of the Father and the Son.[8]

---

[5] Moses 6:51, 63-67.
[6] John 3:1-8.
[7] Moses 5:6-15, 58-59.
[8] *Ibid.*, 7:10-11.

Noah, the mighty preacher and great-grandson of Enoch, received a Gospel dispensation, and God commanded him to teach and practice the ordinance of baptism.

And the Lord ordained Noah after his own order, and commanded him that he should go forth and declare his Gospel unto the children of men, even as it was given unto Enoch.

And it came to pass that Noah called upon the children of men that they should repent; but they hearkened not unto his words. . . . Noah continued his preaching unto the people, saying: "Hearken, and give heed unto my words; *believe and repent of your sins and be baptized in the name of Jesus Christ, the Son of God, even as our fathers, and ye shall receive the Holy Ghost,* that ye may have all things made manifest; and if ye do not this the floods will come in upon you"; nevertheless they hearkened not.[9]

FROM NOAH TO JESUS

After the flood, Noah and his family continued to walk in righteousness before the Lord. Surely that great patriarch and his posterity continued the practice of baptism. This is evidenced by the fact that when Christ came into the world, baptism was a common practice of the Jews and the numerous pagan religions.

However, through apostasy a number of vital changes were made from time to time in the ordinance of baptism. One finds in ancient and modern religions numerous ways in which baptism has been interpreted and practiced. Where these variances from the original pattern occur, they are man-made and represent a falling away from the true Gospel ordinance.

BAPTISM AND THE JEWS

When one considers the prevalence of the practice of baptism throughout the Mediterranean world for several hundred years B.C. and on throughout the Christian period, he is surprised not to find the mention of this ordinance in the Old Testament. Was the Hebrew religion the one exception of a prominent religion that did not practice this rite? Or has the record of that particular Gospel doctrine failed to be preserved in Jewish literature for our generation?

Dr. Shirley Jackson Case and other prominent students of religion maintain that at the time of the birth of

---
[9] *Ibid.,* 8:19, 23-24.

our Lord in Bethlehem "baptism was already practiced by Jews."[10] In the words of Dr. Arthur C. McGiffert, who has been one of America's foremost scholars in this field:

> Baptism was entirely in line with the common Jewish rite of purification, and as a symbolical representation of cleansing from the sins or crimes of which they repented, it must seem the most natural thing in the world to them . . . and was never thought of as involving any disloyalty to Judaism, or any departure from its traditional principles.[11]

Dr. Alfred Edersheim states that the Jewish law required:

> That those who had contracted Levitical defilement were to immerse before offering sacrifice. Again, it was prescribed that such Gentiles as became "proselytes of righteousness," or "proselytes of the Covenant," were to be admitted to the full participation in the privilege of Israel by the three-fold rites of circumcision, baptism and sacrifice—the immersion being, as it were, the acknowledgement and symbolic removal of moral defilement, corresponding to that of Levitical uncleanness.[12]

Nephite Teachings of Baptism

Those students of Jewish religion who maintain that the Hebrews baptized corroborate evidence given in the *Book of Mormon*. Jacob, the son of Lehi, shortly after their arrival in America from Jerusalem, gave to the small colony of Israelite exiles the following definite instructions relative to this ordinance:

> And he [Christ] commandeth all men that they must repent and be baptized in his name, having perfect faith in the Holy One of Israel, or they cannot be saved in the kingdom of God. And if they will not repent and believe in his name, and be baptized in his name, and endure to the end, they must be damned; for the Lord God, the Holy One of Israel, has spoken it.[13]

Jacob's discussion and the writings of the other Nephite historians are so definite and explicit that we are sure that Lehi and his family were familiar with the details of the ordinance of baptism very shortly after leaving Jerusalem— probably before leaving. Whether they received their information entirely through special revelation or from the brass plates—the Hebrew scripture similar to our Old Testament, which they had brought with them from Jerusalem— is not discussed by Jacob or by any other Nephite writer.

---

[10] Shirley J. Case, *The Evolution of Early Christianity*, p. 340.
[11] Arthur C. McGiffert, *The Apostolic Age*, p. 59.
[12] Alfred Edersheim, *The Life and Times of Jesus the Messiah*, vol. 1, pp. 273-274; Edersheim states that "In Kerith., 92, 'the baptism' of Israel is proved from Exodus 24:5-8, since every sprinkling of blood was supposed to be preceded by immersion."
[13] 2 Nephi 9:23-24; Mark 16:15-16; Matthew 28:19-20.

But the record does state that Nephi was privileged to see in a vision the coming of Christ and His subsequent baptism.

The plainness and positiveness with which Nephi and Jacob instructed their associates relative to baptism—without once suggesting that their information came entirely as a new revelation—seems to sustain the viewpoint that baptism was practiced by the Jews prior to the time of Lehi's departure from Jerusalem, and the Nephites were but continuing a religious practice well understood by the people.

The *Book of Mormon* points out definitely that baptism is an ordinance of initiation, rebirth and regeneration, that the mode to be used is immersion, that in order to baptize one must hold the Priesthood, and that baptism should be administered only to those who have faith and a desire to become members of the Church of Christ, for "behold, baptism is unto repentance to the fulfilling the commandments unto the remission of sins."[14] A point of significance is that throughout the entire history of the Nephites, whenever their records discuss baptism it is evident that these ancient Americans had the same interpretation of this holy ordinance as did Adam, Enoch and Noah and as was taught by the early Christians and also by the Church of Jesus Christ of Latter-day Saints today. All the details relative to this ordinance which have been revealed to the holy prophets from Adam's day, with the exception of baptism for the dead, are found as teachings of the *Book of Mormon* prophets. For example, Nephi declared:

And now, if the Lamb of God, he being holy, should have need to be baptized by water, to fulfill all righteousness, O then, how much more need have we, being unholy, to be baptized, yea, even by water. . . .

But notwithstanding he being holy, he sheweth unto the children of men, that according to the flesh, he humbleth himself before the Father, and witnesseth unto the Father that he would be obedient unto him in keeping his commandments. . . . And he said unto the children of men, "Follow thou me." Wherefore, my beloved brethren can we follow Jesus save we shall be willing to keep the comandments of the Father? And the Father said, "Repent ye, repent ye, and be baptized in the name of my beloved Son."

---

[14] Moroni 8:11-12.

And also, the voice of the Son came unto me, saying, "He that is baptized in my name, to him will the Father give the Holy Ghost, like unto me; wherefore, follow me, and do the things which ye have seen me do."[15]

Over four hundred years after Nephi's time, Alma baptized his converts by immersion in the waters of Mormon, thereby making them members of the Church of Christ. A detailed description is given in the *Book of Mormon* of this event.[16]

Approximately one hundred and fifty years later the resurrected Lord visited the Nephites. He instructed them definitely concerning baptism. The procedure to follow is more clearly presented herein than in any of the other ancient scriptures, and so we shall quote it:

The Lord said unto him [Nephi III], "I give unto you power that ye shall baptize this people when I am again ascended into heaven."

And again the Lord called others, and said unto them likewise; and he gave unto them power to baptize. And he said unto them, "On this wise shall ye baptize; and there shall be no disputations among you.

"Verily I say unto you, that whoso repenteth of his sins through your words, and desireth to be baptized in my name, on this wise shall ye baptize them: behold, ye shall go down and stand in the water, and in my name shall ye baptize them. And now behold, these are the words which ye shall say, calling them by name, saying:

" 'Having authority given me of Jesus Christ, I baptize you in the name of the Father, and of the Son, and of the Holy Ghost. Amen.'

"And then shall ye immerse them in the water, and come forth again out of the water."[17]

Descriptions are given of their following the Master's instructions.

The message of the *Book of Mormon,* to use the words of the Lord to Moroni, the last of the Nephite prophets, is as follows:

Therefore, repent all ye ends of the earth, and come unto me, and believe in my Gospel, and be baptized in my name; for he that believeth, and is baptized, shall be saved; but he that believeth not, shall be damned; and signs shall follow them that believe in my name. And blessed is he that is found faithful unto my name, at the last day, for he shall be lifted up to dwell in the kingdom prepared for him from the foundation of the world.[18]

---

[15] 2 Nephi 31:4-31.
[16] Mosiah 18:5-22.
[17] 3 Nephi 11:21-41; 19:10-16.
[18] Ether 4:18-19.

Nephites Adulterate the Ordinance of Baptism

But when the Nephite nation dropped into wickedness and apostasy near the close of their history, they adulterated the doctrine of baptism by introducing the unholy practice of infant baptism in their church, just as the Christian church in Rome did, as we shall point out later. It is of interest to note that the doctrine of infant baptism was introduced among both peoples during the same period of history.

Mormon, the famous Nephite prophet and general in whose honor the Nephite record has been named, wrote a letter to his son, Moroni, to help counteract this evil and apostate belief of baptizing babies which had arisen among his people.[19] This letter is one of the most forceful documents condemning infant baptism that has ever been written by a prophet of God. Before writing his letter, Mormon received a revelation from the Lord regarding this subject in which the Savior declared that "little children are alive in Christ even from the foundation of the world; . . . [therefore, they] need no repentance, neither baptism."[20] Thus Mormon forcefully condemned the unholy doctrine of infant baptism and taught as follows:

Behold I say unto you that "he that supposeth that little children need baptism, is in the gall of bitterness, and in the bonds of iniquity; for he hath neither faith, hope, nor charity; wherefore, should he be cut off while in the thought, he must go down to hell."[21]

Conclusions

Enough evidence has been given to show that from the beginning to the end of Nephite history the prophets of this race had a clear and detailed understanding of the holy ordinance of baptism. It has also been shown that baptism was a vital Gospel ordinance first revealed to Father Adam and later to the holy prophets in each dispensation, and that it is definitely requisite for the salvation of mankind. In fact, it is the gateway by which one may enter into the Kingdom of God.

---

[19] Moroni 8:1-30.
[20] Ibid., 8:11-12.
[21] Ibid., 8:14.

SUPPLEMENTARY READINGS—CHAPTER 27

1. *Book of Mormon:* 1 Nephi 10:9-10; 11:27; 2 Nephi 9:23-24; 31:4-21; Mosiah 18:4-22; 21:35; 25:15-18; 26:22-23; Alma 4:4-5; 5:3; 6:1-2; 7:14-15; 8:10; 15:13-14; 32:16; 49:30; 62:45-56; Helaman 3:24; 5:17-19; 16:3-4; 3 Nephi 1:23; 7:26; 9:20; 11:10-41; 12:1-2; 18:5, 11-14, 30; 19:12-18; 21:6; 23:5; 26:17-21; 27:1, 20; 28:18; 30:2; 4 Nephi 1:1; Mormon 3:2-3; 9:22-25; Ether 4:18-19; Moroni 6:1; 7:34; 8:1-30.

2. *Pearl of Great Price:* Moses 6:49-67; 7:10-11; 8:19-25.

Chapter 28.

BAPTISM IN CHRISTENDOM

Christian Baptism Instituted

When John the Baptist came preaching repentance and baptism, and Jesus not only accepted John's symbol, but attached a deeper meaning to it in His reply to John, "Suffer it to be so now, for thus it becometh us to fulfill all righteousness," they were both proclaiming the same Gospel ordinance which had been practiced from the beginning and which had been instituted for the salvation of man before the world was created.

The criterion for truth in Christianity is to be found in the teachings of the Man of Galilee, since He and His Father were the authors of the eternal plan of salvation. When Jesus came to John and requested baptism, the latter seemed to understand that the ordinance was merely for the purpose of cleansing the repentant believer from his sins. The Master, however, enlarged John's viewpoint by proclaiming that the holy ordinance was requisite for entrance into the kingdom of God. Although John recognized Jesus as a perfect man, the Master made it clear that it was absolutely necessary for even the Son of God to be baptized. He—like the least of us—must obey every law of the Gospel if He was to receive all the blessings predicated on obedience. In the following words, Jesus Christ explained to Nicodemus the absolute necessity of baptism as the holy ordinance which serves as the gateway into the kingdom of God:

"Verily, verily, I say unto thee, Except a man be born again he cannot see the kingdom of God."

Nicodemus saith unto him, "How can a man be born when he is old? Can he enter the second time into his mother's womb, and be born?"

Jesus answered, "Verily, verily, I say unto thee, Except a man be born of water and of the Spirit, he cannot enter into the kingdom of God."[1]

MODE OF BAPTISM

Jesus' statement also definitely shows that the proper mode of baptism was immersion. Paul, the famous Christian missionary, confirmed the teachings of the Master by showing that in his day the mode of baptism used was immersion. To quote his famous statement wherein he compared baptism to death, burial and resurrection:

Know we not that so many of us as were baptized into Jesus Christ were baptized into his death? Therefore we are buried with him by baptism into death: that like as Christ was raised up from the dead by the glory of the Father, even so we also should walk in newness of life. For if we have been planted together in the likeness of his death, we shall be also in the likeness of his resurrection.[2]

No symbolism but immersion could fit such a statement. Again, in Colossians, a similar comparison is made: "Buried with him [Christ] in baptism, wherein also ye are risen with him through the faith of the operation of God, who hath raised him from the dead."[3] John did his baptizing in the Jordan river "because there was much water there";[4] "and Jesus, when he was baptized, went up straightway out of the water."[5] Such statements as the foregoing are definite proof that the early Christians practiced baptism by immersion.

It is very definite that the mode of baptism as established by God, as practiced by Adam, by the Nephites, and by Jesus and His followers during the early Christian period was that of immersion. The aggregate evidence presented by the early Christian writers following the Apostolic Age, plus the meaning of "the word 'baptism,' as is generally admitted by philologists to be derived from the Greek *bapto, baptizo,* meaning literally to dip or immerse,"[6] give conclusive proof that there was but one officially recognized mode of baptism during the early Christian centuries. History furnishes ample proof that during and fol-

[1] John 3:3-5.
[2] Romans 6:3-5.
[3] Colossians 2:12.
[4] John 3:23; Matthew 3:5-6.
[5] Matthew 3:16.
[6] James E. Talmage, *The Articles of Faith,* pp. 139-161; for a fuller discussion of this subject see James L. Barker's "The Protestors of Christendom," *Improvement Era,* XLI (Salt Lake City, April, 1938), p. 218ff.

lowing the time of Jesus in mortality, baptism was administered solely by immersion. Tertullian refers to the immersion ceremony common in his day as follows: "There is no difference whether one is washed in a sea or in a pool, in a river or in a fountain, in a lake or in a channel; nor is there any difference between those whom John dipped in Jordan, and those whom Peter dipped in the Tiber. . . . We are immersed in the water."[7] Starbo, a Greek writer who lived during the first century A.D., refers to the buoyancy of certain saline waters in the following words: "These have the taste of salt water, but a different nature, for even persons who cannot swim are not liable to be 'baptized' in them, but float like logs on the surface."[8] And Justin Martyr, a believer in Jesus, who wrote in defense of the church about 135 A.D., said:

After that (repentance) they are led by us to where there is water, and are born again. For unto the name of God, the Father . . . and of Jesus Christ, our Savior, and of the Holy Ghost, the immersion in water is performed because Christ hath also said "Except a man is born again, he cannot enter the kingdom of God."[9]

BAPTISM BY SPIRIT

During the early Christian period the baptism of the Spirit was just as essential for exaltation as was the baptism of water. John the Baptist boldly told the people: "I indeed baptize you with water unto repentance; but he that cometh after me is mightier than I, whose shoes I am not worthy to bear: He shall baptize you with the Holy Ghost, and with fire."[10] Again we read: "They were baptized in the name of the Lord Jesus. Then laid they their hands on them, and they received the Holy Ghost."[11]

THREE POINTS ON BAPTISM

In addition to what has been presented, the accounts of baptism given in the New Testament agree definitely on the following three points: (1) Repentance and baptism were taught only to those who were old enough to commit sin; (2) the only ones who did the baptizing were men who held the holy Priesthood; (3) converts to Christianity

---

[7] Talmage, op. cit., p. 160.
[8] Cited in ibid.
[9] Smith, The Message of the New Testament, p. 48; Justin Martyr, Dialogue With Trypho, xiv, 1.
[10] Matthew 3:11; Hebrews 6:1-16; John 3:5; Acts 2:38-39.
[11] Acts 8:16-17.

were baptized almost immediately after repenting of their sins and asking for admittance into the church.[12] The account given of Philip's converting the Ethiopian eunuch will serve to illustrate these points:

Then Philip opened his mouth, and began at the same scripture, and preached unto him Jesus. And as they went on their way, they came unto a certain water: and the eunuch said, "See, here is water; what doth hinder me to be baptized?"

And Philip said, "If thou believest with all thine heart, thou mayest."

And he answered and said, "I believe that Jesus Christ is the Son of God."

And he commanded the chariot to stand still; and they went down both into the water, both Philip and the eunuch; and he baptized him. And when they were come up out of the water, the Spirit of the Lord caught away Philip, that the eunuch saw him no more.[13]

JESUS' COMMISSION TO HIS APOSTLES

Much of the Christian conception of baptism which we have discussed is found in the Savior's last commission to His apostles, which He gave to them following His resurrection and shortly preceding His ascension. He commanded them:

Go ye into all the world, and preach the Gospel to every creature, (baptizing them in the name of the Father and of the Son, and of the Holy Ghost[14]). He that believeth and is baptized shall be saved; but he that believeth not shall be damned.[15]

The apostles followed the injunction of the resurrected Lord. On the day of Pentecost the Holy Ghost came upon them and they preached the Gospel with great power to a multitude of people. Many believed the teachings, and asked, "What shall we do?"

Then Peter said unto them, "Repent, and be baptized every one of you in the name of Jesus Christ for the remission of sins, and ye shall receive the gift of the Holy Ghost. For the promise is unto you, and to your children, and to all that are afar off, even as many as the Lord our God shall call."[16]

IMMERSION CHANGED TO SPRINKLING

As time passed during the early Christian centuries, many strange and foreign practices crept into the Christian

---

[12] *Ibid.*, 16:19-34; 2:1-3.
[13] *Ibid.*, 8:35-39.
[14] Matthew 28:19.
[15] Mark 16:15-16.
[16] Acts 2:37-39.

baptism, transforming the holy ordinance into a rite which was distinctly different from the original Gospel revelation.

The first point to be presented relative to this apostasy was the changing of the mode of baptism from immersion to sprinkling. This transformation took place gradually.

"The first instance of record [of Christian sprinkling] is that of Novatus, a heretic who requested baptism when he thought death was near,"[17] and the priest granted his request. Tertullian (160-220 A.D.) speaks of Christian baptism as by immersion,[18] but Cyprian (200-258 A. D.), "the learned bishop of Carthage, advocated the propriety of sprinkling in lieu of immersion in cases of physical weakness; and the practice, thus started, later became general."[19] But at the time of Thomas Aquinas (1225-1274 A.D.), "immersion was still the more prevalent form, and had his approval."[20] According to Dr. Williston Walker, "immersion continued the prevailing practice till the late Middle Ages in the West; in the East it so remained."[21]

It should be observed that changing the mode of baptism from the true pattern established by God to sprinkling robbed this holy ordinance of its symbolism of death and rebirth—a concept both prominent and vital in baptism from the very beginning.

INFANT BAPTISM INSTITUTED

The early Christians did not baptize babies. The Gospel plan as established by Jesus and as practiced during the Apostolic Age provided initiatory rites only for those who were "accountable and capable of committing sin."[22] Dr. Walker maintains that "till past the middle of the second century, they (who received this ordinance) were those of years of discretion. The first mention of infant baptism, an obscure one, was about 135 A.D., by Irenaeus."[23] Tertullian, another Christian writer (160-220 A.D.), however, spoke distinctly of the matter, strongly condemning the

[17] James E. Talmage, The Great Apostasy, pp. 118-119; Eusebius, Ecclesiastical History, vol. 6, p. 17.
[18] Barker, op. cit., pp. 218-219.
[19] Talmage, op. cit., p. 118.
[20] Williston Walker, A History of the Christian Church, p. 373.
[21] Ibid., p. 96; James C. Gibbons, The Faith of Our Fathers, p. 277-279.
[22] Arthur C. McGiffert, The Apostolic Age, p. 543; Moroni 8:1-30; Mosiah 3:16-20; 15:25.
[23] Walker, op. cit., pp. 95-96.

baptism of babies.   He felt that it would be best to delay the performance of this rite until character was formed. Two or three hundred years later, however, the baptism of infants became the general practice in the Catholic church. This became confirmed by decrees of the Christian "councils of Olmutz (1318 A.D., canon 19) and Salamanca (1335 A.D., canon 6)."[24]   The gradual changing of immersion to sprinkling as an acceptable mode of baptism did much toward instituting infant baptism; also the Catholic belief of babies being conceived in sin and born in sin was basic in the developing of the false and adulterated doctrine of infant baptism.

The complete original ritual connected with initiation into the Christian church was designed not for infants, but for people old enough to be accountable for their actions and capable of understanding right and wrong; so when infant baptism was adopted by Roman Catholics, the custom of having sponsors or godparents for the children evolved.   One duty of the godparents was to promise for the children those things which the children would promise for themselves if they had sufficient understanding.

DEVELOPMENT OF ELABORATE CEREMONIALISM

Baptism as practiced in New Testament days was a simple rite unaccompanied by elaborate ceremonialism. Gradually additional practices crept into the Christian ordinance, so that by the third century an elaborate ritual had developed.   At that time the Catholic baptismal ceremony began with the formal renunciation of Satan.   Then official exorcisers indulged in "menacing and formidable shouts and declamations" in order to drive out the demons or evil spirits with which the candidates were supposed to be afflicted.[25]   This was followed by a three-fold immersion, the first immersion in the name of the Father, the second in the name of the Son, and the third immersion in the name of the Holy Ghost.   "On coming from the fount, the newly baptized tasted a mixture of milk and honey, in symbolism of their condition as new-born babies in Christ.   To that succeeded anointing with oil," designation with the

[24] Barker, op. cit., p. 319.
[25] John L. Mosheim, Ecclesiastical History, vol. 1, p. 261.

cross, and the use of salt.[26] The initiates "returned home, adorned with crowns, and arrayed in white garments, as sacred emblems; the former, of their victory over sin and the world; the latter, of their inward purity and innocence."[27]

PERIOD OF PREPARATION ESTABLISHED

The baptism of converts was attended to only twice a year at stated times following a long period of trial and preparation,[28] in contrast with the early method of baptizing neophytes almost immediately after their confessing faith in Jesus and showing signs of repentance.[29]

AUTHORITY AND THREE BAPTISMS

In apostolic days only those holding the Priesthood did the baptizing, but this practice was finally supplanted by one which permitted any church member who had received initiation to perform the ordinance in case of necessity. The general practice, however, is for the priest to do the baptizing.

In its altered form, after the many changes had come into Christian baptism, the Catholic church offered three kinds of baptism—that "of water, of desire, and of blood"— two of them unheard of in New Testament literature. We have already discussed the meaning of baptism by water. The second one, that of desire, means that a person had a strong desire to become baptized, but did not have what was deemed ample opportunity. After that person died and after certain conditions had been complied with by relatives and the priest, then he was pronounced baptized by desire. And baptism by blood means that the one so baptized gave his life for the church and for Jesus, or, in other words, died in the cause of the church.

SUPPLEMENTARY READINGS—CHAPTER 28

1. *Bible*: Matthew 3:1-17; 28:19-20; Mark 16:15-16; 1:4; 10:13-16; Luke 3:3; 7:28-30; John 3:1-15, 23; Acts 2:37-38; 8:12, 38-39; 10:34-35, 47-48; 16:25-33; 22:10-16; Galatians 3:27; Hebrews 6:1-2; Romans 6:3-5; Colossians 2:12; 1 Peter 3:21; Revelation 20:12.

2. *Handbook of the Restoration*, pp. 115-121, 534-552.

3. Joseph Fielding Smith, *The Restoration of All Things*, pp. 206-225.

4. James E. Talmage, *Articles of Faith*, pp. 122-160.

---

[26] Walker, *op. cit.*, p. 96; Porphyry, *De Antro Nympharum*, p. 15.
[27] Mosheim, *op. cit.*, p. 262.
[28] *Ibid.*, p. 261.
[29] Acts 2:37-41; 8:26-39; 10:47-48.

Chapter 29.

PAGAN INFLUENCES ON CHRISTIAN BAPTISM

PAGAN RIVALS OF CHRISTIANITY

Whence came all of these changes discussed in the last chapter from the true order of baptism as established by Jesus Christ? What was the intellectual and social heritage of these thousands of proselytes who came into the Christian church during the first four centuries A.D., which brought about this apostasy?

The complete answer to these questions can be found only in a study of all the religions and philosophies that contributed to the complex religious pattern of the Mediterranean world in which Christianity was planted. This is a gigantic task, as the world at that time was literally filled with pagan philosophies and religions — principally those known as Mystery Religions.[1] In the words of Harold Willoughby:

> Broadly speaking, the religious situation in the Graeco-Roman world was as varied and complex and syncretistic as Mediterranean society itself was at this period. All people included as citizens or provincials within the limits of the empire and all previous ages of religious experience in the Mediterranean area made some characteristic contribution to the religious life of Roman times.[2]

Never was the world more completely given over to religious syncretism—that is, mixing of religious beliefs—than during the early Christian era. Many peoples had been brought together and their cultures intermingled and fused.[3]

During this period of intensified religious feeling, thousands and thousands of pagans became followers of Jesus. Especially after 392 A.D. (the date at which Christianity became the only legal religion of the Roman Empire), former pagans flocked into the Catholic church. They

---

[1] Adolf Deissmann, *Lights From the Ancient East*, p. 285.
[2] Harold Willoughby, *Pagan Regeneration*, p. 9.
[3] *Ibid.*, p. 33; S. Angus, *The Mystery Religions and Christianity*, pp. 19, 37; Samuel Dill, *Roman Society From Nero to Marcus Aurelius*, p. 62.

brought with them many of their heathenistic rituals, beliefs, and practices. This process of religious syncretism was accelerated by the Roman government's outlawing all pagan religions and forcing them out of existence. Thus numerous pagans were forced into Christianity without their being really converted to the teachings of the Master. This increased the amount of heathenistic beliefs and practices which flowed into Christianity, thereby becoming an integral part of Catholicism. Christianity of the fifth century, then, was the product of many streams of thought—Jewish, pagan, and the teachings of the Man of Galilee. Its principles, ordinances and practices differed vitally from the true Gospel. An apostasy from the plan of salvation as established by Jesus had taken place.

Two facts of great importance can be observed in a study of the religions of the Mediterranean world during the early centuries A. D. First, much of the golden thread of truth—greatly altered—persisted in the pagan religions from bygone days when their ancestors were followers of the divinely revealed Gospel principles; second, the pagan religions affected Christianity immensely, bringing about what writers have termed the "Great Apostasy."

PAGAN BAPTISM PRACTICES

Hundreds of years B.C. and on down through the Christian centuries until paganism was outlawed, baptism was almost universally practiced by the numerous pagan religions. The Mystery Religions washed away the sins of their converts and initiated them into their various religious cults by baptism. Rebirth, regeneration, and all the other promises made to the Christian proselyte were also made to the believer in paganism by one or another of the prevalent heathenistic religions.

For the purpose of throwing light on the alterations of the Christian doctrine of baptism, a brief presentation of the various pagan baptism concepts which contributed to the religious pattern of the Roman Empire is given here. A scrutiny of the Christian doctrine of baptism at the close of the fourth century A.D. reveals the fact that it was composed of a portion of the baptismal practices of each of its pagan rivals mixed with the doctrine of baptism instituted by Jesus.

IMMERSION AND SPRINKLING

The worshipers of Demeter and Persephone in the Eleusinian Mysteries baptized their candidates both by sprinkling and immersion. At stated times, only once or twice each year, proselytes were initiated. This practice came into Christendom. Origen, a Christian father, quotes Celsus, an Eleusinian worshiper, as giving two formulas of invitation to those who were to become cult members. To quote:

Those who invite people to other Mysteries make proclamation thus: "Everyone who has clean hands and intelligible speech," others again thus: "He who is pure from all pollution, and whose soul is conscious of no evil and who has lived well and justly." Such is the proclamation made by those who promise purification from sins.[4]

It is evident that in this pagan rival of Christianity the candidate must be in a repentant condition and must be one who had lived an acceptable life. The ancient records tell us that Nero, the wicked and notorious Roman emperor, "dared not attend the Eleusinian Mysteries, at the initiation of which impious and wicked persons are warned by the voice of the herald from approaching the rites."[5] Two other Roman emperors, Marcus Aurelius and Commodus, were numbered among the illustrious *mystae*.

In this pagan religion, the immersion always took place in the sea, as salt waves were believed to possess a greater cleansing virtue than fresh water. "Sea waves wash away all sin," said Euripides (480-406 B.C.). Little pigs were also cleansed by immersion preparatory to being sacrificed. Then the blood from these animals was sprinkled on each of the initiates, an act closely resembling an ancient Hebrew religious custom.[6] The *Bible* states that "Moses took the blood [of sacrificial animals] and sprinkled it on the people, and said, 'Behold the blood of the covenant, which the Lord hath made with you concerning all these words'."[7]

The golden thread of religion maintained itself in this pagan cult in such a proportion that Tertullian (160-220 A.D.), a Christian, wrote:

4 Origen, *Contra Celsum*, iii. 59, cited in Willoughby, *op. cit.*, p. 44.
5 Suetonius, *Augustus*, p. 93, cited in Willoughby, *ibid.*, p. 40.
6 *Ibid.*, p. 42.
7 Exodus 24:5-8.

At the Eleusinian Mysteries men are baptized and they assume that the effect of this is their regeneration and the remission of the penalties due to their perjuries.[8]

Tertullian, the Christian lawyer, recognized that the members of the Great Mysteries at Eleusis believed that through baptism they experienced a new birth, but he argued the superior validity of the Christian rite and experience. He definitely pointed out the absolute necessity of baptism being performed by one holding the holy Priesthood or authority from God, which Catholics claimed to possess. He argued thus:

If the mere nature of water, in that it is the appropriate material for washing away, leads men to flatter themselves with a belief in the omens of purification, how much more truly will waters render that service through the authority of God, by whom all their matter has been constituted?

Well, but the nations, who are strangers to all understanding of spiritual powers, ascribe to their idols the imbuing of waters with the self-same efficacy [as Christian baptism]. But they cheat themselves with waters that are widowed. For washing is the channel through which they are initiated into the sacred rites of some notorious Isis or Mithra.[9]

Mithraism entered Rome 63 B.C. and in a little over one hundred years spread from one end of the empire to the other. It maintained itself for three centuries as the most powerful religion of the Roman world. Many years before Christ, and throughout the early Christian centuries, worshipers of this Persian god baptized their proselytes. The mode used was either sprinkling with holy water or complete immersion.[10] During the early centuries A.D., immersion was the only mode of baptism accepted and practiced by Christians, but later both immersion and sprinkling were used, an obvious adoption of Mithraic practices. Even today in the Catholic church either method of baptizing is acceptable, but sprinkling is preferable.[11]

Dr. Willoughby concluded: "Mithraic baptism, like the later Christian rite, promised purification from guilt and the washing away of sins. Christian Fathers noted the similarity and were quick to charge the devil with plagiarism at this point."[12]

---

[8] Tertullian, De Baptismo, p. 5.
[9] Ibid.
[10] Franz Cumont, Textes et Monuments, vol. 2, p. 523ff.
[11] James Cardinal Gibbons, The Faith of Our Fathers, pp. 277-279.
[12] Willoughby, op. cit., p. 160.

In the words of Tertullian:

The devil, whose business is to pervert the truth, mimics the exact circumstances of the divine sacraments in the mysteries of idols. He himself baptizes some, that is to say, his believers and followers; he promises forgiveness of sins in the sacred fount, and thus initiates them into the religion of Mithra.[13]

A more probable reason for the marked resemblance in the Mithraic and the Christian concept of baptism than that offered by Tertullian is that Mithraism had retained from earlier times many of the threads of Gospel truths stemming from the original common source. It is evident that not only did these pagan religions affect Christianity, but Gospel teachings from earlier ages had left their imprint on paganism.

DIET OF "MILK MINGLED WITH HONEY"

A distinctly pagan practice that came into Christianity during the early centuries was the feeding of the baptized worshipers on a diet of milk mingled with honey.[14] This practice, no doubt, came from the Great Mother Mysteries and from Mithraism, two of the most prominent pagan rivals of Christianity. The former gave to the newly initiated "nourishment of milk as if he were being reborn";[15] while honey was applied to both the hands and tongue of the initiates of Mithraism for the purpose of nourishing the new spiritual life of those who had recently been baptized.

According to Porphyry, an ancient writer, the Mithraic devotees believed that honey was a celestial substance produced under the influence of the moon and was the food of the gods themselves.[16] It was the custom among these pagans to put honey into the mouths of new-born babies—so, the Mithraic spiritually new-born were also fed on this substance. It was believed to contain properties capable of nourishing the spiritual life of the initiate and of keeping him from blemishes of sin. The Catholic church adopted this practice of giving a mixture of milk and honey to the newly baptized church members; thus we find the origin of the Christian practice of giving their initiates, following baptism, milk mingled with honey.

[13] Tertullian, *De Praescriptione Haereticorum*, p. 40.
[14] Willoughby, *op. cit.*, pp. 159-160.
[15] Sallustius, *Philosophus*, cited in Edward Carpenter, *Pagan and Christian Creeds*, pp. 44-45.
[16] Porphyry, *De Antro Nympharum*, p. 15.

Baptized Converts Robed in White

As early as the fifth century B.C. and on through the early Christian era, the pagan worshipers in the Orphic cult wore garments of pure white after being baptized, symbolical of purification. The following statement in the writings of Euripides is indicative of this practice: "Robed in pure white, I have borne me clean from man's vile birth and coffined clay."[17] By the beginning of the third century A.D., the worshipers of Jesus had adopted this pagan practice of dressing the newly baptized devotees in white clothing symbolical of inward purity and innocence—of a regeneration and spiritual rebirth.[18]

Arduous Preparatory Training and Isiac Baptism

Probably the most significant contribution of the worshipers of Isis, the Egyptian goddess, to Christianity was the long and arduous preparatory training which was required of initiates into this cult, which practice later was adopted by the Catholic church under the name of *catechumenate.*[19]

The Isiac Mysteries originated as early as 3000 B.C. Many years before the birth of Jesus members of this cult practiced baptism. In the words of Dr. Willoughby:

When Paul began his missionary work in these regions [Syria, Asia Minor and Greece], he everywhere met with Isiac establishments that were already centuries old. . . . Even to the last days of paganism, Isis remained a power in the eastern Mediterranean world.[20]

Lucius Apuleius, an ancient pagan, left us an account of his own initiation into the Isiac religion. Harold Willoughby discusses the Isiac baptism and Lucius' experience as follows:

The great priest produced "out of the secret place of the temple certain books written with unknown characters . . . whereby they were wholly strange and impossible to be read by profane people," and thence he interpreted to Lucius "such things as were necessary to the use and preparation of his order." At the propitious time after the impartation of this instruction, Lucius, attended by a company of initiates, was brought to the place of baptism, and there "demanding pardon of the gods," the priest baptized him and "purified his body according to custom." Christian writers knew of this Isiac baptism and made plain

---

[17] Euripides, *Fragments*, p. 475; cited in Willoughby, *op. cit.*, pp. 102-103.
[18] John L. Mosheim, *Ecclesiastical History*, vol. 1, p. 262.
[19] James L. Barker, "The Protestors of Christendom," *Improvement Era*, XLI (Salt Lake City, April, 1938), p. 219; Willoughby, *op. cit.*, pp. 169-194.
[20] *Ibid.*, p. 180.

that a powerful efficacy was credited to it—indeed the selfsame effect of purification from sin and spiritual regeneration that Christians attributed to their baptismal rite.[21]

In the thought of the Isiac community, the waters of baptism were identified with the life-giving waters of the sacred Nile. . . . So for the initiate these sacred waters had a life-giving power, and Isiac baptism was in effect regarded as a regenerative rite that meant new life to the one who experienced it.[22]

The ceremony of initiation into the Isiac Mysteries was extremely elaborate. Since this religion was widespread throughout the Mediterranean world before Paul proclaimed the teachings of the Master to the Gentiles, it was natural for the Christians, little by little, to adopt much of the Isiac elaborate ceremonialism, part of which was the custom of having sponsors in connection with baptism.[23] The latter practice was adopted by the Catholic church when infant baptism became its most prevalent mode.

ROOTS OF THE ORDINANCE OF BAPTISM

The fact that the practice of baptism is so universal and that there are so many resemblances in the rite as observed by the ancient pagan religions and the true ordinance as revealed to the holy prophets is evidence that the roots of this ritual extend to the distant day when the ordinance was revealed to the first man. Throughout the ages, whenever the Gospel of Jesus Christ has been on the earth, God has established again the holy ordinance of baptism in its purity. Through apostasies, however, men have time and time again adulterated the truth. Yet baptism has retained a semblance to the ordinance as established before man was placed upon the earth; that is, baptism was instituted to be the gateway by which mortals must pass if they enter into the kingdom of God.

SUPPLEMENTARY READING—CHAPTER 29

1. Harold Willoughby, *Pagan Regeneration*, pp. 9, 101-103, 159-161, 187-188, 206.

---

[21] Tertullian, *De Baptismo*, 5; Cf. Firmicus Maternus, *De Errore Profanarum Religionum*, 2.
[22] Willoughby, *op. cit.*, pp. 187-188. Osiris was the "savior-god" in the Mysteries of Isis.
[23] Williston Walker, *A History of the Christian Church*, p. 96.

Chapter 30.

REPENTANCE AND REBIRTH

INTRODUCTORY STATEMENT

It is the purpose of this lesson to show that from Adam's day forward the prophets of God, as well as pagan teachers, have proclaimed the doctrine of repentance, stressing the idea that man must experience a spiritual rebirth—i. e., a complete change in his habits and attitudes of life—and that he must acknowledge this rebirth through compliance with the ordinance of baptism. In the preceding lessons we mentioned that the mode of baptism was symbolical of rebirth, but the purpose of this chapter is to center directly on the doctrines of repentance, rebirth or regeneration.

REPENTANCE AND REBIRTH

The voice of God has come to man in all ages calling him to repentance; in fact, the very basis of the Gospel message is that all men must repent or they cannot see the kingdom of God. In the very beginning God gave the following commandment to Father Adam:

Wherefore, thou shalt do all that thou doest in the name of the Son, and thou shalt repent and call upon God in the name of the Son for evermore. . . .

And the Lord God called upon men by the Holy Ghost everywhere and commanded them that they should repent; and as many as believed in the Son, and repented of their sins, should be saved; and as many as believed not and repented not, should be damned; and the words went forth out of the mouth of God in a firm decree; wherefore they must be fulfilled.[1]

This doctrine was confirmed to Enoch by God's speaking directly to him from heaven, saying:

Enoch, my son, prophesy unto this people, and say unto them— *Repent.* . . . And this is a decree, which I have sent forth in the begin-

---

[1] Moses 5:8, 14-15.

214

ning of the world, from my own mouth, from the foundation thereof, and by the mouths of my servants, thy fathers, have I decreed it, even as it shall be sent forth in the world, unto the end thereof.[2]

REPENTANCE, BAPTISM AND REBIRTH

By repentance the holy prophets meant for man to overcome all of his sins and change his life wherein it was evil to that of spiritual righteousness. Thus repentance is actually a spiritual rebirth or regeneration. Baptism, however, is the Gospel ordinance of rebirth which the man who has repented accepts as a token of his spiritual regeneration; but in order for the baptism to be effective in opening the door into the kingdom of God, it must be accompanied by true repentance.

Whenever the Gospel of Jesus Christ has been on the earth the concept of death to the old life and birth into a new spiritual life accompanying repentance and baptism has been held as one of the cardinal tenets.[3] The Master's statement to Nicodemus—"Except a man be born again, he cannot see the kingdom of God"—is familiar to everyone. Alma taught the Nephites the same Gospel truth. In his own words:

Ye must repent and be born again: for the Spirit saith, if ye are not born again, ye cannot inherit the kingdom of heaven; therefore come and be baptized unto repentance, that ye may be washed from your sins.[4]

In Titus it is written, "According to his mercy he saved us, by the washing of regeneration." Paul the apostle expressed the Christian doctrine of rebirth in his letter to the Saints in Rome as follows:

Know ye not that so many of us as were baptized into Jesus Christ were baptized into his death? Therefore we are buried with him by baptism into death: that like as Christ was raised up from the dead by the glory of the Father, even so we also should walk in newness of life. For if we have been planted together in the likeness of his death, we shall be also in the likeness of his resurrection.[5]

The Gospel has always required of mankind not only to accept the outward act of being baptized, but actually to cast aside all sins of the flesh and be born unto Christ into a new life of the spirit—a life of absolute righteousness. The ultimate goal of being reborn and attaining an

[2] Ibid., 6:26, 29.
[3] Mosiah 27:24-32; Alma 36:5, 18-36.
[4] Alma 7:14.
[5] Romans 6:3-11; Galatians 3:24-29; 2:19-21.

inheritance in the kingdom of God will be reached by following the solemn injunction of the Master of life and salvation wherein He said, "Be ye therefore perfect, even as your Father which is in heaven is perfect."

CONSTANTS IN BAPTISM PRACTICES

As has been pointed out, the ordinance of baptism has been practiced in a variety of ways and with various interpretations placed upon it by the different religions throughout history; but there are certain constants in baptism which have maintained themselves in pagan as well as in Christian religions. These indicate one central source from which they were derived. The roots of these constants extend to the following pregnant statements made by the Lord to Father Adam:

Inasmuch as ye were born into the world by water, and blood, and the spirit, which I have made, and so became of dust a living soul, even so ye must be born again into the kingdom of heaven, of water, and of the Spirit, and be cleansed by blood, even the blood of mine Only Begotten; that ye might be sanctified from all sin, and enjoy the words of eternal life in this world, and eternal life in the world to come, even immortal glory.[6]

It has been the practice in many of the ancient as well as modern religions to baptize converts for the avowed purpose of helping to bring about in the worshipers a regeneration or rebirth. Three types of baptisms have been popular—that of water, of Spirit, and of blood.[7] Although interpreted and expressed in a variety of ways by different religions, yet the doctrine on which they are constructed has a kinship to the three points in baptism and atonement emphasized in the foregoing revelation to Adam.

PAGANS' CONCEPT OF REPENTANCE AND REBIRTH

Many of the teachings in paganism remind one of the true Gospel doctrines of repentance and rebirth taught by Jesus and the holy prophets. For example, in order to attain the rebirth in Hermeticism the convert must replace the following "evil inclinations of the flesh" with the "powers of God": "knowledge of God to replace ignorance, joy instead of sorrow, self-control in place of intemperance, continence where sensuality was, righteousness in lieu of

---

[6] Moses 6:59-60; John 5:5-8.
[7] Baptism in blood was discussed in an earlier chapter.

injustice, generosity to drive avarice away, truth instead of error, and the more abstract qualities of goodness, life, and light to take the place of all the other brutish torments."[8]

The Hermetic prophet, like John the Baptist, summoned men to "Repent and be baptized!" The following call to repentance is quoted from one of the Hermetic sermons:

O people, men born of earth, who have given yourselves up to drunkenness and sleep in your ignorance of God; awake to soberness, cease to be sodden with strong drink and lulled in sleep devoid of reason. . . . O men, why have you given yourselves up to death, when you have been granted power to partake of immortality? Repent, you who have journeyed with error, and joined company with ignorance; rid yourselves of darkness, and lay hold on light; partake of immortality, forsaking corruption.[9]

PAGANS' CONCEPT OF BAPTISM AND REBIRTH

Practically every pagan religion that was a vital rival of early Christianity practiced baptism as one of its rites of initiation;[10] and the doctrine behind this ordinance was death to the old life and regeneration or rebirth into a new life—a spiritual life.[11] It connoted a purging of all past sins of the flesh and a birth into a life of the spirit—a life of immortality—just as the Christian doctrine of baptism did. The fundamentals of the concept were inherited from the true plan of salvation.

"There can be no salvation without regeneration," was emphatically asserted in the Hermetic pagan literature. Plato remarked that "To die is to be initiated." Many different religious practices were employed by the ancient pagans to engender a rebirth in the worshipers. Every serious-minded neophyte, in being baptized into the Mystery Religions during early Christian centuries passed through the solemn ceremony believing that thereby he became twice born—a new creature. This concept of rebirth and regeneration was paramount in paganism as early as the sixth century B.C. and remained so until Christianity absorbed the heathenistic cults during the fourth and fifth centuries A.D. Note the definiteness of this concept as expressed in the following Mithraic literature translated

---

[8] Willoughby, *Pagan Regeneration*, p. 209.
[9] *Corpus Hermeticum*, cited in Willoughby, *ibid.*, p. 211.
[10] Samuel Angus, *The Mystery Religions and Christianity*, pp. 81-83.
[11] *Ibid.*, pp. 95-100; Willoughby, *op. cit.*, pp. 45, 101, 131-132, 159-161, 196-224.

from a papyrus scroll preserved in Egypt from the first century A.D. The opening prayer of the liturgy begins:

"O! First spirit of the spirit that is within me! . . . May it please thee to translate me, who am trammelled by the nature which underlies me, to an immortal genesis . . . that I may be born again in spirit." At other points in the documents are recorded: "Though I was born a mortal from a mortal mother . . . having been sanctified by sacred ceremonies I am about to gaze with immortal eyes on the immortal aeon. . . . O Lord! Having been born again, I pass away, being exalted the while, as thou hast established the law and ordained the sacrament."[12]

Dr. Willoughby thinks that "few if any ancient [pagan] texts contain a clearer" statement of the "religious experience of rebirth to immortal life than does this Mithraic liturgy. By itself alone it is startling testimony to the prominence of the idea in Gentile religious circles. . . . It is certain that the devotees of Mithra viewed initiation as a rebirth to immortality."[13] It should be kept in mind that rebirth as promised in Mithraism was to be achieved at least in part through the rite of baptism.

From the teachings of the pagan rival of Christianity known as Hermeticism, in which the rebirth idea was paramount, the following is quoted:

"No one can be saved without regeneration." . . . The author of the new birth is "the Son of God," "the One Man" . . . Spiritual rebirth is an escape from the delusions of the body in order by "the essential birth" to become "divine and Son of the One." By the will of God the new birth is accomplished by which the "begotten" of God becomes "divine" and "Son."[14]

From what has been presented, it is apparent that in their doctrines of repentance and spiritual rebirth, ancient paganism retained many similarities to the original revelations received from heaven.

SUPPLEMENTARY READINGS—CHAPTER 30

1. *Doctrine and Covenants* 18:9-26, 42-47; 20:29; 33:11; 35:5-6; 49:8, 13; 58:48.
2. *Pearl of Great Price:* Moses 5:8-15; 6:22-67.
3. Harold Willoughby, *Pagan Regeneration,* pp. 45, 101, 131-132, 159-164, 196-224, 209-211.

---

[12] *Bibliotheque Nationale, Supp.,* Gr. 574. See Dieterich, *Eine Mithrasliturgie,* cited in Willoughby, *op. cit.,* pp. 163-164.
[13] Willoughby, *ibid.*
[14] *Corpus Hermeticum,* cited in Angus, *op. cit.,* pp. 95-100.

Chapter 31.

THE TRUE DOCTRINE OF BAPTISM RESTORED

BAPTISM ORDINANCE ADULTERATED

So completely were the ordinances of the Gospel of Jesus Christ—such as baptism—changed by the fusing of the concepts and rites of various religions during the early centuries A.D., that baptism as practiced by the Christians during the third century and following can hardly be recognized as having evolved from the New Testament practice of this rite. But when one studies all the religions that contributed to the complete religious situation of the Graeco-Roman world, one can easily recognize that Christian baptism of 250 or 300 A.D. was a composite of Hebrew, Christian, and pagan thought and practice, with the major contributions coming from the latter two.

EFFORTS AT REFORMATION

Many Christians in Europe recognized during the sixteenth century that the prevailing Catholic practice of baptism did not correspond with the teachings of the New Testament. There was, therefore, a desire and a conscious effort made to revive, as nearly as possible, the original method of administering this ordinance. This reformation was expressed in the Ana-baptist and Baptist movement which began in Germany and spread throughout Europe. It later found its way to America. But this reformation movement did not nor could not officially restore the holy ordinance of baptism. There was no church in existence following the Great Apostasy and preceding the nineteenth century that could officially administer the ordinance of baptism, because the holy Priesthood of God was not in the world during that period.

A Divine Restoration

The "Falling Away" from the Gospel truths necessitated a divine restoration. As has been previously mentioned, this restoration took place during the early part of the nineteenth century. The Lord through divers ways made known to Joseph Smith, the American Prophet, the true plan of salvation, which includes the holy ordinance of baptism.

One beautiful spring day (May 15, 1829), while Joseph Smith and Oliver Cowdery were translating the *Book of Mormon* at Harmony, Pennsylvania, they discovered that baptism by immersion for the remission of sins was mentioned a number of times in the ancient Nephite record. Since the ordinance of baptism was erroneously understood and practiced by the various Christian churches, Joseph and Oliver concluded to inquire of the Lord for light. They retired to the woods near the Susquehanna River and engaged in humble prayer. While they were thus engaged, an angel descended from heaven in a cloud of light and introduced himself as John, known as John the Baptist in the New Testament. He said he acted under the direction of Peter, James and John, the Lord's apostles who held the keys of the Melchizedek Priesthood, and that he had been sent to confer on Joseph and Oliver the Aaronic Priesthood, which holds the keys of the temporal Gospel. He laid his hands upon their heads, saying:

Upon you, my fellow servants, in the name of Messiah, I confer the Priesthood of Aaron, which holds the keys of the ministering of angels, and of the Gospel of repentance, and of *baptism by immersion for the remission of sins;* and this shall never be taken again from the earth until the sons of Levi do offer again an offering unto the Lord in righteousness.[1]

The messenger told Joseph and Oliver that the Aaronic Priesthood had not the power of laying on hands for the gift of the Holy Ghost, but soon thereafter the Melchizedek Priesthood would be conferred upon them. The angel instructed them to go down into the water and baptize each other, and then to lay hands on each other and re-confer the Priesthood which he had bestowed upon them. Following the instructions of the angel, they went down into the

---

[1] *Pearl of Great Price,* p. 56; Joseph Fielding Smith, *Essentials in Church History,* pp. 67-70; *Doctrine and Covenants,* 13.

water, where Joseph first baptized Oliver and then Oliver baptized Joseph by immersion.   To quote the Prophet:

Immediately on our coming up out of the water after we had been baptized, we experienced great and glorious blessings from our Heavenly Father. No sooner had I baptized Oliver Cowdery than the Holy Ghost fell upon him, and he stood up and prophesied many things which should shortly come to pass. And again, so soon as I had been baptized by him, I also had the spirit of prophecy, when, standing up, I prophesied concerning the rise of this Church, and many other things connected with the Church, and the generation of the children of men.[2]

Shortly thereafter Joseph and Oliver received the Melchizedek Priesthood from Peter, James and John. The restoration of the higher Priesthood took place somewhere between Harmony, Pennsylvania, and Colesville, New York, on the banks of the Susquehanna River. The Prophet of God who had been called to usher in the last dispensation of the Gospel now had the authority of God to baptize by water and by Spirit. Only those people who have reached the age of accountability in our day who receive the holy ordinances of baptism and confirmation through the administration of this divine restoration shall inherit the kingdom of God. The Prophet Joseph Smith taught as follows regarding the necessity of baptism by Spirit:

The baptism of water, without the baptism of fire and the Holy Ghost attending it, is of no use; they are necessarily and inseparably connected. An individual must be born of water and the Spirit in order to get into the Kingdom of God.[3]

REVELATIONS RECEIVED BY JOSEPH THE PROPHET

Following the divine restoration of the ordinance of baptism and the authority of God to perform the holy ordinance in a valid and acceptable way, Joseph the Prophet received numerous revelations from Jesus and the Eternal Father relative to baptism. Thus the Prophet gave to members of the Church of Jesus Christ of Latter-day Saints a clear and comprehensive understanding of the doctrine of baptism.

This ordinance as revealed to Joseph Smith contains a number of principal items. First, God gave the commandment in this dispensation, as He had done in previous Gospel dispensations, for all people who had arrived at the

---

[2] *Pearl of Great Price, ibid.*
[3] Joseph Fielding Smith, *Teachings of the Prophet Joseph Smith,* p. 198.

age of accountability to repent and be baptized by water and by fire in order that they might enter the kingdom of God. To quote:

Believe on the name of the Lord Jesus, who was on the earth, and is to come, the beginning and the end; repent and be baptized in the name of Jesus Christ, according to the holy commandment for the remission of sins; and whoso doeth this shall receive the gift of the Holy Ghost, by the laying on of the hands of the elders of the Church.[4]

And this is my Gospel—repentance and baptism by water, and then cometh the baptism of fire and the Holy Ghost, even the Comforter, which showeth all things, and teacheth the peaceable things of the kingdom.[5]

And again, inasmuch as parents have children in Zion, or in any of her stakes which are organized, that teach them not to understand the doctrine of repentance, faith in Christ the Son of the living God, and of baptism and the gift of the Holy Ghost by the laying on of hands, *when eight years old,* the sin be upon the heads of the parents. For this shall be a law unto the inhabitants of Zion, or in any of her stakes which are organized. And their children shall be baptized for the remission of their sins when eight years old, and receive the laying on of the hands.[6]

Verily, verily, I say unto you, they who believe not on your words, and are not baptized in water in my name, for the remission of their sins, that they may receive the Holy Ghost, shall be damned, and shall not come into my Father's kingdom where my Father and I are.[7]

On several occasions the Lord made it clear to the Prophet that any baptism that was valid and accepted by Him must be performed by one ordained to the holy Priesthood and thereby possessing the proper authority.[8] He also explained that the only acceptable mode of baptism was immersion, being "baptized after the manner of his [Christ's] burial, being buried in the water in his name, and this according to the commandment which he has given—That by keeping the commandments they might be washed and cleansed from all their sins, and receive the Holy Spirit by the laying on of the hands of him who is ordained and sealed unto this power."[9] Following baptism, the Church member was commanded to continue to live faithfully all the principles of the Gospel; and if he succeeded in doing so he would be sealed by the Holy Spirit of promise in the

<hr>

[4] *Doctrine and Covenants* 49:11-13, 19-31.
[5] *Ibid.,* 39:6.
[6] *Ibid.,* 68:25-27.
[7] *Ibid.,* 84:74.
[8] *Ibid.,* 13; 84:27; 55:2; 107:20.
[9] *Ibid.,* 76:51-54; 33:11; 128:12; 20:68.

resurrection to be accounted among the members of the Church of the Firstborn to dwell with Christ in Celestial glory forever and ever.

God did not leave the Prophet in the dark regarding who should have the privilege of being baptized and the definite method by which baptism should be performed. In April, 1830, the month during which the Church was organized, the Lord instructed Joseph as follows:

All those who humble themselves before God, and desire to be baptized, and come forth with broken hearts and contrite spirits, and witness before the Church that they have truly repented of all their sins, and are willing to take upon them the name of Jesus Christ, having a determination to serve him to the end, and truly manifest by their works that they have received of the Spirit of Christ unto the remission of their sins, shall be received by baptism into His Church. . . .

No one can be received into the Church of Christ unless he has arrived unto the years of accountability before God, and is capable of repentance.

Baptism is to be administered in the following manner unto all those who repent: The person who is called of God and has authority from Jesus Christ to baptize, shall go down into the water with the person who has presented himself or herself for baptism, and shall say, calling him or her by name: *"Having been commissioned of Jesus Christ, I baptize you in the name of the Father, and of the Son, and of the Holy Ghost. Amen."*

Then shall he immerse him or her in the water, and come forth again out of the water.[10]

BAPTISM FOR THE DEAD RESTORED

God not only revealed the doctrine of baptism for the living to the Prophet Joseph Smith, but He established on earth again the glorious doctrine of baptism for the dead, thereby opening the door to all of His sons and daughters who have ever lived in mortality to come back into His presence on condition of their worthiness. The Lord told Joseph that baptism for the dead should be performed in His holy house; in fact, one of the principal purposes He had in mind in commanding the Latter-day Saints to build temples was for the performance of this holy ordinance. In the revelation the Lord declared: "For a baptismal font there is not upon the earth, that they, my saints, may be baptized for those who are dead."[11] Then God commanded the Saints to build temples in which to perform the

---

[10] *Ibid.*, 20:37, 71-74.
[11] *Doctrine and Covenants* 124:29-39.

ordinance of baptizing for the dead, proclaiming that this ordinance was instituted from before the foundation of the world for the salvation of His children who, for various reasons, would not accept the Gospel while in mortality.

A week following the dedication of the Kirtland temple, April 3, 1836, Elijah appeared to Joseph Smith and Oliver Cowdery in the temple and bestowed upon them the keys of sealing power, that all the ordinances for the dead might be performed in a valid way.[12]   Later the Lord revealed many more details regarding this sacred work,[13] thereby making it possible for the complete purposes of God regarding His children to be accomplished.

BAPTISM FOR THE DEAD IN APOSTOLIC DAYS

This dispensation of the Gospel is not the only one in which baptism for the dead has been practiced. This doctrine was so well known by Jesus' apostles and the members of the Christian Church during the Apostolic Age that Paul need not explain the doctrine in detail when he wrote to the Saints. But the apostle did make the following definite reference to the Christians' well-established practice of baptism for the dead:

Else what shall they do which are baptized for the dead, if the dead rise not at all? Why are they then baptized for the dead?[14]

We are informed in First Peter that while Christ's body was in the tomb preceding His resurrection "He went and preached unto the spirits in prison," giving unto the people who had been destroyed by the flood during the days of Noah another chance to hear and accept the Gospel. We are told in the *Doctrine and Covenants* that those of this group who accepted the Gospel and made themselves worthy in all other respects, received terrestrial glory.[15]   And what were the Gospel principles which Christ preached unto the spirits in prison? Certainly they included faith in the Lord Jesus Christ, repentance, and baptism by water and Spirit. Another reference in the same scripture proclaims the foregoing facts to be true. To quote:

Who shall give account to him that is ready to judge the quick and the dead. For this cause was the Gospel preached also to them

---

[12] *Ibid.*, 110.
[13] *Ibid.*, 128.
[14] 1 Corinthians 15:29.
[15] *Doctrine and Covenants* 76:71-74; Alma 34:32-36.

that are dead, that they might be judged according to men in the flesh, but live according to God in the spirit.[16]

For lack of historical records, we do not know exactly when or why the Christians stopped baptizing for the dead, but this is another example wherein they changed the ordinances of the Gospel.

TEACHINGS OF JOSEPH SMITH

Joseph Smith gave many wonderful teachings on the doctrine of baptism, explaining vividly and in simplicity what the Lord had revealed to him. By way of example, two short quotations from his sermons are given:

Baptism is a sign to God, to angels, and to heaven that we do the will of God, and there is no other way beneath the heavens whereby God hath ordained for man to come to Him to be saved, and enter into the Kingdom of God, except faith in Jesus Christ, repentance, and baptism for the remission of sins, and any other course is in vain; then you have the promise of the gift of the Holy Ghost.[17]

In the former ages of the world, before the Savior came into the flesh, "the saints" were baptized in the name of Jesus Christ to come, because there never was any other name whereby men could be saved; and after he came in the flesh and was crucified, then the saints were baptized in the name of Jesus Christ, crucified, risen from the dead and ascended into heaven, that they might be buried in baptism like Him, and be raised in glory like Him, that as there was but one Lord, one faith, one baptism, and one God and Father of us all, even so there was but one door to the mansions of bliss.[18]

CONCLUSIONS

With the coming of John the Baptist and Peter, James and John to the Prophet Joseph and Oliver Cowdery—giving to them the keys of the Priesthood—the authority to act in God's name in administering the holy rite of baptism by water and by Spirit is again present on the earth. Thus the Church of Jesus Christ is the only church in existence that can officially administer this holy ordinance. The publication of the *Book of Mormon* (which contains a detailed account of baptism as taught by Jesus to the Nephites following His resurrection and also as taught and practiced by the Nephite prophets) plus the revelations on baptism which now appear in the *Pearl of Great Price*, and also the reception of numerous revelations which ap-

---

[16] 1 Peter 3:18-20; 4:6.
[17] Joseph Fielding Smith, *Teachings of the Prophet Joseph Smith*, p. 198.
[18] *Ibid.*, 266.

pear in the *Doctrine and Covenants,* resulted in the Prophet's having as comprehensive an understanding of the doctrine of baptism as was ever possessed by man. Therefore, this holy ordinance as administered by the Church of Jesus Christ of Latter-day Saints today is, in all respects, the same as practiced by Father Adam, by the Nephites, and by Jesus and His apostles in Palestine during the early Christian period. This is the only church in the world which administers to its converts the true ordinance of baptism.

SUPPLEMENTARY READINGS—CHAPTER 31

1. *Doctrine and Covenants* 49:11-13; 19:41-43; 39:6; 68:25-27; 84:27, 74; 76:51-52; 33:11; 128; 13:1-6; 55:2; 107:20; 20:37, 71-73, 68, 41.
2. *Handbook of the Restoration,* pp. 115-127, 164-169, 534-552.
3. Joseph Fielding Smith (Compiler), *Teachings of the Prophet Joseph Smith,* pp. 12, 148, 192, 198-201, 260-266, 310, 314, 360-361.
4. James E. Talmage, *The Articles of Faith,* pp. 148-152.

Chapter 32.

THE SACRAMENT OR THE HOLY EUCHARIST

SACRAMENT INSTITUTED

Whenever the true Gospel of Jesus Christ has been on the earth the worshipers of God have always commemorated the great atoning sacrifice of our Lord and Savior by a holy ordinance. Originally this rite was that of sacrifice, which was practiced down to the advent of the Only Begotten Son of God. At the time of the death of the Master, however, the ancient law was fulfilled in His infinite and eternal sacrifice. He, therefore, gave to mortals a new ordinance known to Latter-day Saints as the Sacrament and to Catholics and some of the other Christian denominations as the Holy Eucharist. Since the latter term has been used so universally throughout the course of Christian history and for sake of word variety, we shall use the two terms interchangeably throughout the chapters which deal with this subject.

The institution of the Sacrament was regarded by the early Christians "as the new and true paschal celebration; as St. Paul wrote, 'Christ our Passover has been sacrificed for us; therefore let us keep the feast'."[1]

The night before the crucifixion of the Man of Galilee, Jesus took bread, and blessed it, and brake it, and gave it to the disciples, and said, "Take, eat; this is my body." And He took the cup, and gave thanks, and gave it to them, saying, "Drink ye all of it; for this is my blood of the new testament, which is shed for many for the remission of sins."[2]

It is true that the wording given by Matthew and Mark is rather mystical, suggesting to the practical-minded westerners the presence of flesh and blood of Christ in the Sacra-

---

[1] Charles Gore, *Jesus of Nazareth*, p. 156.
[2] Matthew 26:26-28; Mark 14:22-24.

ment. But the orientals—the companions of the Nazarene
—could be much better trusted than people of the West to
grasp clearly the full significance of Christ's figurative language. Peter, James, John and the other apostles knew
very well when Jesus said, "Take, eat; this is my body,"
that it was physically impossible for them to be eating of the
Master's physical body, as He had not as yet been sacrificed. He was a living person who had Himself given them
bread and the cup.

"This Do in Remembrance of Me"

Luke threw considerable light on the mystical wording
of Matthew and Mark by quoting Jesus as saying:

He took bread, and gave thanks, and brake it, and give it unto
them saying, "This is my body which is given for you: *This do in remembrance of me.*"[3]

Paul, the apostle to the Gentiles, also wrote an account
of the establishment and significance of the Holy Eucharist.
He received his information by special revelation from the
resurrected Savior. Students of the scriptures affirm that
his account was the first one of those in the New Testament
to be recorded; therefore, because of its accuracy and trust-
worthiness, it is of paramount importance in revealing to us
the early Christians' interpretation of the Sacrament.

Paul agrees with Luke in reporting that the bread and
wine were to be taken in remembrance of Jesus.[4] He cau-
tioned the Corinthian Christians against partaking of those
substances (not flesh and blood) unworthily, stating that
if they did so they were eating and drinking damnation
unto themselves. He quoted Jesus as saying: "This cup
is the new testament in my blood; this do ye, as oft as ye
drink it, in remembrance of me."[5] In other words, Paul
taught that the Sacrament was an ordinance of the *new
covenant of atonement,* brought about through the death
and resurrection of Jesus Christ, in order that man might
attain immortality and eternal life.[6]

Paul regarded the Sacrament as a means of communion with the Lord; also as a memorial of the covenant-
sacrifice of the Lamb of God. Being a Hebrew of He-

---

[3] Luke 22:19. The italics were supplied by the author.
[4] 1 Corinthians 11:17-35.
[5] *Ibid.,* 11:25.
[6] Moses 1:39; 6:58-59.

brews, thoroughly versed in the laws and customs of his people, he conceived of Jesus as the true Paschal Lamb and the partaking of the Eucharist as the Christian Passover. Just as the eating of the Paschal Lamb commemorated the deliverance of the children of Israel from the Egyptians, so did the Christians, eating of the Sacrament commemorate the sacrifice of the Lamb of God, who died to deliver all mortals from death and the grave. The point of significance in the Sacrament doctrine is not the fact that Christ died—but that He lives, as Paul presented so clearly in his discourse on immortality.[7]

The fact that Paul's and Luke's accounts definitely state that the early Christians partook of the Sacrament in remembrance of the sacrifice of the Master indicates that the early devotees of Jesus did not believe that they were actually eating the flesh and drinking the blood of their crucified Lord. That concept came into Christianity as a later development. In the words of Dr. Charles Gore:

There is not a word in St. Paul of that "eating of the god." . . . All his teaching grows out of the thoughts of the Passover and the covenant feast of Exodus 24:1-11, immeasurably deepened and spiritualized by the doctrine of the union of Christ with his people which St. Paul had received from Christ Himself.[8]

True Meaning of Sacrament

Jesus Christ visited the Nephites in America following His resurrection and imparted to them also the same Gospel truths that He had given to the Jews. In order to ascertain the true meaning of Sacrament, a comparison of the *Book of Mormon* and *New Testament* accounts should be made. In the words of the Nephite record:

When the disciples had come with bread and wine, he [Jesus] took of the bread and brake and blessed it; and he gave unto the disciples and commanded that they should eat. . . . "And this shall ye do in remembrance of my body, which I have shown unto you. And it shall be a testimony unto the Father that ye do always remember me. And if ye do always remember me ye shall have my spirit to be with you."

And it came to pass that when he said these words, he commanded his disciples that *they should take of the wine of the cup, and drink of it,* and that they should also give unto the multitude, that they might drink of it. . . .

_____
[7] 1 Corinthians 15:1-40.
[8] Charles Gore, *A New Commentary on Holy Scripture,* p. 423.

And when the disciples had done this, Jesus said unto them, "Blessed are ye for this thing which ye have done, for this is fulfilling my commandments, and this doth witness unto the Father that ye are willing to do that which I have commanded you. And this shall ye always do to those who repent and are baptized in my name; and *ye shall do it in remembrance of my blood, which I have shed for you, that ye may witness unto the Father that ye do always remember me. And if ye do always remember me, ye shall have my spirit to be with you."*[9]

Fortunately the Nephite historian recorded the sacramental blessings given to his people by the Savior and used in their dispensation of the Gospel. These blessings agree exactly in their wording with the revelation on Sacrament received by the Prophet Joseph Smith in April, 1830.[10] This is further evidence that the Gospel has always been the same. If at any time a change should occur in an ordinance, the change could be made officially only through revelation from the Lord Jesus Christ—the co-author of the eternal plan of salvation.

An analysis of the doctrine of the Sacrament as given in the Nephite record reveals definitely several facts. In the first place, it is clear that the sacramental substances were bread and wine—not flesh and blood. Also, the emblems were partaken in remembrance of the body and blood of Jesus which were sacrificed for the redemption of mankind. All who partook of these holy emblems entered into a covenant with their Eternal Father that they would keep His commandments. He in turn promised His Spirit to be with them and to guide them. Therefore, the partaking of the Sacrament officially sanctioned a covenant entered into by the worshipers of Jesus and their Maker to the effect that each party concerned has done, and will continue to do, his share in bringing about the atonement of mankind. In other words, Sacrament is a symbolical representation of the great covenant-sacrifice of Jesus Christ, who died that we might live. His blood was shed in order that we might receive forgiveness of our sins on condition of repentance and that all men might be resurrected into immortality. The Sacrament is also a token of Christian fellowship and of spiritual communion with our Eternal Father and His Only Begotten Son—Jesus the Christ.

[9] 3 Nephi 18:1-12.
[10] *Doctrine and Covenants* 20:78-79; Moroni 4:1-3; 5:1-2.

CHANGES IN CHRISTIAN EUCHARIST

History testifies that, after Jesus established the Sacrament and up to the time of the Reformation, several pronounced alterations took place in the Christians' Eucharistic concept. The first evidence of drastic change appears in the writings of Justin Martyr and Irenaeus, two Christian apologists of the second century A.D. They both accepted as literal the mystical wording of the Gospels, and especially that of Jesus' famous sermon on "the Bread of Life" as recorded in the Gospel of John.[11] Their teachings mark a definite stage in the Christian interpretation of Sacrament from which later Catholic writings differ fundamentally very little, the main difference being the attempts made by theologians from time to time to explain how the great mystery of conversion takes place.

Irenæus (about 185 A.D.) maintained that the Holy Eucharist became endowed with spiritual qualities through the "invocation of God"; thereby, in a realistic way, it engendered potions of immortal life into those who partook of it. Quoting Irenaeus:

For as the bread, which is produced from the earth, when it received the invocation of God, is no longer common bread but the Eucharist, consisting of two realities, earthly and heavenly; so also our bodies, when they receive the Eucharist, are no longer corruptible, having the hope of the resurrection to eternity.[12]

John of Damascus (about 759 A.D.) maintained that the Eucharistic objects (the bread and the wine) were identical with Christ's body and blood—that same body that was born of Mary.[13] Cyril, Bishop of Jerusalem (350 A.D.), attempted an explanation as to how the conversion occurred. He said:

The Holy Spirit, who is a living person within the Godhead, descends upon the bread and wine at the prayer of the celebrant, and changes them into the body and blood.[14]

Gregory maintained that the Holy Eucharist was the greatest of the sacraments,[15] and that it was a repetition of the sacrifice of Christ offered to God by the priest for both the living and the dead. As early as Cyprian's time (?200-

---

[11] Williston Walker, *A History of the Christian Church*, p. 40; John 6:31-70.
[12] Cited in Walker, *op. cit.*, pp. 138-139.
[13] *Ibid.*, p. 99.
[14] *Ibid.*
[15] The Catholic church has seven sacraments which are comparable to some of the ordinances in the Church of Jesus Christ, but the Catholics do not use the term ordinances. The Catholic seven sacraments are as follows: Baptism, Confirmation, Eucharist, Penance (Confession), Extreme Unction (Last Anointing), Orders and Matrimony. See Cardinal Gibbons, *The Faith of Our Fathers*, p. 266ff.

285 A. D.), a rather definite doctrine of the Eucharist as a sacrifice had developed. In his own words:

For if Jesus Christ, our Lord and God, is Himself the chief priest of God the Father, and has first offered Himself a sacrifice to the Father, and has commanded this to be done in commemoration of Himself, certainly that priest truly discharges the office of Christ who imitates that which Christ did; and he then offers it according to what he sees Christ Himself to have offered.[16]

The Christian writers of the fourth and fifth centuries taught that partaking of the Eucharist was absolutely essential to salvation, a teaching not found in the scriptures. Quoting St. Augustine (?354-430 A.D.):

The churches of Christ maintain it to be an inherent principle that without baptism and partaking of the Supper of the Lord it is impossible for any man to attain either to the kingdom of God or to salvation and everlasting life.[17]

Latter-day Saints, however, believe that partaking of the Sacrament is very desirable and should be participated in each Sabbath and on certain other occasions by worthy Church members.

Conversion (Transubstantiation) and Symbolic Theories

During the Middle Ages two Eucharistic theories, conversion and symbolic, were vigorously discussed, each having its advocators. The conversion theory means that the bread and wine actually change into Christ's flesh and blood; and the symbolic theory maintains that the sacramental objects remain bread and wine. Paschasius Radbertus, a monk of the monastery of Corbie (about 831 A.D.), published a thoroughgoing treatise on the Holy Eucharist in which he strongly advocated the conversion theory. Eleven years later Ratramus, also of Corbie, answered Radbertus' arguments and supported the symbolic theory. He maintained:

In the Eucharist bread and wine are received, but Christ's body and blood are understood. The latter, therefore, are received in mystery and figure, not in sensible reality.[18]

Two hundred years passed before another open attack was made on the conversion theory. In 1050 A.D., Berengar, head of the cathedral school of Tours, condemned

---

[16] Cyprian, *Letters*, cited in *ibid.*, pp. 62-63.
[17] Augustine, *Forgiveness of Sin*, 1:34; cited in Walker, *ibid.*, pp. 262-265.
[18] Walker, *ibid.*, pp. 262-265.

the doctrine of Radbertus and defended Ratramus' symbolic theory. Two church councils condemned him and required him to sign a confession of faith to the effect that the consecrated bread and wine are not only a sacrament, but also the real body and blood of Christ, and that these "not only sacramentally, but in sensible reality, are taken in the priests' hands."[19] Berengar conformed temporarily to the demand of the councils; however, in 1069, he published his views at length in a treatise on the Holy Supper, in which he denied "subjective change." Again (1079 A.D.) he was required to sign a declamation affirming that the bread and wine are substantially converted. Berengar subscribed and the conversion theology was victorious.

About the time of the Berengar controversy, the name *transubstantiation* was first used in connection with the Holy Eucharist. It "seems to have been first used by Hildbert (1018-1045 A.D.), archbishop of Tours; and its first authorized admission to the doctrinal vocabulary dates from the Fourth Lateran Council (1215 A.D.)."[20] This council gave it full approval and the highest dogmatic standing.

Thomas Aquinas (1227-1274 A.D.) put the doctrine in its final form, giving to it clearness of definition. He taught that when the priest consecrated the Sacrament the power of God performed a miracle upon it, so that while the "accidents" (the shape, the taste, and the like) remained unchanged, the "substance" was actually transformed into the very body and blood of our Lord and Master.[21] By Aquinas' time the doctrine had developed that the whole body and blood of Christ are present in either element of the Eucharist. Thus the theory of transubstantiation became firmly rooted in Christendom. Although rejected later by most Protestant religions, it remains today a pertinent doctrine of Catholicism.[22]

SUPPLEMENTARY READINGS—CHAPTER 32

1. *Bible:* Matthew 26:17-30; Mark 14:12-26; Luke 22:14-23; John 6:31-71; 1 Corinthians 11:17-35; 15:1-40; Jeremiah 31:31-32; Hebrews 8:13.
2. *Book of Mormon:* 3 Nephi 18:1-12, 26-32; 20:1-9; Moroni 4:1-3; 5:1-2.

---

[19] *Ibid.*
[20] Edward M. Hulme, *The Middle Ages,* p. 361.
[21] Walker, *op. cit.* pp. 263-264, 288.
[22] James Cardinal Gibbons, *The Faith of Our Fathers,* pp. 287-299.

Chapter 33.

PAGAN INFLUENCES ON THE EUCHARIST DOCTRINE

Introductory Statement

In the early part of this lesson we refer to some of the same pagan practices that were discussed in chapter 26, i. e., the pagans' eating of the flesh and drinking of the blood of their savior-gods (animals). The emphasis in the previous chapter, however, was that of shedding of blood for the purpose of atonement from sins. The emphasis in this lesson is on the pagans' practice of eating and drinking divine or sacramental substances, which belief was similar to the Catholic doctrine of transubstantiation. The purpose is to show the influence of the pagans' beliefs and practices on the Christian Holy Eucharist doctrine.

Origin of Transubstantiation

Whence came the concept of transubstantiation? An examination of the pagan contemporaries of early Christianity reveals the fact that the strongest pagan religions, especially the Mystery cults, ate eucharistic meals as part of their religious ritual. This religious practice had been participated in for generations before Christianity was planted by Jesus and His disciples in the world of paganism. The Sacrament doctrine was almost universally accepted by the pagans of the Mediterranean world at the time Christianity was established. There was one belief held in common by most of those ancient heathenistic religions, viz., that their sacramental objects were, in a realistic sense, their savior-gods, and must be consumed in order for the worshipers to obtain the virtues that they believed those deities were able to contribute. The spiritual portion of man must be fed with divine substance, they believed; thus they must eat their god. The methods used in obtaining this sacramental grace ranged from the most barbaric orgies to a highly refined sacrament, similar to the Christian Holy Eucharist.

PAGAN PRACTICES

We shall present briefly only a few examples of pagan eucharistic beliefs and practices for the purpose of showing the heathenistic doctrine which altered Christian Sacrament from "This do in remembrance of Me" to the Catholic doctrine of transubstantiation.

The Dionysian Mysteries promised its devotees immortality and communion with their god through a sacrament of eating and drinking.

Participation in the life of the god was realistically attained by drinking the blood and eating raw flesh of the sacred victim in which the god was assumed to be incarnated.[1]

The victims varied according to the country in which the worshipers resided. It might have been a fawn, a goat, a ram, or a bull—whatever the hapless animal was, the worshipers exhibited a certain ferocious cruelty in tearing it to pieces.

Since during their religious festivities, the god Dionysus was believed to be temporarily resident in the sacramental animals, the underlying philosophy of such pagan eucharistic practices and transubstantiation was basically the same. The principal difference, however, was that the sacramental ritual of the pagans was orgiastic and barbaric, while the other was refined.

Dr. Willoughby concluded in regards to the Dionysian belief that:

By the sacraments of eating and drinking they entered into direct communion with their god, and became partakers of his immortality. In assimilating the raw flesh wherein the god was temporarily incarnate and in drinking the juice of the grape, they received into their bodies an undying substance. In life mystically united with their god, in death they could not be divided, and when the time came for them to go to the invisible world, they were sure of sharing the blessed life of their god.[2]

---

[1] Shirley Jackson Case, *The Evolution of Early Christianity*, p. 299; Samuel Angus, *The Mystery Religions and Christianity*, p. 130; Frazier, *The Golden Bough*, vol. 4, p. 31; Robertson-Smith, *Religion of the Semites*, p. 320; Jane Harrison, *Themis*, p. 123.

[2] Firmicus Maternus, *De Errore Profanarum Religionum*, vol. 6, p. 5, cited in Harold Willoughby, *Pagan Regeneration*, pp. 76, 85; Jane Harrison, *Ancient Art and Ritual*, p. 87; Genesis 9:4; Leviticus 17:10-16; Deuteronomy 12:16, 23; Hebrews 9:10.

The Orphic worshiper also partook of a sacrament by eating and drinking the flesh and blood of his god Zagreus. He maintained that this sacrament was a "divine substance that nourished and strengthened the immortal life within himself";[3] thereby setting the balance of his body more Dionysiac (spiritual) than Titanic (mortal), which would make possible the breaking of the cycle of reincarnation. Thus the partaking of their sacrament was absolutely necessary for the salvation of the worshipers, a belief which came into Christendom, as was pointed out in the last lesson.

Just as the life of Zagreus entered the devotee physically when he partook of the flesh of the bull, so the man's soul entered more fully into the spiritual life of Zagreus by this very physical process. In a mystical sense God and man became one by the communion.[4]

Professor Robertson-Smith gives a very interesting account of a similar sacramental custom among the Arabs of the Sinai region. On certain occasions, these ancient people killed a spotless white camel and ate the uncooked blood and flesh of the animal entirely before daybreak. To quote:

The slaughter of the victim, the sacramental drinking of the blood, and devouring in wild haste of the pieces of still quivering flesh, recall the details of the Dionysiac and other festivals. The plain meaning is that the victim was devoured before its life had left the still warm blood and flesh; . . . and that thus in the most literal way, all those who shared in the ceremony absorbed part of the victim's life into themselves. One sees how much more forcibly than any ordinary meal such a rite expresses the establishment or confirmation of a bond of common life between the worshipers, and also, since the blood is shed upon the altar itself, between the worshipers and their god. In this sacrifice, then, the significant factors are two: the conveyance of the living blood to the godhead, and the absorption of the living flesh and blood into the flesh and blood of the worshipers. Each of these is effected in the simplest and most direct manner, so that the meaning of the ritual is perfectly transparent.[5]

PAGAN AND CHRISTIAN SACRAMENT PARALLELS

The sacraments of several of the very prominent pagan rivals of Christianity furnished close parallels to the perverted Christian Holy Eucharist. One example was that of the Cybele-Attis Mysteries. Firmicus Maternus denounced this paganistic rite because it was so similar to

[3] Willoughby, op. cit., pp. 100-101; Edward Carpenter, Pagan and Christian Creeds, p. 60.
[4] Willoughby, op. cit., p. 101.
[5] Robertson-Smith, op. cit.

Christian interpretation of the Holy Eucharist of his day. "Both were believed to communicate divine life to the devotee and assure him of salvation. Maternus concluded his invective against the pagan rite with the appeal, 'It is another food that gives salvation and life. Seek the bread of Christ and the cup of Christ.' "[6] The Cybele-Attis sacrament consisted of a beverage and a solid food.

It is not unlikely that a corn product, or some other vegetable food in which Attis was believed especially to dwell, formed a part of the sacred repast. In partaking of this meal, the devotee was enabled to share in a naturalistic manner the life of his god.[7]

Clement of Alexandria recorded the password of Eleusinian Mysteries as follows: "I have fasted, I have drunk the barley drink. I have taken things from the sacred chest, having tasted thereof I have placed them into the basket and again from the basket into the chest."[8] This formula is a statement of their eucharistic ceremonial. The drink "was a direct and sympathetic participation in the experiences of the goddess, an action expressive of attained fellowship with the deity. . . . If, as is most likely, the sacred food consisted of cereals, then the assimilation of this food meant a direct and realistic union with Demeter, the goddess of grain. It meant an incorporation of divine substance into the human body."[9]

During the first four centuries A.D., the Mithraic and Christian Eucharists resembled each other so much that Justin Martyr (135 A.D.), a Christian apologist, described the Eucharist and then made the following comment about the Mithraic sacrament: "The wicked devils have imitated this in the Mysteries of Mithra, commanding the same thing to be done. For that bread and a cup of water are placed with certain incantations in the mystic rites of one who is being initiated, you either know or can learn."[10]

RELIGIOUS SYNCRETISM

Sufficient evidence has been given to illustrate the universality of the belief held by the pagan rivals of Christianity that they actually ate the flesh and drank the blood of their

---

[6] Firmicus Maternus, *op. cit.*, 18, cited in Willoughby, *op. cit.*, p. 135.
[7] *Ibid.*
[8] Clement of Alexandria, *Protrepticus*, ii, 21.
[9] Willoughby, *op. cit.*, pp. 59-60.
[10] Cited in Angus, *op. cit.*, p. 129; Carpenter, *op. cit.*, p. 66; Willoughby, *op. cit.*, p. 162.

gods in their various sacraments. It should be kept in mind that in early Christendom the proselytes were obtained primarily from contemporary pagan cults. Thousands of worshipers of Mystery gods flocked into Christianity, bringing with them many of their most cherished beliefs. A very extensive syncretism resulted, reaching its height during the third and fourth centuries A.D. Thus the Sacrament as established by the Son of God was later blended with pagan eucharistic concepts, contaminating to a certain extent the divine ordinance and refining the heathenistic contributions in equal proportion. It was but natural for these pagans, when they became Christians, to believe that the bread and wine of the Sacrament were actually the flesh and blood of Jesus, since they had formerly believed that in their sacraments they had eaten and drunk their gods. Obviously, herein lies the origin of transubstantiation.

Of course, those obvious alterations that came into Christian theology and practice were not adopted from paganism purposely, but crept into Christendom through a natural process of religious syncretism, i. e., blending together of religious beliefs. In the words of Dr. Walker:

> The course of development during the succeeding century was determined by the prevalence of ideas drawn from the Mystery Religions. There is no adequate ground to believe that there was intentional imitation. Christians of the last half of the second and the third centuries lived in an atmosphere highly charged with influences sprung from these faiths. It was but natural that they should look upon their own worship from the same point of view. It is probable that already existing tendencies in this direction were strongly reinforced by the great growth of the church by conversion from heathenism in the first half of the third century. The church came to be more and more regarded as possessed of life-giving mysteries, under the superintendence and dispensation of the clergy.[11]

PROBABLE ORIGIN OF PAGAN SACRAMENTS

It is quite probable that the sacramental beliefs and practices of the pagan rivals of Christianity were adulterated forms of the true doctrine of Sacrament, just as most of their other beliefs were altered forms of the Gospel of Jesus Christ. But, the reader may say, "You have just stated that the pagans' sacraments date many years earlier than the birth of Jesus." That is quite true; but it is prob-

---

[11] Williston Walker, *A History of the Christian Church*, p. 92.

able that in one of the early Gospel dispensations God revealed the ordinance of Sacrament to man even before
the advent of Jesus of Nazareth, in anticipation of the sacrifice that Christ would make for mortals. Yet it is true that
practically all of the tangible evidence has been lost to history.
We do know, however, that such doctrines as the United
Order have been revealed and lived three or four times during certain periods when God's children were unusually
righteous. Could not the same thing have happened in
regards to Sacrament?

The Prophet Joseph Smith's translation of the *Bible*,
called the *Inspired Version*, suggests the foregoing conclusions to have been the case. For example, when Father
Abraham met the great High Priest Melchizedek on a certain
occasion the *Inspired Version* states:

*And Melchizedek, king of Salem, brought forth bread and wine;
and he brake bread and blest it; and he blest the wine, he being the priest
of the Most High God, and he gave to Abraham.*[12]

What interpretation could be given to this statement
of the breaking and blessing of the bread and the blessing
of wine by one holding the proper Priesthood and the serv-
ing of these substances to a Church member other than
the observance of the holy ordinance of Sacrament? Therefore, it seems that again we find the roots of paganism running back for generations to the true Gospel revelations.

SUPPLEMENTARY READINGS—CHAPTER 33

1. *Bible:* Genesis 9:3-4; Leviticus 17:10-16; Deuteronomy 12:16, 23; *The Inspired Version*, Genesis 14:1-40.
2. Harold Willoughby, *Pagan Regeneration*, pp. 59-60, 70-78, 100-104, 134-136,
   161-162.

---

[12] *Inspired Version*, Genesis 14:17.

Chapter 34.

RESTORATION OF THE TRUE
SACRAMENT RITE

REVELATION RESTORING THE TRUE SACRAMENT RITE

After humanity became lost in a maze of blighted religious thought, God the Eternal Father and His Only Begotten Son came to the rescue of mankind by restoring to the Prophet Joseph Smith the Gospel of Jesus Christ. Part of this restoration concerned itself with the true meaning of the Sacrament. Early in April, 1830— shortly after the Church was organized—Joseph the Prophet received a revelation in which Jesus Christ told him that, "It is expedient that the Church meet together often to partake of bread and wine in remembrance of the Lord Jesus."[1] Following this remark the revelation unfolded to the Church the true concept of the Sacrament as previously given by the Man of Galilee to His Apostles prior to His crucifixion and as given to the Nephites following His resurrection. The Prophet, having previously received the holy Priesthood from heaven, had authority to administer the holy emblems. Thus through Joseph Smith, the founder of Mormonism, the true Sacrament rite was restored to mankind.

The revelation definitely pointed out that the prime purpose of Sacrament is "to commemorate the atonement of the Lord Jesus as consummated in His agony and death; it is a testimony before God that we are mindful of His Son's sacrifice made in our behalf; and that we still profess the name of Christ and are determined to strive to keep His commandments, in the hope that we may ever have His Spirit to be with us. Partaking of the Sacrament worthily may be regarded therefore as a means of renewing our covenants before the Lord, of acknowledgment of mutual fellowship among the members, and of solemnly witnessing

---
[1] *Doctrine and Covenants* 20:76-79, 46, 58, 68.

our claim and profession of membership in the Church of Christ."[2]

ADMINISTERING THE SACRAMENT

The revelation also stated that the office of priest of the Aaronic order of Priesthood is requisite in consecrating the holy emblems, and also any man holding the higher order of Priesthood has authority to "administer bread and wine—the emblems of the flesh and blood of Christ."[3] The Lord instructed the elder or priest to administer it after this manner:

"He shall kneel with the Church [or, to express it in other words, in the presence of the Church][4] and call upon the Father in solemn prayer, saying:

"*O, God, the Eternal Father, we ask thee in the name of thy Son, Jesus Christ, to bless and sanctify this bread to the souls of all those who partake of it, that they may eat in remembrance of the body of thy Son, and witness unto thee, O God, the Eternal Father, that they are willing to take upon them the name of thy Son, and always remember him, and keep his commandments which he has given them, that they may always have his Spirit to be with them. Amen.*"[5]

The bread is then distributed to the congregation by teachers and deacons, under the direction of the officiating priest or elder, and then the wine or water is consecrated in the following manner:

"*O God, the Eternal Father, we ask thee, in the name of thy Son, Jesus Christ, to bless and sanctify this wine [or water] to the souls of all those who drink of it, that they may do it in remembrance of the blood of thy Son, which was shed for them; that they may witness unto thee, O God, the Eternal Father, that they do always remember him, that they may have his Spirit to be with them. Amen.*"[6]

An analysis of the prayer given in administering the bread and water (wine) plainly shows that in partaking of the holy emblems a sacred covenant is entered into between the worshipers and God. It makes clear that the sacramental objects remain bread and water, no transubstantiation taking place. The emblems are partaken in remembrance of the sacrifice of Christ which was made "that sal-

---

[2] James E. Talmage, *The Articles of Faith*, p. 179.
[3] *Doctrine and Covenants* 20:38-40, 46, 58, 68.
[4] Of course, it is obvious that the Lord did not mean for the entire congregation, especially when the audience is large, to kneel with the administrators while the sacrament is being blessed. The propriety of performing this sacred ordinance in the spirit of worship would be disturbed and the ceremony would become one of confusion. Therefore, it is proper for the audience to remain seated, and in an attitude of prayer, covenant making, and thanksgiving, while the administrators offer the blessings on the holy emblems.
[5] *Doctrine and Covenants* 20:76-77, compare with Moroni 4:1-3.
[6] *Ibid.*, 20:78-79, compare with Moroni 5:1-2.

vation might come unto the children of men, even through faith on His name, . . . [and] that there shall be no other name given, nor any other way nor means whereby salvation can come unto the children of men, only in and through the name of Christ, the Lord Omnipotent." One of the greatest needs of humanity today is to know that Jesus is the Christ and to understand the marvelous things He did for us in the atonement.

Regarding this subject, the Prophet Joseph Smith declared:

And this is the Gospel, the glad tidings, which the voice out of the heavens bore record unto us—That he came into the world, even Jesus, to be crucified for the world, and to bear the sins of the world, and to sanctify the world, and to cleanse it from all unrighteousness; that through him all might be saved whom the Father had put into his power and made by him; who glorifies the Father, and saves all the works of his hands, except those sons of perdition who deny the Son after the Father has revealed him.[8]

SACRAMENTAL EMBLEMS

When Christ instituted the Sacrament among both the Jews and the Nephites, He used bread and wine as the emblems of His body and blood; and in His first revelation on this ordinance to the Prophet Joseph He instructed Church members "to partake of bread and wine in remembrance of the Lord Jesus." Four months later, the Lord revealed to the Prophet that other forms of food and drink may be used in place of bread and wine.

In August, 1830, Newel Knight and his wife came to Harmony, Pennsylvania, on a visit. Since Emma Smith and Newel Knight's wife had not been confirmed, the decision was reached to hold a meeting, partake of the Sacrament, and attend to those confirmations. Thereupon Joseph set out to purchase some wine for the occasion. He had not proceeded far from his door when he was met by an angel who gave him the following commandment:

Listen to the voice of Jesus Christ, your Lord, your God, and your Redeemer, whose word is quick and powerful.

For, behold, I say unto you, that it mattereth not what ye shall eat or what ye shall drink when ye partake of the sacrament, if it so be that ye do it with an eye single to my glory—remembering unto the Father my body which was laid down for you, and my blood which was

---

[7] Mosiah 3:7-8, 17; *Doctrine and Covenants* 19:16-20.
[8] *Doctrine and Covenants* 76:40-43.

shed for the remission of your sins. Wherefore, a commandment I give unto you, that you shall not purchase wine, neither strong drink of your enemies; wherefore, you shall partake of none except it is made new among you; yea, in this my Father's kingdom which shall be built up on the earth."[9]

"Upon this authority, the Latter-day Saints administer water in their sacramental service, in preference to wine concerning the purity of which they are not assured."[10] The foregoing revelation is an important one, since it makes clear that God is not as concerned with the sacramental emblems as He is with the spirit in which the holy ordinance is observed, and that God forbids the use of alcoholic drinks.[11]

Who Shall Partake of the Sacrament

The Lord has revealed to the holy prophets definite instructions concerning the sacredness of the Sacrament and the consequent need of scrupulous care being exercised lest the ordinance be engaged in unworthily. Through divine revelation the Lord directed the members of the Church in this dispensation to meet together upon the Sabbath for the observance of the Sacrament "that thou mayest more fully keep thyself unspotted from the world."[12] Furthermore, the Lord instructed the Prophet:

Ye are also commanded not to cast anyone who belongeth to the Church out of your sacrament meetings; nevertheless, if any have trespassed, let him not partake until he makes reconciliation.[13]

When the resurrected Lord revealed the ordinance of Sacrament to the Nephites, He definitely stated that it was to be administered only to Church members. To quote:

When the multitude had eaten and were filled, he said unto the disciples, Behold, there shall one be ordained among you, and to him will I give power that he shall break bread, and bless it, and give it unto the people of my church, unto all those who shall believe and be baptized in my name.[14]

After the disciples had passed the wine to the people, Jesus said unto them: "And this shall ye always do to those who repent and are baptized in my name; and ye shall do it in remembrance of my blood, which I have shed for you, that ye may witness unto the Father that ye do

---

[9] Ibid., 27:1-4.
[10] James E. Talmage, The Articles of Faith, pp. 179-180.
[11] Joseph Fielding Smith, Essentials in Church History, pp. 109-110.
[12] Doctrine and Covenants 59:9, 12.
[13] Ibid., 46:4.
[14] 3 Nephi 18:5.

always remember me. And if ye do always remember me, ye shall have my Spirit to be with you."[15] Then Jesus admonished the church leaders to permit none whom they knew to be unworthy to take part in the ordinance:

And now behold, this is the commandment which I give unto you, that ye shall not suffer anyone knowingly, to partake of my flesh and blood unworthily, when ye shall minister it; For whoso eateth and drinketh my flesh and blood unworthily, eateth and drinketh damnation to his soul; therefore, if ye know that a man is unworthy to eat and drink of my flesh and blood, ye shall forbid him.[16]

From divine revelations, therefore, it seems definite that the holy emblems should be given only to Church members who are in good standing, since it is "a sacrament to the Most High."[17] In the words of James E. Talmage: "There is an entire absence of scriptural sanction for giving the sacrament to any who are not members in full fellowship in the Church of Christ."[18]

From what has been presented, it is quite clear that the Sacrament as revealed to the Prophet Joseph Smith and as practiced by the Church of Jesus Christ of Latter-day Saints today is the true eucharistic order of that divine Gospel principle given by the Man of Galilee to His apostles the night before His crucifixion and to the Nephites following His resurrection. It is the holy ordinance commemorating the great atoning sacrifice of our Lord and Savior, Jesus Christ.

SUPPLEMENTARY READINGS—CHAPTER 34

1. *Doctrine and Covenants* 19:16; 20:46, 58, 68, 76-79; 27:1-4; 46:4-5; 59:9, 12; 62:4; 19:16-20; 76:40-43.
2. James E. Talmage, *The Articles of Faith*, pp. 175-183.
3. John A. Widtsoe, *Discourses of Brigham Young*, pp. 254-268.

---

[15] *Ibid.*, 18:11.
[16] *Ibid.*, 18:28-29; 1 Corinthians 11:26-30.
[17] *Doctrine and Covenants* 62:4.
[18] Talmage, *op. cit.*, p. 178.

Chapter 35.

THE GOLDEN RULE

Jesus' Teachings

One of the greatest truths ever uttered, which would result in a happy society and the mutual good of all if followed, is known as "The Golden Rule." It constitutes the very heart of the message of the Man of Galilee. Teachers of religion and sociology are convinced that if this eternal truth were universally obeyed, the most remarkable advancement, evolution and growth, coupled with the most complete happiness of which human beings are capable, would be achieved in this mortal world. War, murder, hatred, and all manner of sins would be completely done away with if all men incorporated into their lives this famous admonition of the Christ's. Two of the Gospels—Matthew and Luke —report the Master's notable statement, each giving its own version. The statement as recorded in Matthew is as follows:

Therefore all things whatsoever ye would that men should do to you, do ye even so to them: for this is the law and the prophets.[1]

Luke records the same thought given by Jesus in the following words:

And as ye would that men should do to you, do ye also to them likewise.[2]

The Savior enlarged on this pertinent doctrine during the Sermon on the Mount in this sublime statement of the principle:

Ye have heard that it hath been said, "Thou shalt love thy neighbor, and hate thine enemy." But I say unto you, "Love your enemies, bless them that curse you, do good to them that hate you, and pray for them which despitefully use you, and persecute you; That ye may be the children of your Father which is in heaven: for he maketh his sun to rise on the evil and on the good, and sendeth rain on the just

---

[1] Matthew 7:12; 3 Nephi 14:12.
[2] Luke 6:31.

245

and on the unjust. For if ye love them which love you, what reward have ye? Do not even the publicans the same? And if ye salute your brethren only, what do ye more than others? Do not even the publicans so? Be ye therefore perfect, even as your Father in heaven is perfect.[3]

Jesus summarized all the teachings of the prophets from Adam's day to Himself in the following words, which He quoted from the holy scriptures:

Thou shalt love the Lord thy God with all thy heart, and with all thy soul, and with all thy mind. This is the first and great commandment. And the second is like unto it, Thou shalt love thy neighbour as thyself. On these two commandments hang all the law and the prophets.[4]

This is my commandment, that ye love one another, as I have loved you. Greater love hath no man than this, that a man lay down his life for his friends.[5]

Such teachings of the Master more fully explain what He meant in His statement of the Golden Rule.

Jesus not only taught that doctrine, but by example He showed throughout His entire lifetime that it was the natural and practicable way of life and could be followed by man. There has never been a more sublime example of this Godlike love in all history than was exhibited by the Master of eternal life as He was hanging on the cross on Calvary between two thieves. While He was suffering the pains of this most terrible of deaths—crucifixion—the blind, ignorant people cast lots for His garments and mocked Him, saying:

"Thou that destroyeth the temple, and buildest it in three days, save thyself. If thou be the Son of God, come down from the cross." Likewise also the chief priests, mocking him, with the scribes and elders, said, "He saved others; himself he cannot save. If he be the King of Israel, let him now come down from the cross, and we will believe him."[6]

It was during this trying condition that the Master gave unto us a glimpse of Godliness by putting into practice all that He had ever taught on this subject. Casting his eyes heavenward, He prayed: "Father, forgive them; for they know not what they do."[7] This indeed is the Golden Rule.

[3] Matthew 5:43-48.
[4] *Ibid.*, 22:37-41.
[5] John 15:12-13.
[6] Matthew 27:40-42.
[7] Luke 23:34.

Universality of Golden Rule

The Golden Rule is another of those eternal truths which is world-old and world-wide. It appears in practically every major religion, many of them antedating the birth of Jesus by hundreds of years. Each of the seven great world religions contains in its sacred writings a version of the Golden Rule. To quote:

"The Hindu: 'The true rule is to guard and do by the things of others as you do by your own.'

"The Buddhist: 'One should seek for others the happiness one desires for oneself.'

"The Zoroastrian: 'Do as you would be done by.'

"The Confucian: 'What you do not wish done to yourself, do not to others.'

"The Mohammedan: 'Let none of you treat your brother in a way he himself would dislike to be treated.'

"The Jewish: 'Whatsoever you do not wish your neighbor to do to you, do not unto him.'

"The Christian: 'All things whatsoever ye would that men should do to you, do ye even so to them.' "[8]

All teachers who have been exponents of this great truth have believed that the best good of each person in society will insure the best good of the whole group, and every effort should be made to insure the welfare of each unit. They seek a happy balance between individual rights and group emphasis. If a social institution is over-emphasized, such as the state, the free agency of the people is curtailed and the result may be one form or another of Nazism. On the other hand, if all the individuals in society acted as they desired, regardless of the rights of others, a condition of gangsterism and lawlessness would prevail. Such philosophers as Nietzsche would push the weak out of the way to make room for the strong. That type of philosophy is materialistic, based entirely on the principle of competition. But the Golden Rule, as taught by the great religious leaders, is a philosophy of cooperation, proving that the earth life of an individual is merely part of that larger life of eternity. To these leaders the worth of every human soul is great in the sight of God. In the words of Hugh M. Woodward:

---

[8] Alfred W. Martin, *Seven Great Bibles*, p. xvi.

The Golden Rule represents the parting of the ways between the materialistic philosophy, with all its unlovely selfishness, competition, and ruthless destruction on the one hand and the spiritual philosophy with its cooperation, altruism, love, and eternal helpfulness on the other.[9]

This perfect balance between the individual and the social group is found best in the Gospel of Jesus Christ as taught by the Master in Palestine, or as revealed to the Prophet Joseph Smith in our day. Politically, the most ideal type of government extant today which makes possible the practicing of the Golden Rule is the government of the United States of America or other political systems kindred to or patterned after it. The government of the Church of Jesus Christ of Latter-day Saints also furnishes a good example of the practical application of the Golden Rule in human society.

TEACHINGS OF OUTSTANDING RELIGIOUS LEADERS

It would be well at this point to give additional teachings of the leaders in the outstanding world religions which confirm and amplify the Golden Rule. Nearly 1,500 B.C., Krishna was teaching such philosophy as the following:

> This is the sum of all true righteousness,
> Treat others as thou wouldst thyself be treated.
> Do nothing to thy neighbor which hereafter
> Thou wouldst not have thy neighbor do to thee.
>
> In causing pleasure or in giving pain,
> In doing good or injury to others,
> In granting or refusing a request,
> A man obtains a proper rule of action
> By looking on his neighbor as himself.[10]

Zoroaster (about 600 B.C.), the famous Persian religious teacher, laid down this rule to his followers: "Break not the contract, neither the one that thou hadst entered into with one of the unfaithful, nor the one that thou hadst entered into with one of thy own faith. For Mithra stands both for the faithful and for the unfaithful."[11]

From distant China we receive truths similar to those uttered in Palestine and Persia. On one occasion Confucius (551-479 B.C.) was asked to sum up his teachings in one word. "He chose the word 'shu.' This term ex-

---

[9] Hugh M. Woodward, *Humanity's Greatest Need*, p. 253.
[10] Cited in *ibid.*, p. 254.
[11] Cited in *ibid.*, p. 255.

presses the Golden Rule in such poetic way that it is almost impossible to convey it to the people of the West. The word has been translated in English as meaning 'my heart responds to yours, or my heart's desire is to meet your heart's desire, or I wish to do to you even as I would be done by'."[12]

Lao Tze, another Chinese teacher—an ethical philosopher and a contemporary of Confucius—is credited with having said: "To them that are good I am good, and to them that are not good, I am also good, thus all get to be good. To them that are sincere, I am sincere, and to them that are not sincere, I am also sincere, thus all get to be sincere."[13]

Buddha, i. e., "the enlightened one" (560 to 480 B.C.), carried on his ethical reformation in India during the same period that Confucius and Lao Tze were presenting their teachings to the people of China. Also during that period God was revealing many truths to the Hebrew prophets and to the Nephite leaders who had recently migrated to America. Zoroaster in Persia, the Greek philosophers and religious leaders in other countries were also gleaning certain truths. Some of the teachings of Buddha are as follows:

"With pure thoughts and fullness of love, I will do towards others what I do for myself." "Surrender the grasping disposition of your selfishness and you will attain to that sinless, calm state of mind which conveys perfect peace, goodness and wisdom." Again he says: "Let us, then, live happily, not hating those who hate us; overcome evil with good—a man who foolishly does me wrong, I will return to him the protection of my ungrudging love; the more evil comes from him, the more good shall go from me."[14]

Such teachings of Buddha sound as if they came from Jesus, the Master of truth and light. They are the same as "Love your enemies, bless them that curse you." How much wiser and happier the world would be if mankind would follow this truth given by Buddha: "Conquer your foe by force and you increase his enmity; conquer by love and you reap no after sorrow."

TEACHINGS OF THE PROPHETS

The fundamental doctrine expressed in the Golden Rule constitutes the heart of the message of the prophets

[12] *Ibid.*, p. 258.
[13] Cited in *ibid.*, 255.
[14] Cited in *ibid.*, p. 256.

throughout all dispensations. For example, the voice of God came to Isaiah and to religious leaders of other generations with messages similar to the following: "Wash you, make you clean: put away the evil of your doings from before mine eyes; cease to do evil; learn to do well; seek judgment, relieve the oppressed, judge the fatherless, plead for the widows."[15] The famous discourses on charity given by Paul, King Benjamin, and Mormon contain the essence of this eternal doctrine.[16] The prophet who opened the last dispensation of the Gospel, like all the holy men who preceded him, lived the Golden Rule and taught it constantly.

DIVINE SOURCE OF THE GOLDEN RULE

How did it happen that the Golden Rule was taught by people in far-off India and China hundreds of years before Jesus Christ proclaimed it to His followers in Palestine? How did it happen that this doctrine is so universal, and whence is its source? The answers lie in the fact that all truth comes from one divine source—God the Eternal Father and His Only Begotten Son—and that people of all races are children of the same divine parents. These truths have been declared by the prophets. For example, Nephi proclaimed that God "gave unto the children of men line upon line, precept upon precept, here a little and there a little," and that He reveals His word unto the children of men in all the nations of the earth.[17] Mormon, the ancient Nephite prophet, declared:

Wherefore, all things which are good, cometh of God; and that which is evil, cometh of the devil; for the devil is an enemy unto God, and fighteth against him continually, and inviteth and enticeth to sin, and to do that which is evil continually. . . . For behold, the Spirit of Christ is given to every man, that they may know good from evil.[18]

Thus it is evident that the Golden Rule, like every other truth possessed by mankind, has been revealed from God to His children.[19]

SUPPLEMENTARY READINGS—CHAPTER 35

1. *Bible:* 1 Corinthians 13:1-13.
2. *Book of Mormon:* Mosiah 4:16-30; Moroni 7:43-48.
3. Hugh M. Woodward, *Humanity's Greatest Need,* pp. 250-285.

---

[15] Isaiah 1:16-17.
[16] 1 Corinthians 13:1-13; Mosiah 4:16-30; Moroni 7:43-48.
[17] 2 Nephi 28:28-29, 29:1-14.
[18] Moroni 7:12, 16.
[19] Moroni 7:16.

Chapter 36.

THE STORY OF THE EARTH
(Proclaimed by the Prophets)

INTRODUCTORY STATEMENT

This chapter and the next one deal with the same topic, namely, the story of the earth, presented primarily from the standpoint of the physical changes that the earth has gone and will go through until it becomes celestialized. However, it becomes necessary in describing these physical changes to discuss briefly some of the conditions of human society which have a close relationship to the major physical steps through which the earth passes.

In this chapter we shall present the "Story of the Earth" as proclaimed by the prophets of God; therefore, the material presented will be more or less familiar to the readers. But it is necessary to discuss first the teachings of the prophets in order that we may present in the succeeding lesson, and be in better position to interpret intelligently, similar traditions regarding the earth as they appear in world religions.

THE CREATION

"In the beginning God created the heaven and the earth."[1] In this way the Hebrew record begins its story of the earth. The first two chapters of Genesis give an account of God's creating the heavens, the earth, the seas, plant life, animal life, the heavenly bodies, and mankind. Two other scriptures, accepted by the Mormons, contain similar accounts.[2]

The three scriptural stories of the creation are similar in most respects, yet each of them contains a few additional ideas of its own. For example, the account in Moses makes the contribution of explaining that all things were created

[1] Genesis 1:1; 1; 2.
[2] Moses 2; 3; Abraham 4; 5.

251

spiritually before they were created naturally. The story in Abraham points out that "the Gods" were the creators, rather than only one heavenly being. Moses' writings, as revealed to the Prophet Joseph Smith, indicate that two of these Gods were the Father and His Only Begotten Son.

These three scriptures, however, parallel each other sufficiently to give indisputable evidence that they came from one original source or record, namely, the revelations of the Lord to Father Adam, recorded by that great patriarch. We know it to be a fact that the first man kept records which were handed down from his day through a line of patriarchs.[3] These ancient prophets mentioned the fact in their writings that their records contained a creation story.[4] Thus it is apparent that the people during each of the Gospel dispensations knew definitely that immortal beings were the creators of our universe and its contents, including man.[5]

The Christian denominations have always had as part of their dogma the concept that God was the creator; but in Joseph Smith's day it was almost universally held that the Deity made the world out of nothing. The Mormon Prophet, however, threw much light on this erroneous belief by explaining as follows:

Now, the word create . . . does not mean to create out of nothing; it means to organize; the same as a man would organize materials and build a ship. Hence, we infer that God had materials to organize the world out of chaos—chaotic matter, which is element, and in which dwells all the glory. Element had an existence from the time He had. The pure principles of element are principles which can never be destroyed; they may be organized and reorganized, but not destroyed. They have no beginning and can have no end.[6]

In conclusion, it is a definite fact that from the time of Adam to our day the holy prophets have, each in turn, proclaimed that the Gods were the creators of all that exists.[7]

THE GOLDEN AGE

The scriptures also tell the story of a "Golden Age" when men and beasts were amicable to each other. Adam and Eve lived in a beautiful garden called Eden, which produced fruits of all kinds in abundance. There they walked and

---

[3] See chapter 10, pp. 60-61.
[4] Moses 6:45; Abraham 1:28, 31; Ether 1:3-4, 16; 4:9.
[5] 1 Nephi 17:36; *Doctrine and Covenants* 14:9; 45:1; 76:24; 93:10; 20:18; 29:31; 88:20.
[6] Joseph Fielding Smith, *Teachings of the Prophet Joseph Smith*, pp. 350-351.
[7] 1 Nephi 2:1; 2 Nephi 2:14-15, 22; Jacob 2:21; 4:9; Mosiah 2:20-21; Alma 1:4; 18:28-29; 3 Nephi 9:15; Mormon 9:11; *Doctrine and Covenants* 14:9.

talked with God. The earth was free from thorns, thistles and other noxious weeds. Surely this was a blessed age. God looked upon His creation and declared that it was very good.

THE EARTH TELESTIALIZD AND BAPTIZED

Then came what is known among Christians as the fall and the telestializing of the earth. In other words, our first parents partook of certain fruit and thereby were changed to mortal beings. But the point of importance in this lesson is that the world also became mortal or a telestial realm. Adam and Eve were expelled from the beautiful garden to keep them from eating the fruit of the tree of life and living forever; that is, passing on from mortality into immortality before they had had time to rear children and receive the Gospel plan of salvation. They were made to earn their bread by the sweat of their brows. The scriptures state that God cursed the ground for their sakes, and it brought forth thorns and thistles and all kinds of noxious weeds. Man and beast ceased to be friends. Many among Adam's posterity rejected the Gospel and the earth became corrupted by the wickdness of the children of men.

So wicked did mortals become, the sacred record declares, that God sent upon the earth a great flood or deluge which destroyed all of the human race but one family.[8] In this way the earth received its baptism in water. The scriptures proclaim that God placed a rainbow in the heavens as a sign that He would never again destroy the world by flood. From generation to generation the earth rolled on in its lawful course, with the times and seasons coming around regularly for the benefit of man.

THE EARTH TO BE CLEANSED BY FIRE

The holy prophets also proclaimed that the earth would eventually be cleansed by fire, comparable to a spiritual baptism. Malachi closed the Old Testament prophecies as follows:

For, behold, the day cometh that shall burn as an oven; and all the proud, yea, and all that do wickedly, shall be stubble: and the day that cometh shall burn them up, saith the Lord of Hosts, that it shall leave them neither root nor branch.

---

[8] Genesis, chapters 8 to 8.

But unto you that fear my name shall the Sun of righteousness arise with healing in his wings; and ye shall go forth, and grow up as calves of the stall.[9]

This burning that Malachi spoke of will take place when Christ comes at the beginning of the Millennium. Elder Joseph Fielding Smith explained the situation in the following words:

From the time of Adam's fall until now, and so it will continue until Christ comes, this earth has been subject to telestial conditions, and the telestial dominates the earth. . . . Now, when Christ comes, we will get a new heaven and a new earth and all of these corruptible things will be removed. They will be consumed by fire.[10]

Elder Smith's viewpoint is sustained by direct revelation of the Lord to the Prophet Joseph Smith. These are the words of Jesus Christ to the Prophet when He was describing His second coming:

And prepare for the revelation which is to come, when the veil of the covering of my temple in my tabernacle, which hideth the earth, shall be taken off, and all flesh shall see me together. And every corruptible thing, both of man, or of the beasts of the field, or of the fowls of the heavens, or of the fish of the sea, that dwells upon all the face of the earth, shall be consumed; And also that of element (that is, corruptible element) shall melt with fervent heat; and all things shall become new, that my knowledge and glory may dwell upon all the earth.[11]

THE EARTH TO BE TERRESTRIALIZED

At that time the earth will be renewed or terrestrialized and receive its paradisiacal glory.[12] Drastic physical changes will be brought about. We shall let the prophets inform us regarding some of the earth's physical changes when it is terrestrialized. The Lord declared: "For, behold, I create a new heavens and a new earth: and the former shall not be remembered, nor come in mind. But be ye glad and rejoice forever in that which I create."[13] When these drastic physical changes come upon the surface of the earth, the climate will be altered greatly for the benefit of man. The Prophet Isaiah described the terrestrialized earth as follows:

For the Lord shall comfort Zion: He will comfort all her waste places; and he will make her wilderness like Eden, and her desert like the garden of the Lord.[14]

[9] Malachi 4:1-2.
[10] Joseph Fielding Smith. *The Signs of the Times*, p. 38.
[11] *Doctrine and Covenants* 101:28-25.
[12] Tenth Article of Faith; *Doctrine and Covenants* 45:39-75; Matthew 24:1-51.
[13] Isaiah 65:17-18.
[14] *Ibid.*, 51:3.

Every valley shall be exalted, and every mountain and hill shall be made low; and the uneven shall be made level, and the rough places plain.[15]

Then the eyes of the blind shall be opened, and the ears of the deaf shall be unstopped. Then shall the lame man leap as a hart, and the tongue of the dumb shall sing; for in the wilderness shall water break out, and streams in the desert. And the glowing sand shall become a pool, and the thirsty ground springs of water; in the habitation of jackals, where they lay, shall be grass with reeds and rushes.[16]

The earth will be a terrestrial orb for one thousand years, and during that time Jesus will come to earth and dwell among men. He shall reign as Lord of lords and King of kings. A second Golden Age will be ushered in, which will be discussed in a later chapter as we present the social conditions during the Millennium.

THE EARTH TO BE CELESTIALIZED

At the close of the Millennium the earth is to undergo another drastic physical change. It will die, and all things upon it will die—that is, they will be consumed by fire. The earth will be dissolved and melt with fervent heat; yet that will not be the end of its existence. It will be raised in its resurrection to a glorified, celestialized orb, and will continue on forever in its celestialized condition. It will be the eternal home of the sons and daughters of God who have lived here in mortality and who have merited, through obedience to the Gospel principles, eternal life in the celestial kingdom of God.[17]

We read in Second Peter regarding this great event the following:

But the day of the Lord will come as a thief in the night; in the which the heavens shall pass away with a great noise, and the elements shall melt with fervent heat, the earth also and the works that are therein shall be burned up.[18]

The Lord, speaking of the earth, told the Prophet Joseph:

It must needs be sanctified from all unrighteousness, that it may be prepared for the celestial glory; for after it hath filled the measure of its creation, it shall be crowned with glory, even with the presence of God the Father; that bodies who are of the celestial kingdom may possess it forever and ever; for, for this intent was it made and created, and for this intent are they sanctified. . . .

[15] Ibid., 40:4.
[16] Ibid., 85:5-7.
[17] Isaiah 51:6; Psalms 102:25-28; Matthew 24:35.
[18] 2 Peter 3:10.

Again, verily I say unto you, the earth abideth the law of a celestial kingdom, for it filleth the measure of its creation, and transgresseth not the law—Wherefore, it shall be santified; yea, notwithstanding it shall die, it shall be quickened again, and shall abide the power by which it is quickened, and the righteous shall inherit it. For notwithstanding they die, they also shall rise again, a spiritual body.[19]

We are told by the holy prophets that God dwells in everlasting burnings, enthroned in everlasting power.[20] A celestial world is one comparable to the sun in brightness and glory. It will be like the stars of the firmament, full of light; in fact, it will be a body of light.[21] Joseph, the Prophet, tells us that—

The place where God resides is a great Urim and Thummim. This earth, in its sanctified and immortal state, will be made like unto crystal and will be a Urim and Thummin to the inhabitants who dwell thereon, whereby all things pertaining to an inferior kingdom, or all kingdoms of the lower order, will be manifest to those who dwell on it; and this earth will be Christ's.[22]

This is the story of the earth, briefly told, as it has been given to us by the holy prophets of God.

SUPPLEMENTARY READINGS—CHAPTER 36

1. *Bible:* Genesis, chapters 1 to 10; Isaiah 11:6; 24:19-23; 65:17-18; 35:5-7; 40:4; 51:3-6; Malachi 4; Psalms 102:25-28; Matthew 24:1-51; 2 Peter 3:10; Revelation 21:1-15.
2. *Book of Mormon:* 1 Nephi 2:12, 17-36; 2 Nephi 2:14-15, 22; Jacob 2:21; 4:9; Mosiah 2:20-21; Alma 1:4; 18:28-29; 3 Nephi 9:15; Ether 3:4-9.
3. *Doctrine and Covenants* 14:9; 76; 93:1-18; 43:16-35; 45:16-53; 88:18-27; 101:10-26; 86:1-11; 130:8-9.
4. *Pearl of Great Price:* Moses 1; 2; 3; 8; Abraham 4; 5.
5. Joseph Fielding Smith, *Signs of the Times,* pp. 20-44.
6. Joseph Fielding Smith, *The Restoration of All Things,* pp. 287-300.
7. Joseph Fielding Smith (Compiler), *Teachings of the Prophet Joseph Smith,* pp. 247, 350-351.
8. James E. Talmage, *The Articles of Faith,* pp. 66-75, 384-405.

---

[19] *Doctrine and Covenants* 88:18-20, 25-27.
[20] Smith, *Teachings of the Prophet Joseph Smith,* p. 347.
[21] Brigham Young, *Journal of Discourses,* vol. 7, p. 163.
[22] *Doctrine and Covenants* 130:8-9.

Chapter 37.

THE STORY OF THE EARTH
(Comparative Religious Traditions)

INTRODUCTORY STATEMENT

This lesson is closely related to the preceding one, discussing also the story of the earth as it relates to its physical changes. While the last lesson centered on the teachings of the prophets, this one will present the same Gospel truths in their altered forms as the traditions of various religious groups after they had filtered outward throughout the world and down through the ages.

THE CREATION

Practically every great nation of antiquity has preserved legends or traditions of the creation of the world, of the origin of man, of a Golden Age, of the fall, of the deluge, and of the future rejuvenation of the earth. Some of these traditions are much more valuable than others, since they contain many startling resemblances to the accounts in Genesis and to the teachings of the prophets of God. These resemblances are so numerous and so pronounced that they bear irrefutable testimony to the fact that they are altered forms of the true revelations from God which were first received by Father Adam and later re-revealed during the other Gospel dispensations.

One of the most important documents containing these traditions is the Babylonian creation story. According to the Babylonian creation tradition, even before the beginning of things on this earth, the gods were in existence. Two of them, "Lakhmu and Lakhamu," created the heavens above, and also the earth beneath. After a certain time elapsed another god named Anu became the ruler of the sky. Following this, a terrific conflict between Tiamat and Enlil-Marduk, two other heavenly deities, took place. The latter god was victorious over Tiamat. Thereupon, according to the Babylonian traditions, he took one-half of the body of Tiamat and made a covering for the heavens, and with the other half he made the earth beneath. After this was accomplished, Anu, Enlil-Marduk, and Ea came from their heavenly realm to the earth and made it their abode.

We can see in this Babylonian legend a resemblance to the Gospel teachings of the existence of intelligent beings prior to the time when man was placed on this earth. There are some resemblances to the council in heaven, especially in the conflict between Enlil-Marduk and Tiamat, which remind one of the war in heaven, where Michael (Adam) fought against Lucifer, and Lucifer was defeated. The fact that the earth was created for man and that three of the gods made it their abode can be compared to Adam and Eve in the Garden of Eden before they became mortal beings and that God associated with our first parents in the garden before they partook of the forbidden fruit.

Dr. Ira M. Price quotes the creation traditions as recorded on the ancient Babylonian tablets, and then makes a comparison of the resemblances of the Babylonian and Genesis accounts. His summary is as follows:

(1) Genesis knows a time when the earth was waste and void. The Babylonian accounts mention a time when all was chaos and nothingness.

(2) In Genesis light dispels darkness, and order follows chaos. In the Babylonian records the god Marduk routs and overthrows the demon of chaos, Tiamat.

(3) In Genesis, after a time, the dry land appears. In the Babylonian account, Marduk creates the dust and pours it out by the water.

(4) In Genesis, the sun, moon, and stars are set in the heavens. In the Babylonian, Marduk places these as the stations of the gods.

(5) In Genesis, God created the animals and creeping things. In the Babylonian, the assembly of the gods created animals and living creatures of the field and plain.

(6) In Genesis, God created mankind. In the Babylonian, Marduk is the creator of mankind.[1]

THE GOLDEN AGE

Among the world-wide concepts is a belief in a "Golden Age" in the past. Long before the coming of Christ, the Hebrews recorded a Golden Age in their story of the

---

[1] Ira M. Price, *The Monuments and the Old Testament*, pp. 106-107, 101-107.

Garden of Eden. In Egyptian mythology we have accounts of "the time of the rule of the gods on earth." The Egyptian records speak of that same Golden Age as being under the god Ra. " 'Since the time of the god (Osiris),' and 'since the time of Re' are old formulas for expressing immemorial antiquity."[2] According to the Babylonian tradition, these ancient peoples also believed in a Golden Age as follows:

The Age of Perfection lies at the beginning. Just and pure knowledge, revealed by the godhead, lies at the beginning, so that it is the task of science to discover the original truth by observation of the book of revelation written down in the stars, and to obtain freedom from errors which crept in through human guilt, so also the age of Pure Happiness lies at the beginning.[3]

In further explanation of this Golden Age, the Babylonian records claim that it occurred in *"the time before the flood."* They believed also that, "In the time before the flood lived the heroes, who . . . dwell in the under world, or are removed into the heavenly world. . . . At that time there lived, too, the seven sages."[4] This same people, as well as their neighbors, the ancient Persians, believed in a Garden of Eden which existed in the Golden Age. Of this belief, Ira M. Price has written:

The inscriptions tell us of a primitive sacred garden, in which there was a tree of life. This sacred tree is seen frequently on the seals of prominent personages of Babylon. It also appears among the alabaster reliefs found on the wainscoating of the royal palaces. Approach to it seems to have been limited to the gods or to distinguished persons. Its fruits also were thought to contain qualities capable of granting and maintaining life perpetually.[5]

It is obvious that the Babylonian sacred garden tradition had its origin in the Hebrew account of the Garden of Eden.

The Greeks also had a concept of a Golden Age which was described by such writers as Pindar and Hesid. The former was a poet who lived 522-442 B.C. He wrote about the Islands of the Blest, "where the good lead a blameless, tearless life." Hesid, another Greek writer, who lived about two hundred years before Pindar, spoke of a time when men and animals spoke the same language and lived

---

[2] James Hastings, *Encyclopaedia of Religion and Ethics*, vol. 1, p. 192.
[3] *Ibid.*, p. 187.
[4] *Ibid.*, p. 185.
[5] Price, *op. cit.*, p. 111.

at peace with each other. Following is a summary of some of Hesid's famous writings:

First of all, the Olympian gods made the "golden race of men." These men lived when Kronos was king in heaven. They fared like the gods themselves, always making merry, and untroubled by toil or care, for the teeming earth bore of its own accord an abundance of all good things, and there was no old age. Even death itself, when at last it came, stole upon men like a pleasant slumber. When this race passed away, Zeus made them the good spirits that live above the earth and are the invisible guardians and helpers of mortal man.[6]

Pythagoras, a Greek philosopher who lived about 580-500 B.C., was an expounder of the doctrine that "in the Golden Age men lived upon the fruits of the earth, and that the degeneration of later ages is marked by a departure from this rule."[7] The Greeks, and later the Romans, believed that the race who lived in those happy days where eternal youth and joy abounded everywhere—the Golden Age—still existed somewhere, and that mortals might be able to find them; and, upon finding them, also obtain eternal youth. Hesid, in his "Isles of the Blest," described a place where dwell those sons of gods who have passed alive beyond the grave. Since that day, many a search has been made, similar to the one made by Ponce de Leon, when he was looking for the "Fountain of Youth."

THE FALL OF MAN

A tradition of the fall of man is just as universal as that of a Golden Age. Each of the races of antiquity gives its own version of how it came about that man changed from that condition of eternal youth and happiness into one of misery, sorrow, and eventually death. The Biblical account—with which we are all familiar—tells of Adam and Eve's partaking of the forbidden fruit and being expelled from the Garden of Eden. A remarkable story of the fall of man, the "myth of Adapa," is recorded on four Babylonian tablets. Dr. Price summarized this story as follows:

The resemblances of the ideas in this myth to the so-called "fall of man" in Genesis chapter three are passing strange. This Adapa, like Adam, had a certain amount of inherent wisdom, but was not immortal. He was a kind of a semi-divine person, and was the priest and sage of the temple of the god Ea at Eridu. In carrying out the require-

---

[6] Hastings, op. cit., p. 193.
[7] Recall the Bible account of Adam and Eve living upon the fruits of the Garden of Eden.

ments of his office, he was a fisherman on the Persian Gulf. While [he was] out fishing one day the south wind suddenly swooped down on his craft, overturned it, and, of course, threw him into the sea. Enraged by the insult, he broke the wings of the south wind, and thus destroyed its power for seven days to blow cool air over the hot land. Anu and Ea, the great gods, called him to account and warned him. Ea admonished him that when he should reach heaven's portal he should not eat the food or drink the portions which would be set before him, for fear that they would be the food and drink of death. Such admonition was ill devised, for it was the food and drink of life that were set before him, and this bad counsel robbed him of immortal life, and he was obliged to return to the earth.[8]

THE DELUGE

Genesis, Moses, Josephus (the Jewish historian), Eusebius (an early Christian historian), American Indian traditions,[9] and Babylonian cuneiform inscriptions all proclaim that there was an universal deluge. In vigor of description and details, the Babylonian account stands next to the Biblical record. According to Dr. Price, "This epic is the finest and most beautiful poem that has been preserved for us in the literature of ancient Babylonia."[10] Ira M. Price has published what he terms "the most interesting parts of the translation" in *The Monuments and the Old Testament,* pages 119-127. Dr. Price draws the following conclusions from the Babylonian flood account:

The Babylonian account of the deluge bristles with resemblances to that of Genesis. These have led scholars to think that they are merely two versions of the same original account. At this distance we can set side by side some of these items: (1) There is divine revelation to the main hero of the deluge that a disaster is imminent which no one else knows about. (2) Both records tell of the building of a ship, (a) . . . (b) the embarkation with all living creatures to be saved alive, (c) the terrific storm bringing a deluge of water, (d) the destruction of all not on board the ship, (e) landing of the ship on a mountain, (f) sending out of birds—a dove, a swallow, a raven, (g) the landing, (h) offering of a sacrifice on landing, (i) acceptance of a sweet savior by the (deity) gods, (j) a reference to the possibility of no deluge in the future.[11]

REJUVENATION OF THE EARTH

Certain pagan religions resembled the teachings of the prophets in declaring that the earth was going to be rejuvenated. For example, the Mithraic Mystery Religion's leg-

8 Price, *op. cit.,* pp. 111-112.
9 Josiah E. Hickman, *The Romance of the Book of Mormon,* pp. 88-97.
10 Price, *op. cit.,* p. 120.
11 *Ibid.,* p. 127.

end claimed that after the earth had been re-populated following the flood, a great conflagration consumed most of the habitations of men and of beasts. Through divine protection a few of the creatures escaped.

The Mithraic Religion also taught its cult members that the earth would be rejuvenated, a concept similar to that held by the holy prophets regarding the Millennium. At that time Mithra would come back to earth to dwell. There would be a bodily resurrection of all the dead, and the wicked would be destroyed.[12] Thus the Gospel truths appeared in an altered form in this pagan cult.

CONCLUSIONS

Dr. Ira M. Price gives his conclusion regarding the reasons for so many similarities in the religions of the world. Since his ideas sustain what I have previously written on this subject, we quote his exact words:

The similarities noted above between the records of Genesis and the inscriptions call for further consideration. These are not traditions peculiar to Semitic peoples and religions, which have grown out of their characteristics. They are common to all civilized nations in which they have been preserved and developed. Their common elements seem to point to a time when the human race occupied a common home and held a common faith. The records of Genesis and the Babylonian inscriptions give us two forms of these early traditions.

How, then, is the similarity between Genesis and the inscriptions to be explained? There are four answers sometimes given to this question: (1) The Genesis account is drawn from these traditions; (2) Genesis is the source of these traditions; (3) their likeness is attributable to like ways of thinking—similar traditions having spontaneously arisen in different parts of the earth because of "the natural tendencies of the human mind in its evolution from a savage state"; (4) "Their likeness is due to a common inheritance, each handing on from age to age records concerning the early history of the race."[13]

These theories are elaborated by many writers, and are easily disposed of down to the fourth point. To this very many scholars are now turning as the most plausible solution of the problem. All religions are reducible to a small number of facts. These facts are either individual or common; of the common, some are undoubtedly due to the common nature of man, but others are just as clearly explicable only as an inheritance. Early races of men, wherever they wandered, took with them those primeval traditions, and with the varying latitudes and climes, their habits and modes of life, their intellectual and spiritual de-

---

[12] Harold Willoughby, *Pagan Regeneration*, p. 167.
[13] Recall the evidence given in chapter ten on the Gospel being revealed to Father Adam and records being written and handed down from generation to generation.

velopment, have carried and modified these, through the ages, and present them to us today in their different dresses.   One ancient religion did not borrow these universal traditions from another, but each possessed primitively these traditions in their original form.   A careful examination of all these traditions shows that the Genesis record is the purest, the least colored by extravagances, and the nearest to what we must conceive to have been the original form of these traditions.[14]

In these terms Dr. Price confirms the concept that God revealed the Gospel of Jesus Christ originally to Adam; and that was the common source of all of these religious truths.   From that day forward revelations of divine truths have continued to come to the holy prophets; and these verities have continued to be altered by man-made concepts and human influences.

SUPPLEMENTARY READINGS—CHAPTER 37

1. James Hastings, Editor, *Encyclopaedia of Religion and Ethics,* vol. 1, pp. 183-205.
2. Josiah E. Hickman, *The Romance of the Book of Mormon,* pp. 182-222.
3. Ira Maurice Price, *The Monuments and the Old Testament,* pp. 98-130.

---

[14] Price, *op. cit.,* pp. 129-130.

Chapter 38.

THE HOPE OF A BETTER WORLD

Universality of the Hope of a Better World

The purpose that God had in mind in revealing the Gospel of Jesus Christ to Adam was that man might establish a social order here on earth in which perfection in laws, government, morality, and spirituality would prevail. All of the holy prophets and all good men have conscientiously worked toward the building of a better world. Their central hope has been that some day a state of ideal perfection in human society would be attained. Through divine revelations, many of the prophets were shown glimpses of a future Millennium which should be established on this earth, and God made known to them that after its establishment it would continue one thousand years.

From the teachings of the prophets, the philosophy of establishing the "Good Society" has spread throughout the world and has been handed down from age to age as a golden thread of religious truth. Few ideas in human history have been as universal as the concept that some day human beings would cease warring, murdering, and hating; and in their places universal love and intelligent living would prevail. A "Golden Age" in the future has been just as much a topic for the poet, for the philosopher, for the prophet, and for the teacher as has been the concept of a "Golden Age" in the past.

Examples of the Good Society

Many attempts have been made to establish the good society. Some of the most noble and some of the saddest pages in human history have come about in these attempts. For the purpose of illustrating that it lies within the realm of human possibility for mortals to live in perfect harmony together and in almost absolute righteousness, three examples will be mentioned.

The first was Enoch and his people. They established such a perfect social and economic order that God came down to earth and dwelt with them. After this perfect society had existed for 365 years, the City of Enoch "was taken up unto heaven, and the Lord said unto Enoch: 'Behold mine abode forever.' "[1]

Another example of the perfect society is found in the history of the Nephites. After Jesus' resurrection, He visited the inhabitants of ancient America and taught them His Gospel. Thereafter the political, social, and economic practices of this people became so perfect that for many decades they lived in almost perfect righteousness. Their economic system was one that could be termed the "United Order" or "Order of Enoch," since they had all things in common. This economic system completely did away with poverty.

Through the power of the Priesthood, the apostles healed the sick, caused the lame to walk, the blind to see, the deaf to hear, and even brought the dead back to life. All of these things were done in the name of Jesus Christ. The Nephite historian described the social conditions of the people as follows:

And it came to pass that there was no contention in the land, because of the love of God which did dwell in the hearts of the people. And there were no envyings, nor strifes, nor tumults, nor whoredoms, nor lyings, nor murders, nor any manner of lasciviousness. Surely there could not be a happier people among all the people who had been created by the hand of God.[2]

The natural result of living this way was that the Nephites became prosperous. They reared large families and "became an exceeding fair and delightsome people." They rejoiced in the fact that they were "the children of Christ and heirs to the kingdom of God." The record states that the Lord blessed them in all that they did and prospered them exceedingly. Thus this ancient people set a pattern of life which, if followed by mankind throughout the entire world, would raise humanity from a diseased, sordid, unhappy and sinful condition to one of joy and fullness of life.

---

[1] Moses 7:17-21, 68-69. See also chapter 11, pp. 69-71.
[2] 4 Nephi 1:1-24.

Also, just after the time of Christ in Palestine another body of people successfully formed a good society. Since it was composed of Christians under the direction of Peter, James and John, it operated on the same principles as did the other two good societies discussed. However, such unpreventable factors as persecutions by their enemies forced the Christians to abandon their special economic system which was basic in their good society. Thus the economic phase of this social order was short-lived.[3]

TEACHINGS OF THE OLD TESTAMENT PROPHETS

The doctrine regarding the building of the perfect society declared by the Hebrew prophets had had more inspirational value than any of the secular or religious "Utopias"—theoretical or attempted—with the possible exception of the "Kingdom of God" element in Jesus' teachings. The doctrine of such prophets of Isaiah, Amos, Hosea, Micah, Jeremiah, and Ezekiel have been sources of hope and inspiration to millions of people who have believed in and hoped for social betterment.

Amos and the other great prophets believed that the "Good Society" could come about only when there was a complete change both individually and nationally in the social relationships of the people with each other and in their attitude toward God. Amos' message was: "Seek the Lord and ye shall live."[4] "Seek good and not evil, that ye may live."[5] "But let judgment run down as waters, and righteousness as a mighty stream."[6] He maintained that God's chief attribute was justice, and if the people expected anything but punishment from His hands they must practice justice toward each other. The teachings of all the prophets agree with Isaiah's, namely, that "the nation and the kingdom that will not serve God shall perish—utterly waste shall those nations be laid."[7] In other words, the perfect society will be brought about only through the acceptance and obedience of the divine truths of the Gospel of Jesus Christ.

[3] Acts 2:37-47; 4:32-36.
[4] Amos 5:6.
[5] Ibid., 5:14.
[6] Ibid., 5:24.
[7] Isaiah 60:12.

However, one central theme runs through the teachings of the Old Testament prophets. It is a belief that eventually the time will come when mankind will serve God and thereby establish a perfect society.[8] Jeremiah declared that the day will come when the Lord will make a "new covenant with the house of Israel, and with the house of Judah."[9] At that time, the Lord told Jeremiah:

I will put my law in their inward parts, and write it in their hearts; and will be their God, and they shall be my people. And they shall teach no more every man his neighbour, and every man his brother, saying, "Know the Lord": for they shall all know me, from the least of them unto the greatest of them.[10]

Isaiah's Description of the Millennium

Of the Old Testament prophets, Isaiah's predictions regarding the millennial reign of the Lord are the most illuminating and extensive. In fact, he describes the Millennium in more detail than all of the other Hebrew prophets combined.

An important point which appears in several of Isaiah's prophecies is that the governing power throughout this period of one thousand years of peace will be the Gospel of Jesus Christ. People will learn, love, and obey its precepts. The headquarters of the Church will be Zion.[11] From that point, the law shall go forth, and the word of the Lord shall come from Jerusalem. A Righteous Judge, a descendant of King David, shall reign; and He shall rule with equity.[12] Sorrow and grief will cease, "and the Lord God will wipe away tears from off all faces."[13]

The people of the earth shall live until they are a hundred years old; then they shall be changed in a twinkling of an eye unto a blessed immortality. For God (Christ) "will swallow up death in victory."[14] "There shall be no more thence an infant of days, nor an old man that hath not filled his days: for the child shall die an hundred years old; but

---

[8] Jeremiah 31:9; Amos 9:13-15; Isaiah 42:1-7.
[9] Jeremiah 31:31-34.
[10] Ibid.
[11] According to the Prophet Joseph Smith, America is Zion. The word of the Lord has already gone forth from Jerusalem, as recorded in the holy scriptures; and the Constitution of the U. S. has served as a pattern for many constitutions in the various countries throughout the world. Thus the law has gone forth from Zion and shall continue to do so.
[12] Isaiah 9:6-7; 11:1-6; 16:5; 32:1-7.
[13] Ibid., 25:8; 65:19.
[14] Ibid., 25:8.

the sinner shall be accursed. . . . For as the days of a tree
are the days of my people."[15]

Peace shall reign supreme throughout the entire world.
The people "shall build houses, and inhabit them; and they
shall plant vineyards, and eat the fruits of them." War—
that monster and curse of humanity—shall be completely
done away with. "And in that day the enmity of man, and
the enmity of beasts, yea, the enmity of all flesh, shall cease
from before my face," saith the Lord.[16] For the purpose
of illustrating Isaiah's understanding of the Millennium,
we shall quote some of his teachings:

> The wolf also shall dwell with the lamb, and the leopard shall lie
> down with the kid; and the calf and the young lion and the fatling to-
> gether; and a little child shall lead them. And the cow and the bear
> shall feed; their young ones shall lie down together: and the lion shall
> eat straw like the ox. And the suckling child shall play on the hole
> of the asp, and the weaned child shall put his hand on the cockatrice'
> den. They shall not hurt nor destroy in all my holy mountain: for the
> earth shall be full of the knowledge of the Lord, as the waters cover the
> sea.[17]

> And many nations shall come, and say, "Come, and let us go up to
> the mountain of the Lord, and to the house of the God of Jacob; and
> he will teach us of his ways, and we will walk in his paths. . . .
> And he shall judge among many people, and rebuke strong nations afar
> off; and they shall beat their swords into plowshares, and their spears
> into pruning-hooks: nation shall not lift up a sword against nation,
> neither shall they learn war any more. But they shall sit every man
> under his vine and under his fig tree; and none shall make them afraid:
> for the mouth of the Lord of Hosts hath spoken it. For all people will
> walk every one in the name of his God, and we will walk in the name
> of the Lord our God for ever and ever.[18]

CHRISTIANITY'S HOPE OF A GOOD SOCIETY

Jesus Christ opened His public ministry with the
hope of a good society. He selected as the text for one of
His early public sermons a Messianic prophecy made by
Isaiah. Thus he announced that the course He intended
to follow was "to preach good tidings unto the meek, . . .
to bind up the broken-hearted, to proclaim liberty to the
captives, and the opening of the prison to them that are
bound; to proclaim the acceptable year of the Lord."[19] In

---

[15] Ibid., 65:17-25.
[16] Doctrine and Covenants 101:26.
[17] Isaiah 11:6-9.
[18] Isaiah 2:2-5; Micah 4:1-5.
[19] Luke 4:14-22; Isaiah 61:1-4.

other words, the Savior, like the great prophets of God who preceded Him, knew that the good society could be established only by people learning and obeying the Gospel.

From that day forward the Man of Galilee taught the principles of truth with a power and understanding greater than that with which any man has ever taught. The heart of His message was "Seek first the kingdom of God and his righteousness and all other things shall be added unto you." He summed up all of the teachings of the holy prophets who preceded Him in the following words: *"Thou shalt love the Lord thy God with all thy heart, and with all thy soul, and with all thy mind. This is the first and great commandment. And the second is like unto it, Thou shalt love thy neighbor as thyself."*[20] Through His life and through His teachings, He proclaimed the plan of salvation which, if followed by all of humanity, would bring about that perfect society that the holy prophets have foreseen and foretold from Adam's day down to the present time.

Peter, Paul, and the other great teachers who contributed to the New Testament literature also proclaimed the Gospel of love and peace. They championed the prophets who lived before them in attempting to establish a better society which would ultimately result in the thousand years of peace.

John the Revelator saw in vision the millennial reign of the Lord and the New Jerusalem. Doubtless his writings did much to further stimulate the Christians' hope for the speedy arrival of that great day. (Read John's description of this "holy city Jerusalem" as given in Revelation, chapters 21 and 22.) Following is part of his beautiful word-picture of this glorious event:

And I saw a new heaven and a new earth: for the first heaven and the first earth were passed away; and there was no more sea. And I John saw the holy city, new Jerusalem, coming down from God out of heaven, prepared as a bride adorned for her husband. And I heard a great voice out of heaven saying, "Behold, the tabernacle of God is with men, and he will dwell with them, and they shall be his people, and God himself shall be with them, and be their God. And God shall wipe away all tears from their eyes; and there shall be no more death, neither sorrow, nor crying, neither shall there be any more pain: for

[20] Matthew 22:37; Mark 12:20-21; Luke 10:27; Deuteronomy 6:5; Leviticus 19:18; Psalms 31:23.

the former things are passed away." And he that sat upon the throne said, "Behold, I make all things new."[21]

Jesus had scarcely been resurrected when many of the Christians began to look daily for the second coming of the Son of Man to establish the reign of righteousness, although the Master had told the apostles shortly before His crucifixion of the many events that should occur before His return to earth.[22] During the middle of the first century A.D., the Saints in Thessalonia, whom Paul had converted to the Gospel of Jesus Christ, were definitely expecting the immediate return of the Savior. Paul, however, wrote them a letter, informing them that before the Son of Man should come to earth to reign, an apostasy from the true plan of salvation would take place.[23] Nevertheless, from that time forward Christians by the hundreds have continued to set the date of the Millennium, some of them going so far as to predict an exact year—even the month and day.

The concept of the coming of Jesus Christ to reign upon the earth for a thousand years as Lord of lords and King of kings, and of the perfect society prevailing wherein all hatred, strife, and sin of any nature cease to exist, has been one of the most dynamic and impelling forces in Christian history. Teachers of each generation have felt that it was and is their special calling to prepare the world for that great event—the Millennium.

SUPPLEMENTARY READINGS—CHAPTER 38

1. *Bible*: Galatians 4:26; Hebrews 12:22; Revelation 3:12; 12:1-27; 21; 22; Amos 5; 9:13-15; Jeremiah 31:9-13, 31-34; Isaiah 9:6-7; 42:1-7; 43:5-7; 51:3; 2:2-5; 11:1-9; 16:5; 32:1-7; 60:12; 65:17-25; Acts 1:1-12; Mark 16:9-20; Thessalonians 2:1-5; Matthew 24.
2. *Book of Mormon:* Ether 13:1-12; 3 Nephi 20; 4 Nephi 1:1-27.
3. *Doctrine and Covenants* 42:9, 35, 67; 45:66; 84:2-4.
4. *Pearl of Great Price:* Moses 7:16-21, 27, 58-59.

---

[21] Revelation 21:1-5.
[22] Matthew 24:1-51.
[23] 2 Thessalonians 2:1-5.

Chapter 39.

UTOPIAN AND ZION CONCEPTS

FAMOUS UTOPIAN WRITINGS

Numerous students of society—many of whom were stimulated by the teachings of the prophets—have produced an abundance of literature on the ancient hope for a perfect society which has come to be known as a Utopia. Among these writings are the following classics: Plato, *The Republic;* St. Augustine, *The City of God;* Sir Thomas More, *Utopia;* Lord Francis Bacon, *New Atlantis;* Thomas Campanella, *City of the Sun;* James Harrington, *Oceana.*

Plato (427-347 B.C.) was the most brilliant of Socrates' disciples. In his book, *The Republic,* he pictured a state free from the corruption of extreme license and from the danger of tyranny. Its laws and institutions were the embodiment of the highest moral ideals of individuals united into a socialized state. "He used the myth of an ideal republic in which future mankind was to blissfully abide, as a vehicle by means of which to express these ideas which he could not otherwise openly utter. . . . But, above all, its main argument is the search after justice."[1] Plato was doubtless influenced by Hesid's description of the Golden Age. In *The Republic,* Plato expressed the ideal of a classical philosopher, the best secular thought of that brilliant Greek age.

St. Augustine wrote the *City of God* between the years 413 and 426 A.D. In this book he maintained that the teachings of Christ, if lived by all people, would produce the best and most inviolable state. His writings represent a rather comprehensive expression of his religious and theological beliefs; but the most important parts present his

---

[1] Joyce Oramel Hertzler, *The History of Utopian Thought,* p. 100.

doctrine of the two cities—"the City of Men and the City of God, in respect to their origin, their history, and their destiny." It was Augustine's purpose in his monumental work—*The City of God*—to show that the bond of agreement and the one thing which would produce a righteous society is the love of God. If humanity would love Him deeply, they would renounce all lust and sinfulness and would obey the divine laws, thereby preparing themselves to dwell in the City of God. "This is a beatific vision of a social life in which the personality of the individual is bound to that of other individuals through God, truly the highest stage of moral perfection."[2] On the other hand, Augustine taught that the "City of Men" represented diametrically opposite principles in all respects from the "City of God."

Nearly a thousand years passed following the appearance of Augustine's *City of God,* during which period there was no significant Utopian literature. One big aspect of the Renaissance, however, was the production of a number of Utopian books.

The first and one of the most important of them, known as *Utopia,* was written by Sir Thomas More (1478-1535 A. D.). His writings pictured a perfect communistic commonwealth. More, in his book, "has so surpassed those of his contemporaries and later rivals, not only in vividness and daring, but also in its depth and scientific contribution, that it has given its name to the whole class of literature and has become a word of common parlance."[3] Without doubt, his work was the beginning of a literature that played a prominent part in the social and scientific progress of the sixteenth and succeeding centuries.

Nearly a hundred years after More's death, Francis Bacon wrote the *New Atlantis.* His book "proclaimed with almost romantic enthusiasm that scientific method alone was the ladder by which man was to ascend to perfect living. Its new program to attain Utopia was the rebuilding of society in the light of knowledge and discovery."[4]

The same year (1623) that Bacon wrote his *New Atlantis,* Thomas Campanella wrote the *City of the Sun.* He

[2] *Ibid.,* pp. 84-94.
[3] *Ibid.,* p. 127.
[4] *Ibid.,* pp. 147-148.

was an Italian, born in 1568. The Utopianism in his book
is quite similar in many respects to ideas found in the *Republic* and also to those found in More's works. Here lies
a good illustration of how ideas bridge centuries as a golden
thread of truth coming down from age to age.

James Harrington's political Utopia, called *Oceana,*
which appeared in England in 1656, differed from the others in that it was written to solve the political needs of England during the Cromwell period. Although writing of an
ideal state, the author was presenting a constitution for immediate and practical use, and in order to insure its publication he presented it in the form of what he called a "political romance."

OTHER UTOPIAN WRITINGS

In addition to these famous writings, since the time of
More an abundance of Utopian literature has been produced.
Joyce O. Hertzler gives the following list:

The sixteenth and seventeenth centuries were the richest in speculative treatises of an Utopian nature of any period in history. Among
other works of this age the following are significant: Joseph Hall,
Mundus et Alter Idem (1607); Erycius Puteanus, *Comus* (1608); Jo-
hann Valenti Andreae, *Christianopolis* (1620); Sir John Eliot, *Monarchy
of Man* (1622); John Barclay, *Argenis* (about 1630); Jani Nicii Ery-
thracus, *Eudemiae* (1637); Bishop Francis Godwin, *The Man in the
Moon* (1638); Jacobus Bidermannus, *Utopia* (1640); John Milton and
Samuel Gott, *Nova Solyma, the Ideal City, or Jerusalem Regained*
(1648); Thomas Hobees, *Leviathan* (1651); John Sadler, *Olbia, the
New Island* (1660); Robert Filmer, *Patriarcha* (1680).[5]

UTOPIAN SOCIALISTS

Seven men, all of them Frenchmen but one, are known
by historians as "the Utopian Socialists."[6] They did their
work during the latter part of the eighteenth and early
nineteenth centuries. They are: Abbe Morelly, born about
1720; Francois Noel Babeuf, born 1764; Count Henry de
Saint-Simon, born 1760; Charles Fourier, born 1772;
Etienne Cabet, born 1788; Louis Blanc, born 1813; and
Robert Owen, born in Wales in 1771.

Unlike some modern social reformers, none of these
men were trying to bring about reforms for their own personal benefit. They represented such professions as edit-

[5] *Ibid.,* p. 178.
[6] *Ibid.,* pp. 181-224.

ing, journalism, business, science, and politics. They were really social-conscious men who had inherited from ages past the concept of a Millennium or Golden Age in the future wherein society and the world in general would be a blessed place for all of humanity.

It was the hope of each of these men to do away with disorder, misery, poverty, hunger, and human suffering, which the world at their time presented, and in their places make it possible for wealth, happiness, harmony and beauty to be enjoyed by all mankind equally. This they believed could be accomplished through the establishing of a new social order. It is true that no two of them agreed in the details of this new social order, but they all had a similar purpose and similar basic principles. The following statement, made by one of them, expresses well the purpose of all the others: To "calm the suffering of the peoples, deliver the unfortunate from the anguish of hunger and misery and the fortunate from their egotism, and bring about a marriage upon earth between work and pleasure, between riches and kindly feeling, between virtue and happiness."

Fundamental in their belief was that God had ordained all things to serve the happiness of His children on earth. This was the starting point of their Utopianism. They all believed that men were naturally good and, with proper environment, perfection in society could be brought about.

These Utopian Socialists represent part of that great stream of thought which has come down through the ages proclaiming the establishment of a better society for mankind—a world which would eventually culminate in the millennial reign of Jesus Christ as predicted by the holy prophets since the world began.

RECENT UTOPIAN WRITINGS

Among the more recent Utopian writings which have become somewhat famous are the following: Edward Bellamy, *Looking Backward,* published in 1889; Theodor Hertzka, *Freeland—A Social Anticipation,* written in 1890; and H. G. Wells, *Modern Utopia,* published in 1905. The conception of social growth and development into a more perfect society is fundamental in each of these writings. They were all produced after the world had been affected extensively with the ideas of evolution.

SAVONAROLA'S GOOD SOCIETY EXPERIMENT

Stimulated by divine revelations from God through the holy prophets, religious teachers have constantly attempted to establish the good society. From generation to generation, new leaders arise who put forth renewed efforts to bring about the reign of peace upon the earth.

One outstanding and famous example is "Savonarola's Florentine Theocracy." In 1494, Fra Girolamo Savonarola, the foremost preacher and most influential personage of Florence, Italy, came forth with the idea of establishing in his beloved city a theocracy. It was to be a city-state built upon the pure principles of Christianity. Immorality and all kinds of sin were to be suppressed. Private interests were to be sacrificed to the common good. The social and civic life of the people were to be ruled by divine principles; in fact, God was to reign.

Savonarola preached his fiery sermons from prophetic texts, and called upon the citizens of Florence to put down vice with a vigorous hand, and for each of them to forsake worldly pleasures, and to give themselves in humility to the worship and service of God. A strong political and religious fervor blended together and soon remarkable and unheard-of reforms took place, transmitting Savonarola's dream into a temporary reality. For three or four years' time Florence was lifted from a city of most degrading vices to one of hopeful social righteousness. To quote a contemporary historian:

The whole aspect of the city changed. Finery and jewelry were cast aside; women dressed plainly on the streets; money which had before been spent for ornament and display was now given to the poor; theatres and taverns were empty; cards and dice disappeared; the churches were crowded; alms boxes were well filled; tradesmen and bankers restored their ill-gotten gains; purity, sobriety, and justice prevailed in the city, and the Prior of San Marco (Savonarola) was everywhere hailed as the greatest public benefactor.[7]

Unfortunately this blessed condition was short-lived. The citizens of Florence soon reverted to their former way of living, and the faithful teacher was obliged to look forward to another day for establishment of the good society.

---

[7] Cited in *ibid.*, p. 97.

COMMUNIST AND COOPERATIVE EXPERIMENTS IN AMERICA

After the United States had obtained its independence from England and was fast becoming a nation, religious leaders and social reformers from various lands looked upon America as the place to establish a new Zion, the New Jerusalem. Numerous communist and cooperative colonies were established in America during the nineteenth century.[8] The New World seemed to supply especially fertile ground upon which to build the good society. Prominent among these new societies were the Shakers, the Perfectionists of Oneida, the Dukhobors, Owenite Colonies, Fourierist Colonies, the Free Society of Vaux, the Aiglemont Colony, Robinson's Colonies and numerous other groups who were looking forward for the coming of the Savior.

In practically all, if not all, of these social and economic experiments in America, the people who participated were eagerly looking forward to the second coming of the Master, accompanied by the good society spoken of by the prophets of old. In fact, the millennial hope was the overwhelming religious motivation of the period in American history when Joseph Smith was born and when the Gospel of Jesus Christ was restored to earth through that Prophet. Christians, regardless of which church they belonged to, were anxiously waiting for the time when the Lord would reign.

SUPPLEMENTARY READINGS—CHAPTER 39

1. Charles Gide, *Communist and Co-operative Colonies*, pp. 1-222.
2. Joyce Oramel Hertzler, *The History of Utopian Thought*, pp. 1-320.

---

[8] Charles Gide, *Communist and Co-operative Colonies*, pp. 1-222.

Chapter 40.

THE MORMONS' ZION CONCEPT

INTRODUCTORY STATEMENT

In this chapter we shall present the concept which has been held by the Mormon people in regards to the second coming of Jesus, the millennial reign for one thousand years, and the part that the Church is to play in preaching the Gospel, gathering the children of Israel, and building a holy city preparatory for the coming of the Son of Man. This new city is to be called Zion or the New Jerusalem. The word "Zion" not only means to Church members that one particular city which they are to be instrumental in establishing; but they also believe that in its largest geographical bounds, Zion is the whole American continent.

Another meaning of Zion is "the pure in heart," and the gathering place of the Saints; and so in this respect the term has been applied to the Church wherever its headquarters has been in America. At the present time, however, we speak of the principal concentrations of the Saints as being Zion, but our main emphasis in this chapter shall be the Zion or New Jerusalem which is to be established at Independence, Missouri, and the Mormons' concept of the Millenium.

HISTORICAL SETTING

Joseph Smith and his associates, at the time the Church was organized, were very familiar with the predictions of the holy prophets regarding the Millennium as recorded in the Bible. They knew the ideas that we have pointed out in previous chapters; namely, that Zion was to be established; that Jesus Christ was to reign upon the earth one thousand years; that this period should be one of peace, righteousness, and prosperity; and that it should be a time when enmity between man and man and between man and animal should exist no more. In fact, since these ideas were found in the Bible, they were common property of all Christian churches.

BOOK OF MORMON CONTRIBUTIONS

But the Prophet Joseph and his followers received from the Book of Mormon prophets an added stimulus to the millennial concept and new information that members of other Christian churches did not have. They learned from the Jaredite and Nephite teachers that the American continent was held in favor by the Almighty. It was, indeed, a "land of promise, a land choice above all other lands" upon the face of the earth![1] They also learned that the ancient American prophets had proclaimed that the Lord had blessed this land and dedicated it as the gathering place of Israel in the last days.

Furthermore, Ether, the last of the Jaredite prophets, had predicted that America was to be the land upon which the New Jerusalem was to be built and that it should be "the Holy Sanctuary of the Lord."[2] Those who dwelt in this Holy City, he explained, would be "they whose garments are white through the blood of the Lamb; and they who are numbered among the remnant of the seed of Joseph who were of the house of Israel."[3] Speaking in our terminology, they would be the righteous members of the Church of Jesus Christ of Latter-day Saints who are of the seed of Joseph.

REVELATIONS REGARDING BUILDING OF ZION

Since God the Eternal Father, through His Only Begotten Son and holy angels, was restoring the true plan of salvation to Joseph Smith, the Prophet felt that it was his duty to direct the establishing of Zion—the New Jerusalem —preparatory for the coming of the Savior. During the first few months following the organizing of the Church, therefore, Joseph became deeply concerned over the founding of the City of Holiness. Whenever the Prophet was confronted with any problem, he sought the Lord in humble prayer for the solution. Thereupon, in December, 1830, in response to prayer, God revealed to Joseph the vision

---

[1] Ether 1:42-43; 2:5-12; 1 Nephi 2:20-21; 2 Nephi 1:5-12; 10:10-20.
[2] Ether 13:3-6.
[3] Ibid., 13:10-11.

of Enoch, which is recorded in the "Writings of Moses," now published in the *Pearl of Great Price*. From the words of the ancient prophet, the Mormon leader received additional information regarding the last days and the building of the City of Zion. Joseph learned that the Gospel was to be taken to all parts of the earth for the purpose of gathering out God's elect; and those Church members were to build "an Holy City . . . and it shall be called Zion, a New Jerusalem."[4] This great event was to be preparatory for the coming of the Lord; and at His coming He was to dwell in the New Jerusalem. God revealed the following unto Enoch:

There shall be mine abode, and it shall be Zion, which shall come forth out of all the creations which I have made; and for the space of one thousand years the earth shall rest.[5]

Thereupon, after becoming acquainted with Enoch's vision, Joseph inquired of God as to the place where this Holy City was to be built. The Church was not a year old, in fact, it was in December, 1830, the same month that Joseph had received the revelation regarding the vision of Enoch, that the Lord "announced the revelation that the New Zion would be built somewhere in the West by the borders of the Lamanites." At this time the Saints were residing in New York, Joseph living at Fayette.

Early in the following year, Joseph directed the move of the Saints from New York to Ohio. They had barely arrived at Kirtland when the Mormon Prophet began to look toward another frontier farther west—on which to establish the Zion for the Saints of God.

Parley P. Pratt returned to Kirtland in the spring of 1831 from a mission to the Lamanites in Missouri. He gave a glowing report of the beauty and fertility of that region. Thereupon Joseph inquired again of the Lord relative to the location of Zion. In answer God instructed twenty-six elders, including the Prophet, to travel by twos to Independence, Missouri, stating that after their arrival He would reveal to them the location of the New Zion. All the elders were to go by different routes and preach the Gospel on all opportune occasions *en route*.[6]

4 Moses 7:62-63.
5 *Ibid.*, Galatians 4:26; Hebrews 12:22; Revelation 3:12; 12:1-27.
6 *Doctrine and Covenants* 52:2-5.

The missionaries arrived at Independence in the latter part of July. They had traveled 1,000 miles. Shortly thereafter the Prophet received a revelation which announced Missouri to be Zion, the gathering place for the Saints.[7] Independence was designated as the center—the site for the New Jerusalem, and a holy temple to the Lord was to be erected on a knoll west of the courthouse.

ZION'S FAVORABLE LOCATION

The frontier of western Missouri offered the best possible location for the realization of Joseph's dreams of a "City of God." There in the unsettled West the Prophet contemplated gathering the pure in heart from all parts of the world.[8] Many Lamanites were living on the Great Plains in the region bordering Missouri on the west, and to the eastward throughout the world lived a myriad of Gentiles. God had placed the responsibility upon the Mormons to take the restored Gospel of Jesus Christ to both peoples. Missouri—a spacious fertile frontier country—was centrally located in the United States, as well as being in the heart of the great Mississippi Valley. Extending from Independence—the center of Zion—the Saints of God could build city upon city. The ideas of Zion, i.e., of righteousness and purity of heart, could spread until they eventually filled the whole of the American continent which the Prophet proclaimed to be Zion. To quote:

The whole of America is Zion itself from north to south, and is described by the prophets, who declare that it is the Zion where the mountain of the Lord should be, and that it should be in the center of the land.[9]

At that day when cities of righteousness should be established throughout the whole land, Zion will be great, wonderful, and glorious. The Lord declared to the Prophet Joseph:

Zion [shall] . . . spread herself and become very glorious, very great, and very terrible. And the nations of the earth shall honor her, and shall say: "Surely Zion is the city of our God, and surely Zion cannot fall, neither be moved out of her place, for God is there, and the hand of the Lord is there; and he hath sworn by the power of his might to be her salvation and her high tower."[10]

[7] *Ibid.*, 57; 58:6-14.
[8] *Doctrine and Covenants* 68:24-86; 78:15; 133:4-15.
[9] Joseph Fielding Smith, *Teachings of the Prophet Joseph Smith*, p. 362.
[10] *Doctrine and Covenants* 97:18-20.

ATTEMPTS TO ESTABLISH ZION

Twelve men, representing the twelve tribes of Israel, laid the first log for a Mormon house in Missouri on August 2, 1831. This was done twelve miles west of Independence, now part of Kansas City, where sixty Colesville Saints had settled.

After laying the log for the first house, Sidney Rigdon dedicated the land of Zion for the gathering of Israel, and put the people under solemn covenant to serve God in that land.[11] The following day the Prophet Joseph dedicated the temple site at Independence. On this exact spot the house of the Lord will be erected when the New Jerusalem is built.

As previously suggested, the idea of Zion held by the Prophet was both a condition of the people and a geographical area. The Saints must be "pure in heart."[12] They must live the Law of Consecration, or as otherwise termed, the United Order, as the children of God did in the City of Enoch or as the Nephites did following the advent of Christ. Joseph knew that if a successful Zion city were established, it would require a godlike people—a "Zion people"—to bring it about.

Therefore, the Prophet instructed his followers before he left for Kirtland as to how they should live in Zion. He appointed Edward Partridge to divide unto the Saints "their inheritance," and Sidney Gilbert to purchase all the land in Missouri that the Mormons could pay for. After holding a conference at Kaw Township, where the Colesville Saints had settled, all those who had not been appointed to remain in Zion returned to Kirtland, leaving Independence August 9, 1831. During the next seventeen years, Joseph Smith spent most of his time in Ohio and directed the "Zion Movement" from there.

A general plan for the physical make-up of cities of Zion was prepared by the Prophet in the spring of 1833.[13] A copy of the plan was sent to Independence in June of that year, but the Missourian persecutions of the Saints prevented its being executed at that time. However, the

---

[11] *Ibid.*, 58:57.
[12] *Ibid.*, 97:21.
[13] B. H. Roberts, *A Comprehensive History of the Church*, vol. 1, pp. 311-312.

plan of the "City of Zion" served as the model for the building of Far West in Missouri, and Nauvoo, Illinois, and
later for Salt Lake City and the other Mormon settlements
in the Great West.

Events and conditions that followed the dedication of
the land prevented the Saints from building the New Jerusalem in Missouri; but matters looked well for awhile.
Within a little over a year after Joseph had selected Independence, Missouri, more than a thousand of the faithful
had gathered at that place.

It was not long, however, before their neighbors began
to fear encroachments of this new group which worked and
succeeded in such unified harmony. Gradually the feeling
of jealous antipathy developed into open persecution and
mob violence, and the Mormons, being outnumbered greatly, found resistance futile. They were driven from their
homes in Jackson County. They crossed the river north
into Ray and Clay counties, where they resided temporarily while they sent word to the Prophet in Kirtland regarding their pitiful plight.

The following spring (1834), Joseph organized a vol-
unteer, untrained army from the faithful members in Ohio,
and traveled 1,000 miles westward to Missouri to "redeem
Zion." But upon arriving, Joseph's army, known as Zion's
Camp, was abandoned without restoring the refugees to
their homes in Jackson County. At that time the Lord
revealed to the Prophet that the reason the Saints had not
been restored to their homes and were not permitted to build
the City of Zion at that time was because they had not kept
the commandments of the Lord to the degree requisite for
the building of the City of God—the New Jerusalem.[14]

Four years later the Saints were driven by force from
the State of Missouri. They took refuge in Illinois. There,
under the leadership of Joseph the Prophet, they built a
city known as "Nauvoo—the Beautiful." The Prophet was
now able to put into effect many ideas which he had long
before conceived concerning the plan of the City of Zion.
When Nauvoo was only five years old, however, Joseph and
his brother were martyred by a ruthless mob (June 27, 1844),

---

[14] *Doctrine and Covenants* 105:1-40; 101:1-24.

and less than two years later the Saints were again driven
from their homes.

They were led to the valleys of the Rocky Mountains
by Brigham Young, and here they established their new
home in the solitude of the Great West. But the Saints
have continued to look forward to the day when they would
return to Missouri and participate in the building of the
New Jerusalem preparatory for the coming of the Lord
to reign a thousand years.[15] They firmly maintain that
they shall be the mortals who shall have the main responsibility in building the Holy City, for it is they who hold
the Priesthood of God and who have been divinely authorized to carry forward the Gospel during this the last dispensation. Conditioned on obedience, they are heirs of
the kingdom of God and joint-heirs with Jesus Christ:
thus when the Lord comes the Saints who are worthy shall
dwell with Him in the New Jerusalem.[16]

THE MILLENNIUM AS REVEALED TO JOSEPH SMITH

We have previously discussed the teachings of Isaiah
and the other prophets regarding the Millennium, but our
purpose now is to examine the revelations from God directly to the Prophet Joseph Smith regarding the thousand
years of peace and righteousness.

The heart of the Mormons' concept is the belief in the
Millennium—a perfect society which shall be established
here on this earth. They accept all the teachings of the
holy prophets as given in the scriptures, many of which
have been presented in the preceding chapters. In addition to those revelations given to ancient prophets, Jesus
Christ has made known additional facts to Joseph which
help to clarify the whole picture of the reign of peace and
righteousness. Through direct revelation, the American
Prophet received as complete a knowledge of the millennial
reign of Christ as can be found in the combined teachings
of all the holy prophets as recorded in the *Bible, Book of
Mormon,* and *Pearl of Great Price.* Thus the *Doctrine and
Covenants* and the teachings of Joseph Smith constitute
the Mormons' principal source of information regarding
this glorious event.

[15] *Ibid.,* 101:16-21; 136:18.
[16] *Ibid.,* 45:58-59; 43:29-31; 29:11, 22-23.

Members of the Church of Jesus Christ of Latter-day Saints will participate in the building of the New Jerusalem. They will be joined in that activity by the righteous of the earth who have lived during the various Gospel dispensations from Adam's time forward. Christ, accompanied by the hosts of heaven, shall come to make His abode in Zion. "The Lamb shall stand on Mount Zion, and with him a hundred and forty-four thousand, having his Father's name written on their foreheads. . . . And the graves of the saints shall be opened; and they shall come forth and stand on the right hand of the Lamb, when he shall stand upon Mount Zion, and upon the Holy City, the New Jerusalem; and they shall sing the song of the Lamb, day and night, forever and ever."[17] Father Adam, Enoch and his people who ascended to heaven, Noah, Abraham, Isaac, Jacob, Moses, Elijah, John the Baptist, the apostles of the Lamb, and all the holy prophets of God who have lived from the time of the first man shall come to live in the presence of the Lord.[18]

Even the lost tribes of Israel "who are in the north countries" shall come to Zion, "and they shall bring rich treasures unto the children of Ephraim, my servants. . . . And they shall fall down and be crowned with glory even in Zion, by the hands of the servants of the Lord, even the children of Ephraim."[19]

Thus during the Millennium there shall be both mortals and immortals living upon the earth together. The mortal "children shall grow up without sin unto salvation. For the Lord shall be in their midst, and his glory shall be upon them, and he will be their King and their lawgiver."[20]

Satan shall not have power to tempt any man. And there shall be no sorrow because there is no death. In that day an infant shall not die until he is old; and his life shall be as the age of a tree; and when he dies he shall not sleep, that is to say in the earth, but shall be changed in the twinkling of an eye, and shall be caught up, and his rest shall be glorious.[21]

When the Lord shall come, He shall reveal all things unto man: things which have passed, things regarding the earth, and the heavens, and all the purposes of God.[22]

[17] Ibid., 133:16-25, 46-47, 56.
[18] Ibid., 133:54-55.
[19] Ibid., 133:26-34.
[20] Ibid., 45:58-59.
[21] Ibid., 101:24-34; 63:51.
[22] Ibid., 101:32-34.

At the end of the thousand years of peace and righteousness, men will again begin to deny their God. Satan will be loosed and reign only for a short season, and then the end of the Terrestrial period of the earth shall come. At this time all those who have not heretofore been resurrected shall come forth from their graves to be assigned to their eternal reward or eternal damnation. This shall be another "great and dreadful day of the Lord"—great for the righteous and dreadful for the wicked. Following this, "the heaven and the earth shall be consumed and pass away, and there shall be a new heaven and a new earth."[23] The world shall be celestialized and shall forever become the home of those who have lived righteous lives.

SUPPLEMENTARY READINGS—CHAPTER 40

1. *Bible:* Revelation 20:21; 22. (Review these.)
2. *Doctrine and Covenants* 29:10-30; 43:28-35; 45:22-71; 57:1-5; 58:6-14; 57; 62:4; 63:24-36; 78:15; 97:17-21; 101:1-101; 105:1-41; 133:1-74.
3. Joseph Fielding Smith, *The Way to Perfection,* pp. 278-286, 292-314, 322-327.
4. Joseph Fielding Smith (Compiler), *Teachings of the Prophet Joseph Smith,* pp. 17, 21, 24, 29, 80, 161, 254, 268, 362.
5. James E. Talmage, *The Articles of Faith,* pp. 367-405.

---

[23] *Ibid.,* 29:11, 22-23; 43:29-31. The calamities which shall befall man at the time of the Savior's coming to earth to reign at the beginning of the Millennium has been proclaimed "the great and dreadful day of the Lord."

Chapter 41

THE DYNAMICS OF MORMONISM

INTRODUCTORY STATEMENT

The story of the "Gospel Through the Ages" as given in this book began back in the distant past before man was placed on the earth, and it has moved forward throughout world's history to and including the restoration of the Gospel of Jesus Christ to earth again through the American Prophet—Joseph Smith. It has also continued forward from our day through the periods of the terrestrial and into the celestial stages of the world as revealed by the Lord to the holy prophets.

But since the greatest of all Gospel dispensations and the culminating period of the story of God's dealings and revelations to His children on this earth reside in the Church of Jesus Christ of Latter-day Saints—the one and only completely true and officially recognized religion by the Lord—and since all the power, authority, ordinances and principles of the Gospel (with a thorough understanding of the same) which have been in the world during any Gospel dispensation are and will continue to be present in Mormonism, we shall conclude our story of the history of the Gospel with a discussion of the power, vitality, or dynamics of the Gospel of Jesus Christ—Mormonism. Does this Church contain the requisites to make it the one official organization upon the face of the earth duly endowed by Jesus to bring salvation and eternal life to all of God's children who repent, are baptized, and obey its teachings? Yes, this is the claim made by Mormonism to the whole world. This religion is an ensign, a beacon, which is destined to guide the inhabitants of the earth into the path of light and truth and forward into eternal life.

NEED FOR A RESTORATION OF THE GOSPEL

It has been pointed out throughout this book—and by way of summary it should be restated—that as the Christian Church emerged from the conglomerate social thought and became the universal religion in 392 A.D., it was an adulterated Christianity. A religious syncretism had taken place, fusing many of the best of the pagan beliefs and practices with the teachings of the Master. Many of the grandest precepts given to the world by Jesus were lost. The "Spirit of the Lord was grieved" and He withdrew His holy Priesthood or power from the earth. There was not a church upon the face of the earth at the beginning of the nineteenth century which could officially perform ordinances in the name of Jesus Christ and have those ordinances accepted by God as being valid and binding both on earth and in heaven. Thus a Great Apostasy had occurred, which is evidenced by the rise of hundreds of Christian denominations.

The condition had become such that in the spring of 1820 the Savior declared to Joseph Smith that the creeds of Christendom "were an abomination in his sight; that those professors were all corrupt; that 'they draw near to me with their lips, but their hearts are far from me; they teach for doctrines the commandments of men, having a form of godliness, but they deny the power thereof.' "

THE RESTORATION

God the Eternal Father and His Only Begotten Son felt the necessity of reaffirming the cardinal Christian principles and of re-establishing the divine truths which had been lost through the fusion of pagan and Christian beliefs. If religion was to again become a vital force in human experience, all the principles of Christian living enjoyed by former dispensations, in addition to new principles applicable to our civilization, must be revealed. It was God's purpose, as many prophets of old had foretold, to establish in the last days a glorious dispensation of the Gospel into which all other dispensations would flow; therefore, a dispensation should be established which should be the greatest of all. The Gospel of Jesus Christ was to come to the earth for the last time—the true religion was never to be adulterated again nor given to another people.

Beginning in the spring of 1820, when God the Father and His Only Begotten Son appeared to Joseph, and continuing on from that date, the American Prophet and his successors received revelation upon revelation until all the principles and ordinances of the Gospel requisite for the salvation of mankind—both the living and the dead—were upon earth again. Among the heavenly beings who appeared to Joseph Smith and Oliver Cowdery were John the Baptist, Peter, James and John, Moses, Elias, and Elijah, each coming to restore to earth keys of the holy Priesthood. Thus the Church of Jesus Christ of Latter-day Saints, established by the Prophet under the divine direction of the Savior of the world, contains all the keys, powers, and authority of God, which have been enjoyed by any or all of the other Gospel dispensations. Herein lies the dynamics of Mormonism, and the genius that it possesses to give to its members lives of richness in mortality and an assurance of blessed eternal lives in the kingdom of their God.

THE TRUE AND LIVING CHURCH

In a revelation given to Joseph Smith in 1831—labeled by the Lord, "My preface unto the book of commandments"—Jesus declared that the Church He had established through the American Prophet was "the only true and living church upon the face of the whole earth."[1] The statement "true and living church" is a significant explanation as to the cause of, the moving forces within Mormonism which gives it the aptitude, not only to convert strong intellectual individuals, but to develop and hold forceful characters.

KEYS OF THE PRIESTHOOD

The claim made by Mormonism of its divinity is one of the factors which makes it a "living church." Latter-day Saints maintain that the keys of the kingdom of God and the holy Priesthood are vested in the president of the Church and that all official acts of the Church are per-

---

[1] *Doctrine and Covenants* 1:6, 30.

formed through the Priesthood. In speaking of the Prophet
Joseph Smith, the Lord said: "I have given him the keys
of the mysteries, and the revelations which are sealed, until
I shall appoint unto them another in his stead."[2] Each
succeeding President of the Church has received the same
keys. The Church is endowed, therefore, with Divine Power.

This is indeed the true Church of Jesus Christ, established in this dispensation through divine revelations given
to a Prophet who was also ordained to the holy orders of the
Priesthood by heavenly beings sent from the presence of God
the Father and the Son for that purpose. Therefore, the
ordinances performed by any other Christian denomination,
as well as those performed by non-Christians, are valid only
in this world and only among men. They are not consummated by the holy Priesthood of the Son of God, and so
they are not binding in the world to come.

SERVANTS OF GOD

Faithful individuals affiliated with the Church of
Jesus Christ of Latter-day Saints (and that includes a
vast majority) give freely of their time, talents and money
whenever the authorities ask them to do so, because they
believe that those who preside are appointed by God. No
stronger drive could be conceived than that of a man becoming convinced that he is a servant of the Lord, possessing
authority to speak, act, and officiate in the ordinances for
the Master, and having the right to bless mankind through
the divine Priesthood which he holds. Coupled with that
strong religious drive is the power of Godliness which comes
to the Church members who are honoring the holy Priesthood which has been bestowed upon them. They are indeed divinely endowed servants of the Most High God.

Many individuals not connected with Mormonism marvel over the fact that thousands of Latter-day Saints leave
their homes and friends to go into foreign countries—pay-
ing their own expenses—to proselytize for the Church. The
missionaries do this because they are thoroughly convinced
that they are clothed with the power of the heavens to carry
forward the work of Christ here upon the earth. Having
been ordained unto the holy Priesthood and having been

---
[2] *Ibid.*, 28:7.

called by the First Presidency to fill a mission, they have the authority to speak in the name of the Father and His Son Jesus Christ. In modern revelation, the Lord declared: "Verily, I say unto you, that they who go forth, bearing these tidings unto the inhabitants of the earth, to them is power given to seal both on earth and in heaven, the unbelieving and rebellious."[3]

Officered by the Laity

The fact that the Mormon Church is composed of and officered by the laity is another reason for its being a "living church." When the Savior was establishing His teachings in Palestine, He did not select as His helpers learned rabbis of the Sanhedrin; but He drew His apostles and other disciples from the common people. Men highly trained in the Jewish law, but far removed from the impulses, sorrows, and problems of society, were of no use to Him. Fishermen, tax collectors, and men of similar professions became His devout helpers, because they possessed an intellectual sincerity, honesty and faith which could be vitalized into a tenacious life of adoration and religious worship. To these men He gave the Priesthood and commanded them to go "into all the world, and preach the gospel to every creature."[4] History records morally beautiful yet pitiful stories of how these devout messengers of truth, for the cause of the Master, cheerfully suffered the torture of burning at the stake, of crucifixion, of having wild beasts tear them to pieces, and of all other manners of persecutions. Life actually flowed through the veins of this new church. It was a dynamic religion and remained so until the practice of giving the Priesthood only to a trained group replaced the practice of giving it to all worthy male members of Christendom.

Just as early Christianity was a "living church" because each lay member could function in its ordinances, so is Mormonism forceful today. In accordance with a revelation given to Joseph Smith, all worthy male members of the Church are ordained unto the Priesthood and have the right of advancement to the highest order therein. This is a gift more priceless than the wealth of the world.

[3] *Ibid.*, 1:8.
[4] Mark 16:15.

A learned professor of theology from the East recently visited one of the business men in Salt Lake City and expressed a desire to meet a Mormon bishop. The business man immediately pressed a button. The professor received the surprise of his life when in walked the janitor, who was introduced as the business man's bishop. As long as a church draws its officers from different vocations, it will remain a vital growing concern.

PRODUCES POWERFUL LEADERS

Another evidence of the dynamics of Mormonism is the fact that throughout its history it has distinguished itself as a great institution productive of outstanding leadership. Thousands of obscure individuals have been gathered into Mormonism and recreated. They have been born anew into a God-centered life. What historian today would be classifying Brigham Young as one of the world's greatest colonizers, Jacob Hamblin as a unique frontier scout and "apostle to the Lamanites," Wilford Woodruff as an accomplished missionary, and Orson Pratt as an outstanding religious philosopher, if these men had not been caught in the net of Mormonism? They, like hundreds of other people, while helping create history of the Church were created by the Mormon Church.

The Latter-day Saint program also prepares its youth for leadership. Obedience to the Gospel teachings molds the individual into a character of moral, mental, physical and spiritual strength. Those are the characteristics which are requisite for leadership. An illustration will help to show the power of Mormonism in this respect.

An article entitled "The Production, Retention and Attraction of American Men of Science," by Professor E. L. Thorndike of Columbia University, published in the August 16, 1940, issue of *Science*,[5] shows how effective the Church training and inheritance has been in helping to prepare its youth for leadership in the field of science. Thorndike's statistics are based on the population figures of the forty-eight states in 1890 and in 1900. His study shows that Utah has produced nearly once and a half times as many

[5] E. L. Thorndike, "The Production, Retention and Attraction of American Men of Science," *Science*, XC (Lancaster, Pa., August 16, 1940), pp. 137-141.

"Men of Science" per capita as any other state in the Union. Based on 1,000,000 population, Utah has produced 492 "Men of Science"; Colorado, the next highest of the forty-eight states, has produced, 340, and Georgia, the lowest state in the group, has produced only 44.

A Practical Religion

Another reason for the dynamics of Mormonism is the ability that that institution possesses to care for all the earthly needs of its members and to continue to adjust to a changing world. It fosters all Christian virtues, such as honesty, chastity, temperance, perseverance, reverence, and love. Obedience to these principles immediately brings serenity to the soul, physical and mental health, prosperity and happiness. The Word of Wisdom is the beacon to health. Mormon literature of Utah pioneer days is filled with examples in which the preacher devoted part of his sermon to a discussion of spiritual problems connected with theology and the remainder of his sermon to the giving of advice relative to the building of an irrigation ditch, a bridge over the canal, or a factory for the community. The Church leaders from Joseph Smith on have maintained that true religion is to make people prosperous and happy here and now. Proper thinking and acting towards one's associates are of vital importance in the good life. One glance at the Church school system, at the recreational activities of the M. I. A., at the intellectual religious instructions in Sunday School, at the programs of the Relief Society and Primary, at the activities of a Mormon bishop, and at the Church Welfare program, furnishes sufficient evidence to prove that Mormonism provides for the physical and mental needs of its members in a changing world.

The Doctrine of Progressive Eternalism

Any religion that remains powerful in the lives of the people is a religion which gives to its followers assurance of eternal life. The one thought held uppermost in the mind of the early Christian preacher was the fact that Christ had been crucified, but was alive again. His followers had the assurance that in like manner they, after death, would live again. Mormonism rests upon the fact, as was earlier pointed out, that the work and glory of God are "to bring to pass the immortality and eternal life of man."[6] The whole philosophy of the Church is built around the doctrine of eternal progression. God promised the Saints, "if you keep my commandments and endure to the end, you shall have eternal life, which gift is the greatest of all the gifts of God."[7] To the Mormons, all laws pertaining to religion are spiritual and eternal.[8] Baptism, marriage, family life and temple ordinances are spiritualized and made to endure forever. The deepest loves in human lives and the strongest hopes in the hearts of men are satisfied in this philosophy of progressive eternalism. No wonder Mormonism is the "true and living Church."

TEACHES TRUE CONCEPT OF GOD

Jesus Christ came into the world to give mankind a revelation of the personality of His Father. These two individuals were so much alike in their thoughts, actions, purposes, and personalities that when Philip said, "Lord, show us the Father," Jesus replied, "He that hath seen me hath seen the Father."[9] On another occasion He said, "If ye knew me, ye would know my Father also."[10] His parables are full of the concept of a personalized God who is the Father of the human race. He made the definite claim, "I am the Son of God."[11] Jesus looked upon Elohim as an individual who possessed an unlimited amount of love and compassion for His children and an unbounded interest in their well-being. The vitality of the Savior's personality was that He was God-centered at all times, ofttimes making such remarks as, "I do nothing except that which my Father hath commanded me to do." It is well to read again the Gospel of John in order that we may fully appreciate the intimate relationship that existed between Jesus and God the Father.

But the philosophers of modern Christendom have done away with a personalized God. He is to them an abstraction, making it difficult to get real adoration for and communion with Him. Generally speaking, one who accepts

[6] Moses 1:39.
[7] *Doctrine and Covenants* 14:7.
[8] *Ibid.*, 29:34.
[9] John 14:8-9.
[10] *Ibid.*, 8:19.
[11] *Ibid.*, 10:36.

their creeds cannot experience the beautiful and intimate relationships with the Father that Jesus enjoyed and that Latter-day Saints experience.

Through numerous revelations—including "the First Vision"—the Prophet learned the true character of Deity. This He taught to His followers. One of the strongest factors in Mormonism is its interpretation of God. Latter-day Saints accept and worship their Heavenly Father as taught by Jesus. The only way we can conceive of Him is in personal terms. Yet, we are sure that He far surpasses in love, in charity, in beauty of person, in intelligence and wisdom, and in all other attributes, the most perfect conceptions that the human mind can produce. As has been pointed out, Mormons sincerely believe Jesus' statement. "This is life eternal, that they might know thee the only true God, and Jesus Christ, whom thou hast sent."[12] The complete revelation of Deity will come only to the man who becomes as God is. By living the Gospel of Jesus Christ, there is a possibility of mankind eventually reaching that goal. Therefore, the heart of Mormonism is the God-centered philosophy of the Church revealed by the Savior.

POWER OF TESTIMONY

The last point which shall be mentioned illustrating the dynamics of Mormonism is the conviction which is given to every faithful member of the divinity of the restored Gospel of Jesus Christ. Thousands of men, women, boys and girls stand up at the testimony meetings each month and soberly declare that they know that God lives, that Jesus is the Christ, and that Joseph Smith is a true Prophet of God and one of the greatest Prophets that has ever lived. Through their lives and actions they also bear testimony to the truthfulness of the Gospel. These testimonies come through the gift of the Holy Ghost. It is only through that gift that man can bear absolute testimony to the truthfulness of these things. Many thousands of Latter-day Saints have borne that testimony, and some of them have even sealed it with their lives. The power of individual testimony, therefore, is one of the most forceful things in life and it is the distinguishing power of Mormonism which makes it a "living church."

[12] *Ibid.*, 17:3.

Conclusions

The Church of Jesus Christ of Latter-day Saints is the "true and living Church" because the Lord has again established His work here upon the earth and has endowed it with divine authority. Mormonism provides abundant opportunity for each individual to develop his personality by participating in all Church activities. It also takes into account all the needs of its members, and furnishes a God-centered philosophy which, if obeyed, will produce lives of richness and happiness eternally.

Since God has decreed that the Gospel which was restored to earth through the Prophet Joseph Smith shall never be taken from the earth again nor given to another people, the story of "the Gospel Through the Ages" naturally reaches its climax in a discussion of the dynamics of Mormonism. We are now in the last Gospel dispensation, known as the Dispensation of the Fullness of Times. Thus this religion (Mormonism) will go forward accomplishing the designs of God until the Son of Man comes to earth to assume His position of President of His Church which was named in His honor, namely, the Church of Jesus Christ of Latter-day Saints.

Problems and Activities

PROBLEMS AND ACTIVITIES

General Suggestions: The topics in this book are plainly given in the text of each chapter and so there is no need of repeating them in this outline of suggestions on studying the Priesthood course. But the suggestion is hereby made to each teacher that throughout the entire course he follow the textbook and discuss the various topics as given. At the end of each chapter are to be found "Supplementary Readings," which have been very carefully selected because of their bearing on the subjects under discussion. The teachers of the various classes can enrich their store of information each week by studying as many of the supplementary readings as time will permit. Also, if each member of the Priesthood group can find time to read extensively, such information will be helpful and enlightening to him and to the class. But it is imperative as a minimum requirement that all members of the Melchizedek groups study carefully each week the material presented in the textbook if the course of study is to be pursued with satisfactory results.

CHAPTER 1—THE GOSPEL OF JESUS CHRIST—PAGES 1-5

Discuss: What is meant by the Gospel of Jesus Christ? What is it based on? Where are the best sources of its teachings? Discuss Paul's definition. What is meant by a covenant? What is the origin of the names Old Testament and New Testament? What is meant by the "new and everlasting covenant"? How extensive is the Gospel or what is its scope? Discuss the statements made by Brigham Young and John Taylor on the scope of the Gospel. How old are the Gospel principles and ordinances? What is meant by the laws of God? What is meant by light and truth? What is the source of all light and truth? Through what mediums do light and truth operate? Why do pagan and world religions resemble the Gospel of Jesus Christ?

CHAPTER 2—THE WORK AND GLORY OF GOD—PAGES 6-11

Discuss: For what purpose did God create the world? How? Give evidence that the world was organized by a divine intelligence. What is God's principal work? In what way may we help to enhance God's glory? What is the meaning of immortality? What is meant by eternal life? Distinguish between immortality and eternal life. Explain how immortality is a gift of God through Jesus Christ. Point out what man must do in order to receive eternal life. What is meant by "to know God and Jesus Christ"? What is the purpose of life?

CHAPTER 3—THE PLAN OF SALVATION—PAGES 12-19

Discuss: What is meant by the law of eternal progression? What is meant by "the Great Plan"? Who presided at the council in heaven and was the author of the plan of salvation? What part does law play in the plan of salvation? List three mediums through which we receive revelations from God. What is meant by the first spiritual death? Discuss the need for a savior in the plan of salvation. Do Latter-day Saints believe in foreordination?—Give evidence. Distinguish between foreordination and predestination. What plan did Lucifer present at the council in heaven? What great principle fundamental in growth and eternal progression would Lucifer's plan have interfered with? Did all the spirit children of God attain the same status of development in the pre-mortal life? Describe the war in heaven, stressing leadership, purpose, and results. Show its relationship to similar conflicts in this world. What is the relationship of the Gospel ordinances to the salvation of mankind? To what extent is obedience to the Gospel of Jesus Christ required of man if he is to attain life eternal? Did Jesus have to obey all the Gospel principles and ordinances?

Chapter 4—Jesus and the Gospel—Pages 20-24

Discuss: Why was the Gospel named the Gospel of Jesus Christ? During the early period of earth's history, what was the Priesthood named? Why was the name changed? What part will the Gospel play in the lives of men when the earth is celestialized? How many true Gospels are there? What is the only name by which salvation shall come to the children of men? Describe Jesus' status in the spirit world and His relationship to us. By what names has Jesus been known to mortals? Explain thoroughly in what respect mortal beings may become the sons and daughters of Jesus Christ. In what respect is Jesus the Father of this world? Distinguish between the Fatherhood of Jesus and the Fatherhood of God.

Chapter 5—Religion in Human History—Pages 25-29

Discuss: How old is the Gospel of Jesus Christ? When was it first revealed to mortals? To what extent have human beings searched for God and for salvation? Analyze carefully the various definitions of religion given in the text and formulate definitions of your own. What is the center of all religions? Define theology. Distinguish carefully between religion and theology. What are the definitions of religion given by such holy prophets as James, Amos, Samuel, Micah, and Jesus? How extensive has the quest for religion been among the human family? In what respect do Horace T. Houf's and Joseph Smith's viewpoints agree?

Chapter 6—Man's Quest for Salvation—Pages 30-38

Discuss: What is the author's purpose in Chapter 6? Have human beings fostered numerous religious systems or relatively few? How extensive a part has religion played in the history of mankind? There are approximately how many Christian denominations? List the major world religions, their present approximate memberships, and the dates and places where they originated. Which century in world's history was creative in regards to religious groups? Describe the religious conditions of the Roman Empire during the early Christian centuries. At the time of the birth of Jesus, what was the status of the Greek Homeric religion? What was the status of the ancient Roman Religion? What was the policy of Augustus Caesar regarding religion in the Roman empire? What was the name which applied to several pagan religions which were the rivals of early Christianity? List five factors which contributed to the popularity of the Mystery Religions. What evidence is there to prove that the Mystery Religions were altered forms of the true Gospel as revealed to Father Adam and the holy prophets who succeeded him? Why are the Mystery Religions of great importance in this course of study? Discuss the following Mystery Religions: Mithraism, Hermeticism, Isiac Mysteries, Cybele-Attis (Great Mother) Mysteries, Eleusinian Mysteries, and Dionysian or Bacchus Mysteries. Describe Mystery Religions. Why did Christianity finally become victorious over the Mystery Religions?

Chapter 7—Common Source of Religious Truths—Pages 39-45

Discuss: Make a list of some of the most outstanding similarities between world religions and the Gospel of Jesus Christ. How did Justin Martyr, Tertullian, Las Casas, and others account for the similarities in religious beliefs and customs? Explain what is meant by the "Independent Development Theory." Explain the "Diffusion Theory." What is the common source of all religious truths? Could both the Independent Development and Diffusion theories be explanations for religious practices being world-old and world-wide? Explain how the teachings of the prophets sustain these theories. According to Mormon belief, to whom does God reveal His will?

Chapter 8—Divine Fountain of Eternal Truth—Pages 46-53

Discuss: Are Mormons the only people that receive truth and divine guidance from God? Pay particular attention to President Joseph F. Smith's statement regarding all truths coming from God through the mediation of Jesus Christ. What did the prophets teach regarding the source of truth? Which ones of God's children receive the greatest number of divine revelations? What prevented Joseph Smith on one occasion from translating the Book of Mormon? Through what channels does God reveal His will to man? What part does obedience to law play in man's learning truth? What is the relationship of obedience to law and the receiving of God's blessings? To what extent is God responsible for man's progression? To what extent is man responsible for his own progression?

Chapter 9—Apostasies and How They Occur—Pages 54-57

Discuss: Define apostasy. Explain how apostasies are brought about through sin and ignorance and give examples. What is meant by religious syncretism? Explain how apostasies are brought about through religious syncretism and give examples. Explain how the Gospel has come down through the ages and how apostasies and restorations have occurred as discussed under the topic "World's Stream of Religious Thought."

Chapter 10—The Gospel Given to Father Adam—Pages 58-65

Discuss: Show how "the fall" was a spiritual death. Why has it been absolutely necessary for Father Adam and his posterity to receive divine revelation? Make a list of as many Gospel principles and ordinances as you can that were revealed to Adam. What is meant by the Adamic language? Describe the "Book of Remembrance." Of what importance is Priesthood in the plan of salvation? What position does Adam hold in the Priesthood? Who is Michael the Archangel? Read carefully and analyze the account given in the *Pearl of Great Price* of Adam's receiving the Gospel. What did Joseph Smith and Brigham Young teach regarding Adam's having the Gospel? List all the available evidence sustaining the statement that Adam had the same Gospel that we have today.

Chapter 11—The Gospel Dispensations—Pages 66-71

Discuss: Explain when and by whom the phrase "Gospel dispensations" has been used. Give the meaning of Gospel dispensations. What part in the Gospel plan was played by Adam in the spirit world prior to his coming into mortality? What is Adam's place in the Gospel plan in mortality? Describe the important council meeting which is to be held at Adam-Ondi-Ahman. Describe some of the leading events in the Adamic dispensation. Tell the story of Enoch as found in the Book of Moses. Give evidence which shows that Enoch had the Gospel. Describe Enoch's vision. Describe Enoch's great accomplishments.

Chapter 12—Gospel Dispensations from Noah to Jesus—Pages 72-81

Discuss: In what respects was Noah the second father of humanity? List the evidences which prove that Noah had the Gospel of Jesus Christ. Describe Noah's work. What is meant by the Patriarchal dispensation? How did it come about that Abraham received the Gospel and the Priesthood? List Abraham's righteous desires. From whom did Abraham receive the Priesthood? Explain that the holding of the Priesthood is evidence of one's having the true Gospel. List the items which show that Abraham had the Gospel. What is meant by a covenant? Discuss the nine points given in the text relative to God's covenant with Abraham. In what respect are all members of the Church of Jesus Christ accounted Abraham's seed? Discuss the "Chosen People" concept and show its force in human history. Give a short description of Moses' life. What evidence is available to prove that Moses had the Gospel? What is meant by the Law of Moses? What was its principal purpose? Did the Hebrews have the Gospel from Moses' time to Jesus'? Did they hold the Melchizedek Priesthood? Did any other ancient peoples have the Gospel of Jesus Christ besides the Israelites, Jaredites, and Nephites? Who was Jethro and what proof do we have that he had the Gospel? Answer the foregoing question as applied to Melchizedek.

Chapter 13—Gospel Dispensations in Ancient America—Pages 82-89

Discuss: Which prophet was the religious leader and founder of the Jaredite dispensation? Tell the story of his great vision. List all the evidence available that he had the Gospel. Tell the story of the Jaredite dispensation. Which prophets began the Nephite dispensation? Evaluate the Nephites as a religious people. Give evidence to show that the *Book of Mormon* contained the Gospel. Make a list of the principal Nephite prophets and teachers. Did the Nephites live under the Law of Moses or were they governed entirely by the Gospel? Describe the Church of Christ as it operated throughout Nephite history. According to available records, when in history were people first called Christians? Read the teachings of the Master as recorded in Third Nephi.

Chapter 14—The Meridian and Fullness of Times—Pages 90-95

Discuss: Why is the Christian dispensation of special importance in this course of study? What is meant by "the Great Apostasy"? Give evidence that a Great Apostasy occurred. What is meant by the Reformation? Make a list of as many Protestant reformers as you can. What was the principal reason why the reformers could not establish the true Church of Jesus Christ? What were the views of Ralph Waldo Emerson regarding Christianity of his day? What is meant by the Dispensation of the Fullness of Times? In what respects does it differ from other dispensations? Why has it been declared to be the greatest of all dispensations? List evidences supporting the claim of the restoration of the Gospel to the Prophet Joseph Smith.

Chapter 15—Children of God—Pages 96-103

Discuss: In what respect are men the offspring of God? What is the origin of the "children of God" belief? Describe a spirit-being from the evidence given in the vision beheld by the Brother of Jared and *Doctrine and Covenants*, 129. Give evidence that the Hebrew prophets understood the doctrine that we are spirit children of God. Did Jesus believe literally in the Fatherhood of God? What is the Mormon concept regarding our Heavenly Parents? Study carefully the poem *"O My Father"* for the purpose of observing its teachings of a Mother as well as a Father in heaven. Are there any resemblances between the teachings of the pagans on man's being a child of God and the teachings of the Gospel? Observe one by one the teachings of the various pagan groups on this doctrine. Why should their teachings resemble Mormonism?

Chapter 16—Men May Become Gods—Pages 104-113

Discuss: Why is Jesus sometimes referred to as "the Son of Man"? According to Joseph F. Smith, Orson Hyde, and Daniel H. Wells, what is the principal difference between God and man? Study carefully Joseph Smith's statement on page 105 in which he declares God to be an exalted man. Which Mormon first taught the doctrine that "men may become Gods"? Who is responsible for the following statement: "As man is, God once was; as God is, man may become"? Give the available evidence supporting the doctrine that men may become Gods. What is the evidence supporting the doctrine of the plurality of Gods? Did the early Christian Fathers know of the Gospel doctrine of men's becoming Gods?— Give proof supporting your answer. Compare the pagans' beliefs of deification with the doctrine of men's becoming Gods. Which statement made by one of the Mystery Religions resembles most closely the statement (previously discussed) made by Lorenzo Snow? Study the poem—"Man's Destiny"—for the purpose of getting President Snow's beautifully expressed ideas of men's becoming Gods.

Chapter 17—"Then Shall They Be Gods"—Pages 114-123

Discuss: What are the requirements to reach the exalted station of Godhood? In what respects do Gods differ from other intelligent beings? How did the Eternal Father become God? Describe the personality of God. What did Joseph Smith teach regarding the way in which men may become Gods? Compare the teachings of the Gospel and those of paganism on knowledge of Deity as an avenue to Godhood. Explain how celestial marriage is the crowning Gospel ordinance. Distinguish between celestial marriage and plural marriage. Was celestial marriage practiced by the ancient patriarchs? Have any individuals besides Jesus who have lived in mortality become Gods? What is the principal difference between a God and an angel? Compare the pagans' concept of celestial marriage and the Catholics' practice of the same doctrine. Do the practices of either of them have any relationship to the true doctrine of man's becoming a God? Explain.

CHAPTER 18—THE IMMORTALITY OF MAN—PAGES 124-129

Discuss: How extensive in the world is the belief in immortality? According to Dr. Bennion and Joseph Addison, why do human beings believe that they are immortal? Study carefully the teachings of the prophets, especially Joseph Smith's, regarding immortality. Explain how the life, intelligence, or mind of man is eternally existent. What is meant by an "intelligence"? Describe, as far as we have the information, eternally existent intelligences. If we are as old as God the Eternal Father (both being eternal), then explain how He became our Father. Describe the spirit world and spirit-beings according to the teachings of the prophets. What evidences do we have in mortality that we had a pre-mortal existence? Review briefly the Latter-day Saints' concept of post-mortal life.

CHAPTER 19—UNIVERSALITY OF THE BELIEF IN IMMORTALITY— PAGES 130-137

Discuss: Which mortal received first the knowledge of the immortality of man? Prove your answer. Is there as much information concerning immortality in the Old Testament as there is in the other scriptures? Quote the choice Old Testament statements regarding immortality. Make a list of Jesus' teachings on the subject. Read Paul's entire discourse on immortality given to the saints at Corinth and compare his teachings with those of the other prophets. Compare the teachings on immortality in the *Book of Mormon* with those found in our other scriptures. What did Lao-Tze and Confucius teach regarding immortality? Did the Egyptians believe in immortality? Describe the Sumerian burial practices and compare them with those of the Egyptians. Compare the immortality doctrine of the Mystery Religions with the concept held by the Christians. Do many of the most brilliant modern scientists believe in immortality? Give evidence to sustain your answer. Since it has been pointed out in the text that the belief in immortality is universal, give reasons why such should be the case. As members of the Church of Jesus Christ, what direct evidence do you have that we are immortal?

CHAPTER 20—WE SHALL BE JUDGED—PAGES 138-144

Discuss: Will we literally stand before the judgment seat of God and give account of the lives we have lived in mortality? What did Paul teach regarding our moral responsibility? What is the basis of God's judgment of our actions? Give evidences from the scriptures sustaining the doctrine of a final judgment day. Who will be the principal judge of the human family? Are men to be held accountable for their thoughts as well as for their words and actions? Is the Christian religion the only one which teaches the doctrine of a final judgment? Describe the teaching of a final judgment of the Egyptians, Persians, and the people of India. Compare the teachings of the Old Testament, New Testament and *Book of Mormon* on the final judgment. According to the beliefs in Mithraism, what was Mithra's principal function? Who were Persephone and Pluto? What were their principal functions in the Eleusinian Mysteries? Describe the Orphic beliefs of the next world and the final judgment. What is the source of the belief in a final judgment?

CHAPTER 21—THE MESSIANIC HOPE—PAGES 145-151

Discuss: What is meant by the Messianic hope? What is the origin of such a belief? Have there been any other religions in world's history which believed in a Messiah (Savior) other than the true Gospel? Describe Enoch's knowledge of the Messiah. Give evidence that the Jaredites also knew that a Messiah should come into the world. List all the teachings and practices you can which sustain the thesis that the Hebrews had a Messianic hope. Compare the teachings of the *Bible* and the *Book of Mormon* regarding the Messiah.

Chapter 22—The Belief in a Savior-God—Pages 152-160

Discuss: What is the purpose of chapter 22? Give evidence that the belief in a Savior-God was universal. Compare the traditions regarding Prometheus, Buddha, and Krishna with the prophecies and life of Jesus Christ. What is the contents of the Messianic prophesy found in the ancient Chinese religion as quoted on page 154? Who was Quetzalcoalt? In what respects did traditions regarding him resemble our knowledge of Jesus? Make a list of the savior-gods of the Mystery Religions and compare the beliefs regarding them with our knowledge of the true Savior. Were there any beliefs held by the Mystery Religions which resembled the Gospel concept of God the Father and Mary the mother of Jesus? While reading this chapter, it would be of value to make a list of beliefs regarding the pagan savior-gods and then note the relationship of each of those beliefs with one or another of the teachings regarding Jesus Christ. What is the source of all the pagans' savior-god concepts?

Chapter 23—The One Divine Savior-God—Pages 161-166

Discuss: Why have many modern writers attempted to discredit the divinity of Jesus? Do the most reputable scholars of early Christian history believe that the New Testament accounts give a true history of Jesus? Discuss the evidence that Mormons have in addition to that of other Christian churches regarding the divinity of Jesus. What is the principal purpose of the *Book of Mormon?* Discuss Joseph Smith's testimonies regarding the divinity of Jesus Christ. What were the signs which were to accompany the birth and the death of the Savior according to Samuel the Lamanite? Note the appropriateness of those signs. Which religions held a belief in a new star as a sign of a birth of a savior or a great personage? Compare Zoroaster's prophesy and the story of the wise men as told in Matthew. Discuss the conclusion of this chapter.

Chapter 24—Jesus and the Sorrows of Humanity—Pages 167-176

Discuss: What is the purpose of this lesson? Why do human beings suffer? Discuss the birth of Jesus and the greatness of His personality. What problems did Jesus meet during the earlier years of His life which helped to prepare Him to understand the sorrows of humanity? Did Jesus and the people of Nazareth know when He was a boy that He was to be the Savior of the world? Did Jesus grow and develop gradually as you and I do? How perfect did Jesus become while in mortality? On what occasion did Jesus receive the direct announcement of His Messiahship? What was John the Baptist's testimony regarding Jesus as the Messiah? In what respects did Jesus fail to fulfill the Jewish Messianic hope? Analyze the course of life that Jesus chose to follow. In what ways did the Savior give hope to suffering humanity? What did Isaiah prophesy regarding the suffering of Jesus? Describe Jesus' suffering. What was the purpose of His suffering? Through His victory over sin and death, the Savior assured man of what great blessing?

Chapter 25—Atonement Through Sacrifice—Pages 177-184

Discuss: What part did the use of blood as a means to purge one from sin play in ancient religions? What were the *Bible's* teachings regarding blood? State the purpose of this lesson. What part did the atoning blood of Jesus play in the redemption of man? In what sense have all of us passed through "the fall"? List the qualities which Jesus had which fitted Him to atone for the sins of man. To whom was the atonement doctrine first revealed? Discuss the events connected therewith. What was the purpose of the law of sacrifice as revealed to Adam and practiced in ancient Israel? In what respects may some of the Hebrew priests have misinterpreted the law of sacrifice? Discuss the teachings of the prophets regarding the Hebrew practice of sacrifice. Why was it necessary for the blood of Jesus to be shed? Compare the efficacy of the shedding of Jesus' blood with that of shedding of animals' blood.

CHAPTER 26—PAGAN BELIEFS OF ATONEMENT THROUGH SACRIFICE— PAGES 185-191

Discuss: What is the origin of the pagan beliefs of atonement through sacrifice? Describe the blood atonement practices of the Eleusinian Mysteries. How did the Orphic worshipers attain regeneration? Discuss the extreme practices in the Dionysian Mysteries. What is meant by "The Bacchae"? Who was Euripides? What was the pagans' belief regarding the blood of Dionysus? What was the origin of the pagans' practices of human and animal sacrifices and the principal philosophy back of those practices? Define and describe *taurobolium*, also *criobolium*. What is the true meaning of the phrase "washed in the blood of the Lamb"?

CHAPTER 27—THE TRUE ORDINANCE OF BAPTISM—PAGES 192-199

Discuss: To whom must we look to find the origin of baptism and the other principles and ordinances of the Gospel? Give proof that baptism is essential to our gaining eternal life. Describe Adam's experiences connected with his baptism. Give proof that during Enoch's day the saints of God became church members through the ordinance of baptism. Did Noah know of the ordinance of baptism? Was baptism practiced by God's chosen people during the period from Noah to Jesus? Are there quotations in the Old Testament on baptism? What evidence do we have that the Jews practiced baptism? Did Lehi receive the ordinance of baptism from the Jews? Discuss Nephi's and Jacob's knowledge of baptism. Study carefully the doctrine of baptism as taught in the *Book of Mormon*. What changes did the Nephites make in the ordinance of baptism? Has baptism been a vital Gospel ordinance in the true Church of Jesus Christ from Adam's day to the present time?

CHAPTER 28—BAPTISM IN CHRISTENDOM—PAGES 200-206

Discuss: Tell the story of Christian baptism's being instituted in Jesus' day. What was Jesus' statement to Nicodemus on the necessity of baptism? Discuss the proper mode of baptism. Give evidence from ancient sources which prove that immersion was the mode of baptism practiced in the early Christian period. What is meant by "baptism by Spirit"? What three points on baptism as practiced during New Testament days are listed in the text? What commission did the Savior give to His apostles following His resurrection? Describe Peter's teachings on baptism. Give the story of the Christians' changing immersion to sprinkling. What were the principal causes for the Catholics' instituting infant baptism? What is meant by godparents? Describe the development of elaborate ceremonialism in Christian baptism. What connection does Priesthood have to baptism? What is meant by the three kinds of baptism in the Catholic Church today?

CHAPTER 29—PAGAN INFLUENCES ON CHRISTIAN BAPTISM— PAGES 207-213

Discuss: Whence came all of the changes discussed in the last chapter from the true order of baptism as established by Jesus Christ? What was the social and religious heritage of Christianity of the fifth century A.D.? What were the principal causes of the Great Apostasy? Did the pagans practice baptism? Describe the baptism practices of the Eleusinian Mysteries. What were the fundamental beliefs regarding baptism in this religion? What was the source of those beliefs? Discuss the validity of Tertullian's argument of the superiority of Christian baptism over pagan baptisms. Compare Christian and Mithraic baptism practices. Which pagan religions had the practice of feeding their newly baptized converts a diet of "milk and honey"? What effect did these practices have on Christianity? For what purpose did the pagans robe their baptized converts in white? What is the origin of the arduous preparatory training for baptism which was adopted by the Catholic Church under the name of *catechumenate*? Describe the Isiac baptism practices. What are the roots of the ordinance of baptism?

CHAPTER 30—REPENTANCE AND REBIRTH—PAGES 214-218

Discuss: What is the purpose of this lesson? What part has repentance played in Gospel history? What commandments were given to Adam and Enoch in regards to repentance? In what respects is repentance a spiritual rebirth? What is the relationship of repentance to baptism? List and discuss the constants in baptism practices. Contrast the teachings of repentance and rebirth in Hermeticism with similar teachings of the prophets of God. What is the relationship of baptism and rebirth as taught by the ancient pagans? What is Dr. Willoughby's opinion in regards to the quotation from Mithraic literature found on page 218 of the text?

CHAPTER 31—THE TRUE DOCTRINE OF BAPTISM RESTORED— PAGES 219-226

Discuss: What causes were responsible for adulterating the ordinance of baptism during the Catholic period? Why could not the Protestant reformers restore the true ordinance of baptism? Discuss briefly the principal points in the story of the restoration of the Gospel to Joseph Smith. What keys did John the Baptist restore to Joseph and Oliver? Discuss the events connected with the baptism of Joseph and Oliver. When and where and to whom was the Melchizedek Priesthood restored in this dispensation of the Gospel? What are the principal items regarding baptism which were revealed to the Prophet Joseph? On what conditions are baptisms valid and acceptable to God? Who shall have the privilege of being baptized? Study carefully the doctrine of baptism for the dead. What proof is there that baptism for the dead was practiced in ancient times? Present to the class some of Joseph Smith's teachings regarding baptism. Discuss the contents of the conclusions of this chapter.

CHAPTER 32—THE SACRAMENT OR THE HOLY EUCHARIST—PAGES 227-233

Discuss: What is meant by Holy Eucharist? Give the story of the instituting of the Sacrament. Compare the teachings of Matthew and Mark on Sacrament with those of Luke, Paul, and the *Book of Mormon*. In what respect was Jesus the true Paschal Lamb? Give Dr. Gore's interpretation of Paul's teachings. Examine carefully the *Book of Mormon* record for the purpose of getting an understanding of the true meaning of Sacrament. What interpretation did Justin Martyr and Ireaneus put on Holy Eucharist? Read and discuss Jesus' sermon on "the Bread of Life" for the purpose of finding the Catholic justification for their interpretation of Sacrament. Discuss the interpretation of the Holy Eucharist given by John of Damascus, Cyril, Gregory, and St. Augustine. Tell the story of the controversy during the middle ages over the conversion and symbolic theories. What is meant by transubstantiation? Who is credited with first using the term transubstantiation as applied to the Sacrament? What contributions did Thomas Aquinas make to the Catholic Holy Eucharist doctrine?

CHAPTER 33—PAGAN INFLUENCES ON THE EUCHARIST DOCTRINE— PAGES 234-239

Discuss: What are the principal points of emphasis in this lesson? What is the origin of the Catholic doctrine of transubstantiation? Discuss the eucharistic beliefs and practices in the Dionysian Mysteries and compare those practices with the doctrine of transubstantiation. Tell the story of the Orphic sacrament of eating and drinking the flesh and blood of the pagan god Zagreus. What did Professor Robertson-Smith say was the custom among the Arabs of the Sinai region? Compare the sacraments of the Cybele-Attis Mysteries and of the Eleusinian Mysteries with the doctrine as established by Jesus. What charge did Justin Martyr make against the Mithraic sacrament? Note carefully the religious syncretism that took place during the early Christian centuries for a picture of pagan influences on the Eucharist doctrine. What is the probable origin of pagan sacraments? What evidence do we have that Melchizedek gave the Sacrament to Father Abraham?

CHAPTER 34—RESTORATION OF THE TRUE SACRAMENT RITE— PAGES 240-244

Discuss: Give the reasons for Joseph Smith's instituting the practice of partaking of the Sacrament in the Church of Jesus Christ. According to revelations received by the Prophet Joseph, what are the purposes of the Sacrament ordinance? Explain how Sacrament should be properly administered. Where can we find copies of the blessings on the bread and wine (water)? Why do Mormons usually serve water instead of wine as one of the Sacrament emblems? Who shall partake of the Sacrament?

CHAPTER 35—THE GOLDEN RULE—PAGES 245-250

Discuss: What would be the result in the world if everybody lived the "Golden Rule"? Study carefully Jesus' statements of the Golden Rule and His enlargement on the same doctrine in the Sermon on the Mount. Are there other teachings of the Master and actions which show beyond doubt that He sincerely believed the Golden Rule? Did any other world religions proclaim a doctrine similar to the Christian Golden Rule? Compare the statements of the Golden Rule made by various religious teachers. Why are they so much alike? Contrast the philosophy of Nazism and Nietzsche with the teachings of the Golden Rule. Give examples of practical application of the Golden Rule in governments. Compare the teachings of outstanding religious leaders, such as Zoroaster, Confucius, Lao-Tze, and Buddha with the teachings of the prophets (pages 248-250). What is the source of the true teachings of all of these religious leaders?

CHAPTER 36—THE STORY OF THE EARTH (PROCLAIMED BY THE PROPHETS)—PAGES 251-256

Discuss: What is the purpose of this lesson? Discuss the most vital points in the creation accounts given by the prophets. Contrast the creation stories in the three scriptures. What erroneous concept regarding the creating of the earth was held by various Christian denominations in Joseph Smith's day? What light was thrown on this subject by the Prophet? Discuss briefly the Hebrew golden age story. What is meant by telestializing the earth? Was the earth ever baptized? Discuss the teachings of the prophets in regards to the earth being cleansed by fire. When will the earth be a terrestrial orb? What changes will take place before that condition is realized? What is meant by celestializing the earth? Describe the place where God dwells. Describe the earth after it is celestialized.

CHAPTER 37—THE STORY OF THE EARTH (COMPARATIVE RELIGIOUS TRADITIONS)—PAGES 257-263

Discuss: What is the difference between the contents of this lesson and the previous one? Did the great nations of antiquity other than the Hebrews preserve legends of the creation of the world, of the origin of man, of a golden age, of the fall, of the deluge and of the future rejuvenation of the earth? What was the source of the traditions of antiquity? Compare the Babylonian creation story with the one found in Genesis. Study Dr. Price's summary (page 258). How do we account for the golden age tradition being among practically every people of antiquity? Which tradition of a golden age found among peoples other than the Hebrews do you think is the most striking and true? Make a list of all the items of conditions that existed during the golden age as proclaimed in the traditions of various peoples and compare the list with the *Bible* account. Compare the fall of man account in Genesis and the one recorded on the Babylonian tablets. Which ancient writers recorded a deluge (flood) story? Compare the Babylonian flood account with the story recorded in Genesis. What is meant by the rejuvenation of the earth? Why are there so many similarities in the religions of the world? Study the conclusions made by Dr. Ira M. Price and compare those conclusions with what we have previously pointed out in the text.

CHAPTER 38—THE HOPE OF A BETTER WORLD—PAGES 264-270

Discuss: Give reasons for the Gospel of Jesus Christ's being placed on the earth. Have any other peoples besides the Biblical groups believed that a Millennium would be established? Is it possible for people to establish a "good society" and live in almost perfect righteousness? Study the social conditions that prevailed in the three examples of the good society which are listed in the text. What were the basic principles which made these social groups righteous? Which of the Old Testament prophets predicted the establishment of a good society? Upon what principles did they believe that that society would be founded? Discuss Isaiah's description of the Millennium. What did Christ teach would be the basis of a good society? Study John the Revelator's vision of the millennial reign of the Lord and the establishment of the New Jerusalem. After Jesus' resurrection, did the Christians look for Him to return to earth? What did Paul prophesy would happen before that event occurred?

CHAPTER 39—UTOPIAN AND ZION CONCEPTS—PAGES 271-276

Discuss: Who were the authors of "famous Utopian writings"? What are the main points in Plato's *Republic?* What is meant by *The City of God?* What is the outstanding feature of Sir Thomas More's *Utopia?* What book did Francis Bacon write? What is meant by *The City of the Sun?* What caused James Harrington to write *Oceana?* Look at the list of other Utopian writings on page 273. What is meant by "Utopian Socialists"? What was their main purpose? Have any writers during the past century produced Utopian literature? Tell the story of Savonarola's good society experiment? Why did it finally fail? Of what importance has America been in communist and cooperative experiments? What was "the overwhelming religious motivation of the period in American history when Joseph Smith was born and when the Gospel of Jesus Christ was restored to earth"?

CHAPTER 40—THE MORMONS' ZION CONCEPT—PAGES 277-285

Discuss: What is the purpose and principal viewpoint of this lesson? What was the historical setting of Joseph Smith's millennial hope? What additional information did the Prophet receive on this subject in the *Book of Mormon?* What is the background in regards to Joseph Smith's receiving revelations regarding the building of Zion? What did Enoch prophesy regarding Zion? Tell the story of locating Zion. What conditions contributed to Zion's favorable location? According to Joseph Smith, where is Zion? What does Zion mean? Tell the story of the attempts to establish Zion in Missouri. Why were the Mormons driven out of Independence? What is meant by Zion's Camp? Do the Mormons still expect to build the New Jerusalem in Missouri? Study the details of the Millennium as revealed to Joseph Smith and contrast his knowledge of this great event with what had been revealed to the prophets of old. Who shall participate in building the New Jerusalem? What is meant by "the great and dreadful day of the Lord"?

CHAPTER 41—THE DYNAMICS OF MORMONISM—PAGES 286-295

Discuss: What is the scope of the story of the *Gospel Through the Ages?* Which is the greatest of the Gospel dispensations? Why? List reasons why it was necessary for God to restore the Gospel to Joseph Smith. Discuss briefly the story of the First Vision and the other important incidents connected with the restoration of the Gospel. What is meant by "the true and living Church"? Who holds the keys of the Priesthood? Discuss the belief held by Mormons that they are servants of God. Give examples. What are the strong points of Church government officered by the laity? Give proof that Mormonism produces powerful leaders. In what respects is Mormonism a practical religion? How does the doctrine of progressive eternalism help to make Mormonism a living Church? Give evidence to show that this Church teaches the true concept of God. Of what value is testimony in the Church of Jesus Christ? How do Church members get their testimonies? Discuss the conclusions at the end of the chapter.

Index

INDEX